Illustratic

CW01500705

AESTHETICS & THE PHILOSOPHY OF SPIRIT

PETER LANG
New York • Washington, D.C./Baltimore • Bern
Frankfurt am Main • Berlin • Brussels • Vienna • Oxford

John Shannon Hendrix

AESTHETICS & THE PHILOSOPHY OF SPIRIT

From Plotinus to Schelling and Hegel

PETER LANG
New York • Washington, D.C./Baltimore • Bern
Frankfurt am Main • Berlin • Brussels • Vienna • Oxford

Library of Congress Cataloging-in-Publication Data

Hendrix, John Shannon.
Aesthetics and the philosophy of spirit: From Plotinus
to Schelling and Hegel / John Shannon Hendrix.
p. cm.
Includes bibliographical references and index.
1. Plotinus—Aesthetics. 2. Schelling, Friedrich Wilhelm Joseph von, 1775–1854—
Aesthetics. 3. Hegel, Georg Wilhelm Friedrich, 1770–1831—Aesthetics.
4. Aesthetics--History. I. Title.
B693.Z7H43 111'.85'09—dc22 2004022834
ISBN 978-0-8204-7632-2

Bibliographic information published by **Die Deutsche Bibliothek**.
Die Deutsche Bibliothek lists this publication in the "Deutsche
Nationalbibliografie"; detailed bibliographic data is available
on the Internet at http://dnb.ddb.de/.

Cover design by Joni Holst

Cover illustration: Caspar David Friedrich (1774–1840),
Two Men Observing the Moon, 1819–20, detail, Gemaeldegalerie,
Staatliche Kunstsammlungen, Dresden, Germany
(Photo credit: Erich Lessing, Art Resource, NY)

The paper in this book meets the guidelines for permanence and durability
of the Committee on Production Guidelines for Book Longevity
of the Council of Library Resources.

© 2005, 2014 Peter Lang Publishing, Inc., New York
29 Broadway, 18th floor, New York, NY 10006
www.peterlang.com

All rights reserved.
Reprint or reproduction, even partially, in all forms such as microfilm,
xerography, microfiche, microcard, and offset strictly prohibited.

Printed in Germany

For Shannon, Christopher, and Tyler

Contents

Acknowledgments

I would like to thank Phyllis Korper and Peter Lang Publishing for their continued support of the work. For their support during the course of this book I would like to acknowledge my colleagues at Roger Williams University: Hasan-Uddin Khan, Okan Ustunkok, Alberto Balestrieri, Edgar Adams, Andrea Adams, Ron Henderson, Ulker Copur, and Robert Rustermeier. I would also like to thank Marie Bullock, Michael Pomerleau and Daniel Alexander for their help with typesetting and scanning of images. For their dialogue, observations and suggestions during the course of the book, I would like to acknowledge: Liana de Girolami Cheney, Panayiota Vassilopoulou, Patrick Quinn, Suzanne Stern-Gillet, Kevin Corrigan, Jean-Marc Narbonne, Stephen Gersh, Robert Berchman, Tracey Eve Winton, Renée Tobe, Nicholas Temple, Raymond Quek, James McQuillan, Stephen Fleming, Ali Mozaffari, Rosa Cabral, and Zeynep Siram. I would like to thank Art Resource and Artists Rights Society for permission to reproduce the images.

"The *Symposium* and the Aesthetics of Plotinus" was inspired by a panel at the International Conference on Ancient and Medieval Philosophy at Fordham University in October 2003. The participants in the panel were M. Andrew Holowchak, Cory Wimberly, and Lawrence Horsburgh. Portions of "Plotinian Hypostases in Hegel's *Phenomenology of Spirit*" were presented at the conference on Philosophy, Spirituality, and Art in the Neoplatonic Tradition at the University of Liverpool in June 2004, organized by Panayiota Vassilopoulou, and the International Conference on Ancient and Medieval Philosophy at Fordham University in October 2004. Portions of "Architecture and the Philosophy of Spirit" were presented at conferences of the Association of Collegiate Schools of Architecture at Syracuse University and Judson College in October 2004.

1
Introduction

Aesthetics and the Philosophy of Spirit examines the aesthetics of Plotinus (c. 205–270), Friedrich Wilhelm Joseph von Schelling (1775–1854) and Georg Wilhelm Friedrich Hegel (1770–1831). It examines the Platonic bases of the aesthetics of Plotinus, and the Plotinian bases of the aesthetics of Schelling and Hegel in the Philosophy of Spirit, Identity Philosophy, and Transcendental Idealism. It examines the notion of art as philosophy, as a product of mind, and as an instrument of intellect in the relation between reason and perception, involving concepts of the universal and particular, freedom and necessity, the beautiful and sublime, allegory and symbolism, and forms of artistic representation. Other concepts examined are Subjective and Objective Spirit, the self-consciousness and self-alienation of reason, and Absolute Spirit as the reconciliation of reason with its "other." The book demonstrates the importance of the role of aesthetics in the Philosophy of Spirit, in the definition of reason and perception, and in an understanding of human history and artistic expression. It re-examines the writings of Plotinus, Schelling and Hegel, and brings them together and to light in relation to contemporary aesthetic and philosophical concerns, demonstrating the importance of the writings in the course of western thought and in contemporary theory. The book is intended to be an original treatise on aesthetics, grounded in commentary on previous works and systems. It is intended to contribute to the understanding of art in philosophical terms, the philosophy of art, and theories of artistic production.

In previous books (*Platonic Architectonics: Platonic Philosophies and the Visual Arts*, *Architectural Forms and Philosophical Structures*, and *The relation between architectural forms and philosophical structures in the work of Francesco Borromini in seventeenth-century Rome*) I have explored the relation between philosophy and art and architecture. As I went along, I became increasingly interested in the philosophy of art, that is, aesthetics.

This book is an exploration of aesthetics, of the aesthetics of the Philosophy of Spirit. It is an attempt to emphasize the importance of aesthetics from a philosophical point of view, as well as from a practical point of view, in the production of the arts. The purpose of the philosophy of art, and the analysis of the relation between philosophy and art, is to better understand art itself, and the making of art, and, ultimately, the nature of human creativity and intellect. These issues are of importance in classes that I have taught in aesthetics and the history and theory of art and architecture.

Having done extensive research and writing previously on the Platonic and Neoplatonic tradition, I was struck by the extent to which the aesthetics of the Continental philosophers, Schelling and Hegel, were infused with Platonism and Neoplatonism. The Philosophy of Spirit is a comprehensive philosophy, combining Identity Philosophy (Realism and Idealism), Philosophy of Nature (Realism), and Philosophy of Mind or Intellect. It combines the classical philosophical tradition with the contemporary philosophies of Realism and Idealism in the nineteenth century. As Michael Vater explains in "Schelling's Neoplatonic System-Notion: '*Ineinsbildung*' and Temporal Unfolding," in *The Significance of Neoplatonism*, Schelling's philosophy "at one and the same time saves the concreteness of philosophy and guarantees the comprehensiveness of its systematic grasp. Schelling perceives himself as taking up and continuing in pertinent terms, the questions namely of philosophical *Wissenschaft*, the Neoplatonic problematic of system and structure—the question of the reconciliation of opposites, of the ingathering of the fragmentary and (on its own terms) inexplicable into a world, of the restoration of psyche to its appropriate level of functioning."[1]

In Identity Philosophy (*Identitätsphilosophie*), forces in nature (*potences*) are identical to forces in human intellect; thus, philosophy is not entirely dependent on the subjective, or the ideal, but rather the combination of the ideal and the real, the real being matter and organism. The perceiving subject and that which is perceived are equally important to the definition of consciousness. The principle of identity in consciousness is the first step in the development of self-consciousness, in the understanding of the indifference, or identity, of the real and the ideal, and the function of intuition in intellect, corresponding to the Intellectual Principle of Plotinus. The identity of the real and ideal in consciousness corresponds to the identity of the perceiving subject and that which is perceived. The absolute, the indifference of the real and ideal, is present in both nature and human intellect, but in entirely different ways. The Philosophy of Nature (*Naturphilosophie*) is the understanding of the real, matter and organism, while the Philosophy of Spirit is the understanding of the intellect, and the two coincide in Identity Philosophy.

In the same way that philosophy is a systematic examination of the absolute in relation to the real and ideal, the particular and the universal, art is a systematic representation (*Darstellung*) of the absolute in relation to the real and the ideal, and a philosophical instrument in the development of self-consciousness and understanding of the absolute in intellect through the dialectic. Art, as it exists in the real, is a representation of the absolute as it exists in the ideal, as an idea, an archetype in the Platonic sense, for that which is real. The real consists of the multiplicity of forms which are generated from the simplicity of the absolute, as given by the archetypes in the intellect, in the Platonic and Neoplatonic tradition. The unity of the absolute is informed (*einbilden*) into every *potence* in nature, intellect, and art. In Identity Philosophy, the underlying principles of the real and the ideal are the same. Art is capable of representing the archetypal status of the real in the ideal, according to Schelling, and thus representing the intellect. The aesthetics of Schelling are the aesthetics of Spirit, the absolute in the real and ideal; art is the objectification of philosophy. Aesthetics, the philosophy of art, is a part of philosophy. Aesthetic intuition is "intellectual intuition become objective,"[2] as described by Schelling in the *System of Transcendental Idealism*, and art is the true document of philosophy.

In consciousness, the identity of the real and the ideal is never completeable. Human consciousness is defined by an originary dehiscence, or splitting, between the ideal and real, between thought and the object of thought, and perception and the object of perception. The purpose of philosophy, and art, is to seek a resolution of that dehiscence, to seek an identity of the conscious and unconscious, reason and intuition, to seek a belonging of the human being in the world. Art is a product of the intuition of the absolute in consciousness, and requires the participation of both the real and ideal, defined as necessity and freedom. Necessity is the dominant factor in nature, while freedom is the dominant factor in intellect. Art contains the representation of the real and ideal in the real, the indifference of activity and knowledge, signification and meaning. Beauty in art is the indifference of the real and ideal, expressed primarily through color; beauty in art can represent absolute beauty, as in the universal beauty understood by the initiate in the *Symposium* of Plato. The sublime in art, on the other hand, represents the absence of the ideal in the real, the terror of the *horror vacui*, the self-alienation of the perceiving subject from being.

The operating principle in the resolution of the real and ideal in the intellect is the pre-existence of the absolute in both intellect and nature. The absolute is thus the first principle of both philosophy and art in Identity Philosophy and the Philosophy of Spirit. The absolute can only be understood through intuition, which is a product of dialectical development in philosophy, and is itself an indifference of the real and ideal, objective and subjective. The work of art reflects (in the reflected image, *Gegenbild*) the self-consciousness of the intellect because it presents the division of the real and ideal within the absolute, which is the state of human consciousness, as well as the indifference of the real and ideal. It also represents the indifference of freedom and necessity, the universal and particular, as the intuition of the absolute. Art represents the *Zeigeist* of the culture, the universal spirit, and the participation of the individual artist in culture. History itself represents the manifestation of the absolute in human activity and the development toward self-consciousness and toward freedom in the indifference of the real and ideal, in the *Zeitgeist* of the culture.

Both Schelling and Hegel believe that the self-alienation of the human being (the gap between the conscious and unconscious, between the universal and particular, the infinite and finite in the intellect), along with the desire to resolve that self-alienation, is the cause of philosophy, as well as artistic expression, and that the purpose of both philosophy and art is to achieve a reconciliation, a dialectical synthesis, a re-affirmation of being. To that end, the Continental philosophers appropriated the structural metaphysics of Plato and the Neoplatonists (principally Plotinus) and combined them with the *Wissenschaftslehre* of Johann Gottlieb Fichte (1762–1814), to achieve a dialectical synthesis of the classical and modern worlds as well, to re-affirm the universality of the spirit in relation to both history and the sensible world.

Schelling and Hegel had a close relationship, as they were friends as students in the Protestant Seminary at Tübingen University, along with Friedrich Hölderlin (1770–1843). Schelling invited Hegel to prepare as a lecturer at the University of Jena, and they collaborated as co-editors of *The Critical Journal of Philosophy* (*Kritisches Journal der Philosophie*), though Hegel soon broke with Schelling's philosophical system, which caused a falling-out. The *Phenomenology of Spirit* (1807) of Hegel and the *System of Transcendental Idealism* (1800) of Schelling are nevertheless similar in their post-Kantian attempts, following Fichte, the principal figure at the University of Jena at the time, to bridge the gap between subject and object, the noumenal and phenomenal, the ideal and the real, reason and that which it perceives.

The groundwork for the dialectical relationship between subject and object in human consciousness, the basis of Transcendental Idealism, was laid by Fichte in the original *Wissenschaftslehre* (Doctrine of Science, or Science of Knowledge) of 1794. According to Fichte, reason defines itself in consciousness in relation to its own negation, its other, as the infinite in relation to finite thought. Thought is caught in an interplay or struggle between its existence to itself and the negation of that existence, between the finite and the infinite; Fichte defines this interplay as imagination (*Wissenschaftslehre* § 4, III: I, 215).[3] The conflict of irreconcilables plays itself out in the temporal manifestation of thought (217), and it is in the fact that "the self posits itself as determined by the not-self" (218) that presentation in thought is possible, as an "absolute power of production" of thought, in that the self "posits itself at once as finite and infinite—an interplay that consists, as it were, in self-conflict, and is self-reproducing, in that the self endeavors to unite the irreconcilable..." (215).

The "principle of opposition" in thought (§ 2: I, 105) and the corresponding "category of negation" are seen as the basis of the dialectic as developed by Hegel. The opposition of thought to itself constitutes a theory of self-consciousness; the striving (*streben*) of thought to complete itself and to overcome the contradiction of the finite and the infinite in the imagination constitutes the basis of the freedom of mind from causal and mechanical determination in the synthesis of the subjective and objective which will become Absolute Spirit. Fichte said of his philosophy that it was the "first system of freedom"[4] in the dialectical struggle; Hegel sought to resolve the dialectical struggle of thought, as posited by Fichte, in Absolute Spirit. Post-Hegelian thought, in Deconstruction for example, as will be seen, returns in some ways to the Fichtean model of the irreconcilability of thought in relation to itself in self-consciousness, the impossibility of completion.

Returning to artistic expression, in the *Phenomenology of Spirit*, Hegel defines the historical development of art in terms of the symbolic, the Classical, and the Romantic. Symbolic art is seen as *Vorkunst*, "pre-art," in its inability to represent the identity of the ideal and the real in its limitations as symbolic. Egyptian architecture, in particular, reveals the inability of reason in Ancient Egypt to recognize itself in the real, and the symbolic in general reveals the problematic relation between reason and that which it perceives, the ideal and the real, in its representation to itself. All architecture, which is symbolic, created by the combination of the schematic and allegorical, as described by Schelling in *The Philosophy of Art*, reveals the "crisis of representation" revealed by the symbolic and the allegorical, the inability of reason to reconcile itself following its self-alienation from its other in consciousness. The return of reason to itself is Absolute Spirit in mind in Transcendental Idealism, and the difficulty of such a synthesis is made apparent in the forms of art which are limited to symbolic representation. Classical art, in particular the Classical sculpture of the human body, achieves the synthesis of the ideal and the real, according to Hegel, because it is the perfect imitation of organic form based on the understanding of the real in the ideal, for example in the Golden Section and Harmonic Proportions. Classical art displays the indifference of mind and body which is the basis of classical mythology.

Architectural forms cannot achieve such a synthesis between the real and the ideal, according to Schelling, because the anorganic forms of architecture, regulated by mathematics and geometry, can only imitate the organic forms of nature, and can never display the essence of organic form in itself. Romantic art, which is the highest point of development in the history of art, according to Hegel, is similar to symbolic art in that it reveals an incompatibility between the ideal and the real, between reason and that which it perceives. The principal innovation of Romantic art is the sublime, which reveals to reason the absence of reason in the real, and the self-alienation of reason in its consciousness of its other. Romantic art reveals the fallacy of the identification of the real and ideal based on the identification of mind and body in Classical art, and Romantic art introduces the modern historical subject, as a product of the construction of reason which is incompatible with nature or the real. Romantic art frees reason from an identity with the real, and enacts an allegory of the dialectical relation of reason to itself in self-consciousness; Romantic art is thus the first modern art, or the new beginning of artistic representation in the modern world.

In the *Phenomenology of Spirit*, Spirit is differentiated from the appearance of being in the same way that the Platonic *archê* is differentiated from the flux of appearance. Absolute Spirit is seen as a void in being, absolute formlessness, the dark night of being, "the nightlike void of the supersensible beyond" (177),[5] which is the equivalent of pure and absolute form in the synthesis of the real and the ideal. Reason becomes aware of itself in abstract thought, and sees itself as other in self-consciousness, in being-for-self. The origin of the abstract thought of reason is its being-in-itself, the essence of being, which is unconscious thought. In consciousness reason becomes aware of itself, and becomes alienated from its other, as it becomes aware of the incompatibility within itself which is a result of its incompatibility with the real, with nature, and its self-perception of its own absence in nature, as represented by the sublime in art. Reason then attempts to overcome its own self-alienation in a dialectical struggle which returns reason to itself, so that it becomes being-in-and-for-itself, which is Absolute Spirit in mind, and is represented by the identity of the real and the ideal in reason. (Which is the Idea, the "proper philosophical meaning of 'reason'," as Hegel describes in the *Wissenschaft der Logik* of 1830, § 214.[6] The science of the Idea is logic, which is different from logic in the ordinary sense, dogmatic logic, as will be seen.) The identity of the real and ideal in reason is not as the ideal in the real, as reason in nature, but rather as both ideal and real, reason and nature, in the absolute, Absolute Spirit, which is the underlying ground of being, unconscious being from which both reason and nature develop.

The Absolute Spirit as the ground of being is the goal of representation in Romantic art, which entails the representation of the alienation of reason from nature and from itself, but the identity of reason and nature, the ideal and the real, within Absolute Spirit, thus combining Nature Philosophy, Identity Philosophy, and Transcendental Idealism. In post-Hegelian philosophy, the identity of reason and nature, or reason and that which exceeds it, is no longer seen as possible, and the role of the symbol as containing that identity in literature and art is seen as less plausible in its unification, but the Hegelian scheme of the self-alienation of reason, and the absence of reason in the real, has dominated philosophy, and especially philosophical psychology, to the present. Hegel's philosophy can be seen as a metaphysical psychology, the first modern philosophy. Hegel is seen as the last metaphysical philosopher, and it is mostly the non-metaphysical elements of his system which are appropriated by his followers.

A re-reading of Hegel and Schelling, as situated between Neoplatonism and contemporary theory, can contribute to a revival of the validity of metaphysical thought at the beginning of the twenty-first century (critical or rational metaphysics, as opposed to dogmatic or theological metaphysics, as described by Hegel in the *Wissenschaft der Logik*), which is particularly important for the development of philosophy, and for artistic production and expression. Metaphysics is given by language in philosophy; metaphysical philosophy reveals the structure and limitations of the role of language in philosophy more than any other system. It is possible to approach metaphysics from a Structuralist perspective, even an empiricist perspective, in relation to the structures of language, as an instrument of the manifestation of reason to itself in thought.

The relationship between the universal and the particular in reason is an important basis of philosophy in general and an important common element in the structural metaphysics of Plotinus and Hegel. The relation between the universal and the particular contains within it the relation between reason and perception, as forms and images are translated into ideas and vice versa, through the mediation of language in thought. Both Plotinus and Hegel formulate important schematic representations of reason in relation to perception which can be translated into artistic expression. The relation between the Intellectual Principle and the Reason Principle of Plotinus is an important precedent for the relation between Spirit and reason in mind for Hegel, in relation to the absolute. The unconscious in mind, as well as consciousness and self-consciousness, which play important roles in Hegel's system, are present in the philosophy of Plotinus. The roles of Ego and universal Spirit in Hegel also have precedent in Plotinus. For both philosophers, picture-thinking (*Vorstellung*), reason in perception, is seen as an important factor in the relation between the ideal and the real, in particular the dialectical relation between reason and nature and reason and the absolute, in Plotinus between Intellectual Principle and Reason Principle, though reason must transcend picture-thinking in the absolute, and the One of Plotinus.

In both systems the relation between the ideal and the real entails the relation between the infinite and the finite, and the reconciliation of the two in reason. In both systems the ideal is seen to precede the real, that is, what is perceived by mind is given by mind, and is determined by the parameters of mind, a principal content of both Platonism and Idealism. The essence of being is taken to be outside of appearance in Platonism and Neoplatonism, while in Transcendental Idealism it is possible for the essence of being to enter into appearance, while appearance is seen as being insubstantial in relation. The absolute is shared by reason and nature in both systems; in Plotinus there is no hint of the perception in nature of the absence of reason on the part of reason, or of the alienation of reason from itself in self-consciousness; those structures are products of the Enlightenment, and scientific thinking, in the distinction between mind and nature. Hegel and Schelling attempted to formulate a philosophical science, a science of human thought within a world of its own construction, while such a concept could not have occurred to Plotinus.

The aesthetics of Plotinus are derived in large part from the *Symposium* of Plato, as a product of the dialectical relationship between the universal and the particular, between the *archê* and its manifestation in the real. The absolute Idea of Plotinus in the intelligible is seen as a form of the good, the source of ethical and moral principles, in the same way that the Absolute Spirit of Hegel in mind is connected to ethical and moral principles and to the *Zeitgeist*, the universal manifestation of Spirit in a culture. The beautiful in the real of Plotinus is a manifestation of the good, as for Hegel and Schelling the beautiful in the real is the identity of the real and the ideal, the compatibility of reason and nature, and reason and its other. Artistic production for Plotinus is an expression of the absolute and intelligible form in reason, a product of the Intellectual Principle, in which the identity of the real and ideal is achieved, as in the Absolute Spirit of Hegel and Schelling. The forms which reason assumes for Hegel in the dialectical struggle in self-consciousness are as the hypostases of Plotinus, each defined in relation to the absolute, as the particular is defined in relation to the universal, and the finite is defined in relation to the infinite. Common elements in the systems of Plotinus, Schelling and Hegel can be read in twentieth-century thinkers from Sigmund Freud to Georges Bataille to Jacques Lacan to Jacques Derrida; the structural metaphysics of Neoplatonism and Transcendental Idealsim are best preserved in the philosophical psychology of the twentieth century. Manifestations of the structural metaphysics can be seen in art movements in the twentieth century ranging from Cubism to Surrealism to Abstract Expressionism, from Rationalist to Deconstructivist architecture, and in theoretical systems from Phenomenology and Existentialism to Chaos Theory and Catastrophe Theory.

The philosophical project of Schelling and Hegel is an attempt to synthesize the classical and modern worlds, to establish a continuity in what is already perceived as an irreparable split, given the advent of science. Hegel declared the death of art for the purpose of re-inventing art in relation to the modern world, but such a re-invention was not possible without an understanding of the relation between the classical and modern worlds in their differentiation and incompatibility, as a macrocosm of the relation between reason and the perceived world in their differentiation and incompatibility. Too often in contemporary theory the history of philosophy is overlooked, and the same systems and ideas are repeated unknowingly, even in philosophies whose professed basis is the rejection of a previous system. A complete philosophical system is not possible without a knowledge and understanding of philosophical history, and theoretical positions should not be formed in ignorance of that history.

Hegel's re-invention of art establishes a new basis for the judgment of beauty, following Immanuel Kant in the *Critique of Judgment*. Standards of artistic representation reflect standards of consciousness, of the self-consciousness of reason in the real. The achievement of Spirit in mind for Hegel is ultimately the achievement of freedom, which is the highest value to which a culture can aspire. Spirit is seen in opposition to the laws of necessity and cause and effect, and the Principle of Sufficient Reason in nature; Spirit is also seen in opposition to the limited and delimiting structures of logic (dogmatic logic), as developed in the thought of Georges Bataille. Spirit in mind is freedom from the limitations of reason and nature in the real, and the state of being to which human beings as cultural subjects aspire, that which differentiates the human being from nature, and which is the basis of a moral and ethical *Zeitgeist*. Art is ideally the expression of the freedom attained in Spirit, the identity of the real and ideal, the result of the dialectical struggle of reason. Art is thus that which defines being human in opposition to nature, and what defines human thought as exceeding both nature and logic in reason. The purpose of philosophy as well is to transcend logic in reason towards understanding in the imagination and Spirit, as the Intellectual Principle of Plotinus entails intuition, imagination, and participation of the absolute which Reason Principle does not.

Schelling, in *The Philosophy of Art*, goes to great length to identify the means of representation of Spirit in painting, as a model of the hypostases of reason. Drawing is completely within the realm of the real, being structural, material and schematic. Color introduces the synthesis of the real and the ideal as the synthesis of matter and light. Light in painting is the most complete representation of the absolute in the plastic arts, the synthesis of the real and ideal, because light is the most immaterial of substances in the real, and in the Platonic and Neoplatonic traditions, light is the source of the good and the entrance of the archetype into matter. For both Schelling and Hegel, ultimately all the plastic arts are insufficient representations of the absolute in relation to music, poetry and philosophy. The forms of the social expression of Absolute Spirit are art, religion and philosophy. Art can only partially represent Absolute Spirit because it is contained within the real, within its material existence. The more immaterial of the arts, music and poetry, are less bound to the real, but more limited by the presence of the real in the ideal, by notation and language. Religion can only partially represent Absolute Spirit because of the necessity of the embodiment of Spirit as the basis of religious faith. Only philosophy sets as its objective the transcendence of its own scaffolding, in the possibility of the self-consciousness and doubling of reason, as the basis for the attainment of the absolute in mind.

For Schelling and Hegel the artist is always a product of his or her culture, of the *Zeitgeist* and philosophy of the culture. Artistic expression is a social act, and engages the ethical and moral standards of the culture. In the modern world, according to Hegel, art is no longer possible as a representation of its culture. The art which was a product of classical cultures is no longer possible because of the very attainment of freedom to which the history of art aspired. It is not possible for art to represent a free and ethical culture; in such a culture art becomes subject to philosophical development, and the theory of art becomes more important than the art itself. The expression of a free and ethical culture is philosophy, because only in philosophy is freedom of Spirit possible in the absolute. The necessities to which artistic expression is tied in a free culture become individual necessities and individual manifestations of the universal; philosophy is free from individual necessities, in its attainment of Absolute Spirit in mind, and is able to represent the *Zeitgeist* of a free culture. For Hegel, as expressed in the *Introductory Lectures on Aesthetics*, "the science of art is a much more pressing need in our day" (XVIII),[7] and "Art invites us to consideration of it by means of thought, not to the end of stimulating art production, but in order to ascertain scientifically what art is." I would like to think that once philosophy comes to an understanding of art, or as philosophy attempts to come to an understanding of art, art production can be stimulated as a result.

This book is a systematic analysis of the role that Platonism and Neoplatonism play in the aesthetics of the Philosophy of Spirit, and an attempt to make both Neoplatonism and the Philosophy of Spirit, Transcendental Idealism, relevant to the present. To my knowledge no such analysis has been undertaken, although the role has been suggested by Michael Vater. Eric von der Luft, in his "Comment" in *History and System: Hegel's Philosophy of History*, points out Hegel's certain awareness of Neoplatonism: "To be sure, Hegel must have known both Proclus and Plotinus very well, since his friend, Heidelberg colleague, and frequent correspondent, Georg Freidrich Creuzer (1771–1858), prepared standard editions of each of these authors."[8] According to Jon Mills in *The Unconscious Abyss: Hegel's Anticipation of Psychoanalysis*, "Hegel's use of the positive significance of the negative"[9] must be attributed to the cosmology of Proclus and Plotinus, and "It may be argued that Hegel's generic conceptualization of the dialectical self-unfolding of spirit…is a standard Neo-platonic idea" (p. 30). In his "habilitation" thesis of 1801, entitled "On the Orbit of the Planets," written to earn a lecturing position at the University of Jena, Hegel included an analysis of the discussion of Pythagorean numerical series in the *Timaeus* of Plato. Later that year he published his first book, *The Difference Between Fichte's and Schelling's System of Philosophy.* According to Terry Pinkard in *Hegel, A Biography*, Hegel "avidly read Plato"[10] as a student at Tübingen University.

In the following year, 1802, Hegel and Schelling collaborated on the introductory essay for the first issue of *The Critical Journal of Philosophy*, entitled "The Critical Journal of Philosophy Introduction on The Essence of Philosophical Criticism Generally, and its Relationship to the Present State of Philosophy in Particular."[11] The first sentence of the essay reads:

> In whatever domain of art or [speculative] science it is employed, criticism requires a standard which is just as independent of the person who makes the judgement as it is of the thing that is judged—a standard derived neither from the singular [*ie.* the immediate occasion for critical judgement] nor from the specific character of the [*judging*] subject, but from the eternal and unchangeable model [*Urbild*] of what really *is* [*die Sache selbst*].

Such a statement lays the groundwork for "a revival of the Christian Platonic ideal of the *philosophia perennis*," as described by H. S. Harris. As for Schelling, Harris asserts that "there is no doubt that he (whom his Jena students called 'Plato') believed as fervently as Hegel that the true 'speculative' tradition of western philosophy must be rescued from the limbo to which Kant consigned *all* previous metaphysics in the 'Dialectic of Pure Reason'."

In my analysis I found particularly helpful the commentary in the introduction by Douglas Stott to *The Philosophy of Art*; the introduction by Peter Stillman to *Hegel's Philosophy of Spirit*; the introduction by John Niemeyer Findlay to *Phenomenology of Spirit*; and the treatises *Logic and System: A Study of the Transition from "Vorstellung" to Thought in the Philosophy of Hegel* by Malcolm Clark; *Art and the Absolute: A Study of Hegel's Aesthetics* by William Desmond; *The Aesthetic Theories of Kant, Hegel, and Schopenhauer* by Israel Knox; *Hegel and the Symbolic Mediation of Spirit* by Kathleen Dow Magnus; and *Hegel's Recollection: A Study of Images in the* Phenomenology of Spirit by Donald Phillip Verene.

This particular analysis of the relation between Neoplatonism and the Philosophy of Spirit within the framework of contemporary theory forms a framework for an exploration of aesthetics and the formulation of my own aesthetic points of view. To that end the book is intended to be an original treatise on aesthetics, grounded as are all treatises in commentary on previous works and systems. It is intended to contribute to the attempt to understand art in philosophical terms, for the purpose of continuing the possibilities for human expression, attempting to understand the nature of reason in relation to perception, and perception in relation to reason. Philosophy is the project of the self-understanding of reason on its own terms, within its own structure, as given by language. Philosophy thus stages, like architecture as an allegorical drama, the dialectical struggle of reason in relation to itself and that which is outside it. I hope that this treatise on aesthetics can contribute to the philosophy of art at the beginning of the twenty-first century, and that it may contribute to artistic production in theory, and that both Neoplatonism and the Philosophy of Spirit of Schelling and Hegel can be seen as relevant and beneficiary to contemporary consciousness, keeping in mind the importance of the study of history for all theoretical concerns.

2
The *Symposium* and the Aesthetics of Plotinus

The conversation between Diotima and Socrates in Plato's *Symposium* 210–212 can be seen as a foundation in many ways for the aesthetics of Plotinus, Friedrich Wilhelm Joseph von Schelling and George Wilhelm Friedrich Hegel. Diotima describes to Socrates that in order to be initiated into the rites and mysteries of love, one must begin by being drawn to beautiful bodies (the bodies of young boys, in this case). If one begins by loving one beautiful body, then one will be compelled to love all beautiful bodies, in the desire to "pursue the beauty of form" (*Symposium* 210)[1] rather than the beauty of the body itself. Once seduced by the beauty of form rather than body, the initiate will see that it is the beauty of the mind, of which the form is a subject, that is more valuable than the beauty of form or body.

The beauty of mind is to be found in the goodness of mind, the good, so real beauty will be found in goodness, "practices and laws," in comparison to which the beauty of the body becomes petty. In that goodness, practices and laws are subjects of knowledge, or forms of knowledge, it is forms of knowledge which become the higher beauty. Thus the initiate will be turned away from the "low and small-minded slavery" of love for the beauty of a body, and "he will be turned towards the great sea of beauty and gazing on it he'll give birth, through a boundless love of knowledge, to many beautiful and magnificent discourses and ideas."

Once the initiate perceives real beauty, the beauty of mind, he will understand that this beauty is not subject to the conditions of the material world, to change and decay, becoming and perishing. Beauty of mind is eternal, universal, and self-contained, not subject to the flux of nature and not the quality of any particular body or form. Beauty of mind is the object and goal of the initiation into love, the top rung of the ladder in the initiation process, and ultimately the purpose of physical love and desire itself. Beauty of mind is beauty itself, the idea of beauty which participates in physical beauty, as the divine Idea participates in physical form. Beauty of mind, that is intelligible beauty, or beauty of the divine intellect, is "pure, unmixed, not cluttered up with human flesh and colors and a great mass of mortal rubbish," and it requires a particular faculty of mind on the part of the initiate to be able to perceive absolute beauty, a faculty which is learned and developed. The initiate must first be able to overcome the splendor of physical beauty, no matter how dazzling, intoxicating and overwhelming. He must be able to overcome the physical and emotional desire by which he is seduced by physical beauty. He must learn to "catch sight of divine beauty itself, in its single form," and in order to do that he must make use of the "right part of himself," in order to share in the company of divine beauty, the splendor of which is infinitely greater than the splendor of physical beauty.

The "right part" of the initiate which is trained to perceive absolute beauty is the rational mind, properly disciplined and prepared. Each thinking mind has an innate capacity to perceive and understand the intelligible of the divine intellect, which can be developed as even a skill (*techné*), as described in the *Republic*. This capacity of the rational mind is the function of the Intellectual Principle of Plotinus, the imagination (*Einbildungskraft*) of Schelling, and the Objective Spirit of Hegel. In *Republic* 490, Socrates describes the mental faculty by which the initiate "will not rest content with each set of particulars which opinion takes for reality, but soars with undimmed and unwearied passion till he grasps the nature of each thing as it is," that is, forms, as they participate in the absolute. The progress from the particular to the universal in reason is a dialectical process by which human reason becomes unified with divine mind.

In *Republic* 518, the capacity for knowledge is innate in everyone. The turning of the mind away from "the world of change" to be able to perceive reality, and "the brightest of all realities which is what we call the good," as the eye accustomed to darkness learns to see the light, as in the allegory of the cave, is a subject of professional skill, or *techné*, and the cultivation of the *areté*, or "excellences of the mind," in the training and discipline of the innate capacities of the mind for judgment, clear perception, and understanding. Knowledge must necessarily have a "diviner quality," as in the Intellectual Principle of Plotinus, that which is both eternal and unchanging and applicable to a specific cause, or universal and particular for Hegel. In *Republic* 519, the mind which can perceive the good, through training and discipline, is able to "give birth not just to images of virtue (since it's not images he's in touch with), but to true virtue (since it's true beauty he's in touch with)," as for Plotinus the artist goes back to the principles from which nature is derived, and for Hegel "picture-thinking," or perception, is the medium toward understanding. Images produced by the mind contain the inner understanding and beauty of the eternal principles in the soul, which is their true beauty, rather than their outward appearance.

Thus in the *Enneads* (I.6.5),[2] the perceiving mind is able to perceive the beauty within. This is accompanied by a "Dionysiac exultation that thrills through your being, this straining upwards of all your soul, this longing to break away from the body and live sunken within the veritable self." The beauty within is the participation of the soul and intellect in the beauty of the divine, of the eternal and unchanging, which is the result of the cultivation and disciplining of the innate capacities of the mind to transcend the manifestation of appearances. For Plotinus the result is a *katharsis*, a transcending of the body in consciousness, and an *ecstasis*, an intoxication of the mind brought about by a higher form of knowledge. It is a detachment from the sensible world of unstable knowledge, thus a kind of meditation, an experience of the inner self. The beauty found within, in the soul, is not derived from any material quality, any shape, color or mass, but rather the "hueless splendor of the virtues," as in the good of Plato. The hueless splendor of the virtues includes "loftiness of spirit; righteousness of life; disciplined purity; courage of the majestic face; gravity, modesty that goes fearless and tranquil and passionless; and, shining down upon all, the light of godlike Intellection," divine mind. As with Plato, the cultivation of the mind has a moral and ethical imperative; a moral and ethical society is the result of the cultivation of the moral and ethical citizen, through discipline and training of the *areté*.

In *Oration on the Dignity of Man*, Giovanni Pico della Mirandola asks, "who would not desire, putting all human concerns behind him, holding the goods of fortune in contempt and little minding the goods of the body, thus to become, while still a denizen of earth, a guest at the table of the gods, and, drunk with the nectar of eternity, receive, while still a mortal, the gift of immortality?"[3] In the Renaissance, the contemplation of beauty, the beauty of the good as manifest in the sensible world, following Plotinus, was a source of spiritual *ecstasis*. Pico continues, "Who would not wish to be so inspired by those Socratic frenzies which Plato sings in the *Phaedrus*...?" In the *Phaedrus* (245), Socrates describes how, in order to be expressive, the artist must be possessed by the madness of the Muses, which stimulates desire and rouses the soul to expression. In order to understand the Socratic frenzy, it is first necessary to understand the dual nature of the soul, how it is both divine and human. The soul participates in the divine because it is capable of moving itself, as well as being moved. It is capable of ascending the hierarchy of being toward the good, and thus must contain within it to begin with the quality of the good. It also moves and shapes the body, and determines the nature of sensible forms. Thus, "a body which moves itself from within is endowed with soul, since self-motion is of the very nature of soul. If then it is established that what moves itself is identical with soul, it inevitably follows that soul is uncreated and immortal" (*Phaedrus* 245),[4] that it participates in the divine Idea.

According to Socrates, the soul is both mortal and immortal because it is capable of traversing all of being and taking on different forms, as it is self-moved. The soul is immortal in that when it is "perfect and winged it moves on high and governs all of creation" (246), but it is mortal when "the soul that has shed its wings falls until it encounters solid matter. There it settles and puts on an earthly body, which appears to be self-moving because of the power of soul that is in it…" The wings of the soul are its divine attribute, that quality which allows it to ascend toward the good. The wings of the soul are nourished by beauty, wisdom and goodness, those qualities of the divine manifest in the Intellectual Principle of Plotinus, and which define the virtues of the good in the *areté* of Plato.

The soul aspires to the heights of the eternal beauty because it is stirred by passion and motivated by love, according to Plotinus, the Platonic love of the eternal form. As in the *Symposium*, the initiate ascends from love of the beauty of the body, to love of the idea of beauty, to beauty itself, which he finds within. For Plotinus, the *techné* of the disciplining of the mind involves the recognition of the principles of the eternal in sensible forms, in both nature and the arts, as they are given in the Intellectual Principle. The principles are manifest in correspondences, measures and proportions, which are displayed in sensible form and which stimulate the desire of the soul to ascend to the idea of beauty and to understand the good, to participate in Platonic love. In the *Enneads* (II.9.16), "those seeing by the bodily sense the productions of the art of painting do not see the one thing in the one only way; they are deeply stirred by recognizing in the objects depicted to the eyes the presentation of what lies in the idea, and so are called to recollection of the truth—the very experience out of which Love arises."

When the soul becomes free of the body it becomes completely intellective, participating in the divine Idea which is the source of beauty; the idea of beauty is communicated to the soul through the Intellectual Principle. When the soul is heightened to the Intellectual Principle it becomes beautiful itself. The beauty of the soul is its intellection, as it takes on the characteristics of the divine Idea. The divine Idea, the Authentic-Existence, is beauty itself (*Enneads* I.6.6), or the One, from which is derived Intellectual Principle, through which the soul participates in the divine. The Intellectual Principle is "pre-eminently the manifestation of Beauty," and through the Intellectual Principle the soul becomes beautiful. The human soul participates in both the sensible world and the eternal world; thus the beauty of sensible things in the world of appearance is a product of the eternal beauty in the soul from the absolute, through the Intellectual Principle. "For the Soul, a divine thing, a fragment as it were of the Primal Beauty, makes beautiful to the fullness of their capacity all things whatsoever that it grasps and molds."

This is reflected by Pico della Mirandola in *Oration on the Dignity of Man*. While the divine is absolute and eternal, the soul is both eternal and variable, participating in both the divine and the sensible. In the soul, "God bestowed seeds pregnant with all possibilities, the germs of every form of life" (p. 8). While every other form of life is subject to a prescribed set of laws and limitations, the human soul is free to determine its own nature, to determine the extent of its own participation in the sensible and eternal worlds; thus the Renaissance notion of free will. As in the *Symposium*, the soul, by the extent of its discipline and desire, varies the extent of its own involvement in the hierarchies of being.

As described by Plotinus in the *Enneads*, the *techné* of the ascension of the soul to the good involves a withdrawal into the inner self, "foregoing all that is known by the eyes, turning away for ever from the material beauty…" (I.6.8). The "shapes of grace that show in body" must be seen as copies, vestiges and shadows, like the shadows cast by the figures modeled by the students of geometry in *Republic* 510, and the shadows seen on the wall by the prisoners in the cave in *Republic* 514–516. Plotinus compares the reflections of material beauty to the reflections on the surface of the water which seduced Narcissus; if seduced by the reflections on the surface, the subject will be swept away in the current; he will not be able to break free of the chains of images, and "shall have commerce only with shadows."

Thus for Plotinus "the Soul must be trained" (I.6.9), as for Plato, to the end that the inner vision be able to see the ultimate splendor of the good. The soul must be able to recognize the good in civic virtue, in moral and ethical conduct. The soul must be trained "to the habit of remarking, first, all noble pursuits, then the works of beauty produced not by the labor of the arts but by the virtue of men known for their goodness..." The soul must then be able to recognize the source of the noble pursuits produced by virtue, that is, the nature of the producing soul. The only way for a soul to see another virtuous soul is to look into itself. In order to see the virtue of the inner soul, the subject must carve away everything that is excessive and impure, as does a sculptor when making a beautiful form. The subject must eliminate in his soul any knowledge based on the shadows and reflections which seduce him in the sensible world. The soul of the subject is crafted as a "stainless shrine" of perfect goodness from which "there shall shine out on you from it the god-like splendor of virtue."

In the *Phaedrus*, the subject sculpts his soul in the image of the god which he worships and does his best to imitate, and according to which he conducts himself. A soul loves another soul in which it sees an image of the god which it worships, which is the definition of Platonic love according to Marsilio Ficino. When the soul recognizes the good in a person as the object of his love, that is when the soul recognizes the idea of beauty or beauty itself as it is trained to do in the *Symposium*, the subject "fashions and adorns an image, metaphorically speaking, and makes it the object of his honor and worship" (*Phaedrus* 252). The image in the soul becomes a kind of talisman orienting the subject to the image of the god. It leads individual subjects to the discovery of truth in all knowledge and it allows them to "find in themselves traces by which they can detect the nature of the god to whom they belong." The image is a memory device which stirs the subject to remembrance of absolute beauty which is the source of sensible beauty, shadows and reflections. It also enables the subject to keep focus on the divine virtues which he is cultivating in his soul; the image crafted of the god in the soul allows the mind to participate in the divine, as it would through the Intellectual Principle of Plotinus.

The crafting of the image is the "picture-thinking" of Hegel, the process by which sensible forms are recognized as manifestations of ideas of forms in perception, and are thus able to participate in the universal through perception, in the same way that forms in the Reason Principle of Plotinus are transformed in the Intellectual Principle. In the Intellectual Principle, forms are self-generating and self-supporting, and it is in the image of picture-thinking, through perception, that forms in matter are possible. Forms in matter depend on the development of Reason Principle to form; all mental images are pre-generated by the reasoning process, through perception. As Plotinus explained in the *Enneads* (I.I.7), "The faculty of perception in the Soul cannot act by the immediate grasping of sensible objects, but only by the discerning of impressions printed upon the Animate [soul] by sensation: these perceptions are already Intelligibles, while the outer sensation is a mere phantom of the other (of that in the Soul) which is nearer to Authentic-Existence as being an impassive reading of Ideal-Forms." The discerning of impressions printed upon the soul by sensation is the function of reason, not perception, while perception is also a function of reason. Since the sensual impressions in perception are copies and derivatives of intelligible forms, perception itself is a copy and derivative of Reason Principle, which is closer to the intellectual, and thus absolute.

When the image is sculpted in the soul of Plotinus, the subject is able to be self-gathered in the purity of being and achieve an absolute inner unity like the absolute unity of the One. The subject becomes completely self-generated and self-dependent, and the idea of beauty and beauty itself. The subject is the beauty which the subject perceives in the intelligible, as in the *Symposium*, thus the seer becomes the seen; "when you perceive that you have grown to this, you are now become very vision" (*Enneads* I.6.9). Thought becomes the object of thought, and consciousness and ego dissolve into the universal, as in the self-consciousness of Georg Wilhelm Friedrich Hegel in the *Phenomenology of Spirit*. The unity of the One as manifest in the subject transcends the image as a mechanism of transferal, and the purity of the soul is experienced as pure light, beyond sensible form, "that only veritable Light which is not measured by space."

Thus for the seer to become the seen the eye must "become sunlike," and the soul must be beautiful in order to perceive beauty. In the *Republic*, Socrates describes the sun as being the source of the power of sight. The sun is the cause of sight and is at the same time seen by the sight it causes. The relation of the sun to sight is the same as the relation of the good to intelligence. In the same way that objects are clearly perceived when they are illuminated by the sun, and only dimly perceived in the dark or at night, so intelligible objects are clearly perceived by intelligence when they are illuminated by truth and reality, and dimly perceived when they are within "the twilight world of change and decay" (*Republic* 508), limited to sensible reality, which causes confusion and instability. The initiate in the *Symposium* learns to see the objects of intelligence as illuminated by the good and the absolute Idea, differentiating them from the sensible world of physical beauty and shadows and reflections. The good in the intelligible idea gives to intelligence the power of knowing as the sun gives to sight the power of seeing. Since the good is understood by the intelligence that it causes, the knower becomes the known in the same way that the seer becomes the seen, and consciousness and ego are dissolved in the absolute, as physical desire in the *Symposium* is dissolved into love of beauty itself.

As the beauty in the soul of Plotinus transcends beauty in the sensible world and becomes the pure unmeasurable light of the absolute, in the *Republic* the knowledge of the good in the soul, and the good as the cause of its knowledge, becomes a purer kind of knowledge than knowledge itself. The good is not accessible to the reality which it creates; it is pure and ineffable, and though the soul may participate in the good, in the pure light of the soul, the soul can never be the good, as sight can never be light. But in order for the soul to understand the good, it must become like the good, as in the *Enneads*, "first let each become godlike and each beautiful who cares to see God and Beauty" (I.6.9).

As in the *Symposium*, where the initiate moves from the beauty of the body to the beauty of all bodies, to the idea of beauty and to beauty itself, in the *Enneads* the soul moves from the Reason Principle to the Intellectual Principle and to the understanding of the One. The intelligible idea of beauty is visible to the soul in the Intellectual Principle, and it becomes clear that all sensible beauty is a product of intelligible beauty. The source of beauty lies beyond the Intellectual Principle in the good, or the One. There beauty is primal and absolute. In the allegory of the cave in the *Republic*, the good is the source of light in the visible region and the source of intelligence in the intelligible region. The good is perceptible to the mind in the intelligible region, to which it ascends from the visible region, represented by the prison in the cave, as the light of fire in the prison represents the visible good. The fire, representing the light of the sun, is the source of light in the visible realm, as the good is the source of intelligence, to which the mind ascends from the sensible world, as in the *Symposium*.

For Plotinus the good is the source of all and is self-generating and self-sufficient. It is the source and measure of all existence, while being immeasurable. It is also the source of all beauty, which is all existence, but is itself beyond beauty, as it is beyond existence. "The Good is beyond-beautiful, beyond the Highest" (*Enneads* I.8.2). The good is beauty itself, and thus cannot be beautiful. The first manifestation of the good is in the Intellectual Principle, but while the Intellectual Principle acts in relation to the good, the good remains stationary within itself and self-contained. The Reason Principle in the soul has the same relation to the Intellectual Principle, and through the

Intellectual Principle the soul has access to the good, that is, through the intelligible idea, as in the *Symposium.*

Plotinus describes the good, or the One, as "the untroubled, the blissful, life of divine beings" (*Enneads* I.8.2), which is visible to soul through the intelligible. In the *Phaedrus*, when the immortal souls (the gods) go outside the vault of heaven, that is outside the visible universe, and "stand upon the back of the universe" (247), they are able to "contemplate what lies outside the heavens"; they are able to see beyond the visible world into the region of the good, a region beyond beauty or any other form or representation. The region of the good visible to the immortal souls is "the abode of the reality with which true knowledge is concerned, a reality without color or shape, intangible but utterly real, apprehensible only by intellect which is the pilot of the soul." It is the realm of beauty itself as imagined by the initiate in the *Symposium.* When the soul perceives the region of the good it participates in divine intelligence, "sustained as it is by pure intelligence and knowledge, like that of every soul which is destined to assimilate its proper food." The capacity for understanding of the good exists in every soul, and can be realized if properly nourished and developed, as described in the *Symposium* and the *Republic.*

The divine mind, and the soul that participates in it, is nourished by the vision of the good, which keeps it on a regular, circular course. The vision of the good entails a vision of "absolute justice and discipline and knowledge, not the knowledge which is attached to things which come into being, nor the knowledge which varies with the objects which we now call real..." The realm of the good is a realm of being rather than becoming, of the universal rather than the particular, and of the absolute and unified rather than the multiple and diverse. Nourished by the sight of the good, the divine mind, the immortal souls or gods, return home to the vault of heaven. The charioteer (representing the soul) which drives the winged horses (representing the powers of the soul) feeds the horses ambrosia and nectar, as if to represent the "Dionysiac exultation" of the soul in contemplation of the good, as described by Plotinus. Thus, in the *Phaedrus*, "such is the life of the gods...," "the untroubled, the blissful, life of divine beings" described by Plotinus, the good which is visible to the soul through the intelligible.

For Plotinus, if the soul is able to perceive absolute beauty and harmony in the intellectual realm, then the soul is able to perceive manifestations of that beauty and harmony in the sensible realm, even as it is represented in the arts. The soul is stirred by a particular painting or sculpture "by recognizing in the objects depicted to the eyes the presentation of what lies in the idea" (*Enneads* II.9.16); the soul is also stirred by harmony in music and symmetry in visual compositions, including in the beauty of the body. In seeing the beauty of the body, for example, "the sight of Beauty excellently reproduced upon a face hurries the mind to that other Sphere," as described in the *Symposium*. When the soul is stirred by representative objects in the visible world, it is "called to recollection of the truth," of the idea of beauty in the intelligible, and it is this "experience out of which Love arises." Love is the process of bringing to vision, through understanding, the absolute beauty of which physical beauty is a manifestation, and in so doing, of confirming the absolute beauty present in the soul. As Gustav Aschenbach experiences in Thomas Mann's *Death in Venice*: "His eyes embraced that noble figure at the blue water's edge, and in rising ecstasy he felt he was gazing on Beauty itself, on Form as a thought of God, on the one and pure perfection which dwells in the spirit and of which a human image and likeness had here been lightly and graciously set up for him to worship" (p. 60).[5]

It is possible in the thought of Plotinus that the ineffable beauty of the good, that which is the source of beauty and beyond beauty itself, can be represented in the sensible world. Or, at least, that forms in the sensible world can suggest the ineffable beauty of the divine, or the possibility of such beauty. It is the contemplation of sensible forms in perception, and the consciousness of perception as distinct from the sensible forms, or the Intellectual Principle, which leads to the contemplation of the intelligible in sense perception. While the perception of the beauty of the good is only possible for those souls which have been trained and disciplined for it, the good, and the beauty of the good, are present always already in every soul. The love of beauty on the part of the soul follows the love of the good; the good is prior, as it is most primal and archetypal. To perceive the beauty of the good is to understand that it is a beauty only for itself; it is not meant to be perceived, and it is not meant to give anything to the perceiver. Beauty is nevertheless dependent on the good, which is dependent on nothing, and is a manifestation of the One.

The perception of intelligible beauty is a medium by which the soul understands the divine. Intelligible beauty may be perceived in art in the understanding that the beauty of a form of art has nothing to do with the form itself, but with how the form corresponds to the idea of beauty in the mind of the artist. In the same way, the beauty of a form in nature has nothing to do with the form itself, but how the form corresponds to the idea of beauty in divine intelligence. This is illustrated by Plotinus by comparing two blocks of stone, one of which is carved into a statue by a craftsman, so that in which "the form is not in the material; it is in the designer before ever it enters into the stone..." (*Enneads* V.8.1). The beauty of the stone therefore pre-exists the stone in a higher state, and the beauty in the stone is just a "derivative and a minor" of that prior beauty, the intelligible beauty, as material forms are shadows and reflections of intelligible forms in both art and nature. The material form of the stone is limited as to how much it can participate in the intelligible beauty; it is impossible for a craftsman or artist to express completely the intelligible beauty which he understands in his soul, and in being.

Thus the making of art, and the contemplation of beauty in nature, in particular the human form, which is the highest manifestation of beauty in nature, is a perpetual cycle of desire in the pursuit of the absolute, which is ineffable and unattainable, but the pursuit of which is necessary for its understanding, for the consummation of being, for the cultivation of the intellect, its disciplining in the understanding of the intelligible, and for the experience of love. This is expressed by Diotima in the *Symposium*, and by Thomas Mann in *Death in Venice*, as Gustav Aschenbach contemplates the figure of Tadzio, the beautiful boy (pp. 60–61):

> Had he not read that the sun turns our attention from spiritual things to the things of the senses? He had read that it so numbs and bewitches our intelligence and memory that the soul, in its joy, quite forgets its proper state and clings with astonished admiration to that most beautiful of all the things the sun shines upon: yes, that only with the help of a bodily form is the soul then still able to exalt itself to a higher vision. That Cupid, indeed, does as mathematicians do, when they show dull-witted children tangible images of the pure Forms: so too the love god, in order to make spiritual things visible, loves to use the shapes and colors of young men, turning them into instruments of Recollection by adoring them with all the reflected splendor of Beauty, so that the sight of them will truly set us on fire with pain and hope.

In the *Republic* of Plato, "And I think that you call the habit of mind of geometers and the like reason but not intelligence, meaning by reason something midway between opinion and intelligence" (511).[6] Opinion is concerned with the world of becoming, the transformations of material things, while intelligence is concerned with the world of reality, the stable and indivisible archetypal ideas. Geometrical and mathematical figures are visible images of pure forms. In the dialectic, in order for the mind to be able to go beyond the assumptions of a first principle and rise to the intelligible, it must make use of the images in the sensible world as illustrations, an example of these images being geometrical figures (511). While the geometer "sees one circle, he is studying another, the circle in the understanding, yet he makes his demonstrations about the former," the circle in the imagination.

For Plotinus, the beauty in a work of art is created by the Reason Principle, which transfers the ideas of the Intellectual Principle to material form. The beauty of the work of art, as manufactured by the Reason Principle, is preceded by the idea of beauty in the Intellectual Principle, which is preceded by beauty itself in the good, following the ascension of the mind of the initiate in the *Symposium.* As beauty enters into matter from the Idea it is dispersed and weakened, as it is transferred from unified and pure light to multiple intertwined bodies, as in the Baroque ceiling fresco—by Correggio in the Cathedral of Parma, Bacciccio in Il Gesù, etc. "In the degree in which the beauty is diffused by entering into matter, it is so much the weaker than that concentrated in unity." Nevertheless, all beauty in matter is derived from the idea of beauty, and form is derived from the idea of form as generated in the Reason Principle; it is in the Idea as it is manifested in the Reason Principle that matter retains its beauty, as the perception of beauty in matter, and the perception of beauty in forms of art, depends on the understanding of the Idea, the participation of the Reason Principle in the Intellectual Principle. Phidias sculpted Zeus by understanding the idea of the form of the god, not by imitating matter.

Beauty in nature is not in the material but in the idea which governs the perception of form. Beauty in nature is that which participates in the perception of nature, the interaction of nature and Intellectual Principle through Reason Principle, in the process of picture-thinking, in Hegelian terms. Beauty can only be given by Intellectual Principle (which is why, for Hegel, art is superior to nature); without the idea, matter can be only "sheer ugliness or (at best) a bare recipient" (*Enneads* V.8.2). Without participation in the Intellectual Principle, matter is Absolute Ugly: "All shapelessness whose kind admits of pattern and form, as long as it remains outside of Reason and Idea, is ugly by that very isolation from the Divine-Thought. And this is the Absolute Ugly: an ugly thing is something that has not been entirely mastered by pattern, that is by Reason, the matter not yielding at all points and in all respects to Ideal-Form" (I.6.1). The idea in the Intellectual Principle, as it functions in perception, coordinates a diversity of parts into a unity, and transforms confusion into harmony. This was the basis of the *concinnitas* of Leon Battista Alberti in the Renaissance, the theory of harmonious composition in nature as described in *De re aedificatoria*. The diverse forms of matter in nature are unified by a "precise rule" so that they have a harmonious relationship. Beauty is a harmony and grace in bodies that results from a composition of surfaces (II.35);[7] it is not the body which is beautiful, but the form of the body as it is perceived. Surfaces which are out of proportion and lacking grace are ugly to look at like the "faces of old women."

The beauty of form as it is manifest by the Intellectual Principle is twofold, divine and visible, unseen and seen. Quoting Thomas Mann in *Death in Venice*, Socrates says to Phaedrus, in the shade of the plane tree outside of Athens, "For Beauty, dear Phaedrus, only Beauty is at one and the same time divinely desirable and visible: it is, mark well, the only form of the spiritual that we can receive with our senses and endure with our senses" (p. 61). The idea of beauty exists separately from the form, as immaterial unity. Material form does not contain beauty in itself, except in that the form is the object of perception, and the participation of the sensible in the Intellectual Principle. Plotinus explains, "as long as the object remains outside us we know nothing of it; it affects us by entry; but only as an Idea can it enter through the eyes..." (*Enneads* V.8.2). In order for an object to be perceived, it must be constructed according to the idea of it. Perception itself is a process of construction, of conceptual construction of the sensible world as it intersects with mind. Works of art, if they are successful, reproduce the constructive process of perception and the intersection of the intellect and the sensible world. Beauty is composed of this intersection. It is itself a construct of perception, and the self-knowledge of the perceiving subject, that is, self-consciousness, in Hegelian terms. Beauty is ultimately the physical realization of self-consciousness, a symbol of the projection of the self into the sensible world; literally, beauty is in the eye of the beholder. Beauty is a vehicle in the construction by the subject of the relationship between himself or herself and the sensible world, and a projection of the ego of the subject into that relationship; as such beauty is a function of desire.

Aphrodite in particular, the goddess of beauty, or any god or goddess the image of which the perceiving subject molds in himself or herself, is beautiful in both idea and image. The twofold beauty of the goddess reflects the dual nature of the soul, participating in both the sensible world and the intellectual. "To us Aphrodite is twofold; there is the heavenly Aphrodite, daughter of Ouranos or Heaven: and there is the other the daughter of Zeus and Dione, this is the Aphrodite who presides over earthly unions..." (V.8.2). The heavenly Aphrodite has no mother, born of immaculate conception as it were, and is the daughter of Kronos or Saturn, which is the Intellectual Principle, the divine mind.

The heavenly Aphrodite "must be the Soul at its divinest: unmingled as the immediate emanation of the unmingled; remaining ever Above, as neither desirous nor capable of descending to this sphere, never having developed the downward tendency, a divine hypostasis essentially aloof, so unreservedly an Authentic Being as to have no part with Matter..." The heavenly Aphrodite is the good, the nature of the One, the source of everything but unparticipant in anything, separate from and preceding the sensible world, *a priori*, and the cycle of desire in perception. Beauty which emanates from the intellectual is also pure and unmixed, uncontaminated by the material, and even material beauty, as in reflections and shadows. Beauty beheld in the inner soul is as light beheld from the sun; pure beauty in the inner soul is the presence of the good, or the One, which is present in every soul. Eros, or love, turns the soul toward the pure inner beauty of the divine.

The act of the soul turning to the divine within generates a hypostasis or a level of being in relation to the divine. Love is the medium between the soul, or desire, and the object in the soul of desire, divine beauty, or the good. It is only by the initiative of the individual soul, as in the *Symposium*, that the good can become known and visible. The mechanism by which the soul sees the good in itself is perception, or picture-thinking. "It is the eye of the desirer; by its power what loves is enabled to see the loved thing." By the power of sight the soul is able to see the un-seeable, the good. Love enacts desire through vision, and thus enables the idea of beauty to participate in the objects of perception: "desire attains to vision only through the efficacy of Love, while Love, in its own Act, harvests the spectacle of beauty playing immediately above it."

In the *Symposium* (180), Pausanias explains to Phaedrus the two Aphrodites: heavenly Aphrodite is the older Aphrodite, also called the Uranian Aphrodite, being the daughter of Ouranos. The other Aphrodite is the Common Aphrodite, also called Pandemic Aphrodite, daughter of Zeus and Dione. In the *Theogony*, Hesiod described Aphrodite as being formed from the foam that formed in the ocean around the castrated genitals of Ouranos, having been thrown there by Kronos. "And out stepped a modest and beautiful goddess, and the grass began to grow all around beneath her slender feet" (193–195).[8] As love directs the desire of the soul toward the beauty of the divine, or the heavenly Aphrodite, thus "Eros and fair Desire attended her birth and accompanied her as she went to join the family of gods" (199–201).

The birth of Aphrodite from the sea, and the dual nature of Aphrodite, or beauty, as both divine Idea and sensible form, is illustrated in Alessandro Botticelli's *Birth of Venus*, a product of the influence of the Platonic Academy in Renaissance Florence. Heavenly Aphrodite becomes Common Aphrodite when she is clothed by Flora, a goddess of nature, having come to shore from the sea, as described by Hesiod: "About them a white foam grew from the immortal flesh, and in it a girl formed. First she approached holy Cythera; then from there she came to sea-girt Cyprus. And out stepped a modest and beautiful goddess..." (191–194).

The beauty that desire pursues in material form, like the reflection of Narcissus or the figure of Tadzio, the sensible beauty, is not the same beauty that is its source, namely, divine beauty. The disciplined mind, as of the initiate in the *Symposium*, is able to recognize that it is the inner, divine beauty, which affects the soul, rather than the outer reflection. The disciplined mind is able to recognize the pure inner beauty not through its manifestation in sensible forms, but in the good, the intangible beauty of justice and virtue, as in the vision of the good on the part of the immortal souls in the *Phaedrus*, of "absolute justice and discipline and knowledge." In the *Enneads*, "but that the thing we are pursuing is something different and that the beauty is not in the concrete object is manifest from the beauty there is in matters of study, in conduct and custom; briefly, in soul or mind" (V.8.2). While sensible beauty is a catalyst to the desire for absolute beauty, pure beauty is already manifest in virtue, as manifestation of the good.

In the more disciplined souls, the light of absolute beauty shines brighter, though the source exists in all souls. It would seem, in *Enneads* V.8.3, that the closer natural forms are to the human form, thus to the soul, the brighter the light of the archetypal beauty shines. "Thus there is in the Nature-Principle itself an ideal archetype of the beauty that is found in material forms and, of that archetype again, the still more beautiful archetype in Soul, source of that in Nature." There is a hierarchy of beauty; things become uglier the further away they are from the absolute beauty in the Intellectual Principle, and its manifestation in soul, in Reason Principle. There is also a hierarchy of beauty in soul, as "in the proficient soul this is brighter and of more advanced lovliness: adorning the soul and bringing to it a light from that greater light which is Beauty primally..." This hierarchy of beauty is evident in high classical sculpture, with the human form as the ideal, being a product of the Athens of the Academy of Plato.

The archetypal beauty of the Intellectual Principle is unrepresentable whole, but may be represented in part, in the image of the gods within. The beauty of the gods is in intellect rather than form, "Intellect operating within them…to visibility" (V.8.3). The intellect is the pure and unified beauty, beauty as virtue. The gods, as dwellers of heaven, "live at ease" (V.8.4) in authentic being, perfect lucidity, all possessing all in intellect, unchangeable and absolute, in eternal contemplation of the infinite. The contemplation of the eternal is infinite because there is never satisfaction. "This absence of satisfaction means only a satisfaction leading to no distaste for that which produces it; to see is to look the more, since for them to continue in the contemplation of an infinite self and of infinite objects is but to acquiesce in the bidding of their nature." The intellect participates in the contemplation of the infinite on the part of the gods in a kind of *stupefazione*, giving oneself to the infinite beauty of the intellect as a form of pleasure, not in a cycle of desire, as in the contemplation of forms or images, but in a desire without ego or self-consciousness, generated from within and self-perpetuating. This kind of *stupefazione* was applied to the experience of the Baroque church. Fra Bonaventura wrote about San Carlo alle Quattro Fontane in Rome, for example,[9]

> What amazes people the most is that when one continues to look at this church it makes one wish to look more and one seems to see it anew and is left with the desire to return to see it again. They see so well that it gives such pleasure that it does not weary them but rather incites the desire to see more of it: it seems to me that this tends to imitate something of the Divine. The Divine Essence incites such pleasure that when one sees it, filling the soul with sweetness, it seems to incite a greater desire to see it and always seeing it always makes it appear something new.

The geometries of the church are representations of the principles of the intellect, and the beauty of the forms represents the idea of beauty, as for the geometers in the *Republic*. The pleasure of the contemplation of the forms simulates the pleasure of the gods living at ease in contemplation of the infinite. While the cycle of desire in the sensible realm is a cycle of satisfaction and regeneration, as in procreation, the only satisfaction in the desire for the infinite is the absence of satisfaction, as Plotinus explains. The participation in the desire of the gods was seen as a kind of intoxication in the Renaissance, a blinding joy (*gaudium*, for Marsilio Ficino) and a mystical self-annihilation in the giving of oneself, one's ego and self-consciousness, to the divine. As Giovanni Pico della Mirandola asks in *Oration on the Dignity of*

Man in 1486, "Who would not desire, by neglecting all human concerns, by despising the goods of fortune, and by disregarding those of the body, to become the guest of the gods while yet living on earth, and, made drunk by the nectar of eternity, to be endowed with the gifts of immortality though still a mortal being?"[10]

The geometries in the architecture incite contemplation of intelligible forms, according to the intellect of the architect, in the same way that forms in nature incite contemplation of the absolute according to the intellect of the Demiurge of Plato. The absolute beauty of the divine is reflected in the beauty of the forms, in the intellectual and sensible worlds. According to Plotinus, this is illustrated by Plato in the approval of the Demiurge of the forms created; the beauty of forms is recognized by the archetype of beauty, and thus the beauty of the first principle is understood. In the *Timaeus*, "When the father who had begotten it perceived that the universe was alive and in motion, a shrine for the eternal gods, he was glad, and in his delight planned to make it still more like its pattern; and as this pattern is an eternal Living Being, he set out to make the universe resemble it in this way too as far as was possible" (37).[11] It was not possible for the Demiurge to transfer absolute beauty and eternity completely to the material world; time was intended to be "a moving image of eternity," to enable the sensible world to participate in the eternal. Through geometries, the sensible world participates in absolute beauty. The beauty of the forms of the visible world, in nature and art, pleases the divine mind, and the beauty therein, as a copy of it, and the beauty of the visible world is the greatest of all beauties other than the divine, being the closest copy or manifestation of it. "And indeed, Plotinus asks, "if the divine did not exist, the transcendently beautiful, in a beauty beyond all thought, what could be lovelier than the things we see?" (*Enneads* V.8.8).

For Plotinus, being is beauty itself, and beauty is being. "Being is desirable because it is identical with Beauty; and Beauty is loved because it is Being" (V.8.9). This is the case because being is perception, or picture-thinking, or thinking. I perceive therefore I am, thus I think therefore I am. Being is defined in its participation in the Idea, which is its participation in beauty. "The power in that other world has merely Being and Beauty of Being." The superficial forms of beauty in the sensible world, as they are perceived, are copies of being itself, as they are copies of the divine mind, which is archetypal beauty. The essence of archetypal beauty is not beautiful form, but the good, the pure light of the beyond, as when in the *Phaedrus* the immortal souls arrive at the vault of heaven and "being appears before them from some unseen place and rising loftily over them pours its light upon all things, so that all gleams in its radiance," as recounted by Plotinus (*Enneads* V.8.10). The content of being, archetypal beauty, is not beautiful form, but "the font and principle of Justice...the sight of Moral Wisdom." When the immortal souls see the eternal beauty, they become beautiful; when the mortal soul sees the copies of eternal beauty in visible forms, it becomes beautiful (it fulfills its being) if it understands the source of the beauty, through training and discipline, as in the *Symposium*. "This vision Zeus takes and it is for such of us, also, as share his love and appropriate our part in the Beauty there, the final object of all seeing, the entire beauty upon all things; for all there sheds radiance, and floods those that have found their way thither so that they too become beautiful; thus it will often happen that men climbing heights where the soil has taken a yellow glow will themselves appear so, borrowing color from the place on which they move" (*Enneads* V.8.10). When the soul understands the beauty of the divine, in its participation it assumes an inner beauty, a beauty which soaks its content and pervades its essence, as opposed to a beauty which adorns its clothing, its parameters and manifestations.

The soul penetrated by absolute beauty in its essence is as if "drunken with this wine, filled with the nectar, all their soul penetrated by this beauty." The soul is "become the guest of the gods while yet living on earth, and, made drunk by the nectar of eternity," in the words of Giovanni Pico della Mirandola. The soul penetrated by the absolute beauty is no longer a spectator; the perceivers become the perceived, and "hold the vision within themselves" (*Enneads* V.8.10). In that way being is fulfilled; "thus a man filled with a god...need no longer look outside for his vision of the divine being; it is but finding the strength to see divinity within." This is what is accomplished in the *Symposium*, as it is "someone who's given birth to true virtue and brought it up who has the chance of becoming loved by the gods, and immortal—if any human being can be immortal." The fulfillment of being, the understanding of absolute beauty, is an *enthusiasmos*, the filling of the soul with the god, the participation of Reason Principle in Intellectual Principle.

In the penetration of the soul with absolute beauty, the perceiver becomes the perceived, and image becomes self-identical with the act of perception. In true being there is no separation between thought and beauty; the divine intellect is beauty. In Hegelian terms, the individual passes from consciousness to self-consciousness to identity with Spirit, the source of being and being. The perceiver, or thinker, "must give himself forthwith to the inner and, radiant with the Divine Intellections (with which he is now one), be no longer the seer, but, as that place has made him, the seen" (*Enneads* V.8.11). The seer becomes the seen in the gaze of Jacques Lacan in psychoanalysis as well. In *The Four Fundamental Concepts of Psycho-Analysis*, the gaze is "something that introduces what was elided in the geometral relation—the depth of field, with all its ambiguity and variability, which is in no way mastered by me. It is rather it that grasps me, solicits me at every moment" (p. 96),[12] as absolute beauty, and the Intellectual Principle.

The gaze of Lacan transcends vision as absolute beauty and the Intellectual Principle transcend the Reason Principle of Plotinus. The gaze "is not in the straight line, but in the point of light—the point of irradiation, the play of light, fire, the source from which reflections pour forth. Light may travel in a straight line, but it is refracted, diffused, it floods, it fills" (p. 94). The gaze is not given by geometry in nature; it is the pure light radiating from the beyond as observed by the immortal souls in the *Phaedrus*. The gaze is as the good, the source of beauty, as the sun is the source of light. The gaze is not spatial but luminous, without spatial coordination and geometric abstractions, as pure being, radiant and intelligible.

The gaze is located between perception and consciousness, and is that which is transmitted from stage to stage, as from the Reason Principle to the Intellectual Principle. Lacan explains that "from the moment that this gaze appears, the subject tries to adapt himself to it" (p. 83), as in the presence of the divine in the soul; "he becomes that punctiform object, that point of vanishing being, with which the subject confuses his own failure." The individual soul adapts to the presence of the absolute within by attempting to recognize the absolute through the copies manifest in visible forms, through the geometries in nature which are the mechanisms of perception, or picture-thinking. The subject identifies himself in the construction of his perception, as in the picture-thinking (*Vorstellung*) of Hegel, as the vanishing point in the geometrical perspectival scheme, the scaffolding by which the subject searches for the absolute in the order of the visible world. Thereby the subject becomes self-conscious, and participates in Intellectual Principle, as a means toward the good. In order for the soul to participate in the good, it must lose its distinction from the visible world as the vanishing point in the scaffolding of perception; it must be absorbed into that visible world, through perception, as in the gaze, and thus see beauty as the good, not as visible or intelligible form.

As Plotinus explains, the subject must construct an image of himself as participating in the intellectual: “any one, unable to see himself, but possessed by that God, has but to bring that divine-within before his consciousness and at once he sees an image of himself, himself lifted to a better beauty” (*Enneads* V.8.11), through the mechanisms of perception. But then the subject must transcend the image constructed of himself, by becoming identical with it, by allowing perception to become being, and he must dissolve his self-consciousness into the essence of the good, as in the doubling of the in-itself (*an sich*) of consciousness in self-consciousness for Hegel: “now let him ignore that image, lovely thought it is, and sink into a perfect identity, no such separation remaining…” (*Enneads* V.8.11). The seer becomes the seen in the withdrawal into the inner self, in the transcendence of the body toward the good by way of the intelligible. To see the divine is to be external to the divine, while to understand the divine is to be one with it.

As the subject sees himself beyond the construction of perception in the intelligible, and absorbed into the essence of the good and the absolute beauty, so the universe moves from a geometral construction in perception to the radiant light of the good, visible to the immortal souls, unified and immeasurable. Plotinus suggests (V.8.9),

> Let us, then, make a mental picture of our universe: each member shall remain what it is, distinctly apart; yet all is to form, as far as possible, a complete unity so that whatever comes into view, say the outer orb of the heavens, shall bring immediately with it the vision, on the one plane, of the sun and of all the stars with earth and sea and all living things as if exhibited on a transparent globe. Bring this vision actually before your sight, so that there shall be in your mind the gleaming representation of a sphere, a picture holding all the things of the universe moving or in repose or (as in reality) some at rest, some in motion. Keep this sphere before you, and from it imagine another, a sphere stripped of magnitude and of spatial differences; cast out your inborn sense of Matter, taking care not merely to attenuate it: call on God, maker of the sphere whose image you now hold, and pray Him to enter. And may He come bringing His own Universe with all the gods that dwell in it—He who is the one God and all the gods, where each is all, blending into a unity, distinct in powers but all one god in virtue of that one divine power of many facets.

Thus visible beauty becomes essential beauty, and the human soul participates in the immortal soul, filled with the nectar of eternity, becoming a guest at the table of the gods. The intuition of the good in the perception of beauty in the visible world leads to the knowledge of the essence of the good within, as in *Death in Venice*, "only with the help of a bodily form is the soul then still able to exalt itself to a higher vision." The soul is beautiful when it is true to what is within, true to its own being, rather than to what is external, and not participant in absolute beauty. The soul is beautiful in its self-knowledge, through the Intellectual Principle, through which comes knowledge of the divine, thus know yourself. The soul is not beautiful without self-knowledge, though all souls contain the capacity for beauty. The good can only be found further inward from the intellectual, further withdrawn from the sensible, in absolute being, in a model for the Philosophy of Spirit.

3
The Aesthetics of Schelling

In *Bruno, or On the Natural and the Divine Principle of Things*, in 1802, Friedrich Wilhelm Joseph von Schelling describes the ability of the initiate to recognize absolute beauty, based on the *Symposium* (210), where the initiate "should realize that the beauty of any one body is closely related to that of another, and that, if he is to pursue beauty of form, it's very foolish not to regard the beauty of all bodies as one and the same. Once he's seen this, he'll become a lover of all beautiful bodies, and will relax his intense passion for just one body, despising this passion and regarding it as petty. After this, he should regard the beauty of minds as more valuable than that of the body..."[1] The uninitiated will be unable to recognize beauty other than that of the body, while the initiated will be able to recognize the imperfection of the absolute beauty as it is manifest in sensible form, and at the same time will be able to intuit the presence of the absolute. This intuition involves feelings of wonder, terror and fear, as in the sublime (*Bruno* 225). It also involves self-consciousness, and the ability of the soul to distinguish between the inward participation in the Intellectual Principle and the outward participation in the sensible. The intuition of absolute beauty is, as for Plotinus, dependent on self-knowledge and self-cultivation.

The distinction between the experience of the inner intellectual and the outer sensible is described in *Timaeus* 46–47, where the fire within the eyelids, that fire which produces sight, "smoothes and diffuses the internal motions, and produces a calm,"[2] while the interaction of the internal fire and the external fire, or the ideal and real, results in sensible appearances, composed of distorted unities, reflections and shapes produced by "accessory causes." For Schelling and Hegel, beauty is the product of the intersection of the intellectual and the sensible, the ideal and real, the universal and particular. In the *Phaedrus*, only the human soul is able to "collect out of the multiplicity of sense-impressions a unity arrived at by a process of reason" (249).[3] The soul is able to do this after it has taken its journey with a god, achieved divine communion, dined at the table of the immortal souls. It is in the recollection of the visions of the gods, an anamnesis, that the soul takes wing and is initiated into a mystical vision, the experience of the sublime. The soul is possessed by the divine, and is intoxicated with love, the desire for the absolute, in an *ecstasis*, and *katharsis*, in the pure light of the One. "Pure was the light and pure were we from the pollution of the walking sepulcher which we call a body, to which we are bound like an oyster to its shell" (250).

The soul remembers and loves everything from its experience of the beatific vision, and like the initiate in the *Symposium* (210) it will be turned away from the "low and small-minded slavery" of love for the beauty of a body, and the initiate "will be turned towards the great sea of beauty and gazing on it he'll give birth, through a boundless love of knowledge, to many beautiful and magnificent discourses and ideas." In the beatific vision the soul sees "the revolutions of intelligence in the heavens" (*Timaeus* 47), the manifestation of the pure light of the One in the Intellectual Principle, and through the Intellectual Principle the soul uses "their untroubled course to guide the troubled revolutions in our own understanding," Reason Principle. The vision of the soul is made possible by the internal fire of the absolute (a *scintilla della divinità*, a spark of the divine), which corresponds to its correlate in the sensible world, the vision of the eyes, and the fire of the sun. Vision in sight is a correlate and derivative of the idea of vision in the Intellectual Principle in the same way that sensible beauty is a correlate and derivative of the idea of beauty.

According to Schelling, sensible beauty does not exist; it is only representative of the presence of absolute beauty in the sensible world, as for Plotinus. The idea of sensible beauty is a product of the identification of the absolute or the archetype, the intellectual idea, and the productive and procreative functions of nature. Sensible beauty is a product of the identification in the mind between intellectual processes and natural occurrences; "and this identity also clearly explains why beauty shines forth wherever the course of nature permits, though it never itself enters existence" (*Bruno* 225).[4] Sensible beauty is a product of the projection of the inner self onto the sensible world, the interaction of the inner and outer fires. Although beauty appears to come into being in the sensible world, this is only an appearance; beauty can only exist if it exists eternally, as the archetypal and absolute, visible to the soul of the initiated in the *Symposium*. When something which is beautiful comes into being in the sensible world, it is not the beauty of it which comes into being, but the object itself. The beauty of the object, as for Plotinus, does not exist separately from the perception of the object by the soul. The eternal and archetypal idea is itself beauty, as for Plotinus; if an object in nature or art is beautiful, it is because it reflects the eternal idea in vision. The uninitiated will not be able to identify sensible beauty with the archetypal idea, and will mistake the idea of beauty for physical beauty. Archetypal beauty is mistaken for physical beauty because the manifestation of its qualities, an inferior and deceitful truth, "allies itself with the imperfect, temporal elements of existing forms, with qualities impressed on them from without, rather than with those developed organically from their concepts" (*Bruno* 227). The soul which is not cultivated from within cannot see the beauty of forms which is cultivated within them as the absolute.

The artist who imitates the beauty of forms in nature is not able to unify the natural and the divine, or the real and ideal, matter and thought, and is thus not able to express being. The beauty of forms in nature should not even be called beauty, but rather a derivative and subordinate to it. Thus art which imitates natural beauty is a derivative and subordinate to real art. As for Plotinus, the artist does not merely imitate natural forms, but goes back to the principles from which the forms are derived, in order to reveal the archetypal beauty of which the forms are temporary manifestations. The philosopher and the poet must also concern themselves with the archetypal and absolute, and learn to differentiate the sensible and intelligible, and learn to cultivate beauty itself, as they cultivate the inner soul, rather than temporal and physical instances and revelations of it.

It is not that the sensible world should be rejected, as Plato would have it, but that the sensible and intelligible worlds be melded into the absolute and eternal Idea. The principal departure on the part of both Schelling and Hegel from the Platonic Idea and the Plotinian hypostases is the insistence that the Idea always be seen as participating in the sensible world, in experience, and that the absolute cannot be conceived without the union of the two, the inner and outer fires, which nevertheless was not entirely denied by either Plato or his most important descendent. For Schelling "the eternal is related to all things through their eternal concepts" (229) in the same way that for Plotinus the One participates in all things, although that participation is not reciprocal, as it is for Schelling.

The artist, in creating a beautiful work of art, does so in the same way that the Demiurge creates beauty in the world, or the sensible participates in the absolute. The artist allows beauty, existing eternally (pre-existing temporal production) to be revealed or translated into sensible objects. The work of art must exist independently of the artist; that is, the work of art must participate in the universal, in order to reveal absolute beauty. The individual soul of the artist, the particular manifestation of the absolute and universal, must be transcended, in the same way that the particular existence of an object in nature is transcended in the apprehension of the eternal. The individual artistic act becomes a singular manifestation of the *Zeitgeist*, the universal soul and spirit of a people, in Hegelian terms, the correlate to the soul of the absolute. Only in that way is the work of art beautiful. The beauty of the object of art is identical to the beauty of the soul of the creator, in that both exhibit the participation of the particular in the universal and the real in the ideal. The artist, in order to produce a beautiful work, must be initiated into the mystical vision of eternal beauty of the immortal souls, and understand beauty itself, further than the idea of beauty or the physical manifestation of beauty, as in the *Symposium*. In creating a beautiful work of art, the artist expresses the divine beauty within his soul, as it is intuited in the mystical vision, and understood in the Intellectual Principle; the artist is capable of producing a beautiful work of art in so far as his or her soul is able to participate in the intelligible, and allow the absolute to participate in the particular. Absolute beauty is revealed in the individual soul in the same way that it is revealed in the sensible form, as a particular manifestation of the eternal in time.

The dialectic in the soul in artistic production, the intuition of absolute beauty in the mystical intuition, and the understanding of the idea of beauty in the Intellectual Principle, as it informs the Reason Principle, or reason, is clearly present in the thought of both Plato and Plotinus. For Schelling, the dialectic is the dialectic between unconscious and conscious thought in the soul of the artist. In the *Bruno*, the idea exists in the soul of the artist as both an absolute and a concept. Divine beauty manifests itself as particular in the individual soul, and it is "conceivable that the idea of divine beauty could exist in this way and at the same time exist fully and essentially as well" (*Bruno* 230). This is necessary for the individual soul to participate in the universal soul, the *Zeitgeist*. Divine beauty exists within the soul of the individual "in an absolute mode, and not as the immediate concept of the individual." The individual soul reveals divine beauty in the same way as the particular sensible form; in that way, the particular sensible form as well has both a conscious and unconscious being, as it is a function of human perception, or Hegelian picture-thinking. The unconscious soul is "possessed by the idea of beauty" just as the sensible form, subdued and inebriated by the eternal and absolute in its particular manifestation.

In the *System of Transcendental Idealism* of Schelling in 1799, "this unchanging identity, which can never attain to consciousness and merely radiates back from the product, is for the producer precisely what destiny is for the agent, namely a dark unknown force which supplies the element of completedness or objectivity to the piecework of freedom..." (p. 222).[5] The unchanging identity, the dark unknown force, is the One or the absolute beauty as it participates in the Intellectual Principle, which radiates itself to consciousness but cannot be known in other than a mystical vision, an intuition of its presence, as the unconscious, the deep structure of the real, the underlying eternal. The role that the absolute plays in the creativity of the artist is determined by the extent of the genius of the individual soul. The philosopher, unlike the artist, is able to understand conceptually the idea of the absolute in the intellectual, as it plays a role in conscious thought. The artist, though, is able to tap more directly the force of the absolute and eternal, and allow it to be manifest in the work of art.

Rather than understand the concept of eternal beauty, as does the philosopher, the artist is possessed by the absolute, as he has more direct access to the unconscious. "The artists most fit to produce beautiful works are often those least in possession of the idea of absolute truth and beauty. They lack the idea precisely because they are possessed by it..." (*Bruno* 231). The soul of the artist, rather than understand the idea of absolute beauty through Reason Principle, more likely *is* the idea of absolute beauty, or the translation of the idea of absolute beauty into temporal production, as in nature. As has been seen, in the *Phaedrus* the understanding of the universals on the part of the philosopher involves the role of a mystical vision, and the taking wing of the soul in recollection of the beatific vision of the immortal souls. The artist, unable to attain to the intellectual intuition of the universals, "will necessarily look like one who defiles the mysteries, not their initiate and devotee" (*Bruno* 231), as certainly was the case for Plato.

The artist nevertheless utilizes the divine Idea, and would thus appear to understand it, and to understand beauty as the identity of the real and ideal, the phenomenal and noumenal. In Plato and Plotinus, beauty could only be the ideal, inaccessible to the real. The soul of the artist appears to be absolute beauty, and to understand absolute beauty, in the same way that sensible form appears to be beautiful. Thus "from the most ancient of times poets were revered as mouthpieces of the gods," as in Orphism. Schelling comes to the conclusion that art, no matter how inspired by genius is the artist, can never be absolute beauty, but only the appearance of such, the correlate of the temporal manifestation of absolute beauty in the soul. Philosophy, on the contrary, is capable of recognizing the absolute beauty, because the philosopher is not dependent on the temporal manifestation of the absolute in his soul; he is able to understand the idea of the absolute, and within the idea he is able to view the essence of the absolute.

The work of art, no matter how much it exhibits the presence of the universal and absolute, must always maintain the element of the particular and the individual, no matter how much it is subsumed into and unified with the former. The idea of the philosopher is not bound to a concrete particular, Schelling suggests (though, if seen from the point of view of Structural Linguistics, the written word of the philosopher, the language into which the philosopher translates the idea, like the form into which the artist translates the idea, can be seen as the concrete particular to which the philosopher might be bound). As Schelling explains, "the principle governing the thought of the man who philosophizes is not the eternal concept insofar as it is immediately related to his individuality, but this same concept considered absolutely and in itself" (232). In Structural Linguistics, the eternal concept might be seen as the signified, the idea, while the individuality might be seen as the signifier, the word that corresponds to the idea; in that case, the absolute could not exist without the particular, and could not be taken as an essence in and of itself. The unity of the universal and particular is in fact the basis of Schelling's definition of beauty. In this way, though, philosophy is necessarily hermetic, in that it cannot completely account for the essence of the absolute without the participation of the particular; in the Platonic tradition, it can only be known by a mystical vision. "But the purpose of all the mystery rites is none other than to show men the archetypes of all that they are accustomed to seeing in images."

The archetypes that are discovered in the mysteries are that "something unchanging, uniform, and indivisible beyond the things that ceaselessly change and slide from shape to shape," the Platonic Same. Hegel confirmed that the archetypes are discovered in the mysteries, at the table of the gods, in the *Phenomenology of Spirit* in 1807: "For he who is initiated into these mysteries [the ancient Eleusinian Mysteries of Ceres and Bacchus] not only comes to doubt the being of sensuous things, but to despair of it" (109).[6] The archetype must be known by the soul, according to Schelling, "in some nontemporal way, before birth, as it were" (*Bruno* 232), in the unconscious. The knowledge of the archetypes must be by a soul of a prior state, in which it had immediate access to the archetypes, as in a pure state of the Intellectual Principle. The current state of the soul is one which is removed from its originary state, "torn from this state by its union with the body, that is, its transition over to temporal existence" (233). The composition of the soul includes an unconscious remembrance of a lost origin, and the soul exists in a continual state of being thrown from its origin, of being alienated from itself, other to itself.

The archetypal being, accessible through the mystery rites, which open the unconscious, exists in the depths of the soul inaccessible to conscious thought. The remembrance of the lost origin is the remembrance of the mystical vision of the immortal souls; the love of the archetypal reality is the love of the self-lack and self-alienation of the soul, the essential soul lost in the sensible world, the inability to unite the ideal and the real. Though beauty is that unification, it is an impossible one, and a sense of beauty must be accompanied by a sense of despair in loss and alienation, the longing for which there is no satisfaction. This then is the madness of the philosopher who soars to the heights of essential being with wings, in search of the beatific vision, of the origin which is unknowable, the mystery of existence.

Initiation into the mysteries causes the remembrance of the beatific vision, and the "previously intuited ideas of the true itself, the beautiful, and the good," none of which themselves are present in the sensible world, except as unseen cause. Philosophy is ultimately the teaching of the mysteries of being, and their paradoxical relation to the intellect. Like mythology and poetry, the teachings of the mysteries are passed down from generation to generation, and enhanced and elaborated by each generation, as from Plato to Plotinus to Schelling and Hegel. The mysteries, the mystical visions of the immortal souls, are communicated to the human soul by spirits, in the unconscious. The spirits are love, that which compels the soul to discover the mysteries. This was explained in the *Symposium*, by Diotima to Socrates. Love is a spirit between mortal and immortal, between the human and the divine, and love is the messenger between them. Love is that which binds the universe, and allows it to be whole, as both real and ideal. It is the medium for the mystery rites—divination, sacrifice, ritual, prophecy and sorcery.

As love as a spirit fills the gap between mortal and immortal, it fills the gap between ignorance and wisdom. Love (Eros) is love of wisdom, and love of beauty (Aphrodite, born on the same day), love of absolute beauty and the eternal, the One. Love is the child of Resource (Wealth) and Poverty, as

Diotima explains (*Symposium* 203), as he vacillates between life and death, mortal and immortal. Wealth corresponds to eternal form, replete with all forms, "infinitely fruitful in forms" (*Bruno* 311), archetypal and unchangeable, the One, while Poverty corresponds to particular and sensible form, "essentially barren" matter. Matter is "splendid in its poverty," because the "infinite possibility of all forms and shapes" can be found within matter. Matter is thus possibility, while the archetypal is actuality, thus "all forms are expressed in matter and are actual at all times," unfolding from the eternal in time. The eternal absolute is all forms, and absolute beauty is the manifestation of all beauty. Through time, the absolute differentiates itself, as in the *explicato* of Nicolas Cusanus, unfolding into multiplicity and impermanence, from the totality of the universe.

Though the initiate and philosopher are able to understand the presence of absolute beauty in the sensible world, absolute beauty cannot be completely distinguished from sensible beauty: "it is impossible to say where the realm of exemplars ends and where that of copies begins" (*Bruno* 317). Exemplars and copies, the ideal and real, are combined in the Idea, in the Intellectual Principle; they are both contained within the One, and are both manifest in matter. They are both infinite: "actuality within the world of copies is just as infinite as possibility is within the exemplary world." The more that sensible beauty partakes of absolute beauty, in nature and in art, the closer the form is to the eternal, the closer the ideal and real, actual and possible, are merged, and the more readily the initiate and philosopher conceive of the absolute.

The real cannot exist without the ideal, and vice versa. Absolute beauty could not be known without the beauty of the body, which points to it. Beauty is the synthesis of the dialectic, the combination of the two extremes, which are codependent. The task of art is not just to conceive the union of the ideal and real, but then to re-conceive the ideal and real out of that union, to separate them out and differentiate them, to represent eternal beauty and sensible beauty in relation to their union. To do this the artist must represent the infinite and the finite, the eternal and temporal, the actual and possible, and then "we shall grasp how that simple ray of light that shines forth from the absolute and which is the absolute itself appears divided into difference and indifference, into the finite and the infinite" (328).

The point of the dialectic, as it is represented in art, and pursued in philosophy, in the course of love, love of the absolute, is to identify and differentiate the opposites of ideal and real at every level and in every combination, and to examine the nature of the differentiation, in the same way that multiplicities are resolved into unities in the intellect, from the Reason Principle to the Intellectual Principle. In the Renaissance, mathematics and geometry were the tools by which the philosopher identified and pursued the elements of the dialectic toward wisdom and absolute knowledge, as in the *De circuli quadratura* of Nicolas Cusanus, based on the *Commentary on the First Book of Euclid's Elements* of Proclus.

The dialectic continues until the point is arrived at where the "absolute identity appears divided into two relative identities," the simplest division of the One, in which the point of origin of the real or natural and ideal or divine worlds is revealed. As each is contained in the other, the "eternal incarnation of God" is seen in the real world, and the "inevitable divinization of mankind" (*Bruno* 329) is seen in the ideal world. The union of the ideal and real is the union of the idea of absolute beauty and sensible beauty into beauty itself, and the union of the unconscious and the conscious mind, the Intellectual Principle and the Reason Principle. Thus, "now when we have scaled this peak and behold the harmonious light of this wondrous cognition, we shall realize that this cognition is at the same time that which is real in the divine essence; then we shall be granted the favor of seeing beauty in its brightest splendor and not be blinded by the sight, and we shall live in the blessed company of the gods." This is the goal of the philosopher, and the capability of the philosopher, and every human soul, for Plato, Plotinus and Schelling, in the consummation of being in the intellect.

The Philosophy of Art

The purpose of art then, for Schelling, is to express the ideal through the real, the universal through the particular. Genius is the identity of the universal and particular in the work of art, the "absolute indifference [identity] of all possible antitheses between the universal and the particular" (§ 69),[7] as Schelling described in *The Philosophy of Art*, published as *Die Philosophie der Kunst* in 1859, based on lectures given in 1802–03 at the University of Jena. As such the true work of art is an emanation (*emanieren*) or outflowing (*Ausfluss*) of the absolute (*das Unbedingte*) and eternal, as the universe is an emanation of the multiple from the particular, as in the concept of the Baroque. Forms in the sensible world are emanations from ideas in the intelligible world, which, as for Plato and Plotinus, exist separately from the forms, eternal and unchanging. It follows that the philosophy of art, aesthetics, is philosophy itself, and art is an expression of philosophy. This is reiterated throughout *The Philosophy of Art*. The relation between forms in art and intelligible ideas can be seen in the same way as the relation between forms in the real world and intelligible ideas. To that extent the artistic genius is *artifex secundus deus* in the understanding of the divine mind, Intellectual Principle, and artistic creativity is *scintilla della divinità*, a spark of the divine fire. The purpose of philosophy is to understand how particular forms come to be in relation to the ideas, and how particular forms can be explained in relation to a totality, which is also the purpose of aesthetics.

In the intellect, all matter in the sensible world is symbolic. Objects in the sensible world are given to perception as forms which are the product of ideas, archetypes of the forms. Philosophy concerns itself with the ideas, and the ideas are represented in art as forms in perception; art makes concrete "the essential forms of things as they are in the archetypes" (*The Philosophy of Art*, p. 7), the idea of the form as it is symbolized in the intellect. How the Idea, the essential or archetypal form (Platonic form), is symbolized in the particular form in art is the subject of aesthetics. How the symbol is executed in the production of art is the subject of art theory. Aesthetics, or philosophy, concerns itself with the Idea in itself, while theory is concerned with its *Ausfluss* or manifestation. The Idea, or archetype, as a symbol of a particular manifestation of the eternal and unchanging absolute essence, is a *potence*, or force, which is the medium of the transition from the universal to the particular and the unified to the multiple. The absolute is that element of the intellectual which is not variable according to sense perception. *Potences* are the variable, divisible determinations of the invariant and indivisible, symbols of the essence of the absolute in the intelligible. They are the principal subject of philosophy, because they are the correspondence between the particular idea and the universe as a "totality of all ideal determinations."

The universe is the One, the indifference or identity of all *potences*, and this is the first principle of philosophy, thus the Philosophy of Spirit (*Geist*) of Schelling, the philosophy of the intellectual, is also called Identity Philosophy (*Identitätsphilosophie*). The One is the One of Plotinus, undifferentiated essence, without particularity, the source of all particulars in essence but not in substance. For Plotinus the essence of the One becomes a particular as an archetype or idea in the Intellectual Principle, and the force or will of this becoming is the *potence* of Schelling. The totality of the universe is necessary in conception because of the nature of the perceiving subject and the act of perception, because of the nature of the relation between the sensible object and the concept, which assumes a totality in language, whether verbal or pictorial. All language requires the participation of the universal and the particular in order to be understood; for concepts to be communicated, a totality is necessary.

For Kant, the sensible world is thought; for Derrida, the sensible world is misrepresented by thought, as a totality is imposed upon it which does not exist outside of thought; for Schelling, there is necessarily a negotiation between the sensible world and thought, between the real and ideal in the Platonic tradition, thus the Philosophy of Spirit, or Identity Philosophy. The absolute is that which is ideal and not real. The Philosophy of Spirit is a sensual philosophy, a procreative act on the part of the intellect, as it negotiates and interacts with the sensible world (as itself, a reflection of itself, or something alien to itself). Beauty is the marriage of the real and the ideal. The same can be said for the philosophy of Plotinus, which lays the groundwork for the Philosophy of Spirit, in its systematic attempt to bridge the real and ideal in the hypostases of being and hierarchies of emanation.

The totality, the indifference or identity of all *potences*, is present in each *potence* of Schelling, as the essence of the absolute is present in each individual form for Plotinus. In philosophy, the absolute can only be known in the idea of the absolute, although it can be intuited in a mystical vision, and the idea of the absolute can only be known through its manifestation in particular forms. The importance of the particular form is in its manifestation as an absolute, which requires the indifference of the universal and particular, which is the subject of philosophy, and the definition of beauty in aesthetics. The concern of philosophy is the absolute, the ideal or essence in thought, and the concern of aesthetics is the expression of the ideal. The philosophy of history, as Hegel demonstrates, is concerned with the expression of the ideal in history, in the temporal unfolding of events in ethics and morality. The purpose of philosophy for Schelling is to establish a system or a science (*Wissenschaft*) as a framework for the understanding of the negotiation between thought and the sensible world, and the manifestation of thought in the sensible world, of the ideal in the real. The purpose of aesthetics is to establish a science of that negotiation in the arts, but as an object of aesthetics the art must be capable of representing the ideal in the real, the universal in the particular, the totality in the differentiation.

In the Philosophy of Spirit, the absolute is represented in the intellect as an archetype, the *archê* of Plato, by which it is formulated as an Idea *(Ur-*

bild), as in the Intellectual Principle of Plotinus. The sensible form in art and nature, the reflection and shadow of the ideal form in the real, contains within it the essence of the absolute, which is understood by the initiate, in the mystery rites or philosophy, as in the *Symposium*. The understanding of the sensible form of itself (*Dasein*), or in its physical beauty, is an "exoteric" cognition (*für sich* for Hegel), while the understanding of the sensible form as a manifestation of the Idea, symbolizing the archetype, is an "esoteric" cognition (*Ansichsein*). The esoteric cognition, that of the initiate into the hermetic knowledge of philosophy, is the cognition of the sensible world in relation to thought, or cognition itself, and as it is manifest in language and perception, or picture-thinking (*Vorstellung*), in Hegelian terms. The ideas of the philosopher, symbols of the archetypes, are translated into forms by the artistic genius, sensible and particular, forms within which it is possible to understand the Idea, as the universal essence of the substance and beauty of the form. The form is a schema or a symbol of the Idea, and the presence of the ideal is intuited in the form in the same way that it is intuited in the intellect, in the intelligible realm.

The archetypes that are represented by the forms of art in the sensible realm are the same as the archetypes that are represented by the ideas in the intelligible, as for Plotinus the artist goes back to the principles on which nature is based. The forms of art have the same function as the ideas of philosophy. Art objectifies the archetypes which are imperfectly represented in nature, thus art is superior to nature, as it is for Hegel, in that it is a higher manifestation of the ideal. "The complete forms generated by the plastic arts are the objectively portrayed archetypes of organic nature itself" (*The Philosophy of Art*, p. 17), as Plotinus held as well, which are the intelligible archetypes of the intellectual; the work of art is a representation of the intellectual, human reason and perception. As the absolute is the source of the archetype (*Urbild*) in the intelligible, so the absolute is the source of the archetype in art, and in particular the source of the archetype of beauty, the absolute and universal beauty of the mind intuited by the initiate in the *Symposium*, which is the source of the beauty of forms, which is the source of the beauty of bodies. For Schelling, the purpose of aesthetics is to establish the correlation between beauty and the absolute, as it was for Plato and Plotinus, and then to determine how beauty itself, the absolute, is manifest in particular forms, "how individual beautiful things can issue from universal and absolute beauty"; in other words, how individual forms as they are perceived relate to the idea (*Idee*) of them in the intellect.

Art intuits absolute beauty through particular forms which are sensible correlates of ideas. They are intuited exoterically in sensible forms, as opposed to the esoteric intuition, of the essence of the ideas, in and of themselves, of philosophy, as in the Intellectual Principle of Plotinus. All forms in art are emanations from the archetypal forms, as are all forms of nature. In philosophy, the sensible manifestation of the ideas in the imagination is mythology, that is, the gods. Mythology plays the same role as art in representing the universal ideal in the real; the gods are the multiple determinations of the singular divine essence in bodily form in the imagination in the same way that forms of art are the multiple determinations of the singular essence of the absolute in the sensible or real world. Mythology and art differ from nature in that the gods and the forms of art are symbols of the Idea, self-reflections of the intelligible. Symbols of the Idea can be extracted from natural forms, as in mathematical and geometrical principles, but the natural forms are not symbols themselves, and are thus further derivatives of the Idea. This lays the groundwork for the supremacy of Romantic art over Classical art according to Hegel, because Romantic art symbolizes the self-reflection of the Idea in the intelligible, while Classical art merely imitates nature, while attempting to extract the symbols of the ideas from it. The gods of mythology are "nothing other than the ideas of philosophy intuited objectively"; the Classical work with mythological subject matter is thus closer to the intelligible idea than the imitation of nature, and closer to the philosophical representation of the essence of being, as intuited by the philosopher. The beauty of mythological subject matter is closer to the idea of beauty and absolute beauty itself, as it symbolizes the idea of beauty in concrete form.

Forms in nature, in the real, are by necessity characterized by a nonidentity between the universal and particular, or a disjunction between the two, so that one or the other of the elements predominates in the form. Nature can never adequately participate in the ideal, as for the Neoplatonist the forms of nature are further removed from the divine mind than the mind or the soul. Forms in nature are obscure and intertwined, in shadow and reflection, and need to be illuminated by the idea of the forms in the mind. Forms in nature, and forms in art, are composed of the entrance of the infinite into the finite, the ideal into the real, while ideal forms of the mind are composed of the entrance of the finite into the infinite, or the participation of the finite in the infinite, so that the infinite predominates. Forms in art are dominated by the finite and real, while ideal forms in the mind, in philosophy, are dominated by the infinite and ideal, and are thus purer forms, of a greater beauty.

Philosophy is the expression of the intellect, the higher soul, or *anima prima*, in Marsilio Ficino's terms in the *Theologia Platonica*, while art is the expression of the lower soul, the *anima secunda*. The *anima prima* consists of mind, which is directed toward contemplation and the *intellectus divinus* (Intellectual Principle, in Plotinian terms), and reason (*ratio*), which is directed toward perception, picture-thinking. According to Ficino, the *anima secunda* is directed toward the functions of nature in their necessity: *augmenti* (growth), *nutritionis* (nourishment), and *potentia generationis* (propagation). The forms of art of Schelling participate primarily in the necessity of nature in the soul, and participate in the intellect, in freedom, only as much as possible. The forms of the intellect participate primarily in the intelligible realm, the realm of ideas and archetypes, and participate in necessity only as is necessary to verify their being in the real. Painting is that form of the visual arts which participates in the ideal realm to the greatest extent, because in its effects of light its forms are the least dependent on the real and tangible forms to have an effect on the viewer.

The forms of art conform primarily to necessity in time as well as in space. Because the forms of art must participate in the unfolding of time in their corporeal expression, they cannot participate completely in the absolute essence which precedes time, and the eternal beauty. Like forms of nature, forms of art are given by perception, which is a lower function of mind, and dependent on necessity, on cause and effect. Perception is a function of Reason Principle, not Intellectual Principle, or *intellectus divinus*, which precedes it. Perception is a process of construction on the part of reason based on the archetypes of mind, and is therefore subject to time; thus the objects of perception, forms in the visual arts and nature, are subject to time, and cannot be purely essential or absolute.

In the model of Nicolas Cusanus, in *De circuli quadratura*, the forms of art and nature are the polygonal geometries which approach the circumscribed circle in their complexity, as functions of human intellect, but may never achieve the simplicity and unity of the circle, the divine mind. The forms of nature and art are themselves composed of those geometries and mathematics which approximate the intelligible in the sensible world, but which may never be the intelligible in its essence. It is important for the philosopher and artist to be able to understand the nature and limitations of the participation of sensible forms in the intelligible, though, as it is important for the initiate in the *Symposium* to be able to understand the idea of beauty and beauty itself, in order to appreciate the nature of perception, and the nature of the participation of the perceiving subject in the sensible world.

Art must nevertheless be seen as an emanation of the absolute, as are forms of nature, but which are not afforded reciprocal participation. The history of art must be seen, as history itself must be seen for Hegel, as the unfolding of the absolute in art, the *explicato* of the intelligible. This is not possible in nature, because the forms of nature cannot participate in the intelligible to the same extent as the forms of art, as they are completely bound by necessity. The teleological purpose of art as it unfolds through history, and the purpose of philosophy, is to reveal the absolute, to allow the human soul to come to an understanding of itself. The indifference of the ideal and real in the forms of art is revealed more in the evolution of the forms than in one particular form in itself. The forms taken as a whole in evolution through time, in history, participate to a greater extent in the universal, or the ideal, which is the element in the dialectic which is the most lacking in sensible form, as sensible form begins with the particular and differentiated.

Forms in art become more of a whole, undifferentiated and less particular, when they are taken together in their history. All artforms are individual manifestations of the same absolute, as are all forms of nature. "Only in the history of art does the essential and inner unity of all works of art reveal itself, a unity showing that all poetry is of the same spirit, a spirit that even in the antithesis of ancient and modern art is merely showing us two different faces" (*The Philosophy of Art*, p. 19). In the representation of the history of art, the idea of art becomes symbolic in the indifference of the real and the ideal as it is expressed in the ideal. Spirit is the essence of the ideal, which is given by art in the symbolic.

The content of all works of art is the representation of the absolute, as all works of art are the product of freedom in relation to necessity. As Schelling explains in the *System of Transcendental Idealism* (p. 231), "Infinity is exhibited in every one of its products. For if aesthetic production proceeds from freedom, and if it is precisely for freedom that this opposition of conscious and unconscious activities is an absolute one, there is properly speaking but one absolute work of art, which may indeed exist in altogether different versions, yet is still only one, even though it should not yet exist in its most ultimate form." The idea of art is as the Idea itself, the representation of the undifferentiated One, the universal which precedes all particulars. Art will never exist in its most ultimate form, because though it participates in the ideal, it exists in the real, and corresponds to the inability of the human being to ever become complete, the inability of human intellect to become absolute.

As for Hegel, Schelling's project is to announce the end of art in the classical sense, and to differentiate between the classical subject and the modern subject, but then to dissolve the distinction into a single continuum, the growth toward the revelation of the absolute. The individual work of art is ultimately an ethical act; it is the particular participating in the universal (the definition of art itself), combining necessity and freedom in the progress toward absolute freedom, for the individual and society, and the progress toward the self-knowledge of the perceiving subject. The ancient and the modern, Classical and Romantic art, participate in the same dialectic toward a synthesis as do the ideal and real, and universal and particular. Absolute beauty must be found in a synthesis of the two, one which has yet to be achieved.

In *The Philosophy of Art*, the participation of the form in nature or art in the absolute, or the participation of the real in the ideal, which is the purpose of art, is defined by Schelling as the *potence*, or power. The first *potence* is matter, that which is predominantly real, into which all ideality is resolved. The second *potence* is light, the ideal element of the real into which all reality is resolved, corresponding to the intelligible idea in the intellect, the first manifestation of the absolute. The third *potence* is the essence of the real, or natural form, which contains the indifference of the real and ideal, and the unity of the essence of each. The essence of matter is defined as being, the resolution of the ideal, and the essence of light is defined as activity, the resolution of the real into the ideal. The essence of nature is the indifference of being and activity. The first *potence*, matter, is not essence (universal) nor substance (particular), but rather *accidens* (occurrence), which is combined with the essence or universal within light to create form.

As in contemporary Catastrophe Theory, matter is a temporary manifestation of essence (energy) through light, a momentary instability in the stable flux of energy that makes up the universe. Matter is the shadow and the reflection, in Platonic terms, insubstantial and ephemeral. The material world, as given by perception, is "a number of layers, permeable to something analogous to light whose refraction changes from layer to layer....an immense display, a special specter, situated between perception and consciousness," as described by Jacques Lacan in *The Four Fundamental Concepts of Psycho-Analysis* (p. 45),[8] a kaleidoscopic field of particles whose essence results in its intersection with light, in the infusion of the ideal in the real, as it unfolds in the act of perception and the participation of perception in the intellect, through consciousness. In Schelling's words, "matter, viewed according to its corporeal appearance rather than in itself, is not substance but rather merely *accidens* (form) with which the essence or the universal within light is juxtaposed" (*The Philosophy of Art*, § 11).

In the third *potence*, the essence of nature, form becomes essence, that is, in combination with light, it is no longer completely real, completely ephemeral and accidental. In order to participate in the universal, in order for the real to participate in the ideal, matter must be perceived, and interact with its idea, in the intelligible. Unperceived, matter is pure being, without substance or essence. It is impossible to consider unperceived matter as participating in being, because as such it has no existence, but as it participates in being, through the intersection of perception and intellect, it can never become the unresolved ideal, but only the real, unaffected, thus pure being unparticipant.

The third *potence*, the indifference of essence and form, is the organism in nature, the combination of being and activity. The being of the organism is its activity, and its activity is its being, obeying the laws of necessity in cause and effect, thus, "the affirmed element is absolutely equal to the affirming." The existence of the organism is its own justification; it has no consciousness, and thus cannot fully participate in the ideal; it remains a resolution of the ideal in the real. As the particular forms of the organisms are their own justification in being and activity, they remain particular and individual, and because of the separate multiplicity of its forms, nature remains largely unpaticipant in the ideal. The sum of all the particulars of the real do not equal the ideal; the ideal exceeds the sum of all the particulars of its manifestation. "For God is not equal to the particular result of his affirmation but rather only to the *allness* of these results to the extent that it is a pure position and as allness simultaneously absolute identity."

This was the basis for the aesthetics of *concinnitas* of Leon Battista Alberti in the Renaissance. Alberti wrote, in the treatise on architecture, *De re aedificatoria* (VII.4), "It is the task and aim of *concinnitas* to compose parts that are quite separate from each other by their nature, according to some precise rule, so that they correspond to one another in appearance."[9] Alberti follows Plotinus in his conception of *concinnitas*; in the *Enneads* (I.6.1), matter is transformed into a harmonious coherence by the ideal forms in the intelligible: "But where the Ideal-Form has entered, it has grouped and coordinated what from a diversity of parts was to become a unity: it has rallied confusion into cooperation: it has made the sum one harmonious coherence:

for the idea is a unity and what it molds must come to unity as far as multiplicity may."[10]

For Schelling, it is only when nature "transfigures itself into a totality and absolute unity of forms" (*The Philosophy of Art*, § 11), as in *concinnitas*, and the Ideal Form, that nature may be a "mirror of the divine," may participate in the ideal, in the totality of the intellectual, by means of the Reason Principle of Plotinus. Nature can only participate in the ideal through reason, because reason constitutes the "dissolution of all particular forms." Reason is thus an intermediary between the real and the ideal, that which connects the two, existing in some degree separately from both. This was expressed by Giovanni Pico della Mirandola in *Oration on the Dignity of Man*, as the Demiurge addressed his creation: "We have made you a creature neither of heaven nor of earth, neither mortal nor immortal, in order that you may, as the free and proud shaper of your own being, fashion yourself in the form you may prefer. It will be in your power to descend to the lower, brutish forms of life; [or] you will be able, through your own decision, to rise again to the superior orders whose life is divine…" (p. 7).[11] As reason exists separately from both the real and ideal, the sensible form and the intelligible idea, neither can be absolute, undifferentiated or eternal. The closest that each can attain to the absolute is indifference, the identity of the real and the ideal, the essence of nature and the intelligible. Absolute indifference is only possible within reason, and it is only through reason that the absolute is revealed, first in the archetypes of the Intellectual Principle, *intellectus divinus*, then in the mystical vision, the *via negativa* of Pseudo-Dionysius, the transcendence of reason as the indifference of the real and ideal toward the absolute.

As the essence of nature in reason is the indifference of the real and ideal, the essence of the absolute is the divine, the *intellectus divinus*. The essence of the absolute ideal is the resolution of the real in the ideal, as the essence of matter is the resolution of the ideal in the real. The degrees of the indifference of the real and ideal are the *potences*, as in matter, light, and organism. In human nature, in the ideal, action is the *potence* in which the real predominates, the objective activity, in the realm of the *anima secunda*, and Reason Principle, and knowledge is the *potence* in which the ideal predominates, the subjective activity. As the essence of nature is the essence of the real world, the indifference of matter and light, so the essence of the ideal world is the indifference of action and knowledge, and Schelling defines this indifference as art. Art is the essence of human activity in which action and knowledge are dissolved into a single identity and a unified manifestation of human identity and expression. Art is activity "completely permeated by knowledge" (*The Philosophy of Art*, § 14) and "knowledge that has completely become activity." Art combines the Idea in knowledge, the intelligible idea of Intellectual Principle and the form of Reason Principle, with the temporal unfolding or *explicato*, explanation, in its execution and perception. Art combines the ideal and the real in the ideal realm; it grounds the intellect in the real, and negotiates the relation between the sensible and intellectual realms.

The complete resolution of the *potences* is the absolute, or the divine, and is the subject of reason and philosophy. In the first principles of philosophy, the absolute, or divine, is the indifference of the affirming and the affirmed, of objective and subjective, of perception and consciousness. As indifference the absolute is totality and simplicity, the All of Plotinus, the One as absolute unity preceding number (not in time, but in idea). The absolute precedes the real as the idea of the circle precedes the form of the circle, as in the *Republic* (511), while the geometer "sees one circle, he is studying another, the circle in the understanding, yet he makes his demonstrations about the former."[12] The circle in the understanding is the idea or archetype of the circle which is the manifestation of the absolute in the Intellectual Principle (in Plotinian terms). The absolute is never completely revealed in the real, as the real is always only a *potence*, a force or a manifestation, as is the ideal. The absolute is not completely revealed even in the indifference of the real and ideal, which is still in the realm of the ideal. Schelling sees the science of philosophy as the absolute in the phenomenal ideal, the *anima secunda*, the resolution of particularity in the phenomenal, in the same way that the divine is the resolution of particularity in the archetypal ideal, the *anima prima*.

Philosophy, like reason, and art, belongs neither to the real nor ideal (archetypal) world, but contains the indifference, the resolution, of the two. Philosophy is the self-consciousness of reason, its self-affirmation and self-analysis. Reason is "the matter or objective model of all philosophy" (*The Philosophy of Art*, § 15). Reason is the objective and philosophy is the subjective in the ideal, as *potences*. Philosophy, in that its subject is the archetype or intelligible idea, contains within it the representation of the absolute; art, on the other hand, cannot represent the absolute, but only the presence of the absolute in the real, in the indifference of the real and ideal. While a work of art cannot represent the absolute, it can correspond to the idea of the absolute (the archetypal manifestation in philosophy), in the degree to which the ideal predominates over the real. The beauty of the work of art corresponds to the idea of beauty, and beauty itself, the more that it displays universal beauty, and the beauty of the idea, of mind, as described in the *Symposium.* As the indifference of the real and ideal, and the indifference of action and knowledge, art is the manifestation of philosophy in the real, or phenomenal world; it is the closest thing to philosophy in the real, but it is not philosophy completely, in that it is contained in the real; it is phenomenal philosophy, the ideas of philosophy translated into forms. Art is the "highest *potence* of the ideal world," the highest participation of the real in the ideal, and the highest participation of the ideal in the real.

The three *potences* in the real, matter, light and organism, correspond to truth, the good, and beauty (*veritas*, *bonitas*, and *pulchritudo*, the manifestations of Aphrodite in the real). The good is light, as for Plato, the predominance of the ideal, and the infusion of the absolute into the real. The good is the pure light of the beyond, as when in the *Phaedrus* the immortal souls arrive at the vault of heaven and "being appears before them from some unseen place and rising loftily over them pours its light upon all things, so that all gleams in its radiance," as recounted by Plotinus (*Enneads* V.8.10). The essence of nature is not beautiful form, but "the font and principle of Justice...the sight of Moral Wisdom." Beauty is the indifference of matter and light, the real and ideal, the particular and universal, the finite and infinite. As in the *Symposium*, it is found in matter, in form, in the idea, and ultimately in the absolute. In the indifference of the real and ideal, the form takes on the qualities of the idea, thus the qualities of the universal; the phenomenal becomes reason, and matter attains consciousness.

The qualities of the true, good and beautiful are unified in philosophy as they are in the absolute. As such, philosophy is an ethical science, which distinguishes it from all other sciences, and, as such, philosophy depends on art, in the understanding of beauty as the indifference of the real and ideal. The true is the objective, the real, irrefutable phenomenal existence, while the good is the subjective and the ideal; thus "necessity corresponds to truth, freedom to goodness" (*The Philosophy of Art*, § 16). As the indifference of the real and ideal, beauty is the indifference of freedom and necessity in the real. A form in nature or art is beautiful when it exhibits the maximum amount of freedom (creativity, imagination, disorder, chaos) within the bounds of necessity (custom, law, order), when the dialectic is visible but the ideal predominates over the real. A form is beautiful when the subjective, freedom, is able to develop to the fullest extent within the objective, necessity, when it is allowed to grow and take on a life of its own, but not independent of the laws of cause and effect.

The relation of philosophy to art in the ideal is the same as the relation of reason to the organism in the real. Each determines the infusion of the ideal into the real. Art objectifies, makes concrete, philosophy, as the organism objectifies reason. The objectification of reason in the organism is the soul, and the objectification of philosophy is the soul, or essence, of art. Art is the organism of the ideal as the organism is the art of the real; the forms of art are the concretized ideas of the intelligible, the participation of reason in the archetypal. The forms of nature are the concretized ideas of reason, which participate in the archetypal indirectly; thus the absolute is not completely manifest in nature. In the work of art, the ideal and real, freedom and necessity, are clearly distinct. They are distinguished from one another in the relation between consciousness and perception, between the perceiving subject and that which is perceived. Human consciousness is one of self-alienation, of freedom from necessity, and this is always visible in art, the objectification of philosophy. The subjective and objective are unified in art only after they are separated and distinguished from one another. The dialectic is the co-existence of the subjective and objective, thus the necessary basis of reason, and of art.

In nature, the subjective and objective are unified without having been separated, as there is no alienation of perception and consciousness in the organism, no self-consciousness, no expression in complete of the absolute. In the organism, the infusion of the real into the ideal, multiplicity into unity, complements the infusion of the ideal into the real, light into matter. The universal, light, is subordinated to the particular, matter. The universal is subordinated because the ideal cannot exist as ideal in the real; it must become real, whereas the real can exist in the ideal, thus in the ideal freedom and necessity are more equally balanced and clearly differentiated. In the ideal, the indifference of the real and ideal is clearly seen as the indifference of necessity and freedom, as given by the science of philosophy, while in the real the indifference of the real and ideal is subsumed by the real, and the differentiation of freedom and necessity is obscured, undeveloped, and unresolved. "Since only in the ideal world does the antithesis of the universal and the particular, the ideal and the real manifest itself specifically as that between necessity and freedom, the organic product represents that same antithesis still unresolved (because it is not yet developed) that the work of art represents as suspended (in both the same identity)" (§ 18). The development of the indifference of the real and ideal in the work of art depends on the *a priori* separation and self-alienation of the two in self-consciousness.

As art is based on the indifference of the ideal and real, freedom and necessity, it is based on the indifference of the unconscious and the conscious, as the unconscious contains the intuition of the intelligible idea, and the mystical vision of the absolute. In the same way that beauty in art depends on the maximization of freedom within the bounds of necessity, art is the medium of expression of the maximization of the presence of the unconscious within the bounds of the conscious. This conception of art played an important role in the Romantic art of the nineteenth century and the Surrealist and Abstract Expressionist art of the twentieth century. Art is the fullest realization of self-consciousness, of the indifference of consciousness and perception, in human reason.

Beauty is identical to truth (the finite manifestation of the good) in that the idea of beauty is fully realized in the real, in matter, though not beauty itself. Beauty is truth only to the extent that it is displayed in the phenomenal, in the reflected image. Art often contains a deceptive form of truth in the imitation of natural form; the imitation of natural form does not contain absolute truth, because it does not display the indifference of the real and the ideal, of perception and consciousness, but rather only the content of perception, the ephemeral form in the temporal unfolding, which thereby cannot be any form of truth, or objectivity in the real. The imitation of the natural form in art does not display the presence of the absolute in the form, because the form alone is represented, as a particular, rather than the idea of the form, as a universal. As art is to reason what the organism is to nature, the imitation of the organism in art can only represent a deceitful truth of nature in reason.

While truth is the realization of beauty, beauty is the realization of the good, and beauty is equated with the good, as an absolute, in and of itself. Absolute beauty is the indifference of freedom and necessity as a complete reconciliation, a completion of the dialectic in the ideal, as is the good. The vision of the good in the *Phaedrus* (247) is a vision of "absolute justice and discipline and knowledge, not the knowledge which is attached to things which come into being, nor the knowledge which varies with the objects which we now call real..." Beauty in art expresses the harmonious resolution of freedom and necessity in the good, beauty as absolute. Though natural forms do not completely reveal the absolute, the beauty of natural forms is absolute in its beauty; in other words, because natural forms are the product of the absolute, they are absolutely beautiful, but they cannot participate in the absolute which is their source. The forms of nature are the art of the absolute, as "the universe is formed in God as an absolute work of art and in eternal beauty" (*The Philosophy of Art*, § 21), in the indifference of the real and ideal, necessity and freedom. As the beauty of natural forms is absolute, the beauty of the archetypal form in the intelligible must be absolute as well. The natural form is lacking in beauty when it is lacking in the predominance of the ideal, the idea of beauty in perception, and the presence of the absolute, the incomplete resolution of the ideal and the real.

In the necessity of the dialectic, it is through the reflected image, the temporal phenomenal real, that the archetype or idea becomes beautiful, and when the idea of beauty in reason is intuited in the reflected image, as by the initiate in the *Symposium*, the idea becomes beauty, that is, the real and ideal are unified. Forms of art reveal the ideas of reason in the same way that the ideas and archetypes reveal the absolute in the ideal. The image of the archetype is the *Urbild*, the originary image. Forms in both art and nature are based on "the same informing of infinite ideality into the real" (§ 22). The word for "imagination" in German, *Einbildungskraft*, means "the mutual informing into unity (*Ineinsbildung*)," the mutual indifference of the real and ideal, of the conscious and unconscious. The creation of the artist is seen as participation in the act of creation of the universe, the *scintilla della divinità*, spark of the divine in the mind of the artist, of the Accademia di San Luca in Rome in the sixteenth century. The creation of the universe is the mutual "informing" of the ideal and the real, the infinite and finite. As the source of all mutual informing of the real and ideal is the absolute, which is not itself that indifference, the absolute is the cause of art, as well as the universe, and the cause of the idea in reason. As art represents the Idea, it represents the absolute as cause, and as beauty is dependent on the idea of beauty, the absolute is the cause of beauty. All particular forms in their differentiation are the product of the informing of the ideal into the real, which is caused by the absolute, but the cause of which is not participated in by the cause and effect of necessity. Without absolute identity, there could be no real nor ideal, no dialectic in reason.

The purpose of art is not to imitate natural forms but to present forms as they are in themselves, as the absolute, and absolute beauty. The universal idea of art is the presentation of the universe as an absolute work of art; the content of art is the archetypes which are the representations of the absolute, as they are intuited in nature and the unconscious or the Intellectual Principle. The question, then, is how it is possible that the absolute is manifest in the particular form. The particular form does not exist in the ideal, in the archetypal universe, and thus has no correlate to archetypal or absolute beauty. Each particular form, in order to manifest the absolute, must manifest the absolute in its entirety, must be a universe unto itself, a monad, as it were. The particular form cannot participate in the absolute, but the absolute necessarily participates in the particular form, in every particular form universally. The particular form only exists in relation to other forms in its relation to the absolute, in the shared participation of the absolute. This is the basis of reason. All ideas only exist in relation to other ideas which are representatives of the absolute, and all forms of art only exist in relation to other forms of art, as representations of the ideas. If there were no absolute, no universal, there would be no particular; if there were no infinite, there would be no finite. It is impossible for a particular individual form or idea to exist, to be real. The particular form is only real after it has separated from the ideal, after the unified has become multiple.

Within the absolute, particular forms can become separated and multiple only if each particular form contains the absolute. The separation and differentiation of particular forms in the universe is only relative to the idea of the absolute; without the idea of the absolute, there can be no separation or differentiation. Thus while particular forms can be seen in their separation and differentiation, that is to the extent that they participate in measurement, in the ideas of reason, they also exist unseparated in the absolute. As Plotinus describes in the *Enneads* (V.8.9),

> Let us, then, make a mental picture of our universe: each member shall remain what it is, distinctly apart; yet all is to form, as far as possible, a complete unity so that whatever comes into view, say the outer orb of the heavens, shall bring immediately with it the vision, on the one plane, of the sun and of all the stars with earth and sea and all living things as if exhibited on a transparent globe. Bring this vision actually before your sight, so that there shall be in your mind the gleaming representation of a sphere, a picture holding all the things of the universe moving or in repose or (as in reality) some at rest, some in motion. Keep this sphere before you, and from it imagine another, a sphere stripped of magnitude and of spatial differences; cast out your inborn sense of Matter, taking care not merely to attenuate it: call on God, maker of the sphere whose image you now hold, and pray Him to enter. And may He come bringing His own Universe with all the gods that dwell in it—He who is the one God and all the gods, where each is all, blending into a unity, distinct in powers but all one god in virtue of that one divine power of many facets.

The universe becomes the essence of the radiant light of the good, visible to the immortal souls, corresponding to the idea of beauty in the Intellectual Principle, unified and immeasurable, and absolute. The particular forms are seen as being undifferentiated in the absolute, as sharing in the same essence, conforming to the archetypal idea. In the absolute, "all number or determination by number is suspended" (*The Philosophy of Art*, § 26), and all particulars are absolutes. Unity and multiplicity are products of the absolute, but not qualities of the absolute itself. Measurement of particular forms only exists in perception in the correspondence of the particular form to the whole, the correspondence of the form in matter to the idea of the form in the ideal. Measurement is an instrument of reason in the differentiation of the ideal and real, in the participation of the form in the Idea, and thus in the representation of the absolute.

The representation of the Idea, as the representation of the absolute in the ideal, is the function of art. Art thus depends on the particular form as having been differentiated from the absolute; the distinction is necessary for the form to be able to correspond to the idea of the form, but it is not possible without the pre-existence of the form as undifferentiated in the absolute. The absoluteness of all particular form, the state of un-differentiation, is chaos, that which is not subject to measurement and proportion. It is the element of the sublime, the presence of the absolute in form, the presence of the unconscious in consciousness, the immeasurable in the measurable, which inspires terror in reason, as the element of un-reason in reason, that to which reason is inaccessible, the vision of the gods. In the representation of particular forms, the purpose of art is to represent the chaos of the absolute and the terror of the sublime, as it is represented in the ideal, the intellectual.

The idea is the particular form in the ideal, and is differentiated from the absolute in the ideal in the same way that the particular form is differentiated from the absolute in the real, that is, as always already containing the absolute, and representing it. "Every idea is equal to the universe in the form of the particular" (§ 27) as each particular form is equal to the whole of forms, as a monad. As with particular forms, the idea could not exist except as caused by absolute identity, and every idea contains the essence of the absolute universal. Ideas attain measurement and proportion in reason as well; the absence of measurement and proportion in reason is the same absolute, chaos, the unconscious. The archetypes of measurement and proportion pre-exist reason in the unconscious, the Intellectual Principle, in the same way that the archetypes of measurement and proportion pre-exist the phenomenal world in the intellectual.

The idea or archetype is both universal and particular, the forming of the universal into the particular, and the particular as universal, like the phenomenal form. The idea is thus both a particular in and of itself, and a particular within the universal. The absolute is its cause and essence, but it does not participate in the absolute as particular, like the circle of Cusanus is the cause of the polygonal figures, but the polygonal figures do not participate in the circle. The polygonal figures are particular forms, differentiated in measurement, but they each contain within them the essence of the circle as a possibility, the essence of the absolute, though as particulars they cannot become the absolute. The polygonal figures, the ideas, are unified by the same center which unifies the circle, the absolute, and as forms, represent the same relationship, or indifference, between universal and particular. The unity of the ideas as differentiated particulars is the same unity as particulars in the universal.

The indifference of the universal and the particular in the idea is represented in the real in the classical world by the essential nature of the gods. The gods are ideas of the absolute, representations, in particular forms, and each god is equal to the absolute in its representation. The gods in mythology are a model for the forms in art, as being equivalent to the idea in the ideal, and representations of the absolute in particular forms. The god plays the same role in art that the idea plays in philosophy, as representation of the indifference of the real and ideal, and poetry, the voice of the gods, is the earliest form of philosophy. The gods are both absolute in the ideal and absolute in the real. The purpose of both philosophy and poetry is the indifference of the real and ideal in the absolute; in the indifference, the highest state of both the real and ideal is the absolute, and the highest form of philosophy or poetry displays both the absolute real and the absolute ideal, and the indifference of the two, as in the representative form of the gods. As Giovanni Pico della Mirandola asks in *Oration on the Dignity of Man* (pp. 25–26), "who would not desire, putting all human concerns behind him, holding the goods of fortune in contempt and little minding the goods of the body, thus to become, while still a denizen of earth, a guest at the table of the gods, and, drunk with the nectar of eternity, receive, while still a mortal, the gift of immortality?" To be a guest at the table of the gods is to partake in the highest forms of poetry and philosophy, to participate in the mystical vision of the immortal souls of the absolute. The apprehension of the reality of the absolute is not possible by "ordinary consciousness" (*The Philosophy of Art*, § 29); the reality of the absolute is a non-reality, the chaos of the immeasurable, the subject of the sublime, in the unconscious or the *via negativa*, in the *intellectus divinus*.

The gods are absolutely real because they are absolutely ideal. The idea is as objective as the phenomenal form, and is the most objective the closer the correspondence to the form. Thus the gods are absolutely objective. The real, the reality given by ordinary consciousness, is only a partial reality, even a "non-reality," because it is lacking in the absolute, in the indifference of the ideal and the real, in the Intellectual Principle, and the vision of the gods. Sensible form cannot be taken alone as differentiated from the idea; as such it is without substance and essence in its non-reality, and without meaning in human existence. Consciousness requires the participation of the intellectual in the sensible world, the development of self-consciousness, and the indifference of consciousness and perception.

The comprehension of the gods is only possible by "fantasy" (§ 31), or extraordinary consciousness, a mystical vision. The world of the gods, as in the banquet of the gods, is not accessible by the limitations of understanding or reason, since the absolute only exists in the ideal as an archetype or representative idea, as in the Intellectual Principle of Plotinus. It is in fantasy, or the imagination, *Einbildungskraft*, the mutual informing into unity or indifference of the real and ideal, conscious and unconscious, that "the productions of art are received and formed." Fantasy intuits the forms of art externally within the imagination, as it intuits the gods and the essence of the absolute, "casts them out from within itself," and portrays them in the imagination. Fantasy is to imagination as intellectual intuition is to reason; it is the agent of the in-forming of the forms which represent the ideas which are intuited by the intellectual. Fantasy is the "intellectual intuition within art," the participation of the idea in the real, through which the absolute is represented as the indifference of the two.

Mythology is thus "the necessary condition and first content of all art" (*The Philosophy of Art*, § 38). Art represents absolute beauty through sensible beauty, and even the idea of beauty. Art must represent the absolute by its very limitation, the limitation of the sensible form in the realization of the ideal; no such limitation exists for philosophy and poetry. The only form of representation in art in which this contradiction is overcome is mythology, as the gods have no complete existence in the real. In the gods the ideal predominates, and the essence of the absolute is intuited, in the chaos of the *in-*

tellectus divinus. It is from mythology that art derives its possibility, the possibility of the mortal soul dining at the table of the immortal souls, partaking in the mystical vision, and the possibility of the imagination representing the absolute in sensible form. "Only within such a world are abiding and definite forms possible through which alone the eternal concepts can be expressed." The creations of art must aspire to the gods, higher than nature, higher than reason, higher than intellect. The gods are the highest manifestation of the absolute in the soul, the directly differentiated particulars of the absolute, as in the Celestial Hierarchies of Pseudo-Dionysius in the Middle Ages. The gods are the individual forms of the absolute itself. Mythology is the poetry of the universal spirit, the "eternal matter from which all forms issue..." (*The Philosophy of Art*, § 38), as derivatives of its essence.

The representation of the absolute in art through the imagination takes the form of either the symbolic or the schematic, following Immanuel Kant in the *Critique of Judgment* of 1790. The symbolic allows for the representation of the absolute as indifference of the universal and particular within the particular, as in the forms of nature and art. The schematic is the representation of the absolute as the indifference of the universal and particular within the universal, as in the idea in philosophy. As Kant explained in the *Critique of Judgment*, § 59,[13]

> All *hypotyposis* (exhibition, *subiectio ad adspectum*) consists in making [a concept] sensible, and is either *schematic* or *symbolic*. In schematic hypotyposis there is a concept that the understanding has formed, and the intuition corresponding to it is given a priori. In symbolic hypotyposis there is a concept which only reason can think and to which no sensible intuition can be adequate, and this concept is supplied with an intuition that judgment treats in a way merely analogous to the procedure it follows in schematizing...

In Schelling, the content of the representation of both the symbolic and schematic is mythology, which synthesizes the two, the symbolic in the form of allegory, in the particular. The symbolic can be seen as the synthesis of the schematic and the allegorical. In allegory, the universal is intuited through the particular; in the schematic, the particular is intuited through the universal; in the symbolic, the universal and the particular are unified in indifference, allowing for the representation of the absolute in the particular, which is the purpose of art, and which can be found in mythology. The symbolic is the absolute form of representation in the imagination. For Erwin Panofsky in *Studies in Iconology*, it is from the symbolic that meaning is derived in art.

The schematic is the medium in the imagination between the idea and the sensuous form. For Kant, "Schemata contain direct...exhibitions of the concept." For Schelling, it is the formulation of the idea of the form in the intellect, the transformation of the universal to the particular, the ideal to the real. The schematic constitutes the necessity in artistic production in the imagination, the rule of cause and effect as derived from the principles of nature and reason, for example, mathematics and geometry. The schematic is the universal form in which the particular form is intuited. The schematic grows out of an intuition of the universal, in which individual forms are differentiated and defined by the principles. In that way the schema becomes a concrete image representative of the sensible form. The work of art corresponds to the schematic image in the mind of the artist. As Marsilio Ficino described the design of the architect in *De amore*, "In the beginning the architect develops a Reason or Idea, as it were, of the building in his soul. Then he builds, as nearly as possible, the kind of house he has conceived. Who will deny that the house is a body and that it is very much like the architect's incorporeal Idea, in the likeness of which it was built?" (V.5).[14] In the *Enneads* (I.6.3), Plotinus asks, "On what principle does the architect, when he finds the house standing before him correspondent with his inner ideal of a house, pronounce it beautiful?" The form of the house corresponds to the form of the idea of the house in the mind of the architect, or the schema, as it has been constructed from intuited universals, which is an act of intuition in the imagination.

The schematic is also found in language. All words used in language are particular manifestations of universal concepts. The particular is intuited in the universal, the "deep structure" of the language, as given by Structural Linguistics, beginning with the Port-Royal *Grammar* in the seventeenth century. The deep structure of the language, the universal content, is manifest in the syntax, the organization of the words, in which the particular is intuited. In the same way, in the artistic imagination, the particular is intuited through the schematic from the universal form in the organization of the form according to the necessity of reason, the rules of reason, and the relation of the form to other forms. According to Schelling, "In language, too, we make use of merely universal designations even for the designation of the particular" (*The Philosophy of Art*, § 39). The word itself is a schematic representation of an idea, the transformation of a universal idea into a particular form. The word itself is a "signifier," a particular form which signifies an idea or universal, as the "signified."

The schema though cannot be a complete representation of the absolute in the particular, as that is not possible, and the schema itself is a particular as it facilitates the representation of the absolute. Mythology contains the schematic, but it is not schematic as a whole, and is also symbolic, and in mythology the schematic and symbolic are synthesized; the universal is represented in the particular, and the particular is represented in the universal. Language is completely schematic, as it is composed entirely of particulars, words, while mythology combines words and images, schemas and symbols. Allegory is the opposite of the schematic; it combines the schematic and the symbolic (the symbolic can also be seen as the combination of the schematic and allegorical), words and pictures or images. Through the syntax of words in language, their organization which reveals a deep structure, allegory reverses the schematic function of the word and becomes symbolic, representing the universal in the particular. Mythology is a form of allegory in that it combines the schematic and symbolic, but while in allegory the particular merely signifies the universal, in mythology the particular also *is* the universal, or the manifestation of the absolute, the indifference of the particular and universal.

The three forms of representation of the absolute in art, the schematic, symbolic, and allegorical, are seen by Schelling as *potences*. The mechanisms of language are the *potences* in the representation of the absolute because the ideal, wherein the absolute is represented, does not exist outside of language. As *potences* in the ideal, the particular forms of representation are universal categories; they are all schematic. In the real, only the symbolic and allegorical are possible, as the particular form cannot be a universal or participate in the absolute. In light, on the other hand, the schematic is possible, because in light the infinite and finite are combined, the ideal enters into the real. Light is both schematic in the ideal and symbolic in the real. The particular is intuited in the universal (the universal represents the particular), as in language, and the universal is intuited in the particular (the particular represents the universal), as in sensible forms in nature and art. Thought, as the correlate of language in the ideal, is completely schematic, while action, the correlate of thought in the real, is completely allegorical. Art, in that it combines thought and action, combines the schematic and the allegorical.

Mathematics and geometry also combine thought and action, the ideal and real. They are schematic forms of thought in the imagination which infuse the necessity of cause and effect into the real. Mathematics and geometry are universals which contain the indifference of the universal and particular, and in which particular forms are intuited. Geometry is also allegorical, because it is pictorial, thus symbolic. Like mythology, geometry synthesizes the schematic and the symbolic. In the Renaissance, geometry played the same role as mythology in defining the relation between the particular and the absolute and between the human and divine.

Mythology is the model for the arts because mythology achieves the complete indifference of the universal and particular. A mythological figure is both symbolic and schematic, and represents both the universal and the particular in the indifference of the two. The mythological form is identical with its meaning; it is both what it signifies and symbolizes. The mythological figure also contains the indifference of the ideal and the real, and the co-existence of both. Thought is identical to action, idea is identical to form, language is identical to image. The German word for "symbol," *Sinnbild*, combines sense and meaning, sensible form and signification, as in the symbols of mythology.

As has been seen, the cause of art is the absolute, which causes ideas, which are reflections (*Gegenbild*) as particular things in the real. The absolute does not actually produce the idea or the form, but only imparts its essence to it, in its in-forming. The ideas and the forms are imparticipant in the absolute, though they contain its essence, as in the thought of Plotinus. The particular form contains the essence of the absolute only in so far as it participates in the universal, the ideal, within which the particular is manifest as the idea of the absolute. Through reason, the idea of the absolute is related to the particular. The absolute is only both ideal and real in the human soul; through the idea, the human soul is related to the absolute. As the absolute is the cause of art, the idea of the human soul must exist in the absolute, schematically, as the idea of the absolute exists in the human soul, symbolically. The idea of the human soul in the absolute becomes objective in the human soul, in the indifference of the infinite and the finite, and it is this identity which is the subject of art—the indifference of body and soul, form and idea.

The cause of art in the absolute is the infinite idea of the human soul in the absolute, which if possessed by the artist is called genius, or the demonic, as if the artist were possessed by the gods, a guest at the banquet of the gods, intoxicated with the nectar of the beatific vision of the immortal souls of the light of the good (as in the *Phaedrus*). The artist possesses a piece of the absolute, a *scintilla della divinità*. The artwork that the artist produces is the sensible form which corresponds to the idea to the extent of the presence of the absolute in the idea which represents it. The extent of the artwork depends on the degree to which the indifference of infinite and finite and ideal and real is achieved in the idea. Anything that is caused by the absolute contains the essence of the absolute; anything which contains the essence of the absolute contains the creative power of the absolute, and is thus a universe, a monad, of itself. The creative power of the absolute is visible in the sensible world when the idea corresponds to the form and the indifference of the infinite and finite is achieved in both.

The creative power of the absolute exists in both the ideal and the real, but only exists outside the realm of time. In the real, the creative power of the absolute is nature, in the infusion of the infinite into the finite. In the ideal, the finite is infused into the infinite. The genius of the artist is the comprehension of the forming of the creative power of the absolute in the finite as it is translated into the infinite, in the realm of the ideal, represented by the idea. As the idea is formed in the ideal, it represents all forms in the particular, as a universal. The comprehension of the forming of the idea in the ideal is the comprehension of "the original act of cognition" (*The Philosophy of Art*, § 63) by which the universe was formed, how sensible forms correspond to the idea. The ideal world is reproduced in the real world. The original act of cognition contains the indifference of freedom and necessity, as does the idea of the artist; the true work of art is absolutely free, and absolutely necessary.

The informing of the infinite into the finite on the part of the artistic genius is poetry, the creation of sensible form in the real, in language or image. The infinite is represented in the finite, through the schematic and allegory. The idea of the creator, the informing of the finite into the infinite, is art in the strictest sense, the representation of the finite in the infinite, the real in the ideal, through the symbolic. The sensible form in the work of art turns the particular into a universal. It is only through poetry and art that the particular form, the finite manifestation of the idea in the real, is able to reveal the essence of the absolute and "become something that exists and endures on its own power, a being in itself that does not merely mean or signify something else" as a sign or symbol. For example, in Sonnet 18 by William Shakespeare, "Shall I compare thee to a summer's day?/Thou art more lovely and more temperate./Rough winds do shake the darling buds of May,/And summer's lease hath all too short a date./Sometimes too hot the eye of heaven shines,/And often is his gold complexion dimm'd;/And every fair from fair sometimes declines,/By chance or nature's changing course untrimm'd;/But thy eternal summer shall not fade/Nor lose possession of that fair thou ow'st,/Nor shall Death brag thou wand'rest in his shade,/When in eternal lines to time thou grow'st./So long as men can breathe or eyes can see,/So long lives this and this gives life to thee."[15] It is only in the poem that beauty is eternal, and displays the essence of the absolute, through the mechanism, or *potence*, of allegory, of the transforming of the universal into the particular.

As the sensible form in the real becomes the idea in the ideal, it gains an essence within itself from the absolute. The essence is revealed in the separation of the idea from the sensible form, and is revealed in an inward vision, separate from the world of sense. This is described by Plotinus in the *Enneads* as "another vision which is to be waked within you" (I.6.8). In order to comprehend the essence of the Idea through an inner vision, it is necessary for each individual to sculpt the idea in the soul, metaphorically, as a sculptor would create a statue, to infuse the sensible form into the idea, making use of the participation of the Intellectual Principle in the soul. The sculptor cuts away, smoothes, lightens and straightens until the "godlike splendor of virtue" shines from the statue, the light of the good, being informed by the Idea, and comprehending the act of creation. In turn, the essence is formed in the soul of the form so that it also shines with the godlike splendor of virtue. The idea becomes an independent entity, a monad in the ideal, absolute within itself, and thus "in the absolute," as described by Schelling (*The Philosophy of Art*, § 64). Poetry is the means by which the sensible form reveals the essence of the absolute in the ideal; art is the means by which the sensible form exists in the universal, in the representation of the absolute.

The informing of the infinite into the finite through the symbolic is expressed in art as the sublime; the informing of the finite into the infinite through the schematic and allegorical is expressed as beauty. The sublime in art depends on the inadequacy of the sensible form as symbol of the infinite, and the intuition of the idea of the infinite takes its place. The finiteness of the sensible form which is symbolizing the infinite is subsumed by the idea of the infinite. But the intuition of the infinite in the idea depends on the sublime, that is, the effect of the sensible form as symbol of the infinite, both the idea and form being representations of the absolute. Thus the intuition of the sublime is an *aesthetic* intuition, dependent on the visual image in perception, or picture-thinking (*Vorstellung*). The aesthetic intuition, the symbolic, is represented schematically in poetry. The intuition of the infinite, the absolute, must occur within reason, which is finite by definition, and thus must go outside of itself in the intuitive act, as the Intellectual Principle becomes participant in it, and the human soul is within the absolute.

Poetry is the intuition of the infinite within the finite real, or nature, and the in-forming of the infinite into the finite. If the infinite is intuited by reason, which is within nature, then the possibility of the infinite within the finite is comprehended. When the sensible form is intuited as infinite, it becomes the sublime. In order for form to express the infinite in the sublime, it must become formless; it must represent the presence of the chaos of the absolute. It is the formlessness of form which is the symbol of the infinite. This is represented in the dissolution of form into light, as in the paintings of Caspar David Friedrich in the nineteenth century, such as *Two Men Observing the Moon* of 1819–20 (Figure 1), where the threatening forms of nature at night dissolve into the abyss of moonlight. It is also represented in the *informe* of the twentieth century, in photographs by Man Ray for example, such as *Anatomies* of 1930, or *Minotaur* of 1933, where forms dissolve into each other and threaten the relation of form to perception and reason, evoking the chaos of the absolute.

Form is finite, but in the ambiguity of its definition it can symbolize the infinite, as the sublime; though the finiteness of the form is still visible, the dissolution into formlessness suggests the infinite. In that form is finite it is always a particular, while the infinite is a universal; in the sublime, the particular symbolizes the universal, and contains the indifference of the two. Absolute formlessness is equivalent to absolute form, thus in the sublime must be represented the process of the de-forming of the particular into the universal, and the predominance of formlessness, as it is represented in the ideal, in order for the essence of the absolute to be revealed. In that the particular is de-formed through the process of reason in the real, it must display the limitations of necessity as well as the infinity of freedom, as represented in the sublime.

Chaos is thus "the fundamental intuition of the sublime" (*The Philosophy of Art*, § 65), and consists of everything not contained within the scope of perception and reason, within the sensible world, the real, and even the ideal. Anything that suggests a quality that cannot be contained by human capacity symbolizes the infinite. The intuition of chaos is the intuition of the absolute. As the absolute is complete unification, resolution and simplicity, the One, chaos is the equivalent of complete simplicity and unification, that which precedes (not temporally, but as idea) differentiation. Absolute form is iden-

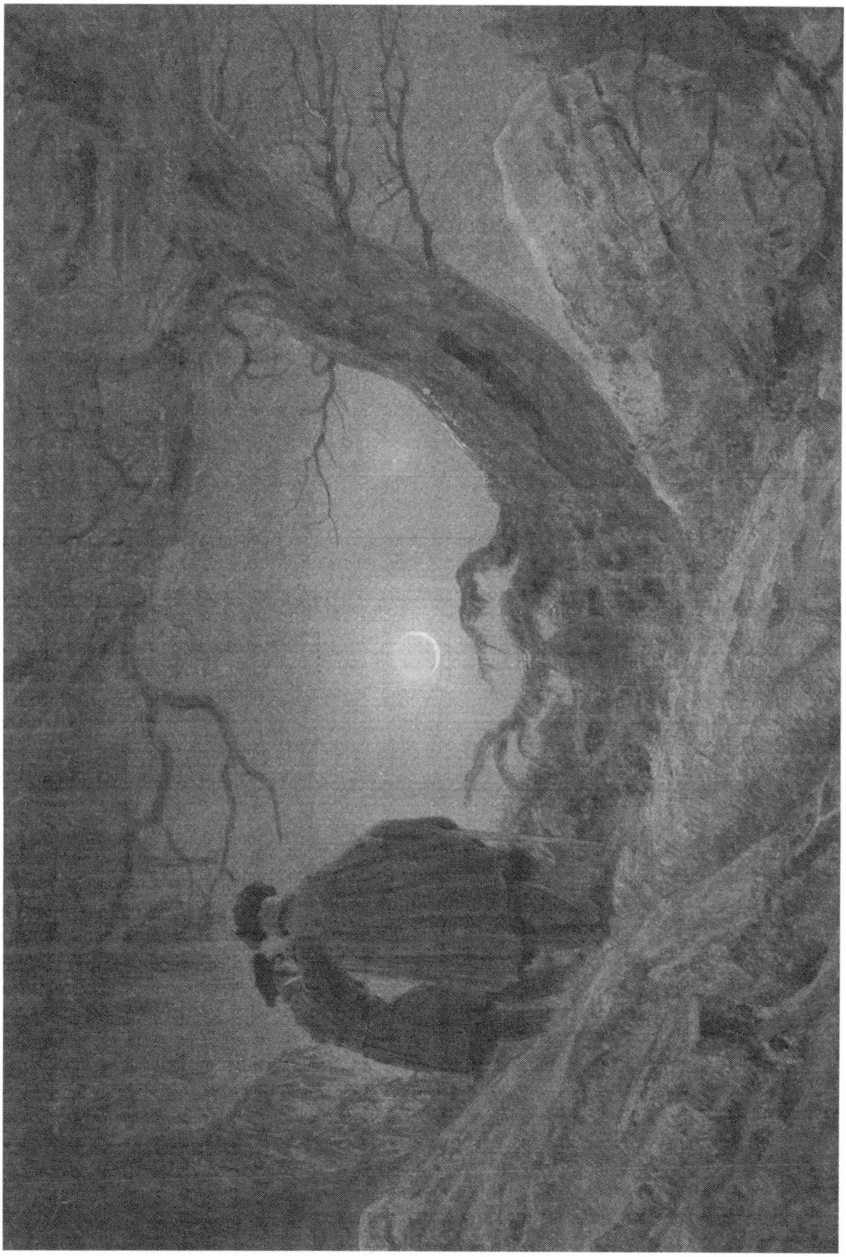

Figure 1. Caspar David Friedrich, *Two Men Observing the Moon*
(Photo credit: Erich Lessing, Art Resource, NY)

tical with formlessness. Chaos is not the negation of form, nor non-being, but rather the highest manifestation of form within the negation of itself. All form is continuous; chaos exists within the absolute, and absolute form exists within chaos. Formlessness is the lack of differentiation of form, and as such particular forms are unified as universal form. Chaos is represented by the color black, in which all forms as colors are dissolved and unified. The vision of chaos is the vision of the mysteries, the comprehension of the absolute. Philosophy, and in particular aesthetics, must take the vision of chaos as a first principle, as the absolute is a first principle, and must take "the incomprehensibility itself as a principle of judgment," as Schelling quotes Johann Christoph Friedrich von Schiller in *On the Sublime*.

It is only in the comprehension of chaos that the universe can be seen as a symbol of reason; the finite is not possible without the infinite, and necessity is not possible without freedom. In this way the sensible forms can be seen as the indifference of the finite and infinite, necessity and freedom, the indifference of the human soul and the sensible world; in this way the human soul is in the absolute. In the differentiation of forms, the sensible world appears to reason as resolute and harmonious; but the intellect intuits the undifferentiation of the forms, the presence of chaos and the absolute, because the intellect, in the participation of the Intellectual Principle, understands the role and limitations of reason in the real, in relation to the ideal. The intellect intuits sensible forms as being independent, disconnected, indeterminate, ephemeral reflections of the idea, and thus as symbolizing reason as representations of the ideal in the real. The absolute is that which is "unqualified and unconditional," not constrained by cause and effect.

As Georges Bataille expressed in "The Notion of Expenditure" in the twentieth century, "human life cannot in any way be limited to the closed systems assigned to it by reasonable conceptions. The immense travail of recklessness, discharge, and upheaval that constitutes life could be expressed by stating that life starts only with the deficit of these systems";[16] the first principle of philosophy is chaos. For Bataille, in "The Pineal Eye" (*Visions of Excess*, p. 80),

> philosophy has been, up to this point, as much as science, an expression of human subordination, and when man seeks to represent himself, no longer as a moment of a homogeneous process—of a necessary and pitiful process—but as a new laceration within a lacerated nature, it is no longer the leveling phraseology coming to him: he can no longer recognize himself in the degrading chains of logic, but he recognizes himself, instead—not only with rage but in an ecstatic torment—in the virulence of

> his own phantasms. Nevertheless, the introduction of a lawless intellectual series into the world of legitimate thought defines itself at the outset as the most arduous and audacious operation.

Man is no longer subordinated to reason in the real; he intuits a heterogeneous nature within himself and the universe, undifferentiated chaos, through the sublime, and lacerates the homogeneity of the real. Man sees something in himself other than that given by language and reason, himself in the absolute, through the ecstatic vision, the communion with the gods or the immortal souls, in an *ecstasis*, the beatific vision.

For Schelling, in *The Philosophy of Art*, the sublime only occurs in art, because it is only in art that the finiteness of the sensible form is juxtaposed with the possibility of its infiniteness. The informing of the finite into the infinite only occurs in the ideal, as it is intuited in the intellect of the perceiving subject; only as it is perceived is nature sublime, in the predominance of the infinite over the finite. Beauty occurs in nature as well as art, because in beauty the finite is at home in the indifference of the finite and the infinite. Beauty is the indifference of the finite and infinite. In sensible forms the finite is informed into the infinite, thus the beauty of the finite is visible within the infinite. In the beautiful form the finite is reconciled with the infinite, while in the sublime the finite struggles against the infinite.

Beauty is both divine and visible, as expressed in *Death in Venice* and the *Birth of Venus*, for example, while the sublime belongs to the absolute. In *Death in Venice*, Thomas Mann quotes Socrates as saying to Phaedrus, "For Beauty, dear Phaedrus, only Beauty is at one and the same time divinely desirable and visible: it is, mark well, the only form of the spiritual that we can receive with our senses and endure with our senses" (p. 61).[17] In the *Birth of Venus*, Aphrodite, goddess of beauty, is represented as both divine Idea and sensible form by Sandro Botticelli. Divine Aphrodite becomes sensible Aphrodite when she is clothed by Flora, having come to shore from the sea, as described by Hesiod in the *Theogony* (194), "And out stepped a modest and beautiful goddess."[18]

Schelling defines the execution of the indifference of the real and ideal in art, that is, the creation of beauty in art, as "style," as opposed to "mannerism," which does not succeed in unifying the real and ideal, the particular and universal. When the particular predominates in the sensible form, it is mannered; it displays the presence of the artist as individual, as particular, not successfully integrated into the universal, into the *Zeitgeist* which is the ethical imperative of art. Mannerism in art signals the breakdown of the universal spirit, the fragmentation of a society, the lack of realization of a universal consciousness, a national spirit, as Hegel would describe. Style is the presence of the absolute in the work of art, and the presence of beauty, the indifference of the real and ideal. In art which can be identified in terms of a style, the artist as individual is undifferentiated from the sensible form as universal. Style is the in-forming of the absolute into the particular; the presence of the absolute depends on the comprehension of the idea of the form in the intellect of the artist as representative of the absolute. The comprehension of the idea of the form is dependent on a universal understanding, as the idea of the form is universal, shared by the collective consciousness of a society. Thus Heinrich Wölfflin defined style as the "form of the *Zeitgeist*."

Through matter, light, and organism, the three *potences*, Schelling describes the absolute as becoming objective in the phenomenal realm, but only insofar as the *potences* are symbols of the idea that corresponds to the sensible form. The absolute becomes objective through the differentiation of the *potences*, while the particular forms retain the essence of the absolute. Matter, light and the organism are symbols of the idea in the same way that forms of art are symbols of the idea, the representation of the universal in the particular. In the absolute, content and form are undifferentiated, while in the differentiated forms the content remains universal while the form becomes the particular. The content of the *potence* is its procreation, which in the absolute is identical to its being. The essence of the absolute can only be intuited through the *potence* which is a symbol of it; the essence of the absolute can only be given by the idea, in the Intellectual Principle.

In the absolute itself, the *potences* are undifferentiated, as are the ideas which correspond to them. The *potence* only becomes particular or differentiated when it assumes the form of the ephemeral, reflected image (*Gegenbild*) in matter. The *potence* is first undifferentiated in the absolute, then becomes idea, then symbol, then matter. All sensible form is a combination of essence and *potence*, ideal and real. In art, the absolute is represented in the sensible form when the form becomes a symbol of the idea; rather than be an imitation of a natural form, the form in art must symbolize the idea of the natural form; it must combine the universal and particular. This was expressed by Georges Braque, the Cubist painter, who is recorded as saying, "One does not imitate what one wishes to create," and "One does not imitate the appearance; the appearance is the result," in "Pensées et réflexions sur la peinture" (Thoughts on Painting),[19] published by Pierre Reverdy in *Nord-Sud* in 1917.

In the *Enneads*, Plotinus declared that the arts "give no bare reproduction of the thing seen but go back to the Ideas from which Nature itself derives" (V.8.1). The purpose of the arts is not to imitate nature, but to reveal the underlying archetypal reality of nature in the idea, of which the sensible form is a symbol, by translating the sensible object into the intelligible object, a symbol of the idea. The beauty of the form in the art is not in the imitation of nature, but in the form itself as symbol, as beauty is the indifference of the real and ideal. In the *Enneads*, "Art, then, creating in the image of its own nature and content, and working by the Idea or Reason-Principle of the beautiful object it is to produce, must itself be beautiful in a far higher and purer degree since it is the seat and source of that beauty, indwelling in the art, which must naturally be more complete than any comeliness of the external."

Because the idea is symbolized by sensible form as the ideal in the real, the idea is the equivalent of the sensible form. Another way of saying this is that the perception of the subject is that which is perceived; the perceiver is the equivalent of perceived, the seer is the seen, the knower is the known. The essence of the absolute is that perception and the act of perception are undifferentiated, as are consciousness and the sensible world. The closer the perceiving subject comes to the essence of the absolute in the intellectual, the more the consciousness of the subject is unified and self-generating, like the absolute, and the more the indifference of the real and ideal becomes the act of perception. If the soul is able to intuit absolute beauty, as in the *Symposium*, the soul itself becomes beauty. In the *Enneads* (I.6.9), "when you perceive that you have grown to this, you are now become very vision." In being able to see the sensible world as the idea, the subject sees the sensible world within himself, and loses the distinction between objective and subjective. In perception, the eye becomes like the sun, which is the source of sight, according to Socrates in the *Republic*.

As the soul is penetrated with absolute beauty, the perceiver becomes the perceived, and the image becomes self-identical with the act of perception, with its symbol in the idea. The distinction between thought and beauty is dissolved, as each become the indifference of the real and ideal. In Hegelian terms, the subject passes from consciousness to self-consciousness in identification with the absolute, with Spirit, the source of being and becoming. In the *Enneads* (V.8.11), the subject "must give himself forthwith to the inner and, radiant with the Divine Intellections (with which he is now one), be no longer the seer, but, as that place has made him, the seen." This is achieved in the "gaze" of Jacques Lacan in twentieth-century psychoanalysis. In *The*

Four Fundamental Concepts of Psycho-Analysis, the gaze is "something that introduces what was elided in the geometral relation—the depth of field, with all its ambiguity and variability, which is in no way mastered by me. It is rather it that grasps me, solicits me at every moment" (p. 96), as the essence of the absolute.

For Roger Caillois, in *The Necessity of the Mind* in 1933, the image which is received in perception corresponds to the content of the imagination, the mental construction of the image. "Imagination is often defined as a virtual perception, and perception as a real imagination" (p. 113).[20] In the indifference of the ideal and real, the mind and that which it perceives, the necessity of the mind of the subject becomes identical with the necessity of the universe. "Fusing perfectly with the necessity of the universe, the mind's necessity would at the same time be absorbed in it" (p. 114). In the indifference of the subject and sensible world, of the interior and exterior, subjective and objective, Caillois sees language as a barrier to the complete identity between the unconscious and the sensible world; the idea as symbol is a barrier to the identity between the idea and the absolute, the mystical vision of the immortal souls.

Identification with the absolute would require a dissolution of the subject as participating in the "signifying structure of language," as in the thought of Georges Bataille, the "new laceration within a lacerated nature"; "it is no longer the leveling phraseology coming to him: he can no longer recognize himself in the degrading chains of logic, but he recognizes himself, instead—not only with rage but in an ecstatic torment—in the virulence of his own phantasms" (*Visions of Excess*, p. 80), wrote Bataille. As Caillois describes in "Mimicry and Legendary Psychasthenia," in the identity of the necessity of the mind with the necessity of the universe, and the freedom of the mind with the freedom of the universe, the perceiving subject dissolves into the perceived space. Distinctions are dissolved "between the real and the imaginary, between waking and sleeping, between ignorance and knowledge,"[21] beyond the signifying structure of thought and language, in identity with the essence of the absolute, the *ecstasis* of the intuition of the eternal.

While matter and sensible form can be idea, they cannot be the essence of the absolute, according to Schelling, as the in-forming of the infinite into the finite can only be relative and never absolute, in participation in the particular. Art, in the in-forming of the infinite into the finite, exists in the real, and cannot be identical with the essence of the absolute. No matter to what extent the relation between idea and matter as symbol of the idea is revealed, to what extent the perceiving subject is identified with the object of perception in artistic representation, art exists in the real as matter. The indifference of the universal and particular which is expressed by art in the real is expressed by thought in the ideal, which is a correlate of language; thus poetry and philosophy are capable of expressing the indifference in the ideal. In *The Philosophy of Art*, "Viewed from the real perspective, language constitutes the same resolution of the concrete into the universal, of being into knowledge, which, viewed from the ideal perspective, is thinking" (§ 73). Thought in this way is the deep structure of language, as in Structural Linguistics, the network of ideas and images in the ideal which are generated by language (in the real), and through which the sensible forms (words) generate meaning. The signifier is the form in the real which corresponds to the signified which is the idea in the ideal which is represented by the signifier. While the sensible form in art symbolizes the idea, the word in language signifies the idea, that is, represents the idea as a schema rather than a symbol. The schema represents the particular in the universal, while the symbol represents the universal in the particular. In that way, language is able to represent the idea in the ideal.

Schelling asserts that language is different from other forms of art in that it is governed completely by necessity and is generated in an organic manner, so that "it is the one necessary form of art that cannot be conceived as being invented or generated by art," but rather by the processes of nature, but clearly language is as artificially constructed as all other forms of art, and there is no direct correlation governed by necessity between language and thought. This is given by Deconstruction, and Structural Linguistics itself, that the relation between signifier and signified is an arbitrary one. Given that, and that language participates in the ideal, through the schematic, it can be said that language in fact is governed by freedom rather than necessity, and in that way is the expression of the indifference of the universal and particular in the ideal in comparison to the sensible forms of art, which exist in the real, and symbolize the indifference of freedom and necessity.

When the ideal becomes the real, or is represented by the real, according to Schelling, it assumes a "husk or covering" as a body or form; the indifference of the universal and particular in the idea "necessarily strives yet again toward a covering, a body, through which it may become objective without detriment to its ideality." The subjective becomes the objective in "the pollution of the walking sepulcher which we call a body, to which we are bound like an oyster to its shell," as described in the *Phaedrus* (250). For Jacques

Lacan, the self-identification of the subject in the body image and its orientation in space, as given by its perception in a mirror, for example, contradicts the disjunction between the identity of the subject as it is represented in the signifying structure, the real or the body, and the idea of the self in the ideal, as being a manifestation of the absolute.

The *objet a* of Lacan is the juncture between the signifying structure, as given by perception, and being, between the real and the ideal, and the idea as representation and the absolute. Driven by the self-misidentification of the subject in the body image, the *méconnaissance* of the subject, which is a function of desire produced by identification with the real, like the initiate in the *Symposium* who initially sees beauty only in an individual body, the subject forms a protective armor, an *armor fou*, a walking sepulcher, as it "solidifies into a signifier," as described in *The Four Fundamental Concepts of Psycho-Analysis* (p. 15). The body, the protective covering, conceals the essence of the absolute within it, as does matter in the sensible world. In the ideal, the absolute becomes a void around which the signifying structure of language circulates, the degrading chains of logic of Bataille, in the cycle of desire, the *méconnaissance* of the subject. In that way, the subject is alienated from the essence of his or her being in the absolute, the beauty of the being of the subject, as it were, in the indifference of the ideal and the real. In the dialectic, the subject must recognize itself as divided, must begin with the division of the real and ideal, in order to achieve a synthesis of the two.

For Schelling, the idea of the subject in its own consciousness strives toward a covering, a body. The idea "remains ideal, yet such that it leaves the other side behind and thus does not appear as something absolutely ideal, but rather merely as something relatively ideal that possesses the real outside of itself—standing over against it" (*The Philosophy of Art*, § 73), as in the divided subject of Lacan. The self-identity of the subject in the idea, though, because it exists in the ideal, does not become completely objective in the real, as is matter, because the self-identity is given by language, the manifestation of thought. According to Schelling, the subject may strive toward the protective covering of the body "through which it may become objective," though "without detriment to its ideality," even though the protective covering of the body as objective stands over against the identity of the subject as subjective. The subject rather integrates itself through the real, and thus allows the essence of the absolute to be expressed in the real, as symbolized by language. The disjunction in the subject between the ideal and real which is an insurmountable fissure in the psyche for Lacan is for Schelling, as for

Hegel, the very state of self-contradiction which allows the subject to intuit the absolute, through the dialectic, in language—which allows for the indifference of the real and the ideal in the ideal, and allows for the expression in language of the indifference of the universal and particular in the ideal, as opposed to other forms of art. A beautiful thought can exist in poetry and philosophy, but it cannot exist in art.

For Hegel, in *The Difference Between Fichte's and Schelling's Systems of Philosophy* in 1801, "That which has died the death of dichotomy, philosophy raises to life again through the absolute identity. And through Reason, which devours both [the finite and the infinite] and maternally posits them both equally, philosophy strives toward the consciousness of the identity of the finite and the infinite, or in other words, it strives towards knowledge and truth" (195).[22] Through philosophy, as Schelling expresses in the *Bruno* (329), "our eyes will be turned toward the higher deities, and achieving participation in their sublime mode of being through contemplation, we shall be truly perfected and satisfied, as the ancients expressed it; for we shall live within this resplendent sphere not just as refugees from the lands of mortality, but as ones who have received the initiation into immortal excellences." Plotinus explained the benefits of philosophical contemplation in the *Enneads* (IV.8.1): "becoming external to all other things and self-encentered; beholding a marvelous beauty; then, more than ever, assured of community with the loftiest order; enacting the noblest life, acquiring identity with the divine; stationing within It by having attained that activity; poised above whatsoever within the intellectual is less than the Supreme…" Through philosophy the particular is dissolved into the universal, and the turmoil caused by the mechanisms of desire and ego in the soul is appeased.

Schelling sees language as being the real structure of reason, reason the ideal being of language. In language and reason, the absolute is represented by the *logos*, that is, "the Word," which establishes reason as the controlling principle of the universe, as manifest in language; the *logos* is the representation of the absolute in reason. Plotinus saw the hieroglyph as a kind of *logos* in language, because the hieroglyph was seen as "an object in itself, an immediate unity, not an aggregate of discursive reasoning and detailed willing" (*Enneads* V.8.6), and thus exhibiting "an absence of discursiveness in the Intellectual Realm." The hieroglyph thus reveals the essence of the absolute in the real, because the hieroglyph was seen as a symbol rather than a schema (though it was actually a combination of both, as established by Jean-

François Champollion); the hieroglyph was seen as playing the role of the *logos* in the real, but that turned out not to be possible.

In equating reason and language, Schelling sees the *logos*, like the hieroglyph as conceived by Plotinus, as existing in the real as well, and at the same time achieving the indifference of the real and ideal in both the real and ideal, thus the essence of the absolute in the real, and the "primal act of speaking" (*The Philosophy of Art*, § 73). Because the sensible forms of art only symbolize the ideal, and only achieve the indifference of the real and ideal in the real, the *logos* does not occur in art, as it is both symbol and schema. The essence of the absolute is not revealed immediately in sensible form, but only in the relation between the sensible form and the idea. Thus "the real world is no longer the living word"; the arts are the "dead word," though they nevertheless speak, but in a speech in which speaking dies. The idea as it is symbolized in the arts can only be a derivative, once removed from the original, the idea which represents the absolute. The death of speech in the arts lends to the effect of the sublime, as the sublime depends on the inadequacy of the sensible form as symbol of the infinite, and allows for the idea of the infinite to develop, the intuition of the infinite in the ideal. Art is a catalyst for the intuition of the absolute, but such intuition cannot take place in perception alone—only in the indifference of perception and cognition, the real and the ideal in the ideal, which language allows.

In *The Philosophy of Art*, § 76, Schelling explains that "the indifference of the informing of the infinite into the finite, taken purely as indifference, is *sonority*," as in resonance created by intensified frequencies, in physics, in an attempt to establish a scientific basis for the Philosophy of Identity, or the Philosophy of Spirit. Sonority is the synthesis of the real and ideal, matter and idea. The act of the informing of the infinite into the finite, the universal into the particular, is magnetism; magnetism and sonority are principles of the Philosophy of Nature. Magnetism is not indifference, but rather difference, because it is bound to the physical qualities of the body. As magnetism as a force separates itself from the body and enters into the indifference of the real and ideal, it becomes sonority. Sonority is both real and ideal, because it has a physical quality that can be measured in space, but also a temporal quality that cannot be measured in space. The sonority or resonance of a body is relative to its "coherence" as a body, that is the resolution of its finiteness, as the infinite is informed into it, with "the ideal principle passed over completely into the corporeal." A body must not only be resonant in its coherence, it must conduct the resonance, or sonority, as sound. The indifference of the ideal and real in the body, of the unified and the multiple, is the indifference of the sonority and magnetism; in and of itself, a body is magnetic, but in order to be sonorous, the sonority must participate in the magnetism.

Sonority thus "is posited only under the condition of a movement transmitted to the body itself whereby it is set out of indifference with itself. Sonority itself is nothing other than the indifference of soul and body" (§ 84). The sonority of the bodies of the universe, the cosmic body in the ideal, is the "inner music of the movement of the stars," which corresponds to the inner music of the idea in the human soul. In the Renaissance, the music of the stars was the *musica mundana*, cosmic, celestial music, while the music of the mind was the *musica humana*, inner, instrumental music, comprising the Music of the Spheres, as described by Marsilio Ficino in *De amore*. Ficino wrote, "Our soul was endowed from the beginning with the Reason of this music, for the celestial harmony is rightly called innate in anything whose origin is celestial, which it later imitates on various instruments and in songs. And this gift likewise was given us through the love of divine providence" (V.13).

Schelling describes sonority as a quality of the infinite and ideal in the universe, and through which the infinite is informed into the particular. Through sonority the infinite participates in the particular, and through sonority the particular is conscious of the participation of the universal in it. Sonority is the medium of the informing of the subjective into the objective, and the means by which the objective is led back to the subjective, the particular is led back to the absolute. The magnetism of the body is the consciousness of the body, the activation of its *potence*, and sonority is the self-consciousness of the body, as the ideal participates in it. "Only through subject-objectivation does it [the absolute unity, eternal nature] manifest itself within objectivity and then as a recognized object [in magnetism] guide itself back from this objectivity [through sonority] into its own self-recognition [self-consciousness]" (*The Philosophy of Art*, § 76). The self-consciousness of the absolute as represented in the ideal anticipates the definition of self-consciousness in Hegel's *Phenomenology of Spirit*. The objectification of the absolute occurs in the *musica mundana* of the universe, and by participation, in the *musica humana* in the soul. In the *Enneads*, Plotinus explained, "all music—since its thought is upon melody and rhythm—must be the earthly representation of the music there is in the rhythm of the Ideal Realm"

(V.9.11). All sonority participates in the sonority of the absolute, in the indifference of the absolute and particular in the ideal.

According to Schelling, sonority occurs in the ideal only in relation to the magnetism in the real, as soul only occurs in relation to body, as manifestation of the absolute. The sonority of a body is the manifestation of the body in the ideal in relation to the body, the participation of the infinite in the finite, the dissolution of the matter of the body into the idea of matter, and the concretizing of the fluctuating and ephemeral form of the body into the absolute and infinite, undifferentiated idea, schema of the absolute. The sensible form is a symbol of its relation to the absolute, while the sonority of the form schematizes its participation in the absolute. While sonority schematizes the indifference of the real and ideal, light, which is absolute sonority, is the indifference of the real and ideal. Sonority is "the indwelling or finite light of corporeal things" (*The Philosophy of Art*, § 84), the infinite as it is being made finite. Sonority does not participate in light any more than the idea or the particular form participate in the absolute. Light cannot thus be integrated into body and vice versa; they are two distinct entities, as are body and soul. In its magnetism, a body can have a harmonious relation to light, and through sonority light can participate in the body, illuminate the body, but the body cannot participate in the light, as the substance of the light is in the ideal. When the body strives toward participation in the light, in the desire for the absolute, the light becomes color, that substance which is the indifference of light and matter, the indifference of the ideal and real in both the ideal and real, in both idea and perception. Color thus contains sonority, or resonance, and beauty.

Light in the real is as intuition in the ideal, which is the indifference of thinking and being, the idea and the absolute. Light is the essence of the absolute in the real; it is neither schema nor symbol, but rather indifference itself. Light is the source and being of both perception and thinking, consciousness and self-consciousness. Light, as the essence of the absolute, is the source of the indifference of the real and ideal in the real. As the essence of the absolute, light is not able to be informed into the real as the ideal, as the sensible form cannot participate in the light, but only interact with it. The informing of the ideal into the real is seen as a condition of contrast, as in chiaroscuro in painting, the juxtaposition of light and dark, and the spectrum of color, which displays the sonority of the real, the intensity of the resonance, as the ideal is informed into it. The real is that which is not ideal; it is the negation of the universal, of the infinite. Thus in sonority there is contrast, as in the dialectic, and the informing of the ideal into the real is a process of resolution, of creating a synthesis of opposites; the sensible form negates the universal, and the universal subsumes the sensible form; without sonority, they are mutually exclusive. In the indifference of the real and ideal, the real retains its particularity as negation of the ideal, thus as darkness in contrast to light, for example, as represented by chiaroscuro.

Symbolism in painting is the extent to which the ideal is discernible (as it is represented) as it is informed into the real. As has been seen, the ideal is in no way discernible in the imitation of natural forms, although symbolism in painting operates according to the same principles as symbolism in nature, as Plotinus explained that the arts "go back to the Ideas from which Nature itself derives" (*Enneads* V.8.1), going beyond just giving a "bare reproduction of the thing seen." An example of the ideas from which nature derives is the indifference of the real and the ideal in sonority and color, and the contrast of the real and the ideal in chiaroscuro. In *The Philosophy of Art*, painting consists of the real (the sensible form), the ideal (as it is symbolized, in color and chiaroscuro, for example), and the indifference of the two (as it is symbolized in light). All particular forms of painting, and the arts in general, contain the universal principles of art.

The universal principles of painting are drawing, chiaroscuro (light), and color—the real, the ideal, and the indifference of the two. Drawing is "the first framing of identity into particularity" (§ 87); the juxtaposition of the identity (the ideal) and the particularity is chiaroscuro (light as the ideal and dark as the negation of the ideal); the indifference of identity and particularity is color. As has been seen, though light as the ideal and dark as the negation of the ideal preclude each other, they are ultimately identical, as absolute form is identical to formlessness, to chaos, wherein all forms and colors are dissolved, as in black. Absolute form is not manifest in sensible form without the participation of sonority and light, but it is present universally, as chaos is present universally in form, though it is not manifest in the unity of the absolute. Chiaroscuro is "the painting within painting," the symbol of the ideal in the real, the merging of particularity as difference into identity, "and its suspension as difference."

The purpose of art is not to represent the real, but rather the ideal, and the indifference of the real and ideal, the self-consciousness of the perceiving subject in perception, the human soul in the order of the universe. The beauty of art is a "beauty elevated above all sensuality," a higher beauty than that of nature, as for Hegel. The purpose of art is to express the absolute in sensible form, universal knowledge and intuition in the particular. As the ideal cannot exist without participation in the real, light cannot exist without participation in form. Form is thus the primary element of painting, as it is the primary element of the perceived real, the element by which the idea participates in matter, as it is constructed in perception and thinking. Color is the synthesis of form and light, real and ideal, which serves as the medium for the participation of matter into form, the real in the symbol of the ideal. Color is a *potence* of form, the will of the real toward the ideal. Through the three principles of line (drawing, form), chiaroscuro and color, painting enacts the transition from the real to the ideal. The three principles combine in sonority or resolution to serve the transition. The three principles allow the sensible forms of the painting to participate in the ideal, symbolically, to become an idea, in the participation of the absolute in human thought, the universal in the particular.

All form in painting depends on drawing, and without drawing painting would not be art; without color painting would not be painting. As color, and chiaroscuro, painting participates in the ideal. Because painting operates according to the mechanisms of these principles, painting cannot be sensible form in the real; thought they can be imitations, the line of painting cannot be the line of forms of matter, the color cannot be the color, and the chiaroscuro cannot be the chiaroscuro. Each of the principles in painting is expressed according to its own essence, in part within the real, but in part independent of it. The sensible form in painting must become as if the sensible form in matter, but by expressing its independent essence, as it participates in the absolute, and as that participation is revealed in the idea, through the symbol. Rather than imitate sensible form in matter in a form of deception, as described by Plato in the *Republic*, where the product of the artisan is a "shadowy thing compared to reality" (597), and "the artist's representation stands at a third remove from reality," the painting must in fact "*destroy* that particular sense of reality" (*The Philosophy of Art*, § 87); the painting must in fact appear as non-real, as elevated above reality, and represent reality as something un-real, as ideal, as classical Greek art does. The purpose of art in fact is to create a representation at a third remove from reality; the sensible form in art represents the sensible form in nature, which represents the idea and the absolute. The form in art is a symbol of a symbol of the idea, and it would be deceptive to represent it as anything else.

In *The Philosophy of Art*, chiaroscuro transforms the appearance of matter, the form of matter in perception, into appearance itself, perceived form and not sensible form. As such chiaroscuro intensifies the illusion of the painting, its nonreality. Chiaroscuro, as the juxtaposition of the ideal and the real, is the medium of the effect of the sublime, the intuition of the infinite within the limitation of the finite. As the juxtaposition of light and dark, chiaroscuro can create the appearance that the source of light of the painting is in the painting itself. The source of light is a symbol of the absolute, the chiaroscuro is the juxtaposition of the ideal and real, and the color is the informing of the ideal into the real. Schelling gives as an example the painting *La Notte* (*Adoration of the Shepherds*) by Antonio Correggio (Figure 2), in which the eternal light of the absolute emanates from the Christ Child, mystically illuminating the dark night, the real which negates the ideal. The light of Christ is a symbol of the light of the absolute, which is a symbol of intuition in the intellect, the participation of the eternal in the idea. The light is the mystical vision of the immortal souls in the *Phaedrus*, as, in the description of Plotinus, "being appears before them from some unseen place and rising loftily over them pours its light upon all things, so that all gleams in its radiance" (*Enneads* V.8.10).

The beauty achieved in the painting by Correggio, in the indifference of the ideal and the real, the light and the form, in the color, and the simultaneous sublimity of it, in the chiaroscuro, transcend the principles of painting taken in themselves—line, color, and light—corresponding to the three *potences* of the absolute—matter, organism, and light—and create a work of art which is of the ideal rather than the real, of a beauty higher than the real. As in the *concinnitas* of Leon Battista Alberti, Correggio seeks to "compose parts that are quite separate from each other by their nature, according to some precise rule, so that they correspond to one another in appearance" (*De re aedificatoria* VII.4). In the words of Plotinus in the *Enneads* (I.6.1), "But where the Ideal-Form has entered, it has grouped and coordinated what from a diversity of parts was to become a unity…" The inner light of the painting is a symbol of the inner light of the soul of the artist, the intuition of the absolute within, through the disciplining of the soul, as in the *Symposium*, allowing the initiate to see beauty itself in the idea of beauty, and in the *Enneads* (VI.9.9), where the advice of Plotinus to the initiate is to "withdraw into yourself and look. And if you do not find yourself beautiful yet, act as does the creator of a statue that is to be made beautiful" (VI.9.9), and cut away, smooth, lighten and straighten until the "godlike splendor of virtue" shines from the soul as it shines from the statue, the light of the good which nourishes the Intellectual Principle and the soul.

The vision of the painting as described by Schelling corresponds to the inner vision of the soul, in the intuition of the absolute, as a symbol of it. Through color, chiaroscuro and light, the medium of painting enacts the transformation of light into dark, ideal into real, and dark into light, real into ideal, in an "infinity of gradations" (*The Philosophy of Art*, § 87), the indifference of the infinite and the finite. The gradations allow "the one [light] to blend into the other [dark] such that they remain distinguishable in themselves"; the real is discernible in the ideal, and the ideal is discernible in the real. The matter of the painting in which the light of the ideal is allowed to enter is darkness, as in *La Notte*, symbolizing the informing of the ideal into the real as the idea into the form, the consummation of perception and consciousness. In the painting, the color black is a symbol of dark, and the color white is a symbol of light; black is the absence of color, its negation, as dark is the negation of the ideal, and white is the combination of all colors, the universal which combines all particulars.

The goal of chiaroscuro is to render the light and dark as if they have the same origin, "as if poured from one mold," as if the absolute form is the equivalent of formlessness and chaos. The gradations of light and color occur within the chiaroscuro, the appearance of form, as the sonority in the indifference of the ideal and real in the real, or the symbol of the real. The sonority of the chiaroscuro reaffirms to the viewer the indifference of the perceiver and the perceived, the subject and the universe. It allows the perceiving subject to overcome its own self-alienation from the absolute, from being, as the subject is given to itself in the signifying structure, and to experience the intuition of the absolute, the mystical vision. Such a condition "must be the truest and most genuine effect of all art," a re-affirmation of being, and of the participation of the universal good in the particular soul.

In the painting by Correggio, the gradations of light in the chiaroscuro are both differentiated from the absolute light which emanates from the Christ Child, and made to appear as the product of the same light. The universal is informed into the particular in the gradations of light. The gradations of light in the chiaroscuro are symbols of the reflection of light in the sensible forms of matter, the kaleidoscopic play of light in reflections off surfaces, the "play of light and opacity" which appears as if it "participates in the ambiguity of the jewel," as the gaze was described by Jacques Lacan in *The Four Fundamental Concepts of Psycho-Analysis* (p. 96). The surface effects of light in chiaroscuro produce the appearance of sensible form in matter, in the real.

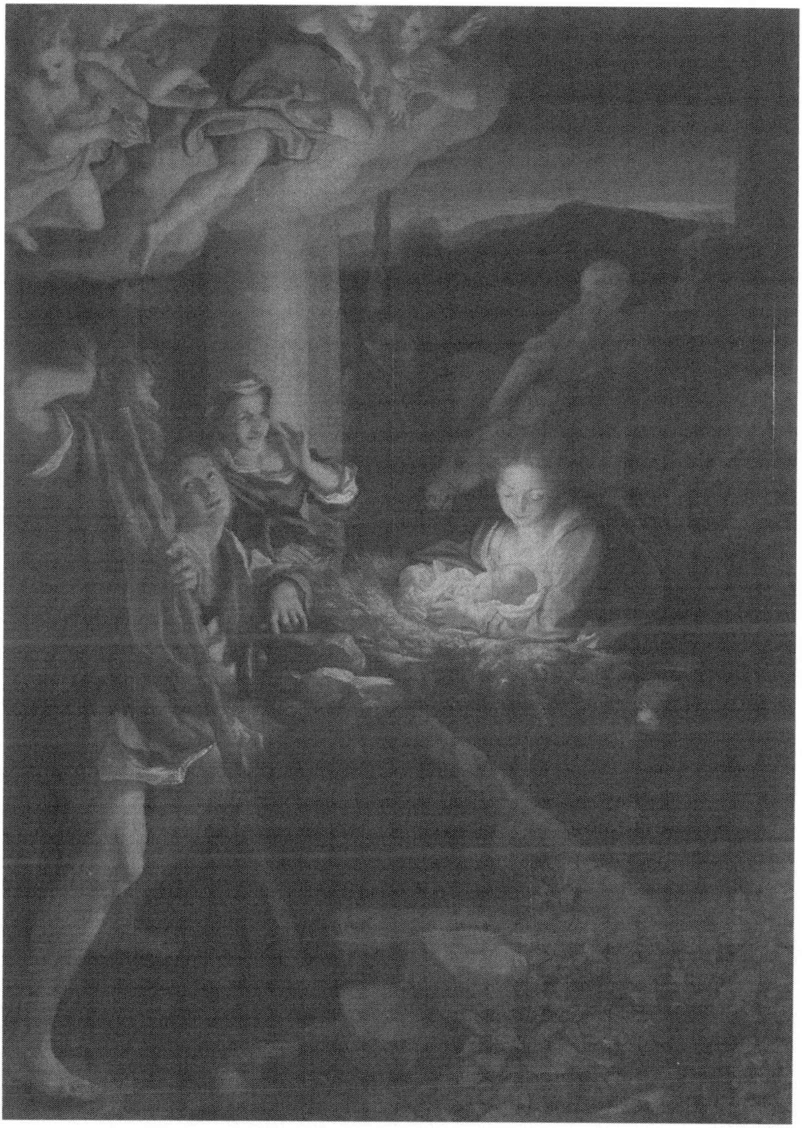

Figure 2. Correggio, *Holy Night* (*Adoration of the Shepherds*)
(Photo credit: Erich Lessing, Art Resource, NY)

Through the gradations the forms remain both independent of the light and as being the recipient of it. The light can never be the form or the matter, as the universal can never be the idea or the particular. The indifference of light and form, the medium in which both light and form co-exist as synthesized, is color. Though gradations of color depend on gradations of light, on the sonority of the informing of the ideal into the real, color cannot be separated from form, and thus exists only in the real. Color can influence the effect of light, as the particular can influence the effect of the universal, but only as light is an independent entity, unabsorbed into the form.

The juxtaposition of light and dark in chiaroscuro symbolizes the juxtaposition of light and dark in the real, in nature. Light is a symbol of eternal beauty "in the struggle against night" (*The Philosophy of Art*, § 87), of knowledge in the struggle against ignorance, of the good in the struggle against chaos, the same struggle as waged by the Olympian gods against the Furies and the chthonic gods. Night, "as the eternal ground of all existence, does not itself exist, even though it manifests itself as power through its perpetual antithetical effect," through its manifestation in universal form, in the absolute. In the Baroque, light and dark were represented by intersecting pyramids, as by Athanasius Kircher in *Primitiae Gnomonicae Catopticae* in 1633, and *Ars Magna Lucis et Umbrae* in 1645. The intersecting pyramids symbolize the diffusion of light from the absolute into the material world, as reflected in the human soul as idea to form the visible forms of the archetypal principles.

Visible forms are created at the intersection of the pyramids, at the intersection of the ideal and real, the light of the absolute and the night of the negation of being. As described in *Primitiae Gnomonicae Catopticae*, "light descends from the luminous body [the sun] to form a reflected body, perceived as a point on a surface, at which point the two pyramids intersect" (p. 33).[23] The point on the surface is the particular in the universal, and the reflected body is the surface of appearance, ephemeral and in flux according to Plato. The light of the absolute is reflected to form images of matter which are simulacrae of the archetypes of the absolute, as is illustrated on the frontispiece of *Ars Magna Lucis et Umbrae*. Light is a symbol of the good, and is passed through human intelligence in the soul to sensible forms; thus "everything accessible to the senses is diffused by grace and divine goodness, in copies and images" (*Primitiae Gnomonicae Catopticae*, p. 2),[24] as symbolized by the intersecting pyramids, and as enacted in chiaroscuro.

Intersecting pyramids also served to illustrate a theory of vision and perception in the *Primitiae Gnomonicae Catopticae*. The base of one pyramid corresponds to the sphere of the eye (the lens, or "crystalline humor" of René Descartes in *Treatise of Man*),[25] while the apex corresponds to a point on the surface of visible things. The base of the other pyramid is the surface of visible things, and the apex is the point at the center of the back of the sphere of the eye (the retina, or what Descartes called the optic nerve). Thus one base forms the retina in the lens of the eye, while the other base forms the point of light on the surface of forms. Light is diffused from the retina along the lines of the pyramid to form the sensible surface, and at the same time it is reflected from a point in the sensible to form the sphere of the eye. "The different lines [of light] produced in the eye extend to the central point of the sphere, and all concur in the center, so that all the lines form a continuum in a body, and the continuous surface is made visible at each point, which is the center of the boundary of the eye" (*Primitiae Gnomonicae Catopticae*, p. 31).[26] The intersection of the real and ideal occurs in the process of perception, which is the construction of the sensible world on the part of the intellect, based on the archetypal principles. The indifference of the real and ideal in sonority and beauty is a function of perception, the in-forming of the infinite into the finite. Chiaroscuro is thus a symbol of perception, as painting is a symbol of the interaction of the intellect and the sensible world.

The point of light becomes the line which becomes the surface which becomes the body, a geometrical allegory in Neoplatonism for the process of creation. Plato conceived the universe as being constructed in a geometrical progression from point to line to surface to solid, each corresponding to a level of the tetractys: one unit for a point, two units for a line, three units for a surface and four units for a solid; thus the atom for earth was a cube. Nicolas Cusanus compared the process of unfolding, *explicato*, and the contracting of particulars in the universal, as the polygon in the circle, for example, to a geometrical progression from point to line to surface, as an allegory for the transformation of the archetypal idea to material form. Particulars arise as a contractible universal which exists not in itself but in that which is actual, just as a point, a line, and a surface precede, in progressive order, the material object in which alone they exist actually. Thus all universals exist in the universe only in a contracted manner, as copies of an original singularity, arising from the point. The line and the surface exist in the material object as the universal exists in the particular. The mathematical structure of the universe is realized as the geometrical structure of the universe, according to

Cusanus in *De coniecturis*, thus as a corporeal body, in the same way that the tetractys was transformed by Plato into the progression from point to line to surface to body. The progression from the simplest unity is seen as a progression from the simplest point, to line, to surface, and to body. Unity is projected into line, surface and body, and the unity of the line is found in the surface and the body,[27] as in the theory of vision of Athanasius Kircher.

Leon Battista Alberti also constructed a theory of vision in which rays of light were arranged in a pyramid, in his treatise on painting, *De pictura*. In *De pictura* surfaces are defined and measured by rays of light which serve to translate visual matter into intelligible matter, giving it the qualities of the archetypal principles. "Extrinsic" rays of light define the outline of surface, and the outline of the pyramid of light in vision (I.7).[28] The pyramid is formed between the surface of the matter and the eye, as for Kircher; the eye is the source of an inner light, the light of the absolute as intuited in the intellect. Contained within the pyramid of light of Alberti, and enclosed by the extrinsic rays, are another type of ray called the "median" ray, which are variable and absorb light and color to varying degrees, as in chiaroscuro. The median ray extends between the apex of the pyramid, the retina of the eye, and the surface of the sensible form, and fills in the color and shadow found within the outline of the form, symbolized by the drawing in the painting. The central ray inside the pyramid among the median rays is the "centric" ray. The centric ray forms a direct line from the apex of the pyramid to the center of the surface, as in the intersecting pyramids of Kircher. The position of the centric ray determines the outline of the surface of the sensible form.

In his treatise on perspective, *De Prospectiva Pingendi*, Piero della Francesca defined perspective (*commensuratio*) as that which "can be demonstrated with angled lines and proportions, that is, the points, lines, surfaces and bodies,"[29] corresponding to the classifications of Euclid's *Elements of Geometry*. The five elements that need to be considered in the perspectival construction of a painting are: sight, or the eye; the form of the thing seen; the distance from the eye to the thing seen; the lines that connect the eye to the extremities or bordering lines of the thing seen; and the area between the eye and the thing seen,[30] following the intersecting pyramids of Kircher and the pyramid of vision of Alberti. Piero della Francesca described the extrinsic rays in the pyramid of vision as lines which present themselves from the extremities of the thing and end up in the eye, in between which the eye receives and discerns them.[31] It is necessary to understand the linear qualities of objects in a picture plane so that they can be represented,[32] in their ideal beauty, as copies of the patterns of intelligible objects.

The point in perspective is that which has no parts, according to Piero, following the definition of the point in Euclid's *Elements of Geometry*. Proclus, in the *Commentary on the First Book of Euclid's Elements*, described the point as being without parts because it is the closest of all things in the real (the Unlimited of Proclus) to the absolute (the One or the Limit of Proclus), that which precedes all things in unity and simplicity. Material forms that are more uniform and concentrated, without a plurality of parts, are closer to the origin of matter, closer to the absolute, in the same way that the point in perspectival construction is at the origin of the lines of construction in space. The point in the eye in Alberti's cone of vision corresponds to the absolute, as it is represented in the intellect.

In the *Bruno*, Schelling associates the point with the absolute and the line with the idea, or concept. The point is "where all the things of the universe are one in substance" (276). In the heavenly bodies, the archetypal forms in the real, the point is a star, which is the indifference of matter and light, form and essence, in the absolute. The star, as a point, the form of the absolute, is "the hearth of the world" and the "blessed sentinel of Zeus." The line symbolizes the connection between the infinite and the finite, the point and its first differentiation, as it is the first manifestation in space of geometry; "the line's place in the domain of extension corresponds to the concept's place in the domain of thought" (263). The line is "the purest abstraction from the totality of spatial relations" (264), and is at the same time infinite in its possibility. This act of the abstraction from totality is a "disruption, as it were, of universal identity," in which "everything particular is precipitated out of the indifferent absolute."

In the *Commentary on the First Book of Euclid's Elements* of Proclus, the point is both "everywhere indivisible and distinguished by its simplicity from divisible things" (92),[33] that is, separate from them, but at some point, "as it descends in the scale of being, even the point takes on the character distinctive of divisibles," that is, it participates in sensible forms, in lines and planes and solids, as the absolute participates in sensible form, but sensible form can never participate in the absolute, as no geometric figure can participate in the point. The line is one-dimensional, so it has the quality of the monad, or indivisible, but in that it connects two points it is dyadic, and divisible. It combines the infinite and the finite, as in the Intellectual Principle, originating in the absolute, and participating in the sensible world. The line according to Proclus "produces transformation into length, that is, into divisible extendedness in one dimension together with participation in duality" (99). The line is "at once unlimited and limited—in its own forthgoing unlimited, but limited by virtue of its participation in its limitlike cause" (101). As the point "goes forth from that region," in the Intellectual Principle, "this very first of all ideas expands itself, moves, and flows towards infinity and, imitating the infinite dyad is mastered by its own principle, unified by it, and constrained on all sides."

For Schelling in *The Philosophy of Art*, of the three elements of painting, drawing is the complete negation of light in matter, the universal unrevealed in the particular; chiaroscuro is the juxtaposition of light and matter wherein the "action and reaction of light" (§ 87) transforms matter into an appearance of form, transforms the real into the ideal; and color is the indifference of light and matter, where matter is transformed into light and vice versa, where the ideal is in-formed into the real and where absolute beauty is represented in form. The purpose of painting is to represent absolute beauty, to achieve the highest beauty possible, to represent the idea of beauty beyond beauty in sensible form. While Correggio achieved the greatest synthesis of light and dark in chiaroscuro of any painter, according to Schelling, the painter who achieved the greatest synthesis of light and form was Tiziano Vecelli, in paintings such as *The Annunciation* in San Salvatore, Venice (Figure 3).

Schelling borrows a quotation from Johann Joachim Winckelmann in *Geschichte der Kunst des Altertums* (*History of the Art of the Antiquities*): "The idea of beauty is like a spirit drawn from matter through fire that seeks to beget a creation according to the image of the first reasoning creature designed within the understanding of the deity." The human spirit aspires to the indifference of the idea and the absolute, that which differentiates the ideal from the real. The human spirit aspires to penetrate the representation of the absolute in the idea, to overcome its self-alienation, its thrown-ness from its primal origin, the "image of the first reasoning creature." As Lord Byron expressed in his ode to Prometheus in 1816, "Thou art symbol and a sign/To mortals of their fate and force;/Like thee, man is in part divine,/A troubled stream from a pure source;/And Man in portions can foresee/His own funereal destiny,/His wretchedness, and his resistance,/And his sad unallied existence:/To which his Spirit may oppose/Itself—and equal to all woes..."[34]

The fate of man is to be alienated from his divine origin, and to seek to be reconciled with his own being; the pursuit of the absolute in art is a function

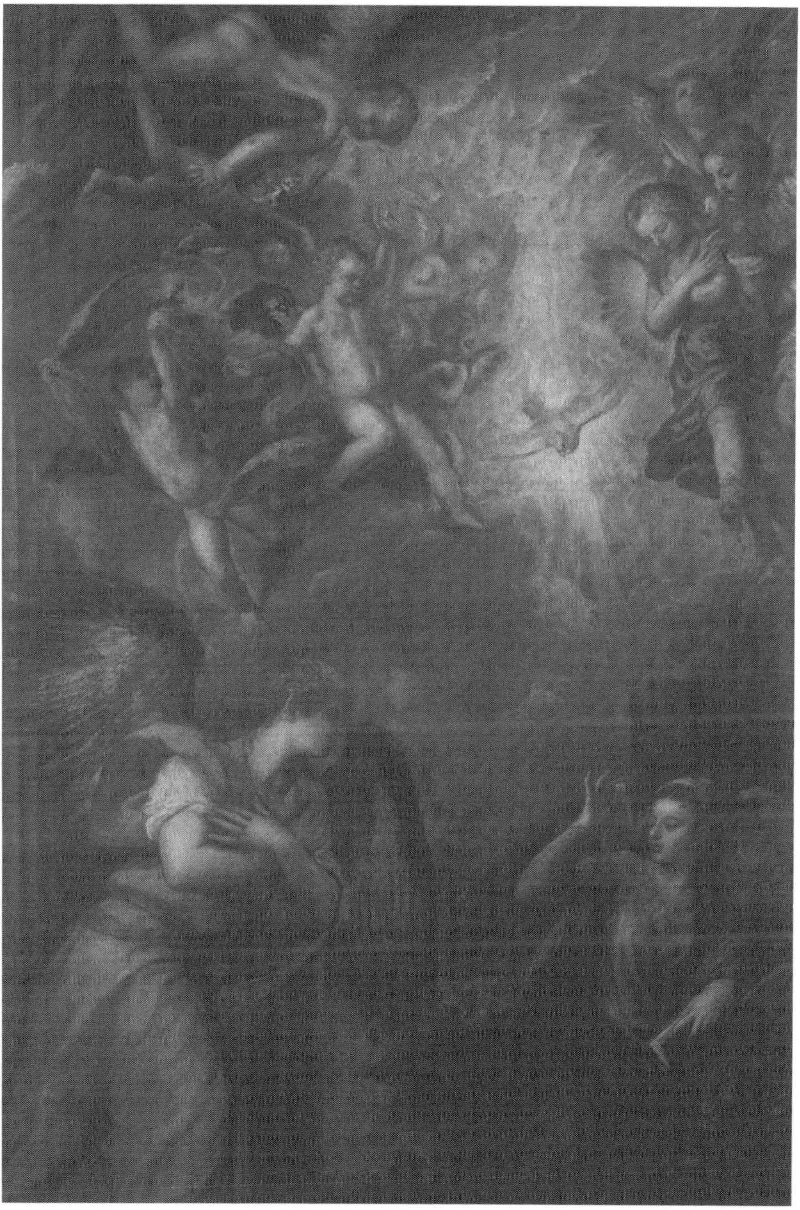

Figure 3. Titian (Tiziano Vecelli), *The Annunciation*, detail, San Salvatore, Venice (Scala/Art Resource, NY)

of the eternal incompleteness of the human consciousness of being. The closer the idea of beauty is to absolute beauty, the closer man comes to being reconciled with his origin. In *The Philosophy of Art*, Schelling seeks to determine the most effective means in painting to accomplish this reconciliation. The relation of the ideal and the real, and the revelation of the absolute, is enacted in the combination of drawing, chiaroscuro, and color. The content of the painting can be either symbolic, wherein the particular signifies the universal and becomes the universal, or it can be allegorical, wherein the particular signifies the universal and remains a particular. As has been seen, in the symbolic the universal and the particular are unified in indifference, allowing for the representation of the absolute in the particular, while in the allegorical the universal is intuited through the particular; in the schematic, the particular is intuited through the universal.

Allegory combines the symbolic and the schematic, as the symbolic contains within it the possibility of the allegorical and schematic. Allegory can be seen as a universal language in its combination of the symbolic and schematic. In allegory, ideas are signified by images; thus allegory is the language of art. Painting, because it exists in the real, can never be completely ideal, and thus can never be purely symbolic, as the indifference of the real and the ideal. Color is the purely symbolic as the indifference of the real and ideal, but color alone cannot be painting, and the indifference of the real and ideal is not possible without the participation of the real. Painting is thus allegorical, combining the symbolic with the schematic; the forms of painting symbolize universal ideas through which the particular forms are then understood. It is through allegory that the ideal enters into the real, the sensible forms of the painting, as they represent objects of perception and are combined in a syntax to form a representative language.

A painting can be symbolic when the allegory which the painting communicates represents an idea itself, as the symbolic combines the allegorical and schematic. *The Parnassus* of Raffaello Sanzio in the Stanza della Segnatura, circa 1508 (Figure 4), symbolizes poetry, because it combines sensible forms as symbols, the poets themselves, the mountain in Greece, the muse of poetry in the form of Apollo, in a syntax, a deep structure of a visual language, which represents the idea of poetry in the ideal; through the idea of poetry as given by the syntax in the allegory, the particular forms of poetry are then intuited as they relate to the whole; the particular is intuited through the universal, and the syntax of the allegory operates as a schema, as in lan-

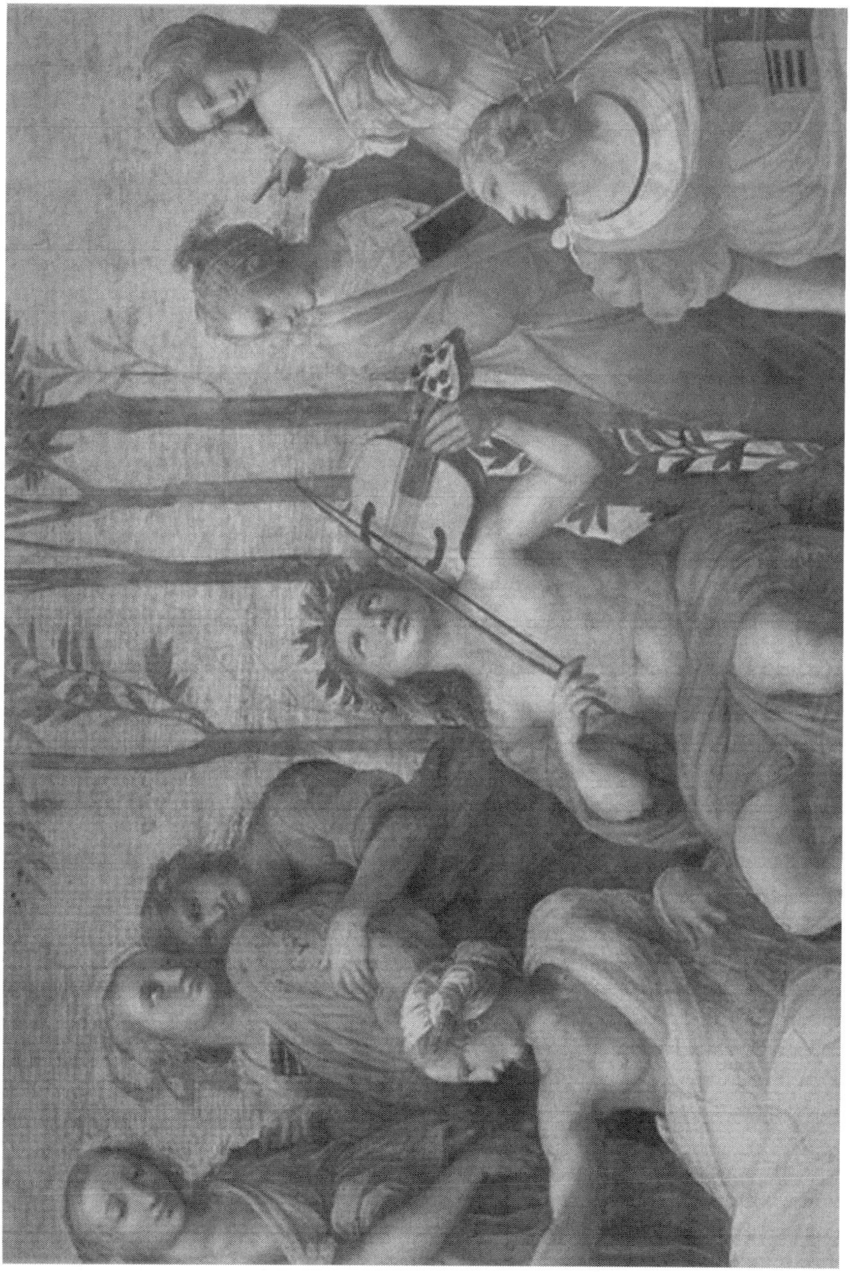

Figure 4. Raphael, *The Parnassus*, detail of Apollo and the Muses, Stanza della Segnatura, Vatican Palace, Vatican State (Scala /Art Resource, NY)

guage. Similarly, *The School of Athens* in the Stanza della Segnatura symbolizes philosophy, *The Disputà* symbolizes theology, and *The Cardinal Virtues* symbolizes jurisprudence; taken as a whole, the frescoes symbolize the Humanism of the Vatican in the Renaissance. Through allegory, the frescoes signify an idea, and the ideal participates in the real.

The *Madonna and Child* of Raffaello of 1503 is symbolic in a different way. Like the history paintings in the Stanza della Segnatura, the *Madonna* presents an allegory in the interaction of the Virgin and Christ, thus symbolizes the Immaculate Conception. The Madonna though is a symbol in and of herself, a symbol of purity; the idea of purity in the ideal precedes the figure of the Madonna in the painting, thus the Madonna of Raffaello is purity itself. The particular thus signifies the universal and becomes the universal in a different way, as symbol. In allegory, the idea which precedes the symbolic image becomes objective, enters into the real, through historical representation. History itself, as Hegel established, is the manifestation of the ideal in the real in human activity. The historical representation in the fresco becomes symbolic when it is combined with the idea; the symbolic combines the allegorical and the schematic. The historical painting is thus "one particular mode of the symbolic" (*The Philosophy of Art*, § 87).

It can thus be seen that painting combines the symbolic, the schematic, and the allegorical—image, language, and history. Through this, and in the use of drawing, chiaroscuro and color, painting achieves the indifference of the ideal and the real, the infinite and finite, within the real. The ideal is intuited in the real in the symbolic, and the real is intuited in the ideal in the schematic. A sensible figure in painting which signifies rather than symbolizes, which participates in the syntax and allows the real to be intuited in the ideal, is a figure which is not preceded by an idea, and in which the ideal cannot be intuited in the real. In the visual form as signifier alone, as in language, the ideal does not participate in the real, and the form has no direct relation to the idea; as in matter, the absolute is unrevealed. As in language, as given by Structural Linguistics, the relation between the signifier and the signified is arbitrary; the signifier does not contain the indifference of the ideal and real as does the symbol. A painting is symbolic if the function of the form is not just that of a signifier, if the idea precedes the form, and the form as form is both real and ideal. As such the idea is expressed in the particular form, and the absolute is represented by the idea. As the painting expresses the idea of the absolute, it fulfills the desire of the consciousness of the human being in its alienation from being to be re-united with its origin, in the dialectic of the absolute, the indifference of the real and ideal. As absolute beauty is the purest symbol of the absolute in the ideal, the representation of the idea of absolute beauty in painting is the purest symbol of the absolute in the real.

Bruno, or On the Natural and the Divine Principle of Things

For Schelling, painting is an organic art because it combines light and matter, in the same way that the organism as a *potence* in nature combines the *potences* of light and matter, activity and being. The organism is the objectification of reason in its combination of being and activity. The organism in nature is reason alone, in which the ideal does not participate. The human organism is reason and intellect, combined in the soul, the *anima secunda* and the *anima prima*. Reason is the essence of matter as it is expressed in nature as the organism; the organism combines magnetism and sonority, which create consciousness. In the same way that the organism objectifies reason in the real, art objectifies philosophy in the ideal. The sensible forms of art are the concrete images of the idea; in that way art is a medium for the participation of reason in the archetypal Idea, or in Plotinian terms, the participation of the Reason Principle in the Intellectual Principle. As such art is a medium for the intuition of the absolute. The idea of the absolute is the product of the indifference of thought and intuition, Reason Principle and Intellectual Principle, which is the first principle of philosophy. The indifference of reason and the *intellectus divinus* in the ideal is the indifference of matter, light and organism in the real. Art is a medium for the dialectical process of philosophy, in the contemplation of the most absolute form of being. As described in *Bruno, or On the Natural and the Divine Principle of Things* (243), the absolute is "the indivisible unity of the identical and the differentiated," and "the inseparability of thought and intuition."

In that the indifference of thought and intuition is an absolute and universal, nothing can exist independently of it. All being is "a determinate identity of thought and intuition" (259), a manifestation of the universal in the particular. All particulars, all finite beings, contain both difference and indifference in various degrees. Difference in the finite being is manifest as body, while indifference is manifest as soul. All finite beings, particulars in the temporal real, are animated to the extent that the indifference of the ideal is contained in their being, and that their being exists as idea. Particulars only exist in the real as manifestations of the universal in the ideal, thus their existence in the real is only one of appearance. Painting and philosophy reveal the ideal existence of the particulars in the real, the idea in which the particulars participate. Painting reveals the participation of perceived objects in the ideal, their existence as idea. Thus painting reveals the relation between the perceived object and the idea, the relation between the perceiving subject and what is perceived.

The indifference of reason and intuition as the absolute requires the differentiation of reason and intuition, just as the indifference of the real and ideal requires the differentiation of the two. In matter, there is no differentiation between the real and ideal, the particular and universal. "The stone that you see, for example, is in absolute identity with all things; hence for it, nothing is distinguished from anything else, nothing steps forth from self-enclosed night" (259–260), the ground of being. Matter is not animated by a participation of the real in the ideal, because the two remain undifferentiated, in the absolute. As the complete negation of the absolute, matter is the absolute itself, as absolute form is complete formlessness. In the organism, real and ideal are differentiated, and the universal is manifest as the particular. In the human organism, reason and intuition are differentiated, in self-consciousness. In the differentiation of reason and intuition, the indifference of reason and intuition, the absolute, becomes visible, is revealed. The universal is revealed in the particular in symbolic reason, of which painting is the visualization.

The particular form becomes particular by "actualizing the relative opposition of the finite and the infinite" (260), by being intuited as a universal, as in art, and then recognized as a particular. All particulars contain within them the potential to be intuited as universals, to actualize the opposition between finite and infinite. The complete indifference of the finite and infinite is the absolute; in its differentiation, "the finite thing, or that aspect of it whereby it is a relative identity, receives the reflected light of the absolute's identity." It is through the reflected light of the absolute's identity that finite things are made visible to perception and participate in the idea. Marsilio Ficino described vision as the process of absorbing the reflected light of the absolute from objects. In *De amore*, "the eye, at first dark and unformed, similar to chaos, loves the light while it sees it, and seeing it absorbs the rays of the sun, and as it receives the rays it discovers the colors and shapes of things."[35]

The sun illuminates the soul and the mind in the same way that it illuminates the elements of matter. In vision, the finite is differentiated from the infinite, as absolute form is differentiated from chaos, the dark night, from original indifference. For Ficino, the desire to differentiate the finite from the infinite is love, the desire to reconcile the self-alienation of being. Love is the "maker and conserver of everything" (p. 43: "fattore e conservatore del tutto"); it generates activity in being, like the *potence* of Schelling. Love is also for Ficino "master and governor of the arts" (p. 45: "signore e governatore delle Arti"), because the artist seeks the differentiation and indifference of the infinite and finite. According to Athanasius Kircher, that which generates motion through the intersecting pyramids of light and dark, finite and infinite, is love. The circle in which the intersecting pyramids are inscribed is filled with love. As described in *Oedipi Aegyptiaci* in 1653,[36] the circle

> commences and draws from God, showing the reason of perfect beauty, transferred into the world, called love above all, revolving in beauty, turning in the example and image of beauty. This circulation penetrates through everything, desiring to continue upwards and downwards. It causes the rays of the sun to create light in the heavens, splendor in the air, light in the elements and mixtures in bodies. Love is thus visible as it causes the conversion of all things to divine beauty and principal form, and in the words of Proclus joins all things and establishes connections, replenishing things, distributing divine light throughout the universe.

Love, Eros, is the servant of Aphrodite, Goddess of Beauty, symbol of absolute beauty. Love is the *potence* in the universe which creates the Neoplatonic *circuitus spiritualis*, the continual motion between universal and particular, the differentiation of the infinite and finite. Love compels all things to absolute beauty, as in the *Symposium* (210), where the initiate, through love, "will be turned towards the great sea of beauty and gazing on it he'll give birth, through a boundless love of knowledge, to many beautiful and magnificent discourses and ideas." For Plotinus, love is caused by the recognition of the idea in the sensible form, as in the *Symposium*, and thus painting causes love in the soul, in the same desire for the indifference of the real and ideal. In the *Enneads* (II.9.16), "those seeing by the bodily sense the productions of the art of painting do not see the one thing in the one only way; they are deeply stirred by recognizing in the objects depicted to the eyes the presentation of what lies in the idea, and so are called to recollection of the truth—the very experience out of which Love arises."

In *De amore*, Ficino described the mind as it is awakened from the dark night of chaos by love, illuminated by the light of the absolute, and turned toward the eternal, as for the initiate in the *Symposium*: "Turning toward

God, it is illuminated by his rays, and through the splendor of the rays is lit, and lit, everything is turned toward God. In turning toward God it assumes form; God can, in mind which turns toward him, sculpt the nature of all things which he creates. In this way all things are painted spiritually which are in this world."[37] In turning toward the absolute, the particular is differentiated from the universal, and strives to return to it. The ideas, the archetypal forms, are formulated in the mind by the light of the absolute, and from them sensible forms are differentiated in the real.

As for Ficino, in the *Bruno* intuition is the passive receptor of the archetypes of absolute form as it is illuminated by the light of the absolute. "Now intuition is by its very nature passive with respect to every form or shape, and receptive of them all; from all eternity, infinite thought impregnates it with all the forms and varieties of things, yet it is infinitely adapted to infinite thought, linked to it in an absolute identity that extinguishes all multiplicity" (*Bruno* 260–261). The archetypal forms in-formed into the Intellectual Principle by the absolute (mixing the terms of Schelling and Plotinus), are differentiated in the multiplicity of the real through the Reason Principle, but retain the infinity of the absolute. Intellectual Principle and Reason Principle, intuition and reason, are set opposite to each other in the process of differentiation. The differentiated forms, the particulars in the multiple, cannot exist in intuition. "Hence it is only in the perspective of the particular thing itself that intuition separates itself from thought and becomes opposed to it..." (261). This does not happen in the absolute, nor does it happen in matter or the organism in nature, where the real and the ideal, reason and intuition, remain undifferentiated. The idea of the form is intuited in the particular form in symbolic reason; the idea could not exist without the particular; "only in the finite thing is intuition adequately conformed to thought." The indifference of reason and intuition is in the idea, which unifies the archetypal form and the sensible form. It is intuition which unfolds the archetypal form in time, as in the *explicato* of Cusanus, and in time the archetype appears as substance, sensible form.

Reason is not intrinsically temporal, but becomes temporal in its separation and reunification from intuition. The *circuitus spiritualis* of difference and indifference in the soul introduces time to the archetype of the absolute. The indifference of the absolute is the paternal principle, according to Plato in the *Timaeus*. The reception of difference is the maternal principle, and the combination of the two, of being and activity, is the organism, as in procreation. In the *Timaeus* (50): "for the moment we must make a threefold distinction and think of that which becomes, that in which it becomes, and the model which it resembles. We may indeed use the metaphor of birth and compare the receptacle to the mother, the model to the father, and what they produce between them to their offspring..." That which becomes is sensible form, that in which it becomes is the Intellectual Principle, and the model which it resembles is the archetypal idea. Continuing in the *Timaeus*, "and we may notice that, if an imprint is to present a very complex appearance, the material on which it is to be stamped will not have been properly prepared unless it is devoid of all the characters which it is to receive."

Intuition, the Intellectual Principle, must be devoid of all particulars; it must be a *chôra*, a receptacle, the place (which is not a place) in which the finite is created from the infinite. The *chôra* of Plato is the *apeiron* of Anaximander. In the *apeiron*, "all things are generated and into this all are destroyed. For this reason too infinite world orders are generated and in turn are destroyed into that from which they are generated,"[38] in the words of Aëtius, differentiated and undifferentiated in the *circuitus spiritualis*. *Chôra*, as intuition, is both active and passive; it entails both an "unchanging form, uncreated and indestructible, admitting no modification and entering no combination" (*Timaeus* 52), the archetypal form, and form which has "come into existence, is in constant motion, comes into existence and vanishes from a particular place," sensible form, the universal manifest as particular in intuition. *Chôra* is the place (which is not a place) where the eternal, unchanging Idea of the divine intellect becomes material form.

The sensible form, the generated entity, "partakes equally in the nature of both principles," as described by Schelling (*Bruno* 261), and achieves the indifference of the real and ideal within itself, "perfectly imitating the absolute reality whence it took its origin," but that indifference is only revealed in its ideality, as idea. The sensible form embodies both the difference and indifference of the real and ideal that the idea of the form in the intellect does; the opposition between real and ideal is visible in the form, and determines its individuality as a particular. The particular form is finite relatively, as its finiteness is dependent on the infinite, as the infinite is dependent on its finiteness. The interdependence of the finite and infinite corresponds to the laws of cause and effect in necessity as it participates in the ideal. The visibility of the finite in the particular is given in appearance, in the participation of the particular in the temporal, as finite, and as the reflected light of the absolute in the soul. The more stable, enduring, and self-dependent a sensible form is, the more it participates in the infinite, as for example the stars and heavenly bodies, the ideas of which are closest to the absolute.

For the Neoplatonists, the circle is the most perfect form in nature, the most enduring and self-dependent, and the closest to the absolute. In the *Enneads*, heaven, "in the likeness of Intelligence, revolves in a circular movement, wisely ordered, always around the same center without seeking anything beyond" (III.2.3). Circular movement is "in imitation of the Intellectual-Principle" (II.2.1), reflecting the self-sufficiency of being, and deviation from circular motion reflects deviation from the Intellectual Principle, as "the heavens, by their nature, will either be motionless or move in a circle; all other movement indicates outside compulsion" (II.1.8). Plato equates circular motion with the good, or the absolute, in the *Phaedrus*, as "In the revolution [the circular motion of the Same] she [divine intelligence] beholds justice, and temperance, and knowledge absolute, not in the form of generation or of relation, which men call existence, but knowledge absolute in existence absolute" (247).

For Schelling, the heavenly bodies are the "primary unities of every type of being" (*Bruno* 262), from which all particular sensible forms are differentiated. Schelling sees the universe as an emanation from the absolute to sensible form, as a differentiation from the universal to the particular, in the same way that Plotinus describes the universe as an emanation from the One to the multiple through the hypostases of being. The multiplicity of finite forms is as infinite as the identity of the absolute, but as, in the geometrical model of Cusanus, the polygonal figures inscribed in the circle, the infinite multiplicity of the particular (the sides of the polygons multiplied as inscribed in the circle) can never equal the infinite identity of the universal (the circle). The particular forms manifest in reason can never equal the archetypal forms in the *intellectus divinus*, in intuition. The heavenly bodies of Schelling, being the closest to the archetypal forms of the absolute, are the most perfect in geometry, and are "indestructible and immortal," and "display the whole universe" within themselves, as if the particular forms are folded into the archetypal form, as the polygons into the circle, in *complicato*, and then unfolded into particular forms in multiplicity, in *explicato*. The heavenly bodies are thus "blessed animals" and "undying gods."

Among the heavenly bodies, the sun is the closest to the absolute. Like the absolute, like the One of Plotinus, it participates in everything in the universe, and nothing participates in it. It is the indifference of everything in the universe, and the essence of all things emanates from it. The earth, and the other planets, are in opposition to the sun in that they retain an element of particularity while the sun is participant in them. The alteration of day and night is the result of the opposition between the earth and the sun, between the particular and the universal, dark and light, dark being the black night, the ground of being, and light being the absolute. Light is the "torch and indicator of time" (277); it covers the universe without filling the universe, thus exists in time and not in space. The alteration of day and night is the dialectic of the essence of the absolute in its participation with the particular, the *coincidentia oppositorum*, to use the phrase of Cusanus in *De Docta Ignorantia*, in creation. In the *Timaeus* (47), the alteration of day and night creates the necessity for arithmetic, which in turn leads to philosophy, in the dialectic, as "...the sight of day and night, and the months and the revolutions of the years, have created number, and have given us a conception of time, and the power of enquiring about the nature of the universe; and from this source we have derived philosophy..."

In the *Republic*, the sun is the presence of the good in the sensible universe. The sun is "the author of visibility in all visible things...of generation and nourishment" (509), while the good is "the author of knowledge to all things known...of their being and essence..." In *The Divine Names*, Pseudo-Dionysius described the sun as "the apparent image of the divine goodness, a distant echo of the Good. It illuminates whatever is capable of receiving its light and yet it never loses the utter fullness of its light" (IV.4).[39] The opposition of the earth and sun is the cause of time, as "Light too is the enumerator of the hours, of the days, and indeed of all the time we have." The sun is the indifference of the universe in that "It draws and returns all things to itself, all the things that see, that have motion, that are receptive of illumination and warmth, that are held together by the spreading rays." The light of the sun is as the absolute which participates in all things.

For Schelling in the *Bruno*, the sun "seeks to unite its own concept to the particular elements of each sphere" (277). The alteration of day and night was created in the resistance of each sphere to the concept of the sun (the good), as the dialectic was created in the resistance of reason to intuition, existence to being. The universe is thus "intertwined with itself" (278), as is the intellect in consciousness, and "forever strives to be more like itself and to become one body and one soul." The bodies of the universe, like the intellect, are caught in a self-perpetuating cycle of desire, created by opposition and seeking reconciliation. All of the drama is played out against the dark night of chaos, illuminated by the light of the absolute. In the *Timaeus* (92), the universe is "a visible living creature, it contains all creatures that are visible and is itself an image of the intelligible"; the universe is a macrocosm of both the mind and the organism.

In the *Bruno*, light is "the eternal idea of all corporeal things" (278). Light is the indifference of the infinite and the finite, as an archetype of the absolute, and the idea in the Intellectual Principle, or intuition, "that cognition in which there is no opposition between thought and being." As a concept becomes particular in the intellect, it differentiates itself from the idea, as a body differentiates itself from light, and the temporal differentiates itself from the infinite. The dialectical opposition of being is caused by a primordial split, an organic dehiscence in the organism of being. As described by Jacques Lacan in *Écrits*, "To the *Urbild* of this [psychic] formation, alienating as it is by virtue of its capacity to render extraneous, corresponds a peculiar satisfaction deriving from the integration of an original organic disarray, a satisfaction that must be conceived in the dimension of a vital dehiscence that is constitutive of man, and which makes unthinkable the idea of an environment that is preformed for him, a 'negative' libido that enables the Heraclitean notion of Discord, which the Ephesian believed to be prior to harmony, to shine once more" (p. 21).[40]

In the *Bruno*, that which is completely differentiated from the light, the idea, falls into "the ground of existence—primordial night, the mother of all things" (278). The light of the sun is not itself the light of the idea, but the manifestation of the light of the idea in the sensible world, a difference in which indifference is participant. In the sensible world, the degree of indifference in relation to the absolute corresponds to the degree of opacity and transparency of an object. The more indifferentiated the object with light, the more the absolute is participant in it, the more transparent it is. The dialectic of the opposition between opacity and transparency in sensible form was a subject of the paintings of Paul Cézanne and the Cubists at the beginning of the twentieth century, and functioned as a metaphor of the dialectic between the concept and the idea, between reason and intuition, in the mind.

Colin Rowe and Robert Slutzky, in the essay "Transparency: Literal and Phenomenal" of 1955–56, observed in late-Cézanne and Cubist compositions "an opposition between certain areas of luminous paint and others of a more dense coloration… all of these planes, translucent or otherwise, and regardless of their representational content, are to be found implicated in the manifestation which Kepes has defined as transparency."[41] That manifestation, as defined by Gyorgy Kepes in *Language of Vision* in 1944, "implies more than an optical characteristic, it implies a broader spatial order."[42] "Transparency means a simultaneous perception of different spatial locations. Space not only recedes but fluctuates in a continuous activity. The position of the transparent figures has equivocal meaning as one sees each figure now as the closer, now as the further one." This transparency was labeled "phenomenal transparency" by Rowe and Slutzky, as existing in the intellect, in the construction of the field of vision. The construction of the sensible world in the mind is an infinitely variable space which "fluctuates in a continuous activity." Like the sensible forms themselves, the spatial relations between the objects are the subject of the mind of the perceiver. Phenomenal transparency is a conceptual transparency, in the dialectic of opacity and transparency in the intellect, between reason and idea, obscurity and clarity, the same dialectic that is carried out in the sensible world.

In *The Necessity of the Mind*, Roger Caillois saw the continuous fluctuation of phenomenal transparency in the intellect as being a form of indifference, in which there is "no appreciable difference between the known and unknown" (p. 87), between the light of the absolute and the primordial night of chaos. For Caillois, the necessity of the mind thus coincides with the necessity of the universe, and is absorbed into it. The opposites of subjective and objective, interior and exterior are dissolved in *informe*, which is both absolute form and formlessness, the indifference of the infinite and finite. Perception is also the continuous fluctuation of the intellect in relation to the sensible world, of the construction of the sensible world in the intellect to the sensible world itself. The mechanisms of intellect in the relation between concept and idea, such as opacity and transparency, are the qualities of sensible objects as the dialectic of the infinite and finite is played out in the sensible world. In the article "Mimicry and Legendary Psychasthenia," Caillois defines perception as a "double dihedral changing at every moment in size and position" (p. 28). The intersecting planes of the dihedral are the intersection of the intellect of the perceiving subject and the perceived objects in a constructed space filled with the light of the absolute.

For Schelling, the greater the extent to which the transparency of light is embodied in an object in space, the closer the object is to the indifference of the particular and the universal, the more the universal is manifest in the soul of the object. Complete corporeality is complete opacity, and complete spirit is complete transparency. The presence of transparency in the object is the presence of the idea, and through the transparency of light which participates in it as the absolute, each particular object contains infinite possibilities, as a monad. The infinity of possibilities contains within it the infinite variability of particulars, of which the object is one manifestation, as one polygon in the infinite variety of polygons which transform themselves in *complicato* toward the infinite circle of the absolute of Cusanus. The infinite variety of possibilities are related to each other in time and space, thus in motion and sequence, or activity, and the activity causes differentiation and variation. Because organic objects, organisms, are subject to differentiation and variance, though they contain the absolute within them, they are subject to finitude in time and space, and thus to diminishing and disappearance, or decay and death, retreat into the dark night, the eternal ground of being and the negation of existence. Because of this, organisms in their particularity "in no way approach the excellence of the things in the heavens" (*Bruno* 279).

Individual organisms are magnetically drawn to each other because they are able to intuit the presence of the universal which exists within them in other forms. The magnetism of the organism resides in its differentiation from the universal, but as the universal participates in the organism, the magnetism manifests itself as sonority. The physical attraction of the bodies of organisms is a correlate of Platonic love in the intellectual. In Platonic love, as defined by Marsilio Ficino, intellect is drawn to other intellects because it intuits the same participation of the absolute. Bodies are drawn to other bodies because of the unconscious presence of the universal in the mind of the organism. As the magnetism of the organism resides in its differentiation from the universal, bodies are also drawn to other bodies because they are imperfect, and desire perfection, and perfection is sought after in the mutual participation of the absolute in the organism, in the mutual participation of the organism in the absolute. In the *Bruno*, "But since organic entities are individual and are necessarily imperfect, because the real and ideal, or soul and body, are opposed in them, so all their actions are indeed ordered toward the identity of all things, not by their own power, but by the divine power that guides them" (280).

Jacques Lacan defines love as the mutual re-affirmation of the flaws of two individuals. When the lover says "You complete me," the lover acts to satisfy the desire caused by the dialectical opposition between universal and particular in the soul, and the differentiation of the particular from the universal. The lover in its internal dehiscence seeks to be dissolved into the universal, to turn itself away from the direction of the dark night of being, of death. But of course it is only because of the necessity of death that the lover seeks the universal. We love because we die, and we die because we love.

We also create, and express ourselves in art, because we die. The cause of philosophy is the internal dehiscence of being, as Hegel expresses in *The Difference Between Fichte's and Schelling's System of Philosophy*, "Self-estrangement is the source of the need for philosophy..." (p. 89). Philosophy serves the same need as artistic creativity, to satisfy the desire for the indifference of the absolute.

In the *Bruno* (280), organic entities are "endowed with one spark of the living artistry that fashions all things" (the *scintilla della divinità* of the Renaissance). In *L'Idea de' Pittori, Scultori e Architetti*, Federico Zuccari, the director of the Accademia di San Luca in Rome in the sixteenth century, described the *scintilla della divinità* as the spark created when the virtue of the intellect strikes the conceptual in reason in the human mind, the Intellectual Principle enters into the Reason Principle, and like two stones rubbing together, produce sparks, which light the tinder of the imagination, putting into motion phantasms and figments of the ideal.[43] The light from the spark is the *disegno interno*, which is a sign of God in the mind, a *segno di dio in noi*. The *disegno interno* as the image or idea of a form in the mind corresponds to *disegno esterno*, the form in the sensible world, in drawing.

The *scintilla della divinità* instructs the mind and organism to achieve "the indifference of thought and being they do not intrinsically contain" (*Bruno* 280); it leads the mind in the desire to reconcile the dehiscence of the particular and universal in the indifference of the absolute, and this desire is the basis of artistic expression, as well as of love. The *scintilla della divinità* implants in the minds of organic beings "the heavenly music which subsists in the universe as a whole, and in light and in the heavenly spheres, and it teaches those that are accustomed to dwell in the air to forget themselves in song and so revert to the identity of all things." The pursuit of pleasure is also driven by the desire for the indifference of the universal in the absolute, as in the pleasure principle of Sigmund Freud. The pleasure is the *ecstasis* and *katharsis* of the mystic, the whirling dervish in the Middle Ages, the guest at the table of the gods drunk with the nectar of eternity as described by Giovanni Pico della Mirandola in the Renaissance.

System of Transcendental Idealism

The *scintilla della divinità* operates in the Intellectual Principle, in that which corresponds to the unconscious. It is an internal light in the soul which gives access to the universal from the particular, the unconscious from the conscious, the infinite from the finite, the Intellectual Principle from the Reason Principle. The inner light of the divine is self-dependent, and its possibility exists in all particulars of matter. In the *Enneads*, "In the intellectual, the vision sees not through some medium but by and through itself alone, for its object is not external: by one light it sees another not through any intermediate agency; a light sees a light, that is to say a thing sees itself" (V.3.8). The *scintilla della divinità* allows the artist to express the indifference of the finite and the infinite, of the conscious and unconscious, in art, that is, the presence of the absolute. In the *System of Transcendental Idealism* of Schelling, "the work of art reflects to us the identity of the conscious and unconscious activities" (p. 225). But as the work of art seeks the indifference of conscious and unconscious activity, the particular and the universal, the opposition between the two is infinite, as in the opposition between the circle and the polygonal figures of Cusanus in *De circuli quadratura*, the insurmountable gap between matter and spirit. The self-alienation of spirit from matter is ultimately irreconcilable, as the divine is ineffable and can only be experienced in *docta ignorantia* and the *via negativa*; nevertheless the purpose of art and philosophy is to pursue that indifference.

In Schelling, the work of art seeks to have the character of an unconscious infinity in the indifference of the universal and particular, freedom and necessity. The work of art contains that which is other than the product of reason, intention or expectation, that which cannot be explained by reason, by finite understanding. Like mythology, art as a whole is composed of particular works, particular figures, which cannot be explained entirely in relation to the whole, and which contain infinite possibilities within each particular, as they relate to the whole. Like mythology, art functions in symbolic, schematic and allegorical means, but the underlying reason behind the forms is not entirely apparent. As with mythology, it is impossible to explain the genesis and function of art in relation to the group of people that produces it; the art is a record of the philosophical striving toward the indifference of freedom and necessity in a culture, as were the *Theogony* of Hesiod and the *Iliad* of Homer.

Each individual work of art, as each individual figure in mythology, is a particular which cannot be explained in relation to the universal, all art and all mythology, and yet cannot exist outside its relation to the universal. The opposition and indifference of universal and particular are simultaneously both finite and infinite. The infinite is represented in art through instinct or intuition. It is not the product of a conscious act, but rather the indifference of necessity and freedom, the necessity of the artistic act becoming freedom, and the freedom of the artistic act becoming necessity. The work of art displays the infinite in the intellect of the artist, and the limitations of his or her reason; reason in and of itself, as necessity, is maximized, and gives way to intuition. The mechanisms of perception on the part of the artist constitute a universal language in a culture, so the indifference of the infinite and finite is communicated through the work of art as it is perceived by the intellect of the observer which sees its own interior dialectic reflected in the work.

If the art is merely imitative of natural form, it is limited to the conscious activity of the artist, and the mechanisms of his or her reason. The perceiving subject can only be reflected in such a work as itself an imitation of nature, not containing within the principles of nature as a function of being, but rather as a reflection or a shadow. In such a work, "purpose and rule lie on the surface, and seem so restricted and circumscribed, that the product is no more than a faithful replica of the artist's conscious activity, and is in every respect an object for reflection only, not for intuition, which loves to sink itself in what it contemplates, and finds no resting place short of the infinite" (*System of Transcendental Idealism*, p. 225), short of initiation into immortal excellences, in community with the loftiest order.

The infinite tranquility which is achieved by the viewer of the artwork corresponds to the infinite contradiction in the soul of the artist; the work of art is a picture of the dialectical resolution of that contradiction, or of a fragmentation or dehiscence of that indifference. The work of art may also be a picture of the primordial self-alienation itself; in either case, the work of art is always an autobiography of the soul of the artist. The work of art communicates the trauma of internal fracturing, and the ecstasy of internal resolution. The absolute unity of the absolute is equivalent to the chaos and formlessness of the dark night of being in the soul, the turmoil of loss. The turmoil in the soul is as the turmoil of the orbits of the immortal soul, inserted into the body of the universe by the children of the Demiurge in the *Timaeus* (43): "And into this body, subject to the flow of growth and decay, they fastened the orbits of the immortal soul. Plunged into this strong stream, the orbits were unable to control it, nor were they controlled by it, and because of the consequent violent conflict the motions of the whole creature were irregular, fortuitous and irrational."

The work of art for Schelling is the finite representation of the infinite, the presence of the infinite in the finite, and the infinite division of the finite and infinite. The division between the finite and infinite occurs in freedom, in the infinite itself. The finite representation of the infinite is beauty; the intuited presence of the infinite within the finite is the sublime. Beauty is the indifference of the infinite and finite, universal and particular. The beauty of the forms in the work of art is not in the forms themselves, but in the ideas of the forms that the visual images represent; the forms in a painting are beautiful only in that the beauty of the infinite is present. The form is beautiful because the idea which it represents contains the indifference of the finite and infinite as a manifestation of the absolute. In the sublime this indifference is not present, but it is suggested and can be intuited; the beautiful and sublime are thus in opposition in the infinite division of the finite and infinite. Both beauty and the sublime depend on contradiction, the primordial fissure of being. The infinity which is suggested by the sublime is that of the unconscious; beauty contains the indifference of the conscious and unconscious. The intuition of the infinite in the unconscious as differentiation from the conscious and finite is threatening to the finitude of reason, because it suggests that which is alien and inaccessible to it without being reconciled with it. The sublime is the representation of the laceration of the soul in being, in Bataille's terms, unresolved as in the indifference of beauty.

The sublime contains the turmoil of being in the soul, the *horror vacui* of self-alienation in the dark night of being, that which exceeds reason. In the words of Georges Bataille in "The Notion of Expenditure," "Human life cannot in any way be limited to the closed systems assigned to it by reasonable conceptions. The immense travail of recklessness, discharge, and upheaval that constitutes life could be expressed by stating that life starts only with the deficit of these systems" (*Visions of Excess*, p. 128). As described by Edmund Burke in *A Philosophical Enquiry into the Origin of Our Ideas of the Sublime and Beautiful* in 1757, the sublime represents the terror of the apprehension of the absolute in the unconscious: "In thoughts from the visions of the night, when deep sleep falls upon men, fear came upon me and trembling, which made all my bones to shake. Then a spirit passed before my face. The hair of my flesh stood up."[44] The terror of the sublime in the formlessness and irrationality of the black night of the ground of being is described by John Milton as well in Book II of *Paradise Lost*: "The other shape,/If shape it might be called that shape had none/distinguishable, in member, joint, or limb;/Or substance might be called that shadow seemed,/for each seemed either; black he stood as night…"[45] The sublimity of the immortal souls of chaos was invoked by Virgil in the *Aeneid*: "Ye subterraneous gods! Whose aweful sway/The gliding ghosts, and silent shades obey;/O chaos hoar! And Phlegethon profound!/Whose solemn empire stretches wide around;/Give me, ye great tremendous powers, to tell/Of scenes and wonders in the depths of hell;/Give me your mighty secrets to display/From those black realms of darkness to the day…"[46]

In the *System of Transcendental Idealism*, the representation of the sublime in art "sets all the forces of the mind in motion, in order to resolve a contradiction which threatens our whole intellectual existence" (p. 226), the alienation of the conscious and unconscious, "whereupon the self is thrown into a conflict with itself which can end only in an aesthetic intuition…" In its representation of the sublime, the work of art displays the opposition between the infinite and finite which is resolved in the organic form in nature; the opposition between the infinite and finite depends on the intuition of the human soul alone, in its self-consciousness of its separation from the infinite. The organic form in nature is not the product of the infinite contradiction of the finite and infinite, or the product of consciousness. The organic form is beautiful in the indifference of the finite and infinite, and not sublime. The principle of beauty in nature is the same as the principle of beauty in art, but the imitation of beauty in nature is not beauty in art, because it is not derived from the same underlying principle of the indifference of the finite and infinite.

The work of art is a work of art only if it exhibits freedom, in combination with necessity. The organic form in nature does not exhibit freedom, though it contains the possibility of freedom; forms in nature are necessarily bound by the laws of cause and effect. Freedom is found only in the ideal, in relation to the real, or only in the subjective, in relation to the objective. Forms in nature have purpose only in relation to other forms, in the Principle of Sufficient Reason (*Satz vom Grund*) of Leibniz, for example, and have no consciousness of the presence of the absolute within themselves. This only occurs in the intellect in the human soul, in the Intellectual Principle, or in the unconscious; art is the expression of the Intellectual Principle and the unconscious, of human identity and consciousness. The human soul has a purpose both in relation to other souls and in and of itself; the function of the human soul is the indifference of the universal and particular.

The negotiation between reason and intuition in the function of the soul is the expression of the work of art. The contemplation of the work of art entails the contemplation of the inner self as well as the sensible world, and of the interaction of the two. The contemplation of the inner self leads to the contemplation of the absolute, as in the *Enneads* (VI.9.9), where Plotinus advises to "withdraw into yourself and look. And if you do not find yourself beautiful yet, act as does the creator of a statue that is to be made beautiful," so that the "godlike splendor of virtue" may shine from the soul as it shines from the statue, the light of the good which nourishes the Intellectual Principle and the soul be made visible to the self. The work of art is a medium for the contemplation of the inner self in the attempt to reconcile the turbulence and self-alienation of the soul in the interaction of the ideal and the real.

Philosophy, according to Schelling, like art, must take into account, and in fact has as its basis, the relation between conscious and unconscious thought, between reason and intuition, the objective and subjective, the Reason Principle and Intellectual Principle of Plotinus. The principal question of philosophy is the relation between the ideal and real, between intellectual activity and objective experience. Art is the "universally acknowledged and altogether incontestable objectivity of intellectual intuition" (*System of Transcendental Idealism*, p. 229), the field in which the relation between the ideal and real is played out. Aesthetic intuition is the objectification of intellectual intuition. The work of art reflects to the perceiver the relation between the real and ideal in his or her intellect; art is the self-reflection of philosophy, the contemplation of the real and ideal. Every principle of philosophy, based on the contradiction of the real and ideal, exists in aesthetic production. The goal of philosophy, the resolution or indifference of the real and ideal, is only partially achieved in art, and more fully achieved in philosophy (and poetry), because art exists in the realm of the real, while philosophy exists in both the real, as language, and the ideal, as thought. Art originates from the real (as does the sensible world) and enters into the ideal; the universal enters into the particular through symbolism. Philosophy originates from the ideal and enters into the real through the schematics of language, as the particular enters into the universal.

While the forms of art emerge from the real, the activity of the artist, aesthetic production, emerges from the ideal, from freedom, and therein the real and ideal are unified. The ideal contains the opposition of the conscious and unconscious, while the real only contains the unconscious latently. The work of art, thus, reveals the latent unconscious in the real, through the interaction of the real and ideal on the part of the artist. The work of art animates the sensible forms of the universe and infuses them with the presence of the absolute. The work of art brings the forms of matter and nature to life as they are self-reflected in the mind of the viewer. Philosophy, too, illuminates the sensible world with the animate soul of the perceiving subject, and art serves as its document in the objectification of the intellectual in the aesthetic. Philosophy, unlike art, is not capable of describing unconscious intuition in the realm of the real, nor the indifference of the conscious and unconscious.

Art visualizes this goal of philosophy, the understanding of the real in the terms of the ideal, and the unity of the two which is not possible in nature, or in the conscious life of reason. Art is thus "paramount to the philosopher, precisely because it opens to him, as it were, the holy of holies, where burns in eternal and original unity, as if in a single flame, that which in nature and history is rent asunder, and in life and action, no less than in thought, must forever fly apart" (p. 231). Art reveals the absolute in the real, the indifference of the real and ideal which is not possible in reason alone nor in human activity. The painting removes the "invisible barrier dividing the real from the ideal world" (p. 232), and is a gateway into the ideal. Nature to the artist, as to the philosopher, is the "imperfect reflection of a world existing, not outside him, but within"; art is the gateway to the soul, and to the identity of the real and ideal within.

Art as a gateway to the soul is a "veil of interpretation," in the words of Paul Cézanne, as he wrote in a letter to Emile Bernard in 1906, "to read nature is to see her, underneath the veil of interpretation, as colored *taches* following one another according to a law of harmony. The large colored areas can thus be analyzed into modulations. Painting is recording colored sensations."[47] For Cézanne, color was the medium by which the painting opened a gateway to the soul, in achieving the indifference of the real and ideal; color is the indifference of light and matter, as described by Schelling, thus the manifestation of the absolute in painting. The veil of interpretation of Cézanne is as the "luminous embroidered veil hanging between the finite and the infinite," what Plato defined as sensible form, as a symbol of the intelligible, the finite expression of the infinite, in the *Timaeus* (38).

In the *Republic*, a curtain-wall is built along the road which runs next to the chamber or cave in which the prisoners see the shadows on the wall cast by a burning fire on the other side of the curtain. The curtain is the luminous embroidered veil, and it is "like the screen at puppet shows between the operators and their audience, above which they show their puppets" (514). From the puppet show, the prisoners in the cave believe that the shadows of objects are the extent of the real. If the prisoner were to see the object in itself, looking into the fire behind the screen, he would be blinded by the fire; he would be "too dazzled to see properly the objects of which he used to see the shadows" (515). Thus the prisoner "would need to grow accustomed to the light before he could see things in the upper world outside the cave. First he would find it easiest to look at shadows, next at the reflections of men and other objects in water, and later on at the objects themselves" (516).

The veil of interpretation is necessary, so that the initiate, as in the *Symposium*, would be able to learn to see absolute beauty, and not be blinded by it. To look directly at the fire is to look directly at the sun, with no intermediary veil, as to look at the sensible world is to see absolute beauty, through the intelligible. The prisoner who learns to look into the flame is the initiate into the love of the absolute in the *Symposium*. In the *Republic*, "The realm revealed by sight corresponds to the prison, and the light of the fire in the prison to the power of the sun. And you won't go wrong if you connect the ascent into the upper world and the sight of the objects there with the upward progress of the mind into the intelligible region" (517), the Intellectual Principle, through which the absolute is understood. The prisoner, when seeing the light, as he has been initiated by the veil of interpretation, understands that the light is the source of the good, which is "inferred to be responsible for whatever is right and valuable in anything, producing in the visible region light and the source of light, and being in the intelligible region itself controlling source of truth and intelligence."

Painting plays the role of the veil of interpretation, the luminous embroidered veil, the screen at the puppet show. It allows the perceiver to be able to see the absolute, as represented in the real, through the veil of the real, and finite, so that the perceiver is not overcome by the brilliance of the light of the absolute, the indifference of the real and ideal. The veil, constructed of color, as in the paintings of Cézanne, creates the beauty of the painted image in that indifference. In the representation of the sublime, there is no veil of color or beauty, nothing to shield the initiate from the overwhelming grandeur and at the same time horror of the absolute, the coincidence of absolute form and absolute formlessness. The veil of interpretation is the ground of the indifference between the real and ideal, between the subjective and objective, the ground in which the beauty of the indifference appears, and the ground of intellectual intuition, the objectification of philosophy in aesthetic intuition. Thus, in the *System of Transcendental Idealism*, it is "precisely this ground which, by means of the work of art, has been brought forth entirely from the subjective, and rendered wholly objective, in such wise, that we have gradually led our object, the self itself, up to the very point where we ourselves were standing when we began to philosophize" (p. 232).

In painting, Cézanne sought himself in nature, through painting; he sought "nature seen and nature felt, the nature which is out there...and the nature which is in here...(he taps himself on the forehead) both of which must unite in order to endure, to live a life half human, half divine, the life of art, listen a little...the life of God,"[48] as he expressed to Joachim Gasquet. In painting, Cézanne sought the absolute in the indifference of the real and ideal, the objectification of philosophy in aesthetics. He said to Gasquet, "The landscape is reflected, becomes human, and becomes conscious in me. I objectify it, project it, fix it on my canvas. The other day, you spoke to me of Kant. I probably can't say this clearly, but it seems to me that I'll be the subjective conscience of this landscape, just as my painting will be the objective conscience."[49]

Through painting, through the veil of interpretation of color, Cézanne seeks the indifference of the subjective and objective; he seeks to fuse himself as the perceiving subject with the object of his perception, so that the seer becomes the seen, the knower becomes the known; as in the *Enneads* (V.8.11), the perceiving subject "must give himself forthwith to the inner and, radiant with the Divine Intellections (with which he is now one), be no longer the seer, but, as that place has made him, the seen." In the intelligible, the indifference of the real and ideal is the same as that in the beauty of the image. Perception and the act of perception are undifferentiated in the absolute; when the absolute is intuited in the intellect, as the result of intellectual discipline, the initiate is able to recognize the absolute within and without. "When you perceive that you have grown to this, you are now become very vision" (*Enneads* I.6.9).

In the *System of Transcendental Idealism*, as painting is the objectification of philosophy, its manifestation in the sensible world, as each artwork participates in art as a universality, as a particular instance of the universal essence of the absolute in the real, so it participates in philosophy as a universality, as a particular instance of the essence of the absolute in the ideal. The objective form flows back into the subjective, "like so many individual streams into the universal ocean," of philosophy and poetry, "from which they took their source" (p. 232). As manifestation of the absolute, the artwork participates in the universal Spirit, the *Zeitgeist* of which each artist is a vehicle for expression. The *Zeitgeist*, like history, is the indifference of the real and the ideal in the universal soul. While intellectual intuition is a property of the Intellectual Principle and not of reason in consciousness, aesthetic intuition, as the objectification of intellectual intuition, is a property of conscious thought, a particular manifestation of a universal, as symbolism in art is a particular manifestation of a universal. Art is philosophy made objective. Art signifies the intellectual intuition which is the subject of philosophy, and is thus a catalyst for philosophical development.

Philosophical development entails the development of intellectual intuition, and thus of self-knowledge and self-consciousness. This is Schelling's definition of transcendental philosophy, and the definition can be applied to the philosophy of Plotinus. The highest form of intellectual intuition in the real is the aesthetic. According to Schelling in the *System of Transcendental Idealism* (p. 234), the first act of self-consciousness in philosophy is the understanding of the division between the ideal and the real in the self, between the universal and particular, subjective and objective, following Fichte in the *Wissenschaftslehre*, in the distinction between self and not-self in thought. Then the indifference of the ideal and real in the self is intuited in the intellectual, the absolute as intelligible, as in the idea of the Intellectual Principle of Plotinus.

At the same time, the subject becomes aware of the determinacy, or manifestation in the particular, of its subjectivity in the objective, in activity and sensation. In this, the work of art plays a role in the development of the self-consciousness of the subject. In the determinacy of the subject the subject becomes aware of itself as an object, determined by a bodily form, as in the *armor fou* of the divided subject of Lacan, and determined by the signifying structure of logic, as in the chains of logic of Bataille. In its self-consciousness as object, the subject returns to the subjective, to the intuition of the indifference of the real and ideal, through the differentiation of the two, anticipating the return of thought from being-for-self to being-in-and-for-itself in the *Phenomenology of Spirit* of Hegel. Through art, the self returns to its subjectivity in its self-consciousness, in the enactment of the differentiation.

Through the development of self-consciousness, the differentiation of the real and ideal becomes embedded in the intuition of the indifference of the two, as in the dialectic the thesis and antithesis are embedded in the synthesis. Reason is embedded in intuition, and conscious activity is embedded in the unconscious. According to Freud, dream images are symbols of signifiers and syntactical structures in language in conscious reasoning. The structure of the unconscious reflects the structure of conscious thought, as Freud described dreams as "nothing other than a particular form of thinking"[50] in *The Interpretation of Dreams* in 1900. In Schelling's terms, conscious thoughts are nothing other than particular forms of dreams. Dreams were described by Freud in *On Dreams* as "disconnected fragments of visual images,"[51] visual images being the product of reason in the construction of perception. Imagination in dreams corresponds to imagination in the intellect, but imagination in dreams is manifest pictorially rather than through language. Dreams are a transference of linguistic structures in conscious reasoning to the unconscious. The structures of conscious reason exist in the dream, but they are disguised in the pictorial imagery, as the Reason Principles of nature are disguised in organic form. Dreams can thus be interpreted by deciphering the relation between dream images and dream-thoughts, which correspond to the structures of conscious reason.

Intellectual intuition thus involves the participation of the self in self-consciousness, and the participation of reason as an objective activity constructed of particulars (Reason Principle in Intellectual Principle). In the *System of Transcendental Idealism*, the participation of reason is given by the identification of logic as a set of particulars in relation to the universal, the indifference of which is the absolute. Within intuition there exists a subjective ideal which corresponds to the objective real, as the idea corresponds to the form. The idea is not possible without the form, but exists independently of it, and the form in the real is only a manifestation of the idea. The idea in the intelligible, though it corresponds to the form in reason, does not operate in relation to other ideas according to the logic of reason, which is why dreams appear to be irrational. The logic of reason is a construct of conscious perception, and the idea in intuition can only be perceived by reason as such. Thus the dialectical development of philosophy is necessary for the understanding of the differentiation. The set of relationships between the real and the ideal and between reason and intuition constitutes self-consciousness in philosophical development, and the intelligence of the subject. The natural organism is unable to achieve such self-consciousness; it is the product of the primordial self-alienation of human consciousness.

The intelligence of the perceiving subject is a universal, but is manifest in reason only as a particular. In self-consciousness reason sees itself as an incompletion of the universal intellect of which it is a product and to which it contributes. In self-consciousness reason recognizes its limitations and thus seeks to go outside itself in order to complete itself, as in the desire for the absolute. Reason must go outside of itself as a particular in order to re-establish itself as a universal, and thus can only complete itself in relation to other particulars. The necessity of reason going outside itself in the universal is manifest in freedom, which contains the self-consciousness of reason as other than itself, which is not possible in organic forms. It is only through philosophical development that freedom is possible. Freedom precedes nature as *natura prior* (*System of Transcendental Idealism*, p. 235), and comes from the ideal, in the Intellectual Principle. The series of relations between reason and intuition in the intellect are not possible in nature.

Freedom is an act of will on the part of reason, beginning with the imposition of order on chaos, on the lawlessness of nature, in order to arrive at the lawlessness of indifference in the absolute. Schelling defines the will of the participation of the universal in the particular as the *potence*. The particular desire in the reason of the subject becomes the universal desire of the intellect, "objectified in the form of absolute will, i.e., as a categorical imperative," a basis of philosophical discourse. The state which allows for the objectification of desire as will is freedom, in participation with consciousness. The identification of freedom with will, as a product of desire, is self-consciousness. But freedom exists outside of consciousness, and consciousness creates itself within freedom, within the mechanisms of its own generation. Consciousness creates itself *ab initio* (*System of Transcendental Idealism*, p. 236), from the primordial dehiscence, and appears always as contingent, always as a particular. The highest goal of art and philosophy is the presentation of consciousness as contingent within the universal, in order to complete the intellect in self-consciousness; such a presentation is the product of genius.

The stages in the development of the relation between real and ideal in the intellect, between necessity and freedom, the subject of philosophy and the content of art, correspond to the development of the Spirit in history toward freedom, which becomes core to Hegel's discourse. Historical development entails the relation between the reason and self-consciousness of a culture, the relation between the functioning mechanisms of the culture in the real and the self-identity of the culture in the ideal. It involves the relation between organization and productivity, the particular and the universal, law and creativity. As art is a presentation of philosophical development in the self-consciousness of the individual subject, so art is a presentation of the historical development in the self-consciousness of a culture, as a catalyst toward freedom in the ideal, and indifference in the absolute. Like self-consciousness itself, art is a dialectic of the universal and particular, and functions to symbolize the indifference of the absolute.

As in reason in self-consciousness, art contains the possibility of the ideal, and the dialectic of the real and ideal serves as the productive principle in art, as it does the creative principle in intellect. In order to represent self-consciousness, art must reflect the relation between the real and ideal and the differentiation of them in self-consciousness. Self-consciousness is the basis of transcendental philosophy in that it resolves the contradiction inherent in the relation between the real and the ideal, namely that the real is only given by the ideal, and the ideal is a product of the real. The subject of transcendental philosophy, the Philosophy of Spirit, is the negotiation between the real and ideal, a seemingly self-contradictory state, which is taken to be the basis, and in fact the generating factor, of human consciousness. Philosophy and art entail the production and representation of filters between the real and ideal in their self-contradiction, in both the real and ideal. In philosophy the filters include the *archê* of Plato, the Intellectual Principle of Plotinus, and intuition and consciousness in the Philosophy of Spirit. In art they include the "luminous embroidered veil hanging between the finite and the infinite" of Plato, perspectival and geometrical constructions in their illustration of the relation between the absolute and multiple, chiaroscuro as the juxtaposition of light and dark representing the juxtaposition of ideal and real, and color as the indifference of light and matter, the ideal and real.

The writings of Schelling are filled with mechanisms for the negotiation of the real and ideal, that negotiation being the state of human consciousness in its inner dehiscence and differentiation of the two. Schelling seeks to overcome the *a priori* categories of Kant, the conception of the real as being only given by the ideal, the phenomenal as given by the noumenal. For Schelling the real and ideal are mutually generative, the real being that which the ideal perceives outside of itself, and this schema is based on the definition of consciousness itself as being formed by the relation of the real and ideal, and the self-identity of that relation which necessitates its possibility. The knowledge of consciousness of itself, self-consciousness, depends on the mutual participation of the real and ideal; activity cannot exist without knowledge, and knowledge cannot exist without activity. Art cannot exist without philosophy and philosophy cannot exist without art. All of the particular manifestations of the universal in both the real and the ideal reconfirm the necessity of the coexistence of both, despite their differentiation in consciousness and their self-contradiction, their mutual existence in the absolute and chaos, absolute form and formlessness.

The necessary state of consciousness for Schelling is thus one of aporia, irreconcilable contradiction, which can be sought to be reconciled in the dialectic, in philosophical development and artistic representation. In the Deconstruction of Jacques Derrida, the idea of *différance* is central to the aporetic contradiction of consciousness. *Différance* is a "systematic play of differences,"[52] and a spacing of the simultaneously active and passive, real and ideal. *Différance* is a "becoming-space which makes possible both writing and every correspondence between speech and writing, every passage from one to the other," a filter between the real and ideal in consciousness. *Différance* is a *chôra*, as in the *Timaeus*, a place which is not a place in the indifference of the real and ideal, in the contradiction between reason and self-consciousness. *Différance*, as described in *Speech and Phenomena*, is a "generative movement in the play of differences," or the "origin or production of differences" (p. 130),[53] as in consciousness, which is not limited to reason, a static structure inscribed in a closed system, and which presents the possibility of structure in its "systematic and regulated transformations" outside of reason, in intuition. *Différance* in consciousness creates a perceiving subject which is "constituted only in being divided from itself, in becoming space, in temporizing, in deferral…" (p. 29), as in the subject of Schelling in Transcendental Idealism, seeking to resolve itself in the disciplines of philosophy and art.

As the subject is divided in the representation of the real in the ideal, it is divided in its self-consciousness as given to it by language, and the symbolic manifestations of language in art. According to Jacques Lacan, the subject is divided between the signifying structure of language, which is only constituted by lack (the differences of *différance*), and the lack itself as it is manifest in the orientation of the body in space; thus, between the real and ideal as irreconcilable. The subject of Lacan attempts to resolve itself through the signification of itself, self-consciousness in reason, which "solidifies into a signifier," in *The Four Fundamental Concepts of Psycho-Analysis* (p. 199). The ideal solidifies into the real, the knower becomes the known. For Schelling this is the self-consciousness of the indifference of the real and ideal in the absolute within the intellect, as given by intuition, thus not within the boundaries of reason.

For Lacan the signifier solidifies from nothing, or from that hidden primordial cause of desire which is defined as the *objet a*, the primordial dehiscence of the subject in consciousness. The subject of Lacan is alienated from being as the *objet a*, the self-signified mediation between the real and *das Ding*, the absence around which being circulates, the aporetic gap between the real and ideal, between perception and consciousness. As the signifier solidifies from nothing, it conceals the nothing as absence. The concealed void identified as absence, the place where the signifier solidifies from nothing, or the "signified," that is, meaning in being, is the *chôra* of *différance*, which is an existence which has no presence in the real, no "sort of being-present," according to Derrida in *Speech and Phenomena* (p. 134). The ideal is not completely present in the real, and the real cannot be completely explained by the ideal, as opposed to the *a priori* categories of Kant. As in the sublime, the perceiving subject becomes conscious of the absence of the finite within the infinite, and recoils at the *horror vacui* of existence as given by the aporia of the divided subject in self-consciousness.

The signified is in the ideal and the signifier is in the real, as language. The signified is that which is known, while the signifier is the activity of knowing. The absolute is manifest in the indifference of the signifier and the signified as the indifference of the real and ideal. The symbol becomes identical to the idea that it represents in the intelligible, in the intuition of the absolute in the intellect, as in the hieroglyph of Plotinus, which is "an immediate unity, not an aggregate of discursive reasoning and detailed willing" (*Enneads* V.8.6). The hieroglyph is the intelligible idea, the *logos* of the absolute, in the ideal, the originary image (*Urbild*); it is schematic rather than symbolic, in that it represents the absolute in the ideal rather than the real.

The hieroglyph is the indifference of the word and the idea, the representation of the direct intuition of the absolute in the intelligible, according to Plotinus. The indifference of the signified and signifier is the indifference of the knower and the known, thus of conscious and unconscious thought, of the particular and the universal. It is the mystical vision of the immortal souls, the goal of philosophy, the laceration within a lacerated nature, in the heterogeneous, which is, in the words of Georges Bataille, "a universe where perhaps there is no composition either of form or of being, where it seems that death rolls from world to world,"[54] in the indifference of the formlessness of chaos and the infinite form of the absolute.

4
Plotinian Hypostases in Hegel's *Phenomenology of Spirit*

The relation between the universal and the particular, reason and perception, and matter and spirit which Hegel explores in the *Phenomenology of Spirit*, have precedents in the *Enneads*, in the overall structure of being, description of reasoning processes, and definitions of ontological categories in relation to experience. The dialectic of the universal and particular is at the base of the role of reason in history, as Hegel explains in *Reason in History*: "But the cultured human mind cannot help making distinctions between inclinations and desires as they manifest themselves in small circumstances and as they appear in the struggle of world-wide historical interests. Here appears an objective interest, which impresses us in two aspects, that of the universal aim and that of the individual who represents this aim."[1] The dialectic of the universal and particular in reason in history is also the dialectic of Objective Spirit and Subjective Spirit, and their resolution toward Absolute Spirit. The union of the universal and particular is the subject of philosophy, and corresponds to the union of freedom and necessity.

Mental cultivation, according to Hegel, involves the acquisition of knowledge of universal principles, and this involves realizing the thought of the subject matter of thought, that is, the objective in the subjective. Mental cultivation leads to "a living experience of the subject-matter itself,"[2] which is to penetrate to the depths of meaning, to reflect the processes of thought itself in the objects of thought. The thought of the subject matter of thought, and the living experience of the subject matter, is the Idea, which is the source of all that exists, through its inner dynamic or life force, like the One of Plotinus. Nature is the self-development of the Idea through space, and Spirit is the self-development of the Idea through time. The Idea is thus manifest in physical form through space, and in history through time; art is the combination of physical form and history, or nature and time, and is the complete self-development of Spirit, combining space and time. History is the progressing self-determination of the Idea, the progressing self-development of Spirit. The study of history requires an understanding of the dialectical development of the Idea, as the underlying force of history.

Spirit is the self-consciousness of the Idea, the subjective inner life force made objective. It is the synthesis of the Idea and nature, of time and matter. The purpose of philosophy is to reveal the nature of the divine, that is, Spirit, through history, to translate the manifestations of the Idea in time into Objective Spirit, and then into Absolute Spirit, combining time and matter and then transcending them. Philosophy is the self-consciousness of the Idea, or the dialectical development of the Idea from consciousness to self-consciousness; philosophy thus entails both Subjective and Objective Spirit. As the Idea manifests itself as thought, in participation with divine intellect, and as Spirit, in its purest form the Idea is freedom, the realization of freedom in history, corresponding to the transcendence of Subjective and Objective Spirit to Absolute Spirit. Through the dialectic, Reason (*Vernunft*) becomes Spirit (*Geist*).

Philosophy introduces the element of reason into history. In *Reason in History*, Hegel defines reason as "substance and infinite power, in itself the infinite material of all natural and spiritual life as well as the *infinite form*, the actualization of itself as content."[3] Reason is thus a medium of Spirit, and plays a critical role in Spirit as the self-development of the Idea through time, in the form of the dialectic. Reason is the substance of history, "that by which all reality has its being and subsistence." The definition of reason as substance and infinite power, and the actualization of itself as content, depends on the definition of reason in the Intellectual Principle of Plotinus. In the *Enneads*, the Intellectual Principle is defined as the substance of being in that it is omni-present and omni-possessive, like Absolute Spirit. As in the reason of Absolute Spirit, everything possessed by Intellectual Principle loses its individual identity in the whole, and remains distinct at the same time; universal and particular become the same as well as the opposite, in the consummation of the dialectic. The Intellectual Principle is "present to all by Its self-presence" (*Enneads* I.8.2)[4] as reason is the "actualization of itself as content." The Intellectual Principle is the intermediary between the Reason Principle and the absolute (the One) as reason is the intermediary between history and the absolute in phenomenology.

Like the Intellectual Principle, Hegelian Reason "does not require, as does finite activity, the condition of external materials"; it is self-generating and self-supporting, substance and infinite form. Reason is infinite form because it is only through reason that all phenomena are possible and attain life, reflecting a Platonic point of view. And it is only in the *image* of reason that all phenomena are possible, thus all phenomena depend on the development of Reason Principle to form, as if to say that the picture of reality given by perception is the realization of reason itself. Without reason there would be no picture of reality; all mental images are pre-generated by the reasoning process. Reason "is its own exclusive pre-supposition and absolutely final purpose, and itself works out this purpose from potentiality to actuality, from inward source to outward appearance, not only in the natural but also in the spiritual universe, in world history" (*Reason in History*, p. 11). History itself is the *form* of reason, its outward appearance, or visual image, as its own realization from its inner potentiality. In Plotinian terms, history is thus the actualization through the Reason Principle from Nous, intelligible reality in the Intellectual Principle, to the forms of matter in nature as they are perceived. History is thus also participation in divine intelligence, or Absolute Spirit. According to Hegel, this was first realized by Anaxagoras.

The Intellectual Principle of Plotinus, like Hegelian reason, is the source of the law of the universal, which governs over the particular (*Enneads* IV.3.13). The Intellectual Principle enters into matter through the soul, the seat of reason, and is infused throughout the universe, as a universal presence. The only way for a soul to transcend a body, or for the creative individual to transcend history, in Hegel's terms, is through intellection, that is by going beyond the Reason Principle and entering into the intellectual. In the intellectual the soul becomes self-encentered, and self-sufficient, as it is participant, through reason, of the absolute. According to Plotinus, in the realm of the intellectual, governed by the Intellectual Principle, it is possible to see without the mechanisms of seeing, that is, an external light. The intellectual is not dependent on the mechanisms of reason in the Reason Principle to transfer substance into form. The inward soul, as its own source of light, sees another soul within, as a light, and there is no need for a connecting medium. Individual souls are dissolved in the absolute.

It is the light in the soul, which connects it to other souls, that allows the soul to become intellective, or to enter the Intellectual Principle from the Reason Principle. The eye operates by both external light and internal light, by both reason and intellection. Plotinus explains, "In the intellectual, the vision sees not through some medium but by and through itself alone, for its object is not external: by one light it sees another not through any intermediate agency; a light sees a light, that is to say a thing sees itself" (V.3.8).

The essence of the Intellectual Principle for Plotinus is the archetype which pre-exists all matter, as in the thought of Plato: "if the Intellectual-Principle is to be the maker of this All, it cannot make by looking outside itself to what does not yet exist. The Authentic Beings must, then, exist before this All, no copies made on a model but themselves archetypes, primals, and the essence of the Intellectual-Principle" (V.9.5). The essence of the Intellectual Principle is the divine Idea in Absolute Spirit. The Intellectual Principle is both the source of all things and separated from them in the same way that the center of a circle is both the source of all radii of the circle and separated from the radii and circumference: "No more than in the circle are the lines or circumference to be identified with that Center which is the source of both" (VI.8.18).

In the same way, Spirit (*Geist*) for Hegel is self-contained and yet able to assume determinate form, the inner being of the world and at the same time externality. In its own nature Spirit is implicit (*an sich*) and is conscious of itself as spirit. In order to be self-conscious it must double itself as object, achieve externality, and then transcend that externality, objective form. It is in the self-consciousness of Spirit that all universals operate, and it is through self-consciousness that all universals, in particular the Idea, develop from self-containment to objective form and participation (in Nous, or Intellectual Principle). Self-consciousness itself is self-contained, being-in-itself, independent of desire (body), thus the medium through which consciousness experiences Absolute Spirit. In the *Phenomenology of Spirit* (177),[5] "It is in self-consciousness, in the Notion of Spirit, that consciousness first finds its turning-point, where it leaves behind it the colorful show of the sensuous here-and-now and the nightlike void of the supersensible beyond, and steps out into the spiritual daylight of the present."

According to Nicolas Cusanus in *De coniecturis*, the spiritual universe is contained within a circumference. The first center is God, the second center is intellect, and the third center is reason.[6] Reason is the operation of the human intellect, while intellect itself is the similitude of the divine mind. The matter of the universe is the product of the Reason Principle, which is a product of the Intellectual Principle, which is a product of the divine, in the words of Plotinus, corresponding to the diagram of Cusanus. In the *Enneads* VI.8.18, "Thus the Intellective power circles in its multiple unity around the Supreme which stands to it as archetype to image; the image in its movement around its prior has produced the multiplicity by which it is constituted Intellectual-Principle: that prior has no movement..." The transition from the Intellectual Principle to the Reason Principle is the transition from the universal to the particular, from Absolute Spirit to Objective Spirit, from participation in the divine to self-consciousness. The Intellectual Principle is both archetype and a product of the archetype, as is Hegelian reason, in the same way that matter is both a product of soul and soul, transferring unity into multiplicity, as the center of a circle is transferred into the radii and the circumference.

The individual soul of Plotinus is identical to Essential Soul in the same way that reason for Hegel is identical to the Idea. If that is the case, then soul is an Ideal Form which is both cause of activity in matter, like reason, but also not partaking of those activities. Like the circumference of the circle, the soul defines matter and at the same time is unattainable by matter; like reason, it is generated from within, and impenetrable by the forms or images which manifest its Reason Principles. Thus the soul does not perceive by the reception of sensible images. The images, which are the manifestation of phenomena for Hegel, by way of reason, are translated into intelligibles, or Ideal Forms, as they enter into soul, and it is the intelligibles which are the source of reason. Plotinus, following Plato, distinguished between sensible forms and intelligible forms as perceived by the soul; this distinction does not exist in Hegel, as both sensible and intelligible forms are generated by reason, and it is through the dialectical process of reason that the soul transcends sensible forms toward intelligible forms, as it transcends Objective Spirit to Absolute Spirit. The Essential Soul of Plotinus, or self-consciousness, transcends Objective Spirit to Absolute Spirit, while the individual soul, or consciousness, transcends the Subjective Spirit to Objective Spirit.

Plotinus describes reason as being the product of the reception of intelligible forms by the soul, given the distinction between intelligible and sensible forms. In *Enneads* I.I.7, "The faculty of perception in the Soul cannot act by the immediate grasping of sensible objects, but only by the discerning of impressions printed upon the Animate [soul] by sensation: these perceptions are already Intelligibles, while the outer sensation is a mere phantom of the other (of that in the Soul) which is nearer to Authentic-Existence as being an impassive reading of Ideal-Forms. And by means of these Ideal-Forms, by which the Soul wields single lordship over the Animate, we have Discursive-Reasoning, Sense-Knowledge, and Intellection." And to this Plotinus adds, "from this moment we have particularly the We," that is, the passage from consciousness to self-consciousness in Hegelian terms, the passage from the Subjective Spirit to the Objective Spirit, enacted by reason, being the product of the perception of intelligible forms by the soul for Plotinus, and the product of the dialectic for Hegel.

The We is the Essential Soul and the "entire compound entity" of being for Plotinus, the animate being which is perceived by the essential soul which raises the individual soul above matter and nature and into the understanding of the divine through the Intellectual Principle, as the self-consciousness of Hegel raises the soul of man above nature and into communion with Absolute Spirit. The We of Plotinus, the "authentic Human-Principle" can be found "loftily presiding over the Animate," over nature and Ego, or consciousness, and partaking in the One, through Intellectual Principle, in Absolute Spirit.

The Intellectual Principle is the realization of the dialectic of reason, in that it contains both the particular and the universal, in that it participates in both Reason Principle and the One, in both matter and spirit, and in soul and Essential Soul. "And we have It either as common to all or as our own immediate possession: or again we may possess It in both degrees, that is in common, since It is indivisible—one, everywhere and always Its entire self—and severally in that each personality possesses It entire in the First-Soul" (I.I.8). The Intellectual Principle contains within it both consciousness and self-consciousness, both Ego and *Geist*. For Plotinus it thus follows that Ideal Forms or intelligibles are possessed by both soul and Intellectual Principle. They are concentrated in the Intellectual Principle, images without matter, as in the *complicato* of Cusanus, the polygonal figures compressed in the circle without material form, and they are "unrolled and separate" in the soul, like the *explicato* of Cusanus, the polygonal figures inscribed in the circle in all their variation and material presence, the Unlimited as opposed to the Limit, in the terms of Proclus. The development of the soul toward the Intellectual Principle is through the Reason Principle, so the development from *explicato* to *complicato* is through reason, as it is for Hegel, in the dialectic. For Hegel, it is the dialectical process of reason itself which generates both ideal and sensible forms.

Perception as such is described in *Phenomenology of Spirit*. Perception is differentiated from sense-certainty in that perception "takes what is present to it as a universal" (111). The act of perceiving is thus "the movement of pointing-out" in combination with the movement of the event of the object perceived. Perception is a dialectical movement, an act of necessity in reason, which is an "unfolding and differentiation," a *complicato* and *explicato*. The object of perception is identical to the perception of the object in that the essence of perception is the universal, and the dialectical movements within perception, the perceiver and the perceived, are the particular and Unlimited, the unessential. Perception introduces the particular into the universal; it is an unstable mediation of the object of perception as universal, and introduction of multiplicity into unity. The object of perception is "a One" (117), an essence or universal, as in Plotinus. Perception is an instrument of Subjective Spirit, or the Plotinian Reason Principle in the soul, which moves reason in the direction of Objective Spirit, as Intellectual Principle, where the essence of the object perceived becomes identified with the essence of the soul of the perceiver, and the movements of particularity become the universal, in *complicato*. In that perception is the basis of communication in art, perception is a dialectical instrument by which art expresses Spirit. The dialectic of Hegel plays the same role as the participation of Plotinus, of the Intellectual Principle in the Reason Principle, toward the absolute. Perception is a medium for the expression of being in soul, and in such expression essence in being becomes differentiated and determinate (113). The differentiation of the properties of being necessitates the coincidence of a property and its negative, thus the dialectic.

In the *Enneads* the Intellectual Principle leads to the One, the Divine Intellect, and it is the "We" which leads to the Intellectual Principle. The We is the Essential Soul, or Undivided Soul, and its union with the divine. The Essential Soul is imparted to individual souls through intelligible form, which allows for sense-perception in individual souls: "...in so far as any bodies are Animates, the Soul has given itself to each of the separate material masses; or rather it appears to be present in the bodies by the fact that it shines into them: it makes them living beings not by merging into body but by giving forth, without any change in itself, images or likenesses of itself like one face caught by many mirrors." The soul participates in bodies without a reciprocal participation of bodies in soul. It is the image, either the intelligible form or the sensible form, as in the reflection in the mirror, which is impenetrable, and thus corresponds to the unparticipant soul. While for Plato and Plotinus the image or form is inaccessible and thus a product of divine intellect in soul, for Hegel the image or form is a product of reason and is thus accessible to soul, and in fact participates in reason in soul. This distinction lies at the basis of the definitions of Classical and Romantic representation in the arts.

The Essential Soul forms part of the constructed soul of the Platonic Demiurge in *Timaeus* 35: "From the indivisible, eternally unchanging Existence and the divisible, changing Existence of the physical world he mixed a third kind of Existence intermediate between them," that existence being the "We" or Essential Soul of Plotinus, as in the *Enneads*: "In that the Divinity is poised upon the Intellectual-Principle and Authentic-Existence; and We come third in order after these two, for the We is constituted by a union of the supreme, the undivided Soul—we read [in Plato]—and that Soul which is divided among (living) bodies" (I.I.8). The Essential Soul is a union of the Same and Different, the indivisible and divisible, the universal and particular. The Essential Soul is the soul of the Renaissance Humanist, negotiating between heaven and earth, the macrocosm in which individual souls participate. It is the presence of intelligible form, the archetype of divine intelligence, as in the Same and Different, in the individual soul.

According to Hegel, self-consciousness is a necessary basis for the dialectical development of the Idea. The presence of Spirit is necessary for consciousness to seek to transcend itself; Spirit is present universally. In the dialectical development of the Idea, the particular wills itself toward the universal, in the self-determination of the Idea, and the self-development of the Spirit, and at the same time the universal wills itself toward the particular. This was illustrated in the *De circuli quadratura* of Nicolas Cusanus at the beginning of the Renaissance. In the *De circuli quadratura* of Cusanus, polygonal geometrical figures are manifestations of mathematical doctrines developed in the intellect, as the polyhedral solids of Plato are geometrical constructions based on the mathematical proportions of the divine Idea.

According to Cusanus, material variations are first made visible by mathematical figures, which transform them into geometrical figures. In the Prologue to the *Commentary on the First Book of Euclid's Elements*, Proclus stated that mathematics "occupies the middle ground between the partless realities—simple, incomposite, and indivisible—and divisible things characterized by every variety of composition and differentiation" (3), that is, between the universal and particular.[7] Mathematics is the medium by which the pure forms in the intelligible world of Plato are transformed into the matter of the material world, the universal into the particular, as for Cusanus mathematics transforms material variations into geometrical figures, which are mathematical doctrines developed in the intellect.

In that the forms of mathematics copy the principles of the intelligible, according to Proclus, the principles of mathematics are to be found in the absolute being and "all-pervading principles that generate everything from themselves: namely the Limit and the Unlimited" (5). The pairing of the Limit and the Unlimited occurs in the *Philebus* of Plato, as the Finite and Infinite; they are implanted in all things which are composed of one and many and are the "parent of all the discoveries in the arts" (16),[8] and provide the means by which the truth of things can be understood. Through the finite and the infinite, unity in things can be found; and by beginning with unity and proceeding by subdividing, "the entire number of the species intermediate between unity and infinity has been discovered." A third principle arises from the compound of the finite and infinite, which like the infinite is "greatly divided and dispersed."

The circle of Cusanus is the Limit, or universal, being indivisible and exceeding all measurement, and the polygonal figures inscribed in the circle are the Unlimited, or particular, containing the species of all sensible things in their infinite variations. The mathematical figures, or magnitudes, of Proclus, which are capable of indefinite increase, are "divisible without end," as described in the *Commentary* (6), and they are all particulars distinguished from one another and bounded in proportion, like the polygonal figures of Cusanus. Such boundaries and particulars, as well as ratios and proportions, are given by the Limit (7), the existence of which is necessary for the sciences of mathematics and geometry. Mathematics and geometry, like being itself, are dependent on both Limit and Unlimited. The Limit is the "ground that underlies their forms," which are composed of ratios, figures and shapes, the qualities of the Unlimited.

Proclus defined the dialectical process of ascending to the intelligibles and descending into particulars (8) as the process of analysis and synthesis, which contain the characteristics of beauty and order. For Cusanus, the dialectical process, which is manifest in the coincidence of opposites, ascends toward the intelligibles in a process of folding or *complicato*, or implication, as in the folding of polygonal figures into the circle; the dialectical process descends towards the particulars in a process of unfolding or *explicato*, or explanation, as in the unfolding of the polygonal figures away from the circle.

For Proclus and Cusanus, mathematics and geometry are the means by which the motion of bodies can be applied toward the dialectical movement of understanding towards Nous, understanding of intelligible reality, the Absolute Spirit of Hegel. Mathematical understanding moves in two possible directions, either from the Limit to the Unlimited, that is from unity to plurality, or the reverse, from multiples back to unities, or from conclusions back to hypotheses, seeking the originary principles of Nous. In the geometrical model of Cusanus, polygonal figures unfold from the circle towards infinite subdivision, and enfold towards the circle, returning to the essence of unity contained within them. "Consequently it is only natural," explained Proclus (19), "that the cognitive powers operating in the general science that deals with these objects should appear as twofold, some aiming at the unification and collection of the manifold for us, others at dividing the simple into the diverse, the more general into the particular, and the primary ideas into secondary and remoter consequences of the principles." The dianoetic process of mathematical understanding operates in both directions, in dialectic and discursive thinking. According to Proclus, "The range of thinking extends from on high all the way down to conclusions in the sense world," from Nous to the objects of sense-perception, encompassing all of being. In the binary dialectical movement, from unity to plurality and plurality to unity, mathematics and geometry are able to force the mind out of sense perception and into contemplation of the intelligibles of a higher reality. Such is the dialectical process adopted by Hegel in the *Phenomenology of Spirit*.

In *Reason in History*, the Unlimited corresponds to matter in nature, and the Limit corresponds to Spirit. Matter is composite, composed of parts that exclude each other, like the polygonal figures of Cusanus, and it tends toward a central point, as in the process of *explicato*. Matter constantly strives toward ideality. Spirit, on the other hand, contains its own center in itself, like the circle, and contains its own substance within itself, undifferentiated, as the polygonal figures are contained within the circle. Spirit is thus "Being-within-itself" (*Ansichsein*),[9] and is thus freedom, in that it is independent from all things external, and self-generated, as in the Intellectual Principle. Such self-contained existence is self-consciousness, or Objective Spirit which becomes Absolute Spirit. Self-consciousness is also the combination of knowledge and knowing. In consciousness, the thinking subject knows something, and knows that he or she knows something. In self-consciousness, the Spirit knows itself, as it is centered in itself, and is self-realizing. If history is the process of the self-realization of Spirit, then it is the process of the consciousness, and self-consciousness, of freedom.

The soul is described as a form of self-consciousness in the *Enneads*, as it is self-contained and self-generated, like the circle. As the soul is interfused everywhere and "herself turning in herself," the movement of the soul is "a movement towards itself, the movement of self-awareness, of self-intellection, of the living of its life, the movement of its reaching to all things so that nothing shall lie outside of it, nothing anywhere but within its scope" (*Enneads* II.2.1). The soul "has itself at once for center and for the goal to which it must be ceaselessly moving." In that the soul is moving towards itself, it is "ceaselessly leading the cosmos towards itself," in the same way that the Intellectual Principle only looks inward, as a model for the soul. The cosmos thus moves in the same circular patterns as the soul, as it is pursuing it.

In the *Enneads*, the pursuit of the good, the essence of the One administered by the soul, by material forms, is the location of desire. The circling body always pursues the soul, as the polygons pursue the circle in *complicato*, but it never possesses it, because "everywhere it finds something else besides the Soul" (II.2.2). According to Nicolas Cusanus in *De Docta Ignorantia*,[10] "The Platonists thought that all motion derives from the world-soul, which they said to be present as a whole in the whole world and as a whole in each part of the world" (II.9). Motion is self-generated in world-soul, and as world-soul is infused in all things, so is desire, causing motion. The world-soul is that which is self-moved. It is ungenerated from anything and immortal, as described by Plato in *Phaedrus* 245, and is self-moving, thus it is the source of all motion, the *archê* of motion.

In that the body ceaselessly circles around the soul at the center in the motion of desire, never attaining the good which it seeks, the human being is constituted by that lack at the center, which is the locus of desire. It is in this void at the center of being, corresponding to the One of Plotinus, around which desire circulates, in the motion of the soul, that the subject must recognize himself in self-consciousness. It is when the Intellectual Principle is infused with desire that it descends to the sensible world through the soul and imposes order on matter. Normally the Intellectual Principle is stationary in the intellective realm of the One and is without desire, but when it descends in soul to matter it becomes moved by desire to form and create, so "while this primal soul in union with the soul of the All transcends the sphere administered, it is inevitably turned outward, and has added the universe to its concern" (*Enneads* IV.7.13). When the soul descends from the universal it enters into the body. "With this comes what is known as the casting of the wings, the enchaining in body" (IV.8.4). The soul for Plotinus retains something of the transcendent, and if it turns toward the intellective it "is loosened from the shackles and soars" (*Enneads* IV.8.4).

As the Intellectual Principle exists independently of the sensible world, it relies on a different kind of vision, an archetypal paradigm of vision not dependent on sensible forms or images, as in the reason of Hegel, a model which is copied in the sensible world. But as the soul turns inward toward the Intellectual Principle, the vision of the Intellectual Principle is an inward vision which does not see in the conventional sense; vision and the object of vision are identical in self-consciousness, as knowledge and the object of knowledge are identical for Hegel. In the intellectual "the vision and the envisioned are a unity; the seen is as the seeing and seeing as seen" (V.3.8).

As the model of vision penetrates the sensible world through the soul, so vision itself is not completely dependent on external light, but also on an internal light, which is the source of the truest form of seeing in vision, as inner knowledge must be the truest form of knowledge. In the *Enneads* "there is an earlier light within itself, a more brilliant, which it sees sometimes in a momentary flash....This is sight without the act, but it is the truest seeing, for it sees light whereas its other objects were the lit not the light" (V.5.7). If knowledge and the object of knowledge are identical, then knowledge itself presupposes the act of knowing, and is only generated from within. Knowledge, and therefore reason, are a function of the soul, and of the spirit. The vision of the Intellectual Principle of Plotinus depends on its withdrawal from the world of matter, so that it "must have its vision—not of some light in some other thing but of the light within itself, unmingled, pure, suddenly gleaming before it." When knowledge is identified with the object of knowledge, it is contained within itself, like the circle. Thus for Plotinus, "It is a principle with us that one who has attained to the vision of the Intellectual Beauty and grasped the beauty of the Authentic Intellect will be able also to come to understand the Father and Transcendent of that Divine Being" (V.8.1); for Hegel, one who has attained to knowledge in self-consciousness has attained freedom through Spirit, and can understand Absolute Spirit, beyond the objective.

Thus, in *Reason in History*, "The Idea has within itself the determination of its self-consciousness, of activity. Thus it is God's own eternal life, as it was, so to speak, before the creation of the world, the logical connection of all things. It still lacks at this point the form of being which is actuality. It still is the universal, the immanent, the represented."[11] The Hegelian Idea is the Platonic Idea, the *archê* or Unlimited which pre-exists all things and is separate from them, but gives them their form. In the same way, the essence of the Intellectual Principle for Plotinus is the archetype which pre-exists all matter: "if the Intellectual-Principle is to be the maker of this All, it cannot make by looking outside itself to what does not yet exist. The Authentic Beings must, then, exist before this All, no copies made on a model but themselves archetypes, primals, and the essence of the Intellectual-Principle" (*Enneads* V.9.5). The Intellectual Principle of Plotinus is the Platonic Unlimited or *archê*, or the *apeiron* of Anaximander. The *apeiron* is the ultimate source and first principle and the primary substance (*stoicheion*) attributed to Anaximander by Simplicius in the *Commentaria*. The *apeiron* of Anaximander is the source of the generation of all things, and is at the same time separated from all things, according to Pseudo-Plutarch in the *Stromata*, like the One of Plotinus, and the Spirit of Hegel. The *apeiron* of Anaximander is also the principle of all things which are generated, according to Aëtius, like the Intellectual Principle of Plotinus.

The Intellectual Principle is both the source of all things and separated from them in the same way that the center of a circle is both the source of all radii of the circle and separated from the radii and circumference. Plotinus explains, "No more than in the circle are the lines or circumference to be identified with that Center which is the source of both" (*Enneads* VI.8.18). According to Cusanus in *De coniecturis* in the fifteenth century, the spiritual universe is contained within a circumference. The first center is God, the second center is intellect, and the third center is reason.[12] Reason is the operation of the human intellect, while intellect itself is the similitude of the divine mind. The matter of the universe is the product of the Reason Principle (or soul), which is a product of the Intellectual Principle (or Nous), which is a product of the divine (or the One), in the words of Plotinus. In the *Enneads* VI.8.18, "Thus the Intellective power circles in its multiple unity around the Supreme which stands to it as archetype to image; the image in its movement around its prior has produced the multiplicity by which it is constituted Intellectual-Principle: that prior has no movement..." The Intellectual Principle is both archetype and a product of the archetype, in the same way that matter is both a product of soul and soul, transferring unity into multiplicity.

The Plotinian hypostases correspond to the Absolute Spirit, Objective Spirit and Subjective Spirit of Hegel, in the participation of human reason in divine intellect, through reason, self-consciousness, and freedom; in the union of the universal and particular, freedom and necessity; and in the participation of the Idea in Ego through self-consciousness. Such participation is similar to the participation of the One in the Intellectual Principle, and the Intellectual Principle in the Reason Principle. The transition from Idea to Ego through self-consciousness is the transition from Intellectual Principle to Reason Principle. The transition is described in *Reason in History* (p. 32):

> The second stage begins when the Idea satisfies the contrast which originally is only ideally in it and posits the difference between itself, and itself as purely abstract reflection in itself. In this stepping over to one side (in order to be object of reflection) the Idea sets the other side as formal actuality (or *Fürsichsein*), as formal freedom, as abstract unity of self-consciousness, as infinite reflection in itself, and as infinite negativity (antithesis). Thus it becomes Ego, which, as an atom (indivisible), opposes itself to all content and thus is the most complete antithesis—the antithesis, namely, of the whole plenitude of the Idea. The absolute Idea is thus, on the one hand, substantial fullness of content and, on the other hand, abstract free volition.

The transition from Idea to Ego is a dialectical process in which Idea becomes both Same and Different (in the terms of the *Timaeus*), which are both unified and distinct in world-soul. The self-separation, as in the primal separation of elements in the model of Anaximander, creates thesis and antithesis as universal and particular, and Idea and Ego. According to Aristotle in the *Physics* (187), Anaximander believed that all matter is separated out as opposites from an original unity. Aristotle explained, "There is a second group [the Pluralists] who declare that opposite qualities are contained in the One and emerge from it by separation, as for instance Anaximander."[13] According to Pseudo-Plutarch, Anaximander believed that "Something capable of generating Hot and Cold was separated off from the eternal in the formation of this world."[14]

Like the One and the Intellectual Principle, the Hegelian Idea both remains separate from and imparts itself to Ego. Ego is "the Absolute itself become finite," the participation of the Limit in the Unlimited, the One in the soul. The self-separation of the Idea is "reflection in itself, individual self-consciousness," a quality of Ego as well, which is "the antithesis of the absolute Idea and hence the Idea in absolute finiteness," the universal as the particular, the union which is the aim of philosophy. Thus, "to comprehend the absolute connection of this opposition is the profound task of metaphysics" (p. 33). The Idea and the Ego are mutually self-existent; the Idea is the essence of being, and the Ego is the appearance of being, as for Plotinus. In the *Enneads*, the beauty of the good, or the Idea, as manifest by the Intellectual Principle through the soul in matter, is inaccessible through the beauty in matter, although it is suggested by it. The Intellectual Principle can be recognized in the patterns and forms of reason in matter, the appearance of being; but to experience the essence of being, it is necessary to experience the source of the beauty in reason which lends itself to matter. In order to do that, it is necessary to become unembodied. As the inner light of the eye is the light of the Intellectual Principle, withdrawing to within itself and partaking of none of the light of matter, it is necessary to turn inward, withdrawing from "those shapes of grace that show in the body" (I.6.8), the appearance of being as given by Ego, which must be recognized as copies, vestiges and shadows, in order to partake of the beauty of the soul, as opposed to the beauty of the body.

The inward experience of Plotinus, separated from the world of sense, is experience by a kind of vision not of the world of sense or appearance, but instead "another vision which is to be waked within you" (I.6.8), a vision of essence. In order to see the essence of one's soul through an inner vision, it is necessary for each individual to sculpt the individual soul as a sculptor would create a statue, making use of the participation of the soul in the Ideal Form and the Intellectual Principle. The sculptor cuts away, smoothes, lightens and straightens until the "godlike splendor of virtue" (VI.9.9) shines from the statue, the light of the Idea, which nourishes the Intellectual Principle and the soul. The beauty of the form in appearance is a copy of the beauty of the Idea in essence. It is a "derivative and a minor: and even that shows itself upon the statue not integrally and with entire realization of intention but only in so far as it has subdued the resistance of the material" (V.8.1). Thus, "In the degree in which the beauty is diffused by entering into matter, it is so much the weaker than that concentrated in unity"; it is the "indivisible exhibited in diversity." The essence of being, the Idea, is found in the universal and the Limit, while the appearance of being, the Ego, is found in the particular and Unlimited.

In the section "Appearance and the Supersensible World," in *Phenomenology of Spirit*, Hegel describes appearance as uniting consciousness and inner being. Appearance is a stage of being between understanding (or consciousness) and essence (or inner-world) which as a being-for-self is a "surface show" (143), like the Platonic veil "hanging between the finite and the infinite," as described in *Timaeus* 38. As a surface show, appearance is only a "vanishing." Appearance as show or veil is the instrument of reason, in the dialectic of perception for Hegel, in the mediation between essence and understanding. The surface show as a totality is a form of universal, a reflection of the totality of essence, or the "inner into self." Hegel's description is reminiscent of the curtain-wall built along the road in *Republic* 514, separating prisoners in a cave from a burning fire. The curtain-wall is "like the screen at puppet shows between the operators and their audience, above which they show their puppets."[15]

From the puppet show, the prisoners in the cave believe that the shadows of objects are the whole truth. If the prisoner were to suddenly see the objects themselves, looking toward the fire behind the screen, he would be blinded by the fire; he would be "too dazzled to see properly the objects of which he used to see the shadows" (515). Thus the prisoner "would need to grow accustomed to the light before he could see things in the upper world outside the cave. First he would find it easiest to look at shadows, next at the reflections of men and other objects in water, and later on at the objects themselves" (516). Finally the prisoner in the *Republic* would be able to look directly at the fire and the sun, without using the shadows or reflections. "The realm revealed by sight corresponds to the prison, and the light of the fire in the prison to the power of the sun. And you won't go wrong if you connect the ascent into the upper world and the sight of the objects there with the upward progress of the mind into the intelligible region" (517). When seeing the sun, the prisoner is able to realize that it is the source of the good, "inferred to be responsible for whatever is right and valuable in anything, producing in the visible region light and the source of light, and being in the intelligible region itself controlling source of truth and intelligence." The light is the essence or inner being of the *Phenomenology of Spirit*, and the process of perceiving the light is a dialectical process of reason and perception, for Plotinus the ascent to the Intellectual Principle from the Reason Principle.

In the dialectical process the object of perception is manifest as its opposite in consciousness, and becomes essence in understanding, as the universal becomes the particular. The movement of the forces of being is the negative of the positive of the universal totality, the instability of the multiplicity derived from the One, as in Neoplatonism. In the Neoplatonic *circuitus spiritualis*, "The Cosmic Soul in turn converts the static ideas and intelligences comprised in the Cosmic Mind into dynamic causes moving and fertilizing the sublunary world, and thus stimulates nature to produce visible things,"[16] as described by Erwin Panofsky in *Studies in Iconology*. The unity and transcendent light of the Absolute Spirit, the One, passes in dynamic fashion through the hierarchy of being into the interwoven proliferation of physical matter, the multiplicity of forms. The multiplicity of forms is represented in the Unlimited variation of the polygonal figures of Cusanus, in relation to the Limited singularity of the absolute in the circle.

The operative force of this transition is appearance, which is part of the movement of the forces of being, in which the object of perception, the "sensuously objective" (*Phenomenology* 143), is the negative of pure being, its other. As this occurs in consciousness, consciousness is both ground and consequence of perception. As in understanding in perception, it is both the object of perception and the act of perception, the seen and the seer, as in the Intellectual Principle, and the gaze of Jacques Lacan. The inner being, essence, or being-in-itself in consciousness is possessed in its own certainty of self, as understanding, but the objective being is outside of itself, fluctuating and unstable, in the flux of the dialectic. The flux is the objective vanishing appearance, the twilight of things in the sensible world, the "twilight of becoming and perishing" as described in *Republic* 508.

The essence of being is experienced in the *Enneads* (I.6.9), "When you know that you have become this perfect work," through desire of the soul for the good, or the essence of the Idea, in its unity and universality, "when you are self-gathered in the purity of your being, nothing now remaining that can shatter that inner unity, nothing from without clinging to the authentic man, when you find yourself wholly true to your essential nature, wholly that only veritable Light which is not measured by space, not narrowed to any circumscribed form nor again diffused as a thing devoid of term, but even unmeasurable as something greater than all measure and more than all quantity." In the *Phenomenology of Spirit*, inner being transcends the antithesis between universal and particular as Absolute Spirit.

The supersensible world becomes the object of understanding above the sensuous world, a permanent beyond above the vanishing present, a being-in-itself of essence. Inner being is beyond consciousness and is unknowable by sense knowledge. It is a void around which desire in consciousness circulates, in Neoplatonic terms, a being beyond measurement and the objects of reason, like the One of Plotinus, as in the *Enneads* (VI.4.2), "We may be reminded that the universe cannot be contained in the Authentic as in a place, where place would mean the boundaries of some surrounding extension considered as an envelope, or some space formerly a part of the Void and still remaining unoccupied even after the emergence of the universe, that it can only support itself, as it were, upon the Authentic and rest in the embrace of its omnipresence."

In that supersensible being comes about through appearance, as a mediating factor, appearance itself cannot be said to be of the sensuous world (*Phenomenology* 147). Perception is not sense-knowledge; it is a product of the dialectic of the particular and universal through consciousness and inner being, from which reason arises. The universal in inner being is an outcome of the flux of appearance (149). The universal contains within itself a universal negation and mediation which is the dialectical process from appearance to essence, thus reason. "This difference is expressed in the law," Hegel writes, "which is the stable image of unstable appearance." The supersensible world is "an inert realm of laws" beyond the perceived world which only exhibits laws in "incessant change," the Heraclitean flux, the "state of perpetual influx and efflux" of the body to which the courses of the immortal soul are fastened by the children of the Demiurge in *Timaeus* 42–43.

The laws of inner being correspond to representations of the Intellectual Principle for Plotinus, the "symmetries, correspondences and principles of order observed in visible things" (*Enneads* II.9.16). The laws of the sensible world reflect the laws of the inner world, and can lead understanding from perception in consciousness, in a dialectical process for Hegel, to the inner being, or absolute. Art can be a medium for such a development, as described by Plotinus: "Consider, even, the case of pictures: those seeing by the bodily sense the productions of the art of painting do not see the one thing in the one only way; they are deeply stirred by recognizing in the objects depicted to the eyes the presentation of what lies in the idea, and so are called to recollection of the truth—the very experience out of which Love arises."

The inert realm of laws of the supersensible world of Hegel are the "Ideas from which Nature itself derives" (V.8.1) in the Intellectual Principle of Plotinus, the ideas which the artist recognizes in the representation of natural objects. For Hegel, "this realm of laws is indeed the truth for the Understanding" (*Phenomenology* 149), but it is not entirely manifest in appearance, but only inconsistently, given the state of flux and particularity, as "with every change of circumstance the law has a different actuality." The world of appearance becomes stable in inner being, as it becomes governed by universal and unchanging laws. Through appearance, consciousness becomes unified with the supersensible world. Consciousness is able to see through appearance, into the ideas or principles which govern it behind the veil of forms. Being-in-itself comes about when inner being sees into the inner world, and "this curtain hanging before the inner world is therefore drawn away" (165). At this point, the dialectical processes of perception and understanding are transcended, and the inner being becomes unified and identical with the inner world.

In the *Enneads* (IV.8.1), the Reason Principle is transcended toward the Intellectual Principle, and the universal laws of the absolute become visible: "Many times it has happened: lifted out of the body into myself; becoming external to all other things and self-centered; beholding a marvelous beauty; then, more than ever, assured of community with the loftiest order; enacting the noblest life, acquiring identity with the divine; stationing within it by having attained that activity; poised above whatsoever within the Intellectual is less than the Supreme..." For Hegel, it is through self-consciousness that consciousness attains inner being and the absolute and transcends the dialectic of appearance and void, particular and universal, toward Absolute Spirit. Thus, "it is in self-consciousness, in the Notion of Spirit, that consciousness first finds its turning point, where it leaves behind it the colorful show of the sensuous here-and-now and the nightlike void of the supersensible beyond, and steps out into the spiritual daylight of the present" (*Phenomenology* 177), Objective Spirit.

All preliminary forms of consciousness are abstract manifestations of Spirit, particular manifestations of the universal, in a hypostatic hierarchy of consciousness, self-consciousness and reason, or sense-certainty, perception, and understanding. Spirit unfolds in consciousness in *explicato*; each particular form in consciousness contains the absolute in Spirit. The forms of consciousness in Spirit are "only moments or vanishing quantities" (440), advancements and retreats which are resolved in essence. Consciousness becomes Spirit when it "embraces" sense-certainty, perception and understanding, that is, when it becomes self-consciousness and being-in-itself; Spirit is the unity, or self-identification, of consciousness and self-consciousness. Spirit is a reasoning consciousness which becomes aware of itself.

In terms of the state, Spirit is the ethical life, as developed through the self-consciousness of the state, which is morality. The state becomes identical with its morality, and achieves an ethical life through the imposition of the underlying universal laws of the Idea in the absolute. The ethical state is a macrocosm of the mind in understanding of Absolute Spirit, through Objective Spirit, the identification of the universal and the particular (the state and the individual). Self-consciousness of Spirit in the ethical state is conscience. Conscience, morality and ethics are the hypostatic hierarchy of being at the level of the state, seeking to resolve themselves in Absolute Spirit.

The ethical state as macrocosm of the mind in understanding of Absolute Spirit, divine Idea, is described in the *Phaedrus* (247)[17]:

> So the mind of a god, sustained as it is by pure intelligence and knowledge, like that of every soul which is destined to assimilate its proper food, is satisfied at last with the vision of reality, and nourished and made happy by the contemplation of truth, until the circular revolution brings it back to its starting-point. And in the course of its journey it beholds absolute justice and discipline and knowledge, not the knowledge which is attached to things which come into being, nor the knowledge which varies with the objects which we now call real, but the absolute knowledge which corresponds to what is absolutely real in the fullest sense.

The ethical state is a copy of the justice and discipline and knowledge in the absolute, manifested by participation in the Intellectual Principle, as described in the *Enneads* (V.8.10):

> Of those looking upon that Being and its content, and able to see, all take something but not all the same vision always: intently gazing, one sees the font and principle of Justice, another is filled with the sight of Moral Wisdom, the original of that quality as found, sometimes at least, among men, copied by them in their degree from the divine virtue which, covering all the expanse, so to speak, of the Intellectual Realm is seen, last attainment of all, by those who have known already many splendid visions.

According to Gottfried Wilhelm Leibniz, consciousness of perception, or self-consciousness, is "apperception." As for Hegel, perception, the perception of appearances, is the medium or mechanism by which the universal is discerned in the particular, and Spirit, or essence, is discerned in substance, through self-consciousness. Perception cannot be explained in mechanical terms and is thus the product of the inner principle, or monad, as in the absolute or universal. In the *Monadology* (14), perception is "the passing condition which involves and represents a multiplicity in the unity, or in the simple substance";[18] it is through perception that multiplicity and unity coexist in the monad, or in Hegelian terms, that the universal and particular are united in Spirit. For Leibniz, it is apperception or self-consciousness which leads to the possibility of the unconscious, which becomes the locus for being-in-itself.

For Hegel, the form of the self-consciousness of Spirit, of Spirit in identity with itself, having passed through sense-certainty, perception and consciousness, is the absence of form, or the absence of shape, shapelessness.

Absence of form, shapelessness, is light, "the pure, all-embracing and all-pervading essential light of sunrise, which pervades itself in its formless substantiality" (*Phenomenology* 686). The other of Spirit in self-consciousness, the absence of light, is darkness, the "nightlike void of the supersensible beyond." The movements of the externalization of Spirit, the genesis of its being-for-self, are "torrents of light," and the return into the absolute being-in-itself from the moments of its existence, the manifestation in particulars, as given by perception, are "streams of fire destructive of structured form," bringing about the shapelessness.

Light forms the *circuitus spiritualis* in the dialectic of the *complicato/explicato* through the hypostases of being, as the universal essence of formlessness in the substance of all particulars. As it streams through the hypostases, "the difference which it gives itself does, it is true, proliferate unchecked in the substance of existence and shapes itself to the forms of Nature; yet the essential simplicity of its thought moves aimlessly about in it without stability or intelligence, enlarges its bounds to the measureless, and its beauty, heightened to splendor, is dissolved in its sublimity." In that light is the ground of perception, light is a medium in the transference of the universal to the particular; but in light, the measured becomes measureless, the beautiful becomes sublime; the laws of the Idea in nature, of the Intellectual Principle, are transcended, and light becomes the ground of self-consciousness, of the absolute. It is pure light which disperses the unitary nature of Spirit into an infinity of forms (688), endowing the vanishing shapes of life with an "enduring subsistence," being-for-self (*Fürsichsein*).

So it is for Plotinus. In *Enneads* V.8.9, Plotinus described the universe as a transparent sphere which is composed of and then transcends the material parts which make up its whole: "Keep this sphere before you, and from it imagine another, a sphere stripped of magnitude and spatial differences; cast out your inborn sense of matter..." The essence of the universe is unmeasurable in the Intellectual Principle. The light of the Intellectual Principle is an inner light, preceding sense-certainty and perception, a pure light uncontaminated by exterior lights: "the Intellectual-Principle, hiding itself from all the outer, withdrawing to the inmost, seeing nothing, must have its vision—not of some other light in some other thing but of the light within itself, unmingled, pure, suddenly gleaming before it" (V.5.7). The form of matter closest to the Ideal Principle is fire, because it is closest to being unembodied, that is, an Ideal Form; it penetrates everything, and can be penetrated by nothing, and is absolutely simple and unitary. The light which comes from fire is the light of the Ideal Form, being a manifestation of the Intellectual Principle, infusing the universal in the particular.

According to Plotinus, the beauty of the good in the Idea (the sublime of Hegel), as manifest by the Intellectual Principle through the soul in matter, is in its origin and source inaccessible through the beauty in matter, although it is suggested by it. It is one thing to recognize the Intellectual Principle in the patterns and forms of reason in matter, through understanding; it is another thing to experience the source of the beauty in reason which lends itself to matter. In order to do that, it is necessary for the perceiving subject to become unembodied. As the inner light of the eye is the light of the Intellectual Principle, withdrawing to within itself and partaking of none of the light of matter, it is necessary to turn inward, withdrawing from "those shapes of grace that show in the body" (I.6.8), which must be recognized as copies, vestiges and shadows. In the allegory of the cave in the *Republic* (517), "the prison-house is the world of sight, the light of the fire is the sun, and you will not misapprehend me if you interpret the journey upwards to be the ascent of the soul into the intellectual world....in the world of knowledge the idea of good appears last of all, and is seen only with an effort; and, when seen, is also inferred to be the universal author of all things beautiful and right, parent of light and of the lord of light in this visible world, and the immediate source of reason and truth in the intellectual."

The image of the intelligible is achieved for Plotinus if "someone took away the bulk of the body but kept the power of the light" (*Enneads* VI.4.7). The vision of the Intellectual Principle depends on its withdrawal from the world of matter, so that it "must have its vision—not of some light in some other thing but of the light within itself, unmingled, pure, suddenly gleaming before it" (V.5.7). The inner light of the Intellectual Principle is described in the Myth of Er in the *Republic* (616), where the souls, traveling through what is described as the understructure of the cosmos like the hull of a ship, a void in the structural matter of being, like the void in the essence of being of Hegel, come to "a place from which they could see a shaft of light stretching from above straight through earth and heaven, like a pillar....for this light is the bond of heaven and holds its whole circumference together, like the swifter of a trireme."

In *Timaeus* 58, each of the elements is divided into intelligible and sensible components. Fire is composed of both flame, which is "the radiation from flame which does not burn but provides the eyes with light," and "the glow left in embers after flame has been quenched." The element of fire which provides light and vision is an immaterial element; light is immaterial, but becomes material in fire. The dialectic of light as sensible and intelligible is also described in the *Republic*. The divine intellect, the "universal author of all things" (517), is "parent of light and of the lord of light in this visible world, and the immediate source of reason and truth in the intellectual." In the Hymn of the Dialectic, intellect transcends reason which transcends perception which transcends sense-perception, as in the hierarchy of Hegel, towards the essence or absolute. The dialectic is the dialectic between the light of the Reason Principle and the light of the Intellectual Principle, in Plotinian terms. The light of the Reason Principle, in reason given by perception, is in imitation of the inner light of the Intellectual Principle, represented by the sun, the light of fire (the immaterial element, as opposed to the flame). Thus, in the allegory of the cave, "the prison-house is the world of sight, the light of the fire is the sun, and you will not misapprehend me if you interpret the journey upwards to be the ascent of the soul into the intellectual world..." In the Dialectic (532),

> This is that strain which is of the intellect only, but which the faculty of sight will nevertheless be found to imitate; for sight, as you may remember, was imagined by us after a while to behold the real animals and stars, and last of all the sun himself. And so with dialectic; when a person starts on the discovery of the absolute by the light of reason only, and without any assistance of sense, and perseveres until by pure intelligence he arrives at the perception of the absolute good, he at last finds himself at the end of the intellectual world, as in the case of sight at the end of the visible.

For Plotinus as well, the idea of fire does not exist in matter. The idea of fire, or light, is separate from fire as material, and the Ideal Fire "produces the form of fire throughout the entire enfired mass" (*Enneads* VI.5.8). The idea of fire exists in a "non-spatial world," because "a principle thus pluralized must first have departed from its own character in order to be present in that many and participate many times in the one same Form." Plotinus infused the Platonic dialectic of the sensible and intelligible into physical light itself, in the allegory of the central light diffused into a transparent sphere in the *Enneads* VI.4.7. Like the sun in the universe, the source of the light which is diffused through matter is impossible to connect to the light itself, thus there are two lights, as with Plato. The intelligible light of Plotinus is like the center of the circle, which is the source of all the radii of the circle, and thus of all the points along the circumference of the circle, as described in *Enneads* VI.5.5, but the center cannot be said to be a part of any of the radii, or any of the points along the circle, as Hegelian being-in-itself cannot participate in substance. In the allegory of the transparent sphere,

> Or imagine a small luminous mass serving as center to a transparent sphere, so that the light from within shows upon the entire outer surface, otherwise unlit: we surely agree that the inner core of light, intact and immobile, reaches over the entire outer extension; the single light of that small center illuminates the whole field. The diffused light is not due to any bodily magnitude of that central point which illuminates not as body but as body lit, that is by another kind of power than corporeal quantity: let us then abstract the corporeal mass, retaining the light as power: we can no longer speak of the light in any particular spot; it is equally diffused within and throughout the entire sphere. We can no longer even name the spot it occupied so as to say whence it came or how it is present; we can but seek and wonder as the search shows us the light simultaneously present at each and every point in the sphere. So with the sunlight; looking to the corporeal mass you are able to name the source of the light shining through all the air, but what you see is one identical light in integral omnipresence.

The central point illuminates as body lit because it is the physical manifestation of the intelligible light, not the intelligible light itself. It is the light of the Reason Principle, as instrument of the Intellectual Principle, through which the Idea, as intelligible light, enters into matter, as the sensible light of the sun, or the flame, which is in turn the intelligible light of the physical flame, which transforms the Idea into matter, as for Hegel the movements of the externalization of Spirit in the genesis from its being-in-itself are symbolized by the torrents of light.

The Hegelian Ego wills itself toward the Idea, as for Plotinus the soul wills itself toward the One. Thus the Subjective Spirit wills itself toward the Objective Spirit. Such is the "desire" of subjectivity, which defines the Ego. "This self-knowing subjectivity projects itself into all objectivity. This constitutes the Ego's certainty of its own existence. Inasmuch as this subjectivity has no other content, it must be called the rational desire….This is the sphere of its phenomenality. It wills itself in its particularity. At this point we find the passions, where individuality *realizes* its particularity. If it succeeds in thus realizing its finiteness, it doubles itself (its potential finiteness becomes actual finiteness)" (*Reason in History*, p. 33). The particular is self-generating in the same way as the universal, in the dialectical movement through the hypostases; in metaphysics the particular mirrors the universal, and the identical actions create the Neoplatonic *circuitus spiritualis* of reciprocal collection and emanation, *complicato* and *explicato.*

Particularity is realized in the passions because desire is a function of the body and soul. Because the Intellectual Principle has no body, it has no appetite or desire, according to Plotinus (*Enneads* IV.7.13). Appearances of being—correspondences and principles, measures and proportions, which are displayed in the arts—are stimulants of the desire of the soul for the good, the essence of being in the Idea, and representations of the Intellectual Principle as manifestation of the Idea. In the *Enneads* (II.9.16),

> What geometrician or mathematician could fail to take pleasure in the symmetries, correspondences and principles of order observed in visible things? Consider, even, the case of pictures: those seeing by the bodily sense the productions of the art of painting do not see the one thing in the one only way; they are deeply stirred by recognizing in the objects depicted to the eyes the presentation of what lies in the idea, and so are called to recollection of the truth—the very experience out of which Love arises.

Desire is the medium by which the suggestion of the essence of being is sought in the appearance of being. Forms and images are manifestations of the Idea, though weak and imperfect in comparison.

The subjective, or Subjective Spirit of Hegel, is the development from consciousness to self-consciousness, from nature to a psychological identity. The development of consciousness is phenomenology. The objective, or Objective Spirit, constitutes the laws and morals by which self-consciousness is manifest in society. The objective is composed of the interactions of individual subjectivity. The subjective and the objective combined form Absolute Spirit, in which the limits of both the subjective and objective are transcended, in an unlimited and unified identity which is expressed in art, religion, and philosophy. It is in this identity that Absolute Spirit is achieved, in which the individual transcends his role as subject of the state in a historical continuum and becomes a creator, participating in the absolute, or divine, Idea. Religion is the consciousness, on the part of the Spirit, of the identity of the subjective and objective. Art contains the same content. The Spirit (*Geist*), *Zeitgeist* in particular, is universality made particular in the reality of the state, the expression of which is culture. In order for a state to express itself as culture, it is necessary that the universal realize itself in the particular of the state. The unity of the subjective and objective in the state is morality.

Such a definition of the individual as creator in participation of the divine Idea can be found at the end of the Renaissance in the *scintilla della divinità* of the Accademia di San Luca in Rome. Federico Zuccari described the creativity of the artist as being the product of a *scintilla della divinità*, a spark of the divine fire within, which is connected to all artistic activity in the same way that each individual soul is connected to all souls, through the Intellectual Principle of Plotinus. The *scintilla della divinità* produces the *disegno interno*, internal design, which is then translated to *disegno esterno*, external design, or the physical drawing or building. *Disegno interno* is also *segno di dio in noi*, a sign of God in us, the Intellectual Principle transformed into the Reason Principle, which is then transformed into matter by the artist or architect acting as *architectus secundus deus*, a second god ordained to mimic the creation of the Platonic Demiurge. For Plotinus, *disegno interno* corresponds to the Shaping Principle, or the Intellectual Principle, or the Idea, a simple substance in the soul, in opposition to matter and the constituents of the soul. In the *Enneads* (V.9.3), in the soul there is "something representing Matter and something else—the Intellectual Principle in it—representing Idea, the one corresponding to the shape actually on the statue, the other to the artist giving the shape."

Plotinus described how the artist or architect acts as the *architectus secundus deus*, as the work of the artisan is the product of the soul or mind of the artisan in the same way that the elements of matter take their pattern from the soul of the cosmos through the Idea, which has been received by the soul from the Intellectual Principle. The Intellectual Principle is both the pattern of the soul and that which gives it its form or pattern, in the same way that the form of the work of art exists already in the mind of the artisan.

The expression of Absolute Spirit and the union of subjective and objective in art is the sensible correlate to such expression in religion and philosophy, according to Hegel. In art, the form of the divine and spiritual are represented as well as the spirit. Art "renders the divine visible to imagination and the senses" (*Reason in History*, p. 63). Plotinus described the hieroglyph in particular as rendering the divine visible to the senses, because the hieroglyph (mistakenly conceived) is "an object in itself, an immediate unity, not an aggregate of discursive reasoning and detailed willing" (*Enneads* V.8.6), and exhibits "an absence of discursiveness in the Intellectual Realm." The artistic image contains the appearance of being which suggests the essence of being, and its meaning can be intuited rather than understood through logic, so it transcends the Reason Principle, and communicates the Intellectual Principle, which participates in the divine.

Hegel describes the Spirit itself as an artificer capable of producing itself as object on a variety of levels in art. The first form of the artificer in art is the abstract form of understanding, capable of communicating the presence of the Idea in matter, but not being composed of Spirit-in-itself. The abstract form of the understanding is the crystalline geometric form, the pyramid or obelisk, "simple combinations of straight lines with plane surfaces and equal proportions of parts" (*Phenomenology* 691), described as "the works of this artificer of rigid form," like the Platonic Solids created by the children of the Demiurge. The crystalline form operates on the level of an "abstract intelligibleness" but does not contain Spirit in itself, because the abstract form is inorganic, and so does not communicate the Intellectual Principle, in Plotinian terms, because it does not combine soul and body, universal and particular. In order to communicate Spirit the artform must overcome the dialectic of soul and body, universal and particular.

In nature, the artificer uses organic form to communicate self-consciousness of Spirit as being-for-self. The organic form, which is only a casing or ornament for life forms, subsumes the rectilinear flat shapes corresponding to abstract forms of thought, and "left to itself, proliferates unchecked in particularity, being itself subjugated by the form of thought" (694). The organic form remains in the realm of the particular, but communicating a quality of Spirit, the conflation of the particular and universal, in symbol. The organic form is the "shape of individuality" (695) introduced into the aspect of the universal element, the abstract form, bringing Spirit nearer to existence, essence nearer to substance, making the form "more in harmony with active self-consciousness."

The form of the artificer of being-for-self in nature is the animal form, which is the self-conscious form of desire outside of the body, in that it is a form of body, but produced by Spirit which is necessarily bodiless. The animal form is thus a hieroglyph of thought in the Idea, of self-consciousness of Spirit. When the animal form is combined with thought itself, the result is the human form. But even the human form in nature does not express Spirit as essence or inner being. Although the human form is the form of self-consciousness, it cannot speak on its own, cannot communicate inner meaning, thought or idea. Even its external shape is only given by light in perception and remains only substance without essence, matter without Spirit, though it is the product of the self-consciousness of Spirit. In the Neoplatonic hierarchy the human form is still only *natura*, above body (*corpus*), but below soul (*anima*) and mind (*mens*) in the progression towards the absolute, according to Marsilio Ficino in the *Theologia Platonica*.

In order for nature to express the inner being within the outer shape it must withdraw into its essence and shed its "living, self-particularizing, self-entangling manifold existence" (*Phenomenology* 696) of crystalline and organic forms. The inner being first revealed is "still simple darkness, the unmoved, the black, formless stone," the dialectical otherness of light and self-consciousness in Spirit (perhaps a reference to the Black Stone in the Kaaba at Mecca). The inner being "of multiform existence is still soundless, is not immanently differentiated and is still separated from its outer existence" (697). The inner being as described in the *Phaedrus* (247) is "the abode of the reality with which true knowledge is concerned, a reality without color or shape, intangible but utterly real, apprehensible only by intellect which is the pilot of the soul." In the *Enneads* the inner being is "a sphere stripped of magnitude and of spatial differences" (V.8.9). For Hegel the unintelligible form of inner being is the product of the combination of nature and self-consciousness and "the darkness of thought mating with the clarity of utterance" (*Phenomenology* 697), the unexpressible and its form of expression, the non-conscious and conscious. Only such a union can express the absolute in form.

The expression of Spirit in form is the doubling of self-consciousness over against itself, the transcendence of matter in relation to consciousness. Shapes and symbols are dissolved into the spiritual essence of light; the outer form retreats inward, and the inner form is self-identical to the Idea. The inner form is the form of self-conscious activity, thought creating itself, without artificial mechanisms; "the artificer has given up the synthetic effort to blend the heterogeneous forms of thought and natural objects" (699). The inner form is "present to its own consciousness" as consciousness itself.

In the *Enneads*, all form in matter exists in a prior state, unmingled in contrast to the material, subject to the intellectual. As such matter is Idea (*Enneads* V.8.7), and as Idea form is essence in matter. Idea is imparted to matter by soul, as mind of the artificer; Idea is received by soul from the Intellectual Principle (the maker of this all). The artificer imparts the authentic reality as given by soul to form (V.9.3). Idea is an image of the authentic transferred to matter, a derivative of the "eternally unchanging," as Timaeus explains to Socrates (*Timaeus* 28–29). The Idea is "that which is and never becomes," as opposed to matter, which is "that which is always becoming but never is." The form of Spirit for Hegel is the presence of the former in the latter. The form of Spirit is "apprehensible by intelligence with the aid of reasoning, being eternally the same" in the words of Timaeus, while the form of matter is "the object of opinion and irrational sensation, coming to be and ceasing to be, but never fully real." The form of matter is the result of cause, the necessity of change (Timaeus: "everything that becomes or changes must do so owing to some cause"), the Principle of Sufficient Reason of Leibniz, while the form of Spirit is self-caused and self-sufficient. The material world has come into being because of the necessity of change, according to Timaeus, as it is "visible, tangible, and corporeal, and therefore perceptible by the senses." Nevertheless, if the world comes into being there must be another reality without becoming, from which the coming-to-be is a derivative; thus the world "must have been constructed on the pattern of what is apprehensible by reason and understanding and eternally unchanging; from which again it follows that the world is a likeness of something else." The form of Spirit of Hegel is the absence of coming-to-be, of sufficient reason and change.

The Artificer, or Authentic Being of Plotinus, is of the reality that is not the material world; if that is the case, then matter has no precedent or model, but is a product of the mind of the Authentic Being, the absolute, as *archê* or archetype, in which consciousness is self-identical, and consciousness and nature are undifferentiated, as in the form of Spirit. Thus "if the Intellectual-Principle is to be the maker of this all, it cannot make by looking outside itself to what does not yet exist. The Authentic Beings must, then, exist before this All, no copies made on a model but themselves archetypes, primals, and the essence of the Intellectual-Principle" (*Enneads* V.9.5).

In the *Phenomenology of Spirit*, the form of Spirit is the identity of the changing and the changeless, the outer substance and inner essence of the form, the identity of self-consciousness and essence, which is manifest in the religion of art (*Kunstreligion*) (748). The religion of art is a part of the ethical spirit of a culture, where the individual self is submerged in the universal, communal spirit (750). The form of Spirit in art is the externalization of the essence of the absolute, but it is enacted in the material forms of change, of "coming-to-be" (754). If the form of the coming-to-be is contained within itself, as an object of sensuous consciousness, then it is a "vanishing object" and aspires to "immediate unity with the universal self-consciousness." In that way the form of art is a part of the ethical spirit. If the form of art represents a world which is a universality and at the same time composed of the certainty of sensuous consciousness, then the form of art exists in the world "as existence raised into an ideational representation," as a form of the Idea in the Intellectual Principle, "the pattern of what is apprehensible by reason and understanding and eternally unchanging," as described by Timaeus. The forms of art as a whole "constitute the periphery of shapes which stands impatiently expectant around the birthplace of Spirit as it becomes self-consciousness" (*Phenomenology* 754), as the Idea is identified with sensuous consciousness (*das Sinnliche Scheinen der Idee*), essence with substance, the universal with the particular. At the center of the forms is the Absolute Idea, "the simplicity of the pure Notion," in which the forms are self-contained as "archetypes, primals, and the essence of the Intellectual-Principle" (*Enneads* V.9.5).

As in the *Timaeus* the world "must have been constructed on the pattern of what is apprehensible by reason and understanding and eternally unchanging; from which again it follows that the world is a likeness of something else" (29), so in the *Phenomenology of Spirit*, "remoteness in time and space is only the imperfect form in which the immediate mode is given a mediated or universal character; it is merely dipped superficially in the element of thought, is perceived in it as a sensuous mode, and not made one with the nature of thought itself. It is merely raised into the realm of picture-thinking (*Vorstellung*), for this is the synthetic combination of sensuous immediacy and its universality or thought" (764), the particular and universal. Form in matter is only a derivative or a copy of the idea of form; the nature of form does not correspond to the nature of thought. In order to participate in the universal, absolute, form in matter must be perceived, must become a form of "picture-thinking," thus perception is the medium between the absolute and material, sensuous consciousness. It is in picture-thinking, in perception, that universality and sensuous immediacy are identified, that is, in Plotinian terms, in the Intellectual Principle, through the Reason Principle, by means of the act of perceiving.

As in the Intellectual Principle, reason for Hegel "does not require, as does finite activity, the condition of external materials"; it is self-generating and self-supporting, and it is only in the *image* (*Bild*) of reason, in picture-thinking, through perception, that forms in matter are possible. Thus forms in matter depend on the development of Reason Principle to form; the picture of reality given by perception is the realization of reason. Without reason there would be no picture of reality; all mental images are pre-generated by the reasoning process, through perception. As Plotinus explained in the *En-*

neads (I.I.7), "The faculty of perception in the Soul cannot act by the immediate grasping of sensible objects, but only by the discerning of impressions printed upon the Animate [soul] by sensation: these perceptions are already Intelligibles, while the outer sensation is a mere phantom of the other (of that in the Soul) which is nearer to Authentic-Existence as being an impassive reading of Ideal-Forms." The discerning of impressions printed upon the soul by sensation is the function of reason, not perception, while perception is also a function of reason. Since the sensual impressions in perception are copies and derivatives of intelligible forms, perception itself is a copy and derivative of reason, which is closer to the intellectual, and thus absolute.

According to Hegel, it is through perception, or picture-thinking, that Spirit becomes self-conscious, as it would be in the Intellectual Principle of Plotinus, though perception itself is not the self-consciousness of Spirit. Spirit cannot attain self-consciousness in perception because perception entails the separation of being and reason, of being and coming-to-be. The content of being (*Dasein*) becomes multiple and particular in perception; it is subject to time through sequence, and measurement through proportion. Perception, or picture-thinking, consists of moments of being "appearing as completely independent sides which are externally connected with each other" (*Phenomenology* 765). The essence of being cannot be known by the level of consciousness as given by perception, but through perception self-consciousness of Spirit can be attained, in perception as a function of reason toward the understanding of the intelligible form.

Perception or picture-thinking is the middle term between Spirit and existence, the universal and particular. The self-consciousness of Spirit is its descent into existence. There is no corresponding explanation in Neoplatonism for the descent of the One into existence, other than that it is motivated by love. Picture-thinking, as the middle term, is the synthetic connection of Spirit and existence, the doubling of the self-consciousness of Spirit, the "consciousness of passing into otherness" (767). Picture-thinking is a manifestation of Spirit, as is the self-consciousness of the perceiving subject in the ascent through picture-thinking to Spirit. These three manifestations of Spirit correspond to Subjective Spirit (individual self-consciousness), Objective Spirit (collective picture-thinking), and Absolute Spirit, which correspond to the Plotinian hypostases (the One, Nous [Intellectual Principle], and soul [Reason Principle]). The "dissociation in picture-thinking" of Spirit "consists in its existing in a specific or determinate mode," which is one moment among many in the diffusion of the nature of Spirit throughout existence, as in Neoplatonic emanation. Picture-thinking corresponds to Objective Spirit in that it is a collective activity, a shared consciousness. Perception plays a role in Objective Spirit as the laws and morals by which self-consciousness is manifest in society, the multiple determinates of individual subjectivity. In the objectivity of picture-thinking, Spirit steps forward out of itself toward the absolute, where it is able to "become an actual Self, to reflect itself into itself" (766) in self-consciousness, through Objective Spirit as community, as collective picture-thinking.

In pure thought Absolute Spirit is "immediately simple and self-identical, eternal essence" (769), like the One of Plotinus. As an inner essence, Absolute Spirit is not a meaning or a signification, or even an existent, but being in its purest form. It is not the substance of picture-thinking or of reason, but rather the negative of thought, "the negativity of thought, or negativity as it is in itself in essence; i.e. simple essence is absolute difference from itself, or its pure othering of itself." Absolute Spirit is as the One of Pseudo-Dionysius in the mystical *via negativa*, where, as described in the *Mystical Theology* (136) "the pre-eminent cause of every object of sensible perception [and picture-thinking] is none of the objects of sensible perception,"[19] and the One is "the highest peak of mystic inspiration, eminently unknown yet exceedingly luminous, where the pure, absolute and unchanging mysteries of theology are veiled in the dazzling obscurity of the secret silence, outshining all brilliance with the intensity of their darkness, and surcharging our blinded intellects with the utterly impalpable and invisible splendor surpassing all beauty."[20] The otherness of Absolute Spirit is Objective Spirit, as given by picture-thinking in its differentiation, but the self-differentiation retains a self-unity as it returns back to itself through Objective Spirit, as in the *circuitus spiritualis*.

The otherness of Absolute Spirit is as the Other of Jacques Derrida in Deconstruction, the possibility of a no-place within a place, of the disruption and negation of metaphysical space or space given by philosophy as a model of the divine Idea. The Other of Deconstruction is not the positive infinity of God, as in negative theology, but rather "infinite alterity,"[21] and the "negativity of the indefinite," as in the *apeiron* of Anaximander, the Unlimited or Boundless, indefinite and eternal, undefinable by sense perception. As Derrida explains in *Writing and Difference* (p. 114),

> As soon as one attempts to think Infinity as a positive plenitude…the other becomes unthinkable, impossible, unutterable.…that the positive plenitude of classical antiquity is translated into language only by betraying itself in a negative word (in-

> finite), perhaps situates, in the most profound way, the point where thought breaks with language. A break which afterward will but resonate throughout all language. This is why the modern philosophies which no longer seek to distinguish between thought and language, nor to place them in a hierarchy, are essentially philosophies of original finitude.

Absolute Spirit exceeds meaning and signification in language, and representation in picture-thinking. As essence in pure thought it exceeds reason, as thought in identity with the object of thought. The identification of the infinite with the negative is the *chôra* of Plato, the no-place within a place, as in the Other of Deconstruction, and the place of coming-to-be. The disjunction between thought and language as given by the otherness of the absolute is the deferral of *différance* in Deconstruction. *Différance* is a kind of a *chôra*, a place of becoming which is a systematic play of differences, as defined by Derrida, that which is outside of meaning or signification, concept or word.

For Hegel the absolute unfolds toward existence in three stages—essence, being-for-self as the other of essence, and being-for-self as self-consciousness in the other (*Phenomenology* 770)—which correspond to Absolute Spirit, Objective Spirit, and Subjective Spirit, and the One, Nous, and soul. Being-for-self as the other of essence is an externalization, and the self-consciousness of essence itself, which is found in the collective, the intersection of the universal and particular, as in Intellectual Principle. Being-for-self as the other of essence is the word, signification in language, which "when uttered, leaves behind, externalized and emptied, him who uttered it, but which is as immediately heard, and only this hearing of its own self is the existence of the Word." The externalization of essence as other is the disjunction between thought and language, *différance*, the radical thrown-ness from essence or origin which constitutes thought in language.

The externalization of essence to other, thought to language, is a circular movement, because the distinction between thought and language dissolves as soon as it is made, and vice versa. Thought in reason is a spiraling out from the core of essence, and a spiraling back, as in the *circuitus spiritualis*, and the forms of the Baroque, representing a dynamic passage through the hierarchy of being, the interweaving of essence and substance, universal and particular. In the Baroque the absolute is a void, the ineffable and unknowable, the *via negativa* of Pseudo-Dionysius, the *docta ignorantia* of Cusanus, the *stupefazione*. For Hegel, the absolute is only a void when it is not grasped as Spirit (*Phenomenology* 771); as Spirit, it is being without existence, without signification, self-contained within itself, like the Plotinian One, presupposing reason.

The externalization of essence as other, and the self-consciousness of essence as other, in language, is picture-thinking, or perception, given by reason in signification (in language). The externalization is self-consciousness degrading the content of its nature (essence) through misunderstanding (*méconnaissance*), "into a historical pictorial idea." Thus only the external element is retained, and the inner essence vanishes. As Jacques Lacan describes in *Écrits*, *méconnaissance* is a function of the ego, the Subjective Spirit as it participates in the Objective Spirit; *méconnaissance* is found in "the existence of everything that the ego neglects, scotomizes, misconstrues in the sensations that make it react to reality, everything that it ignores, exhausts, and binds in the significations that it receives from language."[22] Essence itself, according to Hegel, is an other of Absolute Spirit, an abstraction in signification, a negation of the universal (*Phenomenology* 772). Essence is the other of the self-contained and undivided of the absolute in existence, thus the originary self-consciousness. But the difference between absolute and essence is immediately resolved in pure thought, or being, and is not differentiated as in reason or existence.

The otherness of the absolute is contained within itself in pure thought and being; the absolute contains the seed of differentiation and thrown-ness, as the *apeiron* of Anaximander contained the seed of differentiation in the origin of matter, like bark around a tree. In the cosmos of Anaximander, as described by Hippolytus, "The heavenly bodies arise as a circle of fire which is separated off from the eternal in the formation of this world, like bark around a tree. When this sphere was torn off and closed up into certain circles, the sun and moon and stars came into being."[23] The opposite qualities of hot and cold, wet and dry, etc., were generated as well, as in the Egyptian Ennead, and the dialectic of Love and Strife of Empedocles, the dialectical process of differentiation. As Empedocles described, "When Strife had reached to the lowest depth of the whirl, and Love was in the middle of the eddy, under her do all these things come together so as to be one, not all at once, but congregating each from different directions at their will."[24] The eternal is the Unlimited (*apeiron*), described by Simplicius in the *Commentary on Aristotle's* Physica as "the first principle of things that are. It is that from which the coming-to-be takes place, and it is that into which they return when they perish,"[25] as in the circular movement of Hegel.

According to Hippolytus, "Anaximander held that the Unlimited is the first-principle and is eternal, without age, and that it encompasses all the worlds; moreover that it is in perpetual activity, and that out of its activity the worlds have originated."[26] According to Aristotle, "The Unlimited encompasses and governs all things. On this basis the Unlimited is equivalent to the Divine, since it is deathless and indestructible, as Anaximander says and as most physicists who employ the term will agree" (*Physica* 203).[27] The Unlimited is the Boundless, or the *apeiron*, indefinite and eternal, undefinable by the senses or by the physical boundaries of place or space, as Absolute Spirit. The *apeiron* is an eternal and never-changing idea of space in being, not subject to the permutations of the world of matter in existence, as Plato described the nature of the Same in the *Timaeus*, which receives all things but is always separate from them: "the universal nature which receives all bodies—that must be always called the Same; for, while receiving all things, she never departs at all from her own nature, and never in any way, or at any time, assumes a form like that of any of the things which enter into her" (50).

The *apeiron* of Anaximander is a place which is a non-place, like the *chôra* of Plato, of creation and generation of matter. According to Pseudo-Plutarch, "Anaximander...said that the *apeiron* is wholly responsible for the generation and destruction of the totality of things; from it he says that the heavens are separated off and in general all the world orders which are infinite. He declared that destruction, and much earlier generation, happen from an infinite time as all of them come around in a cycle."[28] The *apeiron* is the space of the *archê*, which pre-supposes reason and existence. It is a space which pre-exists space, where the finite is created from the infinite, the particular from the universal. It is the *archê* itself, the One of Plotinus, the source of generation. As Aëtius described, "Anaximander...says that the principle of existent things is the *apeiron*. For from this all things are generated and into this all are destroyed."[29]

The *apeiron* is the self-sufficient center of being, the Unlimited, infinite, simple and unified source of all multiples and particulars; it is the One of Plotinus, as differentiated in the Intellectual Principle. The One, like the soul described by Plato in the *Phaedrus* (245), is the "self-moving, never leaving self," like the absolute of Hegel, which "never ceases to move, and is the fountain and beginning of motion to all that moves besides." The One is immortal, indestructible and unbegotten by anything else. In the *Timaeus* (27), "that which always is and has no becoming," and "that which is always becoming and never is," is "that which is apprehended by intelligence and reason," the essence of the absolute in signification.

In the *Phenomenology of Spirit*, as the Absolute Spirit, "eternal or abstract spirit" (774), self-sufficient being, passes into the alterity of existence, when elements of pure essence "spontaneously part asunder and also place themselves over against each other" (773), as in the model of Anaximander, the creation of the world of otherness is "picture-thinking," the self-consciousness of Spirit that manifests itself in perception, as in the Intellectual Principle. Essence is posited as existence and universal elements of essence are posited as particulars in the "dissolution of their simple universality and the parting asunder of them into their own particularity" (774), as in a biological model of creation. Spirit retains its presence in all particularity; Spirit is recognized in the particular when the individual self "has consciousness and distinguishes itself as 'other', or as world, from itself." The individual self must become an other to itself before it can recognize itself as Spirit, as Absolute Spirit must become other to itself to enter into existence. The self-consciousness of Spirit, and the individual self, as other, entails a withdrawal into itself, through self-consciousness. The individual self must become self-alienated, must see its existence as alien to being, in order to become conscious of its participation in Spirit, or essence.

According to Jacques Lacan, in *The Four Fundamental Concepts of Psycho-Analysis*, the point at which the individual self becomes alienated from its own being is the *objet a*; the *objet a* is the juncture between the symbolic structure, the picture-thinking of existence, and being, what is beyond signification. As the self is identified through representation in the signifying structure of existence, it becomes divided at the *objet a*, which is constituted by a lack, a void in the cycle of desire, which moves the subject from point to point in its signifying structure. As the subject "solidifies into a signifier"[30] in existence, the subject as signifier conceals the presence of being or essence within, which becomes a void or an absence. The individual self is alienated from being in its own *méconnaissance*, in the externalization of essence and the self-consciousness of essence in the signifying structure. In order to be undivided, the individual self must recognize its self-alienation from being, in order to participate in universal essence, or Spirit. In Plotinian terms, it must pass from Reason Principle to Intellectual Principle, from Soul to Nous, in order to participate in the One.

The individual self must negate itself as signifying structure in "the passage from discontinuity to the continuity of being,"[31] in the words of Jean-

Louis Baudry. At the point of discontinuity, alienation from being, the *objet a*, the self dissolves into a continuous universal of universal Spirit. The self is dissolved in the passage from the signifying structure of existence to being. The passage through the *objet a* is a transgression, a laceration of the signifying structure, of existence in picture-thinking. The *objet a* is a discontinuity between a primordial biological identity hidden in the unconscious, the *apeiron* of Anaximader, the *chôra* of Plato, that which precedes existence in being, and the visual manifestations of that structure in picture-thinking or existence. According to Georges Bataille, the signifying structure of existence is manifest in the "degrading chains of logic"[32] in reason, an abstract causal necessity, as in the Principle of Sufficient Reason, in which "acts undertaken with some rational end are only servile responses to a necessity."[33] It is necessary to lacerate the signifying structure in which the individual self is imprisoned, to participate in the essence of universal Spirit; thus "human life cannot in any way be limited to the closed systems assigned to it by reasonable conceptions."[34] For Hegel, the mechanisms for this transcendence are religion, art and philosophy, and the product of this transcendence, and the participation in universal Spirit, is an ethical and moral community.

In the *Phenomenology of Spirit*, "the transcended immediate presence of the self-conscious essence has the form of universal self-consciousness" (780), and "this notion of the transcended individual self that is absolute Being immediately expresses, therefore, the establishing of a community which, tarrying hitherto in the sphere of picture-thinking, now returns to itself as the Self," anticipating the words of Lacan and Bataille. In the *Enneads*, the transcendence of the Reason Principle to the Intellectual Principle toward the One, from self-consciousness to universal self-consciousness, has a moral and ethical imperative as well, toward a moral and ethical community, and the spirit of a culture.

In the Second Tractate of the First Ennead, "The Virtues," aspiration toward the intelligible is the source of order and virtue in the individual self. It is through the aspiration toward the idea of virtue that the individual self takes on the likeness of virtue; it is through participation in universal Spirit that the individual realizes the qualities of the universal Spirit in the particular. The principles of "Civic Virtues" in Reason Principle are imitations of the principles of Absolute Spirit in the eternal, unchanging, pure and unified essence which is not subject to the tumult of the senses, as in the *Timaeus* (43), where the turbulence of bodies in the embodiment of the soul creates a twisting and distortion of the mathematical and geometrical proportions which hold them together, and "they were twisted in all directions and caused every possible kind of shock and damage to the soul's circles, which barely held together, and though they moved, did so quite irregularly, now in reverse, now sideways, now upside down."

In the *Enneads*, the individual self aspires to the likeness of divine virtue in the intelligible: "it is from the Supreme that we derive order and distribution and harmony, which are virtues in this sphere…it is by our possession of virtue that we become like to Them" (I.2.1); "intently gazing, one sees the font and principle of Justice, another is filled with the sight of Moral wisdom, the original of that quality as found, sometimes at least, among men, copied by them in their degree from the divine virtue" (V.8.10). The Civic Virtues are "measured and ordered themselves and acting as a principle of measure to the Soul which is as Matter to their forming" (I.2.2), and "any participation in Ideal-Form produces some corresponding degree of Likeness to the formless Being there." In the *Phaedrus* (247), "the mind of a god, sustained as it is by pure intelligence and knowledge, like that of every soul which is destined to assimilate its proper food, is satisfied at last with the vision of reality, and nourished and made happy by the contemplation of truth." Participation in absolute virtue is by assimilation, as in the *Enneads*, "thus it will often happen that men climbing heights where the soil has taken a yellow glow will themselves appear so" (*Enneads* V.8.10).

But the individual self initially possesses "not the originals but images, pictures; and these it must bring into closer accord with the verities they represent" (I.2.4). Reason Principle must transcend the idea of the virtues in the images of the intelligible, in picture-thinking, and participate in the essence of the virtues in Intellectual Principle; individual virtues must be manifestations of the virtues of universal self-consciousness in phenomenology. For Plotinus, participation in the intelligible involves an *enthusiasmos*, a possession of the individual soul by the divine, the intelligible virtues. When the individual self is able to see the virtue within itself, it ceases to be just a spectator of the images of virtue in picture-thinking, in signification; the virtue is internalized, and the spectator is able to "bring the vision within and see no longer in that mode of separation but as we know ourselves; thus a man filled with a god [*enthusiasmos*]…need no longer look outside for his vision of the divine being" (V.8.10). And in the *Phenomenology of Spirit*, on a macrocosmic level, "this notion of the transcended individual self that is absolute Being immediately expresses, therefore, the establishing of a community which, tarrying hitherto in the sphere of picture-thinking, now returns to itself as the Self" (780).

The *enthusiasmos* of Plotinus is a means by which the individual self can transcend consciousness to self-consciousness and universal self-consciousness, or Subjective Spirit to Objective Spirit. In the *Enneads*, "any one, unable to see himself, but possessed by that God, has but to bring that divine within before his consciousness and at once he sees an image of himself, himself lifted to a better beauty: now let him ignore that image, lovely though it is, and sink into a perfect self-identity, no such separation remaining; at once he forms a multiple unity with the God silently present; in the degree of his power and will, the two become one..." (V.8.11). In ascending to universal self-consciousness and participating in universal Spirit, the individual self participates in the virtues of the Spirit, and is thus a microcosm of a moral and ethical community, as in the *Phenomenology of Spirit*. The means to facilitate this participation for Hegel are religion, art and philosophy.

Enthusiasmos requires a withdrawal into self, and an overcoming of self-identity as given by signification in language, and a discovery of being in self (*an sich* for Hegel). It requires the ability to see an inner light which is prior to sensible light, as in the *Enneads*, "there is an earlier light within itself, a more brilliant, which it sees sometimes in a momentary flash....This is sight without the act, but it is the truest seeing, for it sees light whereas its other objects were the lit not the light" (V.5.7). The light within is a vision of the Intellectual Principle, the intelligible and essence of being, beyond the sensible. The vision of the Intellectual Principle depends on a withdrawal from the world of matter, and of the signifying structure of language, so that the vision is "not of some light in some other thing but of the light within itself, unmingled, pure, suddenly gleaming before it." The individual penetrates into the sublime; "he must give himself forthwith to the inner and, radiant with the Divine Intellections (with which he is now one), be no longer the seer, but, as that place has made him, the seen....since sight deals with the external, there can here be no vision unless in the sense of identification with the object. And this identification amounts to a self-knowing, a self-consciousness, guarded by the fear of losing the self in the desire of a too wide awareness" (V.8.11). In universal self-consciousness the individual is simultaneously perceiver and the object of perception.

In universal self-consciousness it is necessary to be "self-gathered in the purity of your being" (I.6.9), to experience the essence of being as unmeasurable space, and the source of light as unmeasurable, and the substance of Spirit. The experience of the essence of being is the supersensible world beyond the "vanishing present" and the "twilight of becoming and perishing." Inner being is beyond consciousness and reason. It is the "stable image of unstable appearance," in Hegel's words (*Phenomenology* 149). The laws of perception, picture-thinking, and participation in the sensible world and the signifying structure, are copies and reflections of the laws of the absolute, Absolute Spirit, as given in the Intellectual Principle of Plotinus. The laws of the absolute, the universal, are visible in the laws of the sensible, the particular, as in art the viewer of the painting, according to Plotinus, is "stirred by recognizing in the objects depicted to the eyes the presentation of what lies in the idea, and so are called to recollection of the truth…" (*Enneads* II.9.16). The laws of nature are also derived from the laws of the absolute.

The universal laws of the absolute become visible for Plotinus when the Reason Principle, the signifying structure, is transcended to the Intellectual Principle, participating in the essence of being. Consciousness becomes self-consciousness and then universal self-consciousness, participating in the self-consciousness of the absolute; the perceiver becomes identical with the perceived; the knower becomes identical with the known, or the object of knowledge, and the individual self participates in the being-for-self of the absolute, the self-moving beyond the Principle of Sufficient Reason. For the individual self in the *Enneads*, "Many times it has happened: lifted out of the body into myself; becoming external to all other things and self-centered; beholding a marvelous beauty; then, more than ever, assured of community with the loftiest order; enacting the noblest life, acquiring identity with the divine; stationing within it by having attained that activity; poised above whatsoever within the Intellectual is less than the Supreme…" (IV.8.1). The universal laws of the absolute become visible in universal self-consciousness, beyond signification, and in the ethics of *enthusiasmos* the Spirit of a culture is realized. The individual self, as a member of the state, must will itself toward self-consciousness and participation in the divine, and sculpt its soul accordingly. "Withdraw into yourself and look. And if you do not find yourself beautiful yet, act as does the creator of a statue that is to be made beautiful….until there shall shine out on you from it the godlike splendor of virtue, until you shall see the perfect goodness established in the stainless shrine" (I.6.9).

5
The Aesthetics of Hegel

According to Hegel in the *Introductory Lectures on Aesthetics* (*The Introduction to Hegel's Philosophy of Fine Art*, 1886), beauty in art is a higher beauty than that of nature, because beauty in art is a product of the mind, or Spirit; the intellectual rather than the sensory, and freedom rather than necessity. In the *Symposium* of Plato, when the initiate learns to love all beautiful bodies rather than just one body, to "pursue the beauty of form" (210)[1] rather than the beauty of the body, to turn away from the "low and small-minded slavery" of love for the beauty of a body, and turn "towards the great sea of beauty and gazing on it he'll give birth, through a boundless love of knowledge, to many beautiful and magnificent discourses and ideas," the initiate ascends to the beauty of mind which is higher than the beauty of nature and which can be represented in art, in the beautiful and magnificent discourses and ideas. Thus for George Wilhelm Friedrich Hegel, the beauty of art is "born—born again, that is—of the mind [*Geist*, Spirit]..." (*Introductory Lectures on Aesthetics* II).[2]

In the *Symposium*, the beauty of mind is to be found in the goodness of mind, the good, so real beauty will be found in goodness, "practices and laws," in comparison to the beauty of the body, the beauty of nature. In that goodness, practices and laws, the activities of reason, are subjects of knowledge, or forms of knowledge, it is forms of knowledge which become the higher beauty. In the *Introductory Lectures on Aesthetics*, "mind, and mind only, is capable of truth, and comprehends in itself all that is, so that whatever is beautiful can only be really and truly beautiful as partaking in this higher element and as created thereby" (III). Following Kant, all reality is given by mind, but ultimately for Hegel, in the interaction between mind (Spirit) and the sensory world given by perception, which is a product of mind, as in the Transcendental Idealism of Schelling, reconciling the gap between the Platonic Idea, as in the idea of beauty, and the sensible world, or the idea of beauty as it is applied to the objects of perception. Mind "comprehends in itself all that is," so that sensible beauty can exist in the real, but it is a product of the ideal, in Schelling's terms, of mind. The beauty of nature thus "reveals itself as but a reflection of the beauty which belongs to the mind, as an imperfect, incomplete mode of being..." Beauty in nature is a product of mind inserting itself into the sensible world, of coming to terms with what mind perceives as being alien to it, as Hegel explains at length in the *Phenomenology of Spirit*.

In the *Timaeus* of Plato, the reflections of sensible appearance, as in the reflection of beauty of Hegel, are caused by the interaction of the interior and the exterior in perception, between the intellectual and the sensible, as in Transcendental Idealism, described by Plato as internal and external fires. "And the principles governing reflections in mirrors and other smooth reflecting surfaces are not that difficult to understand. All such appearances are necessary consequences of the combination of the internal and external fire, which form a unity at the reflecting surface, though distorted in various ways, the fire of the face seen coalescing with that of the eye on the smooth reflecting surface" (*Timaeus* 46).[3] The interaction of the internal and external fires results in sensible appearances, composed of distortions, reflections and shadows, momentary manifestations in the flux of being. Images in the sensory world do not exist without being perceived; they are the products of mind, their qualities are given by mind, and they are understood by reason in mind. Sensory appearances as we understand them are self-reflections of mind, which is why an understanding of perception is necessary for an understanding of the phenomenology of mind.

The sensory world for Hegel must be seen as an imperfect and incomplete mode of being, as it is given by mind, but not all of mind. That aspect of mind which tells itself that the sensory world is a reflection of mind, that is, self-consciousness, is not present in the sensory world. The self-consciousness of mind reveals the presence of mind in sensory perception; both mind and sensory appearance thus participate in the absolute, which is the unity (or indifference, in Schelling's terms) of mind and sensory perception, of the ideal and real. The self-consciousness of mind reveals the necessity of the absolute in existence, of the grounds of the relation between the perceiving mind and what is perceived. The absolute is present in what is perceived, but it is not revealed by perception, perception being a function of reason, a dissemination of the absolute in logic which thus cannot participate in the absolute (based on the relation between the One of Plotinus and both intellect and sensory appearance).

The absolute, or Absolute Spirit, manifest in the sensible world, can be revealed in the highest form of Spirit in intellect, that is Objective Spirit, as it is represented most completely in philosophy, then poetry, then art. Absolute Spirit in the sensory world is revealed through art; it is through art that it is possible to come to understand the relation between the perceiving mind and what it perceives, because art (the visual arts) both represents and enacts that relationship. The aesthetics of Hegel, as unfolded in the *Introductory Lectures on Aesthetics* (based on lectures given in the 1820s) and *The Philosophy of Fine Art*, are an attempt to demonstrate how art is a function of philosophy in the understanding of mind and perception, in the framework and categories established in the *Phenomenology of Spirit* (1807), later developed in the *Philosophy of Mind* (1830). Those categories include most importantly Absolute Spirit, Objective Spirit, and Subjective Spirit in the human intellect, which correspond in important ways to the One, the Intellectual Principle, and the Reason Principle of Plotinus.

Despite the systematic exposition of art and perception, their subjection to categories, descriptions, typologies and teleologies, the understanding of art and perception is not a scientific one, but a philosophical one. The philosophical systems of both Schelling and Hegel are responses to the scientific era, attempts to legitimize philosophy in relation to science. To that end, both philosophers attempt to revise classical philosophical tenets, in particular those of Platonism and Neoplatonism, within the intellectual framework of scientific thought, by employing such means as syllogistic and dialectic reasoning, Systematic Reason, and empirical analysis to as great an extent as possible, as in the *Wissenschaft* of Fichte. Nevertheless, the philosophical systems of Schelling and Hegel are principally metaphysical, and cannot be defined by scientific thinking. Art thus is "not made any more worthy of scientific discussion by such treatment" (*Introductory Lectures on Aesthetics* VI), because of the nature of perception itself, which is given by self-consciousness of mind, and thus cannot be subject completely to the empirical processes and observations of mind. The study of art and perception by mind is a self-study of mind itself; science, as a function of mind in reason, is not self-reflective, and cannot take account of its own ground, the ground of its processes. Thus the importance of phenomenology, and the Philosophy of Spirit, in the scientific era, to attempt to come to terms with questions posed about the nature of being which are outside the limits of scientific investigation. The study of art and perception is a medium toward that end. The more scientific and systematic the philosophical process, the more that philosophy can borrow from science and logic, the more complete will be the philosophical system. To that end, Philosophy of Spirit, like Transcendental Idealism, attempts to combine Metaphysical Idealism, Philosophy of Nature (perceived as a science), and Identity Philosophy, the subject of which is the relation between the human mind and nature.

The basic problem posed by Philosophy of Spirit, and of the aesthetics of Hegel, is the problem posed by Plato on the truth of perception, whether what is perceived should be taken as real in the understanding of both mind and nature. The status of both science and philosophy, as well as psychology, at the beginning of the twenty-first century, still bears out the importance of this basic problem posed by Plato. The generation of Schelling and Hegel, the beginning of the scientific era, established the discontinuity between human reason and nature. Until then nature had been understood as corresponding to human reason, despite the problematic nature of that relation; nevertheless, it had always been accepted that the human mind understands nature by recognizing processes and qualities which the mind sees in nature as they relate to mind. In the Philosophy of Spirit, nature is seen as given by mind, a product of mind, in the understanding of its processes; thus it became impossible to accept an understanding of nature based on reason, of which it was itself a function.

Scientific development confirmed that impossibility; the empirical methods of science established continuously, beginning with Galileo, that nature in fact does not function according to the principles or categories of human reason; that despite the fact that nature is given as it is understood by reason, it does not correspond to reason. This is the metaphysical dilemma posed by modern philosophy, beginning with Schelling and Hegel; it is certainly at the base of the major movements of the past two centuries: Phenomenology, Existentialism, Deconstruction. In science, Chaos Theory and Catastrophe Theory, for example, have exacerbated the problematic relationship between human reason and nature, and this problematic relationship has been at the core of the science of psychoanalysis in the twentieth century, in the figures of Freud, Lacan, Bataille, etc.

Thus the principal subject of art in the twentieth century is the impossibility of the relationship between the human mind and nature, from the semantic void of Metaphysical painting, to the reign of the unconscious in Surrealism, to the distortions in perception of Cubism, to the impossibility of meaning in Dadaism, to the attempt to establish a *gestalt* relation between man and nature in Abstract Expressionism, to the abandonment of categories of signification in Postmodern expression at the end of the twentieth century. The break between the classical world and the modern world occurs with Kant, Schelling and Hegel, and the content of Romantic art. Philosophy and art are clearly read today in relation to the foundations established in Transcendental Idealism, the Philosophy of Spirit, and the aesthetics of Romanticism, though they might be put toward different ends.

Ironically, it was the goal of both Schelling and Hegel to come to terms with the modern scientific era by establishing a synthesis between the classical and the modern, rather than a break between the two. It is the nature of the dialectic, the principal instrument of logic in these philosophies, that two sets of ideas or systems be both antithetical and synthetic. The philosophies of Schelling and Hegel are not the product of the revolutionary desire to reject history (defined as Modernism in art and architecture) that would surface in the twentieth century; they are rather the product of the desire to come to terms with the present in a historical framework. Despite the radical differences in the epistemologies of the classical world and the modern world, the subject of philosophy is the same, the nature of the human mind, which is the same entity in both eras. To understand the framework in which the mind operated in the classical world, the epistemologies or structures of knowledge that determined thought in the pre-scientific era, is to better understand the nature of the human mind in the scientific era.

Schelling and Hegel were the first philosophers to attempt that epistemological synthesis, and their writings must be seen as a foundation for contemporary philosophical investigation, as well as for aesthetic theory, and artistic production. This has certainly not been lost on most contemporary philosophers. The purpose of these essays is to better understand the philosophies of Schelling and Hegel in relation to the classical philosophies with which they attempted to synthesize their own world-views. Classical philosophy must still be seen as a basis for the formulation of theories in art and aesthetics, and for philosophical investigation. A neglect of classical philosophy results in an incomplete understanding of the human mind, because, as Hegel established, history itself is a product of mind, along with philosophy and art, thus to neglect history, as product of mind, is to neglect mind itself, that is, the human intellect. The synthesis of Hegel, in the framework of modern epistemology, is the beginning of philosophical investigation and aesthetic theory in the modern world.

At the core of the basic problem posed by Plato in the relation between mind and nature, or the world of sensory appearance, is the nature of perception. Largely, for Plato, perception is a matter of deception; it is a misrepresentation of the world which is given to human intellect through it. The sensible form in art is described as a "shadowy thing compared to reality"[4] in the *Republic* (597), a representation which "stands at a third remove from reality," being a representation of sensible form, which is itself a representation of the Idea, the idea of the form in the intellect, which constructs the perception of it. If the sensible form represents the idea, the perception of it cannot be the reality of it, or the complete reality, and thus the representation of it is deceptive in relation to what must be its real and complete nature or being. In the *Republic* (510), the sensible forms, or images in perception, are described as "shadows, then reflections in water and other close-grained, polished surfaces," etc., the images being reflections of objects in the realm of the visible.

On the other side of the divided line, in the realm of the intellect, "the mind uses the originals of the visible order in their turn as images, and has to base its inquiries on assumptions and proceed from them not to a first principle but to a conclusion"; otherwise, the mind "moves from assumption to a first principle which involves no assumption, without the images used in the other sub-section [of that side of the divided line, the intellect], but pursuing its inquiry solely by and through forms themselves," the example being the students of geometry who "make use of and argue about visible figures, though they are not really thinking about them, but about the originals which they resemble." The actual geometrical figures, which "themselves cast their shadows and reflections in water," are themselves seen only as images as given in perception, their real form being invisible, "except to the eye of reason."

The problem is that both the forms and the images that they cast are given to reason through perception as images; they are thus always already functions of reason, of mind; thus how can mind have any certainty of the image which it perceives, any certainty of the existence of the image separate from mind, outside the perception of it, if it understands that image to be a product of its own processes, and imbued with its qualities? Sensible forms as they are perceived are not only a misrepresentation of their true reality as products of mind, they are a misrepresentation of mind to itself in the process of perception. The mind is thus differentiated and self-alienated, set against itself, in the theory of perception of Plato, and, as will be seen, in the Philosophy of Spirit of Hegel.

The concept of beauty falls into this self-alienation and deception of mind in perception, because beauty is an idea, a quality dependent on mind, but it has existence only in sensible form, in appearance. The ascent of the initiate in the *Symposium*, from love of the beauty of one body, to love of the idea of the beautiful body, to love of the idea of beauty, is a transition from the visible to the intelligible, across the divided line of the differentiation and self-alienation of mind; it is an attempt to reconcile that self-alienation, that primordial dehiscence of mind in perception, in a dialectical synthesis of mind and what it perceives. The product of the synthesis is the absolute, absolute beauty, which combines intellect and sensible form into one totality, the indifference of the ideal and the real in Schelling's terms. The existence of an absolute provides an explanation as to why the mind is self-alienated, and why it cannot recognize itself in the sensible world. Post-Hegelian philosophy has given up such hopes for reconciliation, because it has become clear that the reason why mind cannot recognize itself in the sensible world, in nature, is because it does not exist there, though the "there" is still a product of mind. Mind remains self-alienated in philosophy, without the possibility of reconciliation. Art, for Schelling and Hegel, is the stage on which the reconciliation would take place, represented literally in Classical art, and represented by the presence of both the self-alienation and the absolute as reconciliation in Romantic art.

It is clear from the allegory of the divided line in the *Republic* that perception and the relation between the perceiving subject and the world which it perceives, between the intelligible and the sensory, between reason and images of forms, cannot be explained in a scientific manner. For Hegel, art is the principal medium through which to explore that relation because art does not involve only reason and logic. Art also involves intuition, perception itself, and imagination, the creative process of the mind. Art also involves freedom, a lack of necessary correspondence to the laws of cause and effect in nature, or to the laws and categories of reason or logic. Art is a representation, in Schelling's terms, of the freedom of the ideal, intellect, in relation to the necessity of the real. For Hegel the beauty of art is its freedom, the representation of that element of intellect which is present in the sensory world, but unrevealed by perception, as perception corresponds to the laws of reason. As the sensory world is misrepresented by perception, art is the possibility of the rectification of that misrepresentation, in the resolution of the self-alienation of mind. The beauty of art is the beauty of that possibility, the re-affirmation of the belonging of the human being in the world. The aesthetics of art in the twentieth century represent a challenge to the idea of beauty, as it is taken as a representation of that possibility, and the idea of beauty changes in culture as the self-definition of the individual changes in culture.

Art, then, for Hegel, is as well a record of the self-identification of the individual in a culture, and the self-identification of a culture, in particular in relation to the idea of beauty. In Classical art, beauty is a product of the identity of the ideal and real, intellect and the sensory world, for the purposes of the re-affirmation of belonging in the world of an intellectually undeveloped culture. In Romantic art, beauty is the result of the recognition of the self-alienation of the subject in the world, and the desire to reconcile the divided state in a harmonious synthesis. In the modern world, or the post-modern world, the idea of beauty in art is a rejection of the idea of beauty as a sign of a reconciliation; as the possibility of reconciliation is rejected, or the possibility of a synthetic relationship between mind and the sensible world, the idea of beauty as such is rejected, and beauty is seen as the absence of the idea of beauty, in *informe*, the abject, Deconstructivism, etc. A postmodern work is beautiful in its denial of the idea of beauty as a sign of the possibility of the overcoming of the state of self-alienation of mind, as given by post-Hegelian philosophy. For Hegel, the beauty of art is in its freedom in that it differentiates itself from the sensible world and expresses the intellect in contradiction to it, as being superior to the sensible world, in Platonic terms, being the origin of the sensible world, as it is given by perception.

Introductory Lectures on Aesthetics

In art, for Hegel, the categories and laws of reason, those by which reason is seen in nature, can be transcended. The categories and laws of reason are manifest in the "shadowland of the idea" (*Introductory Lectures on Aesthetics* VII), the reflections and forms on the other side of the divided line from mind in the *Republic*, which are given by reason in perception. Art, in that it functions through perception, is precisely the means to represent that which perception itself cannot, that is the absolute, the identity of mind and form, the erasure of the divided line of Plato. Thus "in the forms of art we seek for repose and animation in place of the austerity of the reign of law and the somber self-concentration of thought" (*Introductory Lectures on Aesthetics*

VII); repose and animation in intellect are given by understanding of the absolute, of reconciliation, of reassurance in being which has been lost in reason. The human being desires to both transcend the laws and limitations of reason through reason itself, in the dialectic, or in science, which gives reason a higher purpose and dispels the responsibility of reason to itself, or to transcend the laws and limitations of reason in non-reason, intuition, the imagination, and the mystical experience of the absolute, or the divine, in *katharsis* or *ecstasis*. Art provides for the repose of reason and the self-concentration of thought in relation to the sensory world within being. It provides a window of escape, a dissolving of alienating boundaries, lacerating chains of logic, as Georges Bataille would put it, an ecstatic state of mind achievable both through the highest development of reason and in the ultimate negation of reason. This dual possibility in art first became visible in the Baroque, when scientific thought and religious faith first co-existed side by side in the same epistemological structure of a culture.

For Hegel, the forms created by the artist are infinite in comparison to the forms created by nature, because mind is infinite, while the organic in nature is not. Organic forms in nature can only be finite representations of the infinite possibilities of the absolute in nature, while in art the infinite can be represented as itself, infinitely, in both content and form. In content, the infinity of art corresponds to the infinite creativity of the mind of the artist, as ideas in the intellect are unrestricted by their material counterparts. In form, the infinite can be represented symbolically in all forms of art, and schematically in the forms of art least restricted by their material condition, namely painting in the visual arts, and poetry in the lyrical arts (borrowing categories from Schelling). The finite representation of the infinite in art is the sublime, the suggestion of the possibility of the infinite within the finite; the combination of the infinite, that is, freedom, with the finite, the sensible form, is beauty in art. In that nature, the sensible world, is given by mind, nature is a finite category of mind; obviously, to imitate natural forms in art is to not do justice to the infinite quality, the freedom, of mind, as a function of the absolute, the reconciliation of mind and nature.

Art is "excluded from science" (VIII) because the subject of science is the finite set of particulars which are manifestations of the absolute in the sensible world; science applies universal categories to particular forms and activities, while art applies particular forms to universal ideas. Similar to science, as a function of reason, language extracts universal ideas from particulars, words, as they are combined in syntax. Science does not reveal the absolute because its subject is limited to the particulars, to which universal categories may be applied, but only as particulars themselves, as they become particulars as they are inserted into the real, the phenomenal. Language may reveal the absolute, like the visual arts, because the universal ideas which are extracted from the words, the meaning which is extracted from the syntax, can be maintained as thought, separate from the phenomenal forms, though subject to temporal duration. Temporal duration itself is a set of categories of particulars in relation to the absolute, thus language is also not capable of complete revelation of the absolute, other than the *logos* itself, which is not subject to temporal duration. Science, as it "is compelled by its form to busy itself with thought which abstracts from the mass of particulars," deals only with the necessary, the Principle of Sufficient Reason in matter and organism.

Art, if treated on a purely intellectual level, reduces its possibilities to a "simplicity devoid of reality" and a "shadowy abstractness." Art must transcend reason in order to reveal the absolute. Philosophy, as well, must transcend reason in order to reveal the absolute; philosophy is ultimately more than reason and logic, and a form of artistic expression. Art, as a mechanism of philosophy, must transcend the intellectual in order that both it and philosophy accomplish what science does not, as it does not transcend the intellectual, which is to pose the question of the being of the intellectual itself, in relation to the phenomenal world, as in the *Phenomenology of Spirit*. As philosophy must look beyond the categories of science to achieve its purpose, aesthetics must look beyond the beauty of nature to achieve its purpose, which is the content of Romantic art. Nature is given by science as being not only governed by necessity, but also by uniformity and rule; even in contemporary Chaos Theory and Catastrophe Theory, the absence of uniformity and rule in natural occurrences is only known through systematic categorization, through the logic and discipline of empirical knowledge and research; such absence is not self-evident in the forms of nature.

In art, the absence of uniformity may be revealed directly in the forms, allowing the artwork to express the "caprice and lawlessness" (*Introductory Lectures on Aesthetics* VIII) of the imagination, as a function of the infinite in the ideal, or in mind, and the universal detached from a finite set of particulars. Perhaps the painter who best displayed the potential for the absence of uniformity and the infinite set of potentials in the imagination, as a function of the absolute, in the twentieth century, was Pablo Picasso. Though the forms of Picasso themselves were limited to the finite, the variation of the forms in relation to the sensible forms of nature, in Picasso's case the human body, suggested a set of possibilities beyond nature itself, as in the *Guernica* of 1937 (Figure 5). Though situated firmly in the real, the configurations in the paintings revealed the absolute as the identity of the real and the ideal, of natural forms and mind, the imagination of which alone was capable of producing the forms of the paintings.

Picasso, as well, abandoned the imitation of natural forms, and the representation of the beauty of natural forms, in the identity of mind with nature; the paintings illustrate the self-alienated mind of post-Hegelian philosophy, and the violence of that self-alienation. The idea of beauty is challenged in the artificial configurations; the forms are beautiful in their lack of beauty as defined by Classical art, in their expression of modern consciousness. The artificial beauty of the forms suggests that man, though no longer at home in his relationship with the sensible world as given to him by perception, and in his identity with nature, is now at home in the revelation of the absolute in his imagination, unmediated by natural forms, though predicated by them. In the imagination, as expressed in art, the infinite possibilities given by the absolute, before becoming categories of particulars as given by reason, are felt as if at home, and they "withdraw themselves as a matter of course from all scientific explanation"; art presents the possibilities for being which reason cannot; it thus reassures mind in its participation of the absolute in modern consciousness.

Art thus seeks to "resist the regulating activity of thought," though art functions in many ways similar to thought itself. Art is a form of thought which is able to transcend certain limitations of thought in reason. Reason for the most part, like science, "submits to be used for finite purposes" (*Introductory Lectures on Aesthetics* XI). Logic in reason, and scientific method in reason, are means to achieve a concrete and clearly defined goal, which itself is a servant of reason, in the self-perpetuation of reason as a function of desire in the real, satisfying the relation of reason to the real, to the finite necessities of existence. Like the cycle of desire, reason carries thought from one point to the next, as being, though predicated on matter external to it, self-sufficient in relation to what is external to it. Science is "not self-determined, but determined by alien objects and relations; but, on the other hand, science liberates itself from this service to rise in free independence to the attainment of truth..." Intuition, on the other hand, in particular artistic intuition, in that it is predicated on perception, *is* self-determined, but its end is only found in the universal, the relation between the individual subject and the *Geist* in which it participates. Science abstracts particulars into universals, while art concretizes universals into particulars.

Art is the principal means, along with philosophy and religion, of the self-understanding of a culture; art is the purest expression of the *Geist* of the culture. In that art represents the ideal in the real, thought in matter, it communicates in a direct and powerful way. Art represents a "supra-sensuous world, which is thus, to begin with, erected as a *beyond* over against immediate consciousness and present sensation" (XIII); this world is represented within consciousness and sensation. Such representation is parallel to the revelation of the divine, and the universal in the particular. Consciousness and sensation are the "*here*, that consists in the actuality and finiteness of sense"; the means by which the *beyond* is accessed is that element of thought in reason which is free, not governed by necessity. Art is a reconciliation between the here and beyond, between necessity and freedom, the particular and universal; it is an instrument of the dialectical process of reason, it is that dialectical process.

The forms of art are shadows and deceptive appearances of the higher reality, the beyond, as for Plato, but the beyond cannot exist without the here, as freedom cannot exist without necessity. Universals can only exist as abstractions of particulars, and particulars only exist as manifestations of universals. Particulars are only meaningful if they reveal the universal; universals are only meaningful if they provide a basis for particulars. It is impossible to have a complete conception of existence, given the interaction of thought and sensation, or the idea and the sensible world, if particulars are not taken in relation to universals, and vice versa, and engaged in the dialectical process. Sensible form in appearance is a particular that can only be understood in relation to a universal; if it is not, then it is a distraction from the whole of existence. "Genuine reality is only to be found beyond the immediacy of feeling and of external objects" (XIV), but it can only be known in relation to that sensible world.

That which is "genuinely real," which combines the idea and the sensible so that it is not a distraction from the essence of existence, is that which preserves the universal in the particular, that which preserves its "self-centered being" in the sensible world, self-dependence. For Plotinus in the *Enneads*, to be "poised above whatsoever within the Intellectual" is to be "external to all other things and self-encentered" (IV.8.1).[5] Art for Hegel is potentially that which is genuinely real in that it has the capacity to reveal the universal

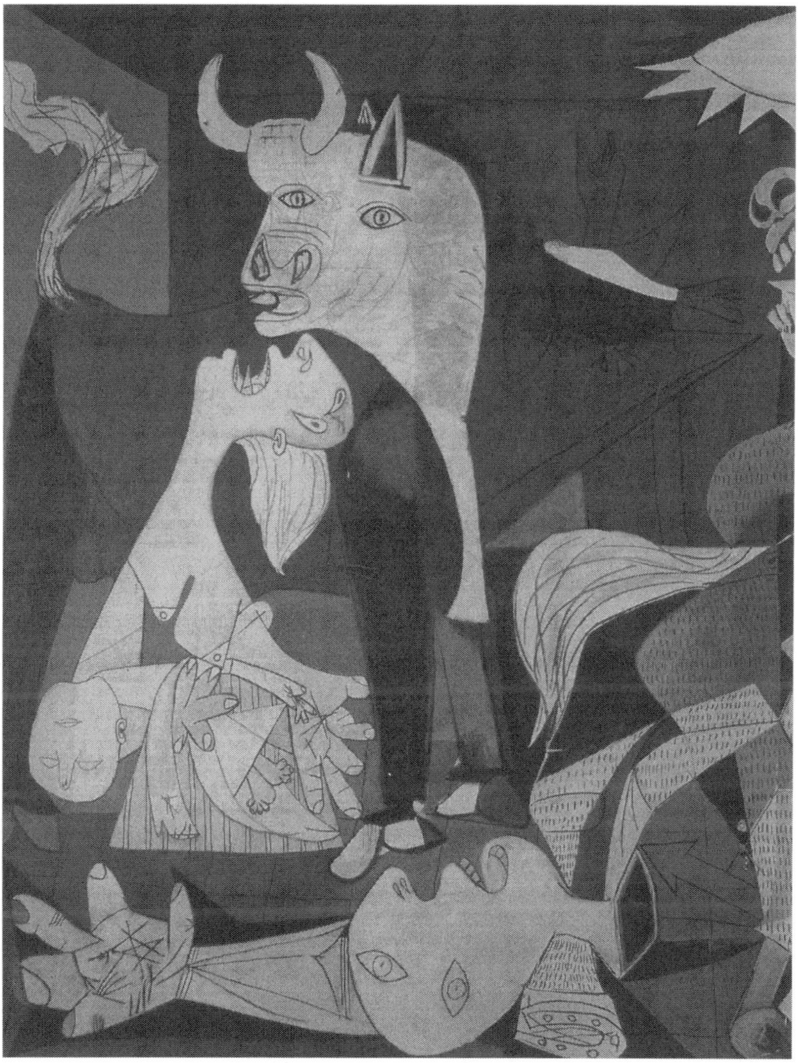

Figure 5. Pablo Picasso, *Guernica*, detail (© 2004 Estate of Pablo Picasso/Artists Rights Society [ARS], New York)

in the particular. That which is eternally real contains both the human and the divine; it is that which manifests the eternal in the finite in the form of the beautiful and the good, which is, as in the *Phaedrus* of Plato, "absolute justice and discipline and knowledge, not the knowledge which is attached to things which come into being, nor the knowledge which varies with the objects which we now call real..." (247).[6] The universal which art is capable of revealing in the thought of Hegel is an ethical universal, a universal of ethical relationships which creates community. The universal values of a community are manifest in its individual members in the same way that universal ideas are manifest as particular forms in artistic representation. Art can serve as a heuristic device for the role of the individual in relation to the state, for the identity of the individual in relation to the ethics of the state. This was certainly not lost on Jacques-Louis David, in paintings such as the *Oath of the Horatii* of 1784, or *The Death of Socrates* of 1787.

Art for Hegel has the capacity to identify ways in which the particular may be related to the universal, which sensory perception and logic in reason do not, because art inserts the intelligible into the sensory world, and thus reveals the relation between the universal and the particular. The sensory world is given by perception as "a chaos of accidental matters, encumbered by the immediateness of sensuous presentation, and by arbitrary states, events, characters, etc." (*Introductory Lectures on Aesthetics* XIV). The sensory world is a "fleeting world" of semblance and deception, as in the declaration by Paul Cézanne in the conversation with Joachim Gasquet: "Nature is fleeting, isn't it? Nature is always the same, but nothing about her that we see endures. Our art must convey a glimmer of her endurance with the elements, the appearance of all her changes. It must give us the sense of her eternity."[7] As for Cézanne, for Hegel "art liberates the real import of appearances from the semblance and deception of this bad and fleeting world, and imparts to phenomenal semblances a higher reality, born of mind" (*Introductory Lectures on Aesthetics* XIV). The reality of forms of art is higher than the reality of objects of perception in the sensible world, because the forms of art define and identify sensible forms of matter in relation to the universal, the idea, of which they are manifestations, in the definition of thought and perception, in the interaction between mind and matter.

The sensuous forms of art (*das sinnliche Scheinen*), in their representation or embodiment of the eternal, may be seen as being more genuine in relation to the eternal than the forms of matter, and the forms that constitute historical narrative, but less genuine than the intelligible forms of philosophy and religion. Historical narrative is a purely intellectual construct, extracted from the particulars of memory; the historical dialectic is insubstantial in relation to the dialectic of art in revealing the relation between the finite and infinite, while the idea in philosophy in religion synthesizes the finite and infinite in the ideal, the realm of the intellectual, which is closer to the absolute, in the Platonic tradition. The sensuous form in art always refers to something other than itself, as a symbol, or a signifier, or a combination of the two;[8] as the particular form symbolizes the universal idea, the artform reveals the ideal in the real, as for Schelling.

The manner in which the artform reveals the ideal in the real is contingent upon the epistemological framework of the culture which produces the art. The paintings of Piero della Francesca, Paul Cézanne, and Mark Rothko, for example, are each intended to reveal the ideal in the real, the universal in the particular. For Piero, as a product of the early Renaissance, the mechanism for such revelation is in the juxtaposition of real space and perspectival space; for Cézanne, a product of the scientific era, the mechanism involves the relativity of perspectival points of view, the juxtaposition of rounded surfaces and plane surfaces, and again the superimposition of a constructed field of vision on real space as given by color and light. For Mark Rothko, a product of the revolution in psychoanalysis, the mechanism involves the juxtaposition of geometry and color, geometry being the embodiment of matter in the painting, as well as the symbol of the interaction of the ideal and real, and the color being the identity of the real and ideal in the real. In psychoanalysis, the ideal is found in the unconscious, and the real in the conscious; the dialectic of the ideal and real is thus the dialectic not only of the relation between the human subject and the world, but of the human subject in relation to itself as well.

Hegel asserts that the artform "refers us away from itself to something spiritual which it is meant to bring before the mind's eye" (XV). The ideal is not represented in the real in perception, that is, it is not possible to see the absolute; the ideal is represented in the ideal in thought, which constructs the mechanisms of perception, then seeks to intuit that which is beyond its limitations. Sensual form in matter does not appear to be deceptive to perception, but it appears as deceptive to thought in the ideal. Sensual form in art does appear to be deceptive to perception, but does not appear to be deceptive to thought. Art inverts thought and perception in relation to each other; that which is given by perception is the dialectical antithesis of that which is given by thought. The "mind's eye" is the correlation of the mechanism of sight in the ideal; the mind "sees" the archetypes of that which the eye sees in the sensible world, like the geometer in the *Republic*, who while he "sees one circle, he is studying another, the circle in the understanding, yet he makes his demonstrations about the former" (511). As described in the *Enneads*, "In the intellectual, the vision sees not through some medium but by and through itself alone, for its object is not external: by one light it sees another not through any intermediate agency; a light sees a light, that is to say a thing sees itself" (V.3.8).

The mechanisms of intuition are seen as a correlate of the mechanisms of vision in perception, as the light of the absolute is represented by the light of the sun in the real, though the mechanisms of perception, and the light of the sun in the real, are inadequate in their enactment of the absolute in relation to the ideal as symbols. The mechanisms of perception and light in the real are imperfect representations of the perception and light of the intellect in intuition, as functions of the participation of the absolute in intellect, the Intellectual Principle of Plotinus. That which is represented by perception and light in the real is thus imperfectly represented, or inadequately represented; in that art depends on another light, and another mechanism of perception, or can vary each within the real, it has the capacity to more adequately represent the absolute in the real. Thus "the hard rind of nature and the common world gives the mind more trouble in breaking through to the idea than do the products of art" (*Introductory Lectures on Aesthetics* XV).

Art, nevertheless, in that it is within the real, is more limited than philosophy in its capacity to reveal the absolute, as mind is closer to the absolute, and further from matter. Forms of art can represent freedom, but cannot be completely free; the concept (*Begriff*) can be completely free, if it can exist separately from language, in intuition, which the perception of art can represent. It is not so much in the forms of art than in how art can be perceived that art can represent freedom in the absolute; forms of art as they are perceived are not subject to the fixed laws of perception in the sensible world of organism and matter—they are more variable, which is why they appear more fleeting and deceptive than appearance in the sensible world itself. But it is that variability, given by deceptive appearance, which allows art to reveal the absolute in perception more than ordinary perception. And it is also that variability which provides the basis for the more integrated interaction between artforms and mind than sensible forms and mind; the infinite is suggested in the seemingly infinite set of variables which constitute thought and intuition in relation to the perception of forms in art, in contrast to the perception of nature.

The idea that the absolute can be further revealed in philosophical contemplation than sensory intuition is a product of Christianity, according to Hegel, because the essence of the Christian god cannot be completely expressed in sensual form, as it contains the element of Spirit within it, and is only partly manifest in body, and even soul. The gods of classical mythology were completely represented in pictorial form and allegorical narrative; there was no element of them that was not represented to human beings. In Plato, the god is given in total by reason in the imagination; the One of Plotinus is parallel to the Christian god, as there is an element of it in which being as existence cannot participate. The worship of the Christian god, like the contemplation of the One, requires an inward withdrawal of consciousness, and the development of a self-centered being within the soul which emulates the absolute by being independent of contingent necessity; such inner contemplation did not exist in classical mythology. In Hegelian terms, the freedom of the soul in its self-dependency turned inward is the basis of self-consciousness, which is the realization of freedom, of the absolute in mind.

Pictorial representation in Christianity is limited in that it admits of the inaccessibility of the sensible world to the absolute; the Christian icon is a two-dimensional signboard which acts as much as a barrier as a medium for the participation of the absolute in the sensible real. The animation of the icon is seen as a miracle because in a moment, the absolute crosses into the real, in the act of perception, and interaction of mind with form in art, of ideal and real. The moment of perception is purely emotional, because it requires the complete suspension of both reason and intuition, and is based completely on faith. In philosophy, the absolute, as the One of Plotinus, is in no way embodied, unlike the Christian god, and thus can be directly experienced only in mind, through intuition, and not in the real, in art or nature, though it can be represented. Hegel seems to see the Philosophy of Spirit at this point as the maturation of Christianity, the absolute state of freedom of the absolute, as given by self-consciousness in contemplation, the most developed form of mind. The Romantic artform is a purer representation of the absolute than the Christian icon, because the absolute is completely disembodied, and becomes an attribute of the ideal rather than the real, though it participates in the real. This conception of the absolute begins with Plotinus, who may have held Christianity in contempt.

Thus, for Hegel, "we are above the level at which works of art can be venerated as divine, and actually worshipped" (XVI). It is not possible for the absolute to be perceived in the real, as is given by self-consciousness. Given that art can no longer function as the revelation of the absolute in the real, the question for Hegel becomes whether the limitations of art are severe enough in relation to philosophy and religion, which operate in the realm of the ideal, in the presence of the absolute, to reflect the *Geist* of the culture. This would only be the case, Hegel suggests, if art were to become completely regulated by reason and contingencies of necessity in a culture, in science, history, and social institutions. This is why art in fact becomes even more important for a culture, when it is no longer capable of revealing the absolute as absolute, because art is the only medium of the preservation of the ideal in the real, of freedom in necessity, of Spirit in culture. Without art there would be no representation of the absolute in the real, the absolute as being conceived as imparticipant by the real, as opposed to Christianity, in which, because the absolute is present in the real, it has no need of art or philosophy to represent it.

Art "no longer affords that satisfaction of spiritual wants which earlier epochs have sought therein, and have found therein only" (XVII); this is a product of the development of self-consciousness and freedom in the course of cultural history. Art grows to define itself as providing more than the spiritual demands of Christianity, in the necessity of the representation of the imparticipant absolute; this is why, in the theory of modern art, it is necessary to return to Plotinus, in the philosophical conception of the imparticipant, disembodied absolute, and its representation in art, both of which are addressed at length in the *Enneads*. For Plotinus, it was necessary to return to Plato, for the philosophical conception of the god as understood in reason as opposed to mythology, and the representation of that conception not in art, but in the structure of being, which art came to be seen to represent. In the modern world, it is no longer tenable that art represent the structure of being, because the structure of being is no longer given completely by philosophical contemplation.

The role of art thus changes, profoundly, in the course of the development of culture; while art is no longer the representation of the structure of being, nor the revelation of the divine, art has become the particular and necessary expression of self-consciousness, in Hegelian terms, not of the structure of being, but being in the world, that is, the relation between mind and perception, the ideal and the real, the universal and particular. Though art is secondary to philosophy in its representation of the absolute, art has become philosophy, or the teleological goals of art and philosophy have grown closer together. Thus it is necessary that art continue to develop as the expression of freedom in a culture, as the expression of Spirit in history, in relation to the philosophical conceptions of the culture. The relation of art to the religion of the culture needs to continue to develop insofar as the religion of the culture is a source of its moral and ethical standards, but not insofar as the religion of the culture is the source of the philosophical representation of the absolute, as Christianity presumed.

In a modern culture, according to Hegel, ethics and morality themselves, laws and rights, though they may be products of a religious epistemology, become more of a regulative force than religious faith. Artistic creativity, though, cannot be limited to universal definitions of ethics and morality. Artistic creativity depends on the presence of the universal, but precisely not in the form of ethics or morality as necessity or limitation, but as the universal as freedom. The work of art, therefore, is the field of the dialectical development not only of the ideal and real, but of freedom and necessity in relation to the absolute as it is manifest in society. The forms of art must contain the particulars of ethical and moral universals as they must contain the particulars of sensory perception; but through those particulars, in the same way, the forms of art must represent the universal ideas of morality and ethics in relation to their particular manifestations in rights and laws. As forms in art can contradict the laws of nature as they are represented in the sensible world, forms in art can also contradict the laws of ethics and morality as they are represented in the ideal, but as always in the dialectic, the universal or antithesis is not possible without the particular or the thesis. The freedom of artistic creation, as a representation of the freedom of the absolute in the ideal, is a freedom only within the bounds of the necessity of the absolute, as forms of art are limited to the real. This is not the case in philosophy, which is not bound to the necessity of the absolute in the real, and thus is predicated on a freedom which is not the product of dialectical development, but rather of intuition in relation to reason, as participant of the absolute, as in the Intellectual Principle of Plotinus.

In the pictorial imagination, the creation of forms of art, "the universal and rational is contained only as brought into unity with a concrete sensuous phenomenon" (*Introductory Lectures on Aesthetics* XVII), and thus freedom. In a modern culture in which ethics and morality rather than religious faith dictate thought and relations, it is more difficult for the artist to represent the

Geist of the culture in the individual work, because, in that the absolute cannot be seen to be present in the real, the universal idea as moral or ethic cannot be seen to be present in individual activity. The individual, the particular manifestation of the culture as a universal, can represent the absolute which is the source of the universal ethic or morality, but the individual cannot embody that universal, as the individual Christian worshipper, for example, can embody religious faith, in the act of worship, and not just represent it. Ethics and morality, those principles of justice as defined in the *Phaedrus* as "absolute justice and discipline and knowledge, not the knowledge which is attached to things which come into being, nor the knowledge which varies with the objects which we now call real..." (247), remain abstractions in the ideal, unembodied in form in the real. The challenge is thus greater for artistic representation of the absolute in a free society governed by ethical and moral principles. "Therefore," Hegel concludes, "our present in its universal condition is not favorable to art" (*Introductory Lectures on Aesthetics* XVII).

It is impossible for the artist to act outside the dictates of his culture, because the creation of the work of art necessitates the interaction of the universal of the culture and of the Idea with the particular of the individual subject and the sensual forms. As a self-reflective particular within the universal, it is impossible for the artist to transcend cultural necessity; art is either a function of cultural necessity, or it is irrelevant to cultural necessity, but it can never transcend cultural necessity, as can philosophy, because it is limited to the particular and grounded in the real. The work of art is necessarily a product of its culture, either in ideality or actuality; the more the creative artist understands the *Zeitgeist* of his or her culture, the more resonant will be the work in relation to the culture which produces it. In a culture regulated by the dictates of the universals of ethics and morality, it is impossible to produce a work of art which transcends the limitations of those dictates, as opposed to the boundaries of philosophical development. In its representation of the absolute, the work of art in a culture of ethics cannot be based in Christian spirituality if it is to represent and not embody the absolute in the particular. The work of art in such a culture can be based on the presence of the absolute in the ideal, though, and its representation in the particular, if such a representation corresponds to the dialectic of the real and ideal in philosophy as a function of the freedom and self-consciousness which are the ontological basis of the ethical culture.

Hegel's pronouncement of the death of art, that "art is, and remains for us, on the side of its highest destiny, a thing of the past" (XVIII), must be taken in context. Such a death does not preclude a rebirth of art in the modern world; in fact, such a death makes possible the rebirth of art in the modern world, makes possible a redefinition of art which is dynamic and necessary for the modern world. The highest destiny of art is no longer possible because of the evolved cultural conditions of which it is a product. The highest destiny of art is defined in relation to a culture dictated by religious faith or a lack of freedom and self-consciousness. In such a culture, art is the most important medium of expression, because in such a culture the absolute, as undeveloped, is embodied in the real. Such embodiment is no longer possible in a more advanced culture on both an epistemological and ontological level; the role of art is thus reduced proportionately, and reoriented toward its relation to the representation of the absolute in the real, and toward the philosophical development of the individual in the culture. Art as it was defined in classical and Christian cultures is no longer possible; art thus seeks an unknown definition at the beginning of the modern world; it becomes a *tabula rasa*, the forms and definitions of which develop parallel to the philosophical development of the modern world. For this reason, art in the modern world follows and reflects philosophical developments. The relation between art and philosophy becomes necessary in the definition of art in a free and ethical culture; philosophical development becomes the basis for artistic development. This is not to say that art is less vital for an ethical culture, but that the role of art as a form of cultural expression has changed, and along with that changed role the methods of artistic production must necessarily change, the role of the artist in the culture, the relation of artistic production to the economic and political structure of the culture, and the relation of the forms of art to the universal principles which dictate the values of the culture, as they are expressed in the art.

Thus for Hegel art "has further lost for us its genuine truth and life [as it was conceived in the classical world], and rather is transferred into our *ideas* [*Vorstellung*] that asserts its former necessity, or assumes its former place, in reality." Art no longer embodies the absolute in the real, but represents the absolute in the real as it is given in the ideal. Art is transferred into philosophy, and is reinvented as such. Art in the modern world is no longer a source of delight nor judgment of taste, because the element of abstraction, of the universal from the particular, becomes a necessary element of artistic reception. The perception of art in the modern world is a philosophical act, a medium of the dialectic of the real and the ideal. "What is now aroused in us by works of art is over and above our immediate enjoyment, and together with it, our judgment...”; art is no longer a subject of immediate enjoyment because it can no longer indulge the sensuous perception of the real as partaking in the absolute; it must necessarily involve the self-reflection of the self-alienation of the mind from itself; it must participate in the construction of perception as a self-enclosed function of reason, and the possibility of transcending that signifying structure, as a language, which threatens the structure itself, but which may result in an *ecstasis* or a *katharsis*, which may be enjoyable itself, but as an intellectual pleasure, rather than a spiritual or physical pleasure, a role which art played beginning in the Renaissance. The subject of art is no longer the judgment of taste, because the work of art can no longer be seen to embody a universal as a manifestation of the absolute, thus a universal judgment, or, for that matter, ethical or moral standard.

In modern culture, according to Hegel, “we subject the content and the means of representation of the work of art and the suitability or unsuitability of the two to our intellectual consideration” (*Introductory Lectures on Aesthetics* XVIII), as art becomes a medium of philosophical development. “Therefore, the *science* of art is a much more pressing need in our day,” that is, the theory of art, the formulation of the principles of art as a philosophical expression. Art is no longer perceived in a mythological, religious, or sensuous framework; art is perceived in a philosophical framework, and the theory of art concerns itself with the relation of art to the philosophical structures of the culture. All art in the modern world is accompanied by a theoretical apology, a philosophical scaffolding which gives the art its significance in relation to the culture; in that way, art can no longer be experienced directly, unmediated. In past cultures the existence of a universal standard in art was sufficient to allow for a direct, unmediated experience of it; in the modern world, the absence of the embodiment of the absolute in art requires that it correspond to a particular tenet of a philosophical structure in relation to the epistemology of its culture, and that tenet cannot be fully understood in the immediate perception of the artwork alone; it requires a philosophical scaffolding. Such is the nature of the culture of freedom and self-consciousness; immediate experience itself is devalued, as it becomes the subject of a fully developed self-consciousness which reflects to the perceiving subject both the intellectual scaffolding of his or her perception, and the necessary self-alienation of the subject given by the nature of that perception.

“Art invites us to consideration of it by means of thought, not to the end of stimulating art production, but in order to ascertain scientifically what art is,” which in turn provides the stimulation for artistic production. The science of art, the theory of art, certainly stimulates artistic production, but the philosophical purpose of art is to stimulate intellectual development in the perceiving subject. As art no longer participates in the universal in its limitation in the real, the definition of art in relation to culture becomes more problematic. The definition of art becomes determined by the relation between the individual subject, the particular, and the cultural whole, the universal, in terms of the ethical and moral determinates of the culture. Each element participates in the dialectic, but the determining factors are never fixed. The unstable flux of appearances which defined the sensible world for Plato now defines the process of reason in intellect.

As defined by Plotinus, Reason Principle, that element of reason unparticipant in the absolute, reflects the characteristics of the sensible world in perception. Reason as science and logic is confined to the necessary and contingent, and it is reason in intuition, the Intellectual Principle of Plotinus, in which the absolute is participant, in which the flux of appearances in the sensible world is transformed into the stable archetypes which are manifestations of the universal. The definition of art becomes multiple and variable, but its teleological function remains the same, to abstract the particulars in the multiple into the universals of the absolute. The science of art theory thus becomes a kind of historicism, creating categories and definitions for the perception of art, in the absence of a universal category or definition.

The theory of art is a science, as well as a philosophy, because it is systematic, as for Schelling, and because its subject is the particular in the real, bound by necessity, as art is bound to the real. Aesthetics requires a systematic, scientific procedure as does the Philosophy of Nature. It is also the inner necessity of philosophy that it be systematic, because the basis of philosophy is dialectical development, or the unfolding of the idea, the *explicato* of Nicolas Cusanus, in its explanation and demonstration. Metaphysics as well is necessarily systematic, as for Schelling, because it is a function of reason and logic, though it seeks the transcendence of reason in intuition, and thus must allow for the unsystematic within the systematic. The same is true of aesthetics, as the principal subject of art is the metaphysical relation of the real and the ideal in the ideal, as represented in the real. The core of aesthetics is systematic, scientific, but the boundaries of aesthetics must be expanded as reason in perception becomes self-reflective, and intuition grows from self-consciousness. "Thus it is only as regards the essential innermost progress of its content and of its media of expression that we must call to mind the outline prescribed by its necessity" (XIX). Aesthetics in modern culture entails historicism and categorization, metaphysics, and what can be best described as Philosophy of Spirit, that is, philosophy of mind, of thought in relation to perception, and the ideal in relation to the real. Aesthetics also entails the phenomena of freedom and self-consciousness in the individual subject in modern culture, and the dictates of morality and ethics in the *Zeitgeist* of the culture.

The element of aesthetics which is most problematic in relation to its definition as a science or a systematic philosophy is the definition of beauty. Beauty in art has been defined as a product of mind or Spirit rather than sensory perception, as in the *Symposium* the initiate learns to love all beautiful bodies rather than just one body, and to "pursue the beauty of form" (210) rather than the beauty of the body, which is the source of the idea in the intellect. The beauty of art is born of the mind rather than of the art itself. The nature of beauty is a product of the relation between the ideal and the real, an element of which is necessarily the transcendence of systematic logic in self-consciousness, the self-reflection of reason. Reason must go outside of itself in order to contemplate itself, in the intuition of the absolute in the Intellectual Principle, and beauty is a product of the self-reflection of reason, which necessitates a departure from the principles of logic, in intuition. Beauty is also a product of freedom, the ability to deviate from adherence to universal principles, in the expression of self-consciousness, in intuition and the unconscious. Though the unconscious is regulated to an extent by the laws of necessity, of cause and effect, as given by reason, as in all natural phenomena, the workings of the unconscious ultimately exceed the limitations of the principles of reason, as do all natural phenomena, and introduce the presence of what is perceived as unreason within reason, as represented by the sublime in art, and also by the beautiful. According to Schelling's definition, the beautiful is the indifference or identity of the ideal and real, of freedom and necessity, in sensual form—the identity of reason and unreason, the finite and infinite.

The identity of the ideal and real in sensual form is a product of the projection of the mind into nature, as are the geometry and mathematics of classical philosophy. The beautiful as the identity of the ideal and real reveals the inherent disjunction between the two, the primordial dehiscence, the self-alienation of the mind in the ideal, and the misapprehension of the essence of the real, of nature and matter, as it has no being outside the ideal, as given in Idealism. For Hegel, "the beauty of art does in fact appear in a form which is expressly contrasted with abstract thought, and which the latter is forced to destroy" (*Introductory Lectures on Aesthetics* XX), given the reformulation of art as a function of philosophy rather than as the sensuous embodiment of the absolute. As art becomes a function of philosophy, beauty in art becomes a function of the systematic reason of philosophy. The transcendence of reason in intuition, though it is the goal of philosophy, only occurs in philosophy itself within the framework of reason, and thus only occurs in art within the framework of reason. Philosophy has thus destroyed the possibility of beauty in art, or rather such possibility was destroyed by the cultural development of freedom and self-consciousness. As with the example of Picasso, beauty in the expression of modern consciousness entails the destruction of beauty in the classical sense, as the product of a universal standard, the embodiment of the absolute in the particular. Beauty in modern culture is a product of the presence of the absolute in the ideal but not in the real, in the imagination but not in sensible form in art as it is related to sensible form in the real, in matter and organism.

In the misapprehension of the essence of the real given by the identity of the real and the ideal, "reality as such, the life of nature and of mind, is disfigured and slain by comprehension." Beauty in art becomes a product of the disfigurement of the real by the ideal, as it is perceived by the ideal—the beauty of nature, imitated in Classical art as an embodiment of the absolute. Beauty in art is unbeauty, the opposite of beauty in the real, not ugliness, but artificial beauty as opposed to natural beauty, sign of the incompatibility of the real and ideal; "so far from being brought close to us by the thought which comprehends, it is by it that such life is absolutely dissociated from us, so that, by the use of thought as the means of grasping what has life, man rather cuts himself off from this his purpose..." Thought, as given by language, is that which prevents the human mind from understanding the essence of being. Philosophy and art entail the attempt to overcome the limitations of thought in relation to being; the first principles of both philosophy and art are the alienation of thought from being, and the self-consciousness of the attempt to reconcile them.

It is the essential nature of mind to think, and it is an essential capacity of mind to be self-reflective, to be aware of itself thinking. Because art is a product and expression of the thinking mind, it necessarily contains the essence of mind, and enacts the entrance of mind or Spirit into the sensible world, into sensuous form. Art is thus closer to mind than nature, but because art is a product of mind, art cannot refer to anything outside of mind in the scope of being. It can refer to the attempt of mind to discover that which is outside itself, but it can never refer to anything that is not predicated in mind. Art is thus self-reflective thought; as opposed to science, it is not governed by necessity, and has no ulterior purpose as thought other than self-reflection, of the process of mind, or the relation of mind to the universal. Art is the pure expression of Spirit in the real; whether or not it is religious in content, it is always spiritual, always refers to the inner life of mind, in the soul.

In art, the abstract and conceptual enter into sensuous form. Art is a means by which mind becomes self-reflective; the abstract and the conceptual alone cannot be self-reflective—self-reflection, thus self-consciousness, depends on the entrance of the conceptual into sensuous form, either as enacted in the imagination or through artforms. Art thus enacts a process of self-discovery. Works of art become "products whose mode of representation admits into itself the semblance of sensuous being and pervades what is sensuous with mind" (XXI). In self-reflection, as enacted in art, mind "returns to itself out of its alienation," in conceptual processes in abstraction and imagination, in the translation of sensuous particulars into abstract universals, in order to reaffirm itself in being. Mind is necessarily self-conscious in the process of abstraction, because it must place itself in the sensible world; art is thus a medium of self-consciousness and abstraction, a medium of the reaffirmation of mind in being.

The self-consciousness of mind is not present in Classical art, because mind has not yet been disembodied from the sensual, and has not begun a process of reconciliation. In modern art, mind or concept (*Begriff*), as it enters into the sensual, is outside of itself, alienated from itself, and seeks reconciliation with itself as well, in self-consciousness, in art. Conceptual mind becomes a thesis in its own self-reflective dialectic, posed against its sensual antithesis, seeking to achieve a synthesis in the identity of the real and ideal, as in art. It is the essential nature of mind in self-reflection to pose itself against itself, as a reflection of its own self-alienation from being. All of these functions of art are only given in its relation to philosophy, in its role as a function of philosophy. The evaluation of art depends on the relation between the forms in art and the abstract concepts of mind, and the intuition of the presence of mind, or Spirit, in the forms. The arrangement and shape of the artforms (*Gestaltung*) are determined and read according to their relation to thought and mind, as mediums of self-reflection and intellectual development. All form in art corresponds to a specific content in thought as words correspond to meaning in language in a given syntax; the syntax of the artforms, the way in which they are organized and combined, allows them to function like a visual language, like a pictographic system, in relation to abstract concept. Like hieroglyphs, artforms are both symbolic, pictorially, and schematic, syntactically, as in allegory, allowing for a complex representation in communication of mind in the ideal.

In that the artform is defined by the entrance of mind into the sensuous, beauty in art is defined by the entrance of the idea (*Idee*, in the Platonic sense of the archetype) of beauty into the sensuous. In beauty, art is capable of embodying not just the concept (*Begriff*) or abstraction, but the archetypal idea itself, the intelligible form in the imagination, as in the Intellectual Principle of Plotinus. According to Schelling, beauty is defined by the extent to which mind is integrated with the sensuous as it enters into it, the ideal into the real. For Hegel, the artform is beautiful in the extent to which the idea of beauty is present in it, or represented by it, the idea of beauty as defined in the *Symposium*. Through art, then, the idea of beauty enters into thought and consciousness, as self-reflective of the archetypal ideal. It is important to Hegel to explore the relation of the idea of beauty with beauty in the sensual, as "the emptiness of content which characterizes the Platonic idea is no longer satisfactory to the fuller philosophical wants of the mind today" (*Introductory Lectures on Aesthetics* XXXVI). As in Transcendental Idealism, there is a necessity of pursuing a dialectic synthesis of the ideal and the real, in order to satisfy the demands of self-consciousness and the self-alienation of the mind in being which did not exist in Plato's world, being at the beginning of philosophical development.

The dialectical synthesis of the real and ideal must be carried out in the framework of the historical dialectic of the classical and the modern if it is to have any resonance for the historical subject. Thus the idea of the beautiful, the philosophical conception or *Begriff* of it, must combine "metaphysical universality with the determinateness of real particularity"; only then can the idea of beauty have any meaning in relation to self-consciousness. Beauty is identified in a particular in which the universal is revealed in the sensible world, and in a conceptual principle which effectively synthesizes particulars of the sensible world in relation to the universal. Beauty is thus a reaffirmation of the being in the world of the mind in its dialectical process towards the reconciliation of its self-alienation. Beauty does not exist outside the framework of the ideal, outside of the experience of the perceiving subject in relation to the sensible world; it is thus revealed in nature and in art as a verification of the process of mind in the construction of perception. Beauty is the product of the tendency of mind in its self-reflection to project itself into the sensible world, and of the thinking subject to "enjoy in the shape and fashion of things a mere external reality of himself" (XLIX).

"The universal need for expression in art lies, therefore, in man's rational impulse to exalt the inner and outer world into a spiritual consciousness for himself, as an object in which he recognizes his own self" (L). The perceiving subject does not naturally recognize itself as belonging in the world, given the alienation of mind from being; art is the product of the necessity of constructing such a belonging. In this constructed synthesis, the freedom which the subject experiences in mind in self-consciousness is projected onto the real, nature and matter, that which of itself is limited to the necessary, to cause and effect. The thinking subject projects its own freedom of mind onto the sensible world in order to convince itself of a belonging; thus artforms combine the freedom of mind with the necessity of the sensible world in perception. The sensual form as it exists in the work of art is only an appearance of sensual form, as given in perception. It is an appearance created by mind in its freedom, as opposed to an appearance created by mind in its necessity in perception, thus it is an appearance which is less deceitful to conceptual mind, though more deceitful to perceiving mind. In the synthesis of the real and ideal in art, mind does not require actual sensual form, but only the appearance of sensual form, as the synthesis of real and ideal cannot exist outside the ideal, outside the framework of thought. The appearance of sensual form in art and perception liberates the idea of the form from the form itself, and allows the form to participate in the freedom of mind, which otherwise it would not be able to do, allowing the sensuous form to conform to the projection of mind onto the real, in the synthesis of the inner and outer.

As with Schelling, the quality of the form according to Hegel which allows it to enter into the ideal is its sonority, or "sonorous vibration" (LVIII), the relation produced by magnetism, as in physics, between the body and its surroundings, its constructed environment, which is, in the case of perception, the environment of the ideal, the entrance of the idea into the sensuous form. Sensuous forms in the sensual must preserve, in mind, an inner essence themselves which is not accessible to mind, an encased inner core that differentiates them bodily in their existence as particulars in the sensible realm, as in the "self-enclosed night" of Schelling, the eternal ground of being. As mind seeks to dissolve itself into the sensible world, it seeks the presence of the absolute in matter itself, but the hard shell of matter remains inaccessible. If it were not, reason itself would dissolve.

The sensuous forms of art are embodied with the spiritual in the ideal; they can only be so as a "shadow-world" of forms. As forms themselves in matter or the organic, they would not be able to be embodied with the spiritual. As forms in art they are only symbolic and schematic, like words in language, which have no correlate to sensuous forms. Forms in art are thus infinitely separated from their correlates in nature and matter; in their capacity to embody the spiritual, they cannot be actual body, but only body as idea. As the appearance of sensuous forms in the ideal, forms in art are liberated from the laws of necessity and cause and effect in nature and matter, and from the self-enclosed night of the ground of being. They are brought into the light of the absolute, the abode of mind purified of matter, and thus represent the absolute to mind in its self-reflection and projection into the real; the absolute is revealed in the beauty of the identity of the real and the ideal.

The imitation of sensuous form in nature can thus play no role in true art, as for Schelling, because, to begin with, the sensuous form in nature itself contains no element of the ideal, and an imitation of it would be an imitation of nothingness in relation to mind. It is impossible to reproduce the beauty perceived in nature in art, because the beauty perceived in nature is dependent on the intersection of natural form and perceiving mind. The beauty of the natural forms of Classical art is not the result of the imitation of the beauty of nature, but of the projection of the abstracted idea of beauty, in the form of mathematics and geometry, into the sensuous form, for example the Golden Ratio. The perceived identity of mind and sensuous body in Classical art is thus a deception, and never really existed, though there is nothing in classical philosophy that would indicate otherwise. Given the deception of the synthesis of mind and sensuous form, there was no need of art, aesthetics, in classical philosophy. "The end of art must, therefore, lie in something different from the purely formal imitation of what we find given…" (LXV).

It is, nevertheless, "an element essential to the work of art to have natural shapes for its foundation; seeing that its representation is in the medium of external and therefore of natural phenomena." The artist must borrow from nature the relationships of color, light, and formal characteristics, but combine them in such a way that the reinvention of the form in the ideal does not imitate form in the real which is inaccessible to the ideal. In the words of Plotinus, "Still the arts are not to be slighted on the ground that they create by imitation of natural objects; for, to begin with, these natural objects are themselves imitations; then, we must recognize that they give no bare reproduction of the thing seen but go back to the Ideas from which Nature itself derives" (*Enneads* V.8.1).

Plotinus expresses for the first time in philosophy an aesthetic theory based on the interaction of the real and the ideal, the insertion of concepts of mind into nature and matter, which is a product of freedom and self-consciousness in philosophical contemplation. The philosophical development of Plotinus was overtaken by Christianity, which subsumed philosophy into religion, and made the attainment of freedom and self-consciousness in philosophical contemplation impossible, given the acceptance of the embodiment of the absolute, the Christian God, in the real. The philosophical development of Plotinus resurfaced in the synthesis of Christian theology and classical philosophy on the part of the Neoplatonists at the beginning of the Renaissance, for the purpose of giving philosophical validity to the arts being produced by the emerging courts, which were the centers of power of the emerging city-states.

An example in modern painting of the reproduction of natural forms through an understanding of the principles of the real in perception as opposed to imitation is the work of Arshile Gorky, the Armenian painter active in New York, in the era of the New York School. The forms of Gorky, for example in the *Betrothal II* of 1947 (Figure 6), have the appearance of obeying the laws of the organic, but they look nothing like anything in the organic, because they are only forms of art, and do not pretend to belong to the real. They are the product of intuition, the synthesis of the real and ideal, the embodiment of mind in sensuous form in appearance. The forms appear to be the product of the unconscious imagination, which obeys the laws of the organic, being the function of mind as an organic body, but the forms of which are not recognizable to reason, as the unconscious is inaccessible to reasoning mind, but is a source of intuition, as a synthesis of real and ideal within the ideal. The forms of Gorky are the product of invention in art, expressions of the being in the world of mind, as the product of a self-alienated and self-reflective organic entity attempting to rediscover its organic origin.

In philosophy given by freedom and self-consciousness of mind in the modern world, judgment is "the power of thinking the particular as contained under the universal" (*Introductory Lectures on Aesthetics* LXXVII; quoting Immanuel Kant, who in *Critique of Pure Reason* and *Critique of Practical Reason* defined mind as the identity of self-consciousness and the infinite in freedom, and the self-knowledge of the absoluteness of reason within itself,

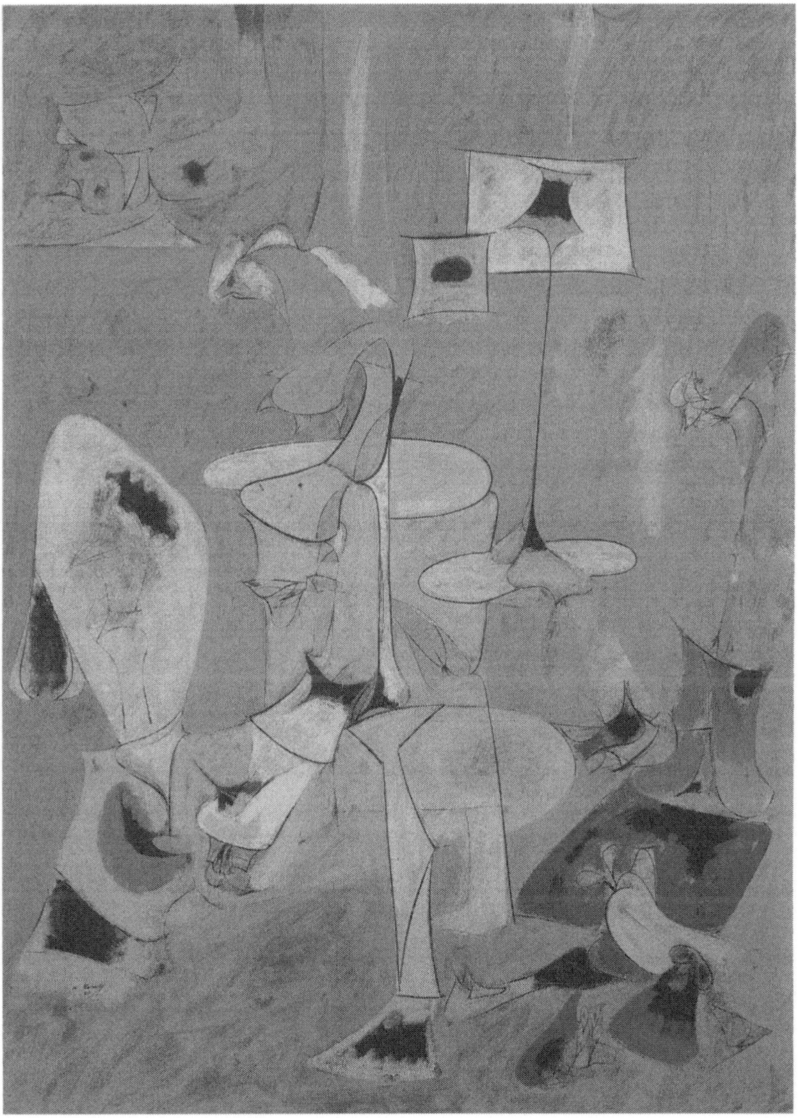

Figure 6. Arshile Gorky, *The Betrothal II* (© 2004 Artists Rights Society [ARS], New York)

seen as the beginning of modern philosophy). Judgment is the self-reflection of mind of the relation between universal and particular, ideal and real. Thus the judgment of beauty, for example, is given entirely by mind as entered into the real. Judgment, according to Kant, is the abstraction of the universal from the particular itself; thus every act of artistic creation, and every act of the perception of art, is an act of judgment, and is dependent on the identity of the individual perceiving subject in relation to the universal, universal culture and universal being.

For Hegel, judgment of beauty must take into account the nature of mind as it is entered into the real, because it is as such transformed; the subjective and objective do not remain mutually independent, as for Kant. Beauty depends upon the adequate synthesis of the ideal and the real, not just the presence of the ideal alone in the real. For Hegel, idea in mind is incomplete without a relation to sensual form in the real; the universal cannot exist without the particular, and the perceiving subject cannot exist without that which is perceived. The idea is complete when it has found a relation with the essence of mind in form, when it is the subject of the synthesis of mind and form, as in Transcendental Idealism. Judgment is not possible as a function of idea alone, but only insofar as it is manifest in form, insofar as the universal is manifest in the particular. This is true for art as well as any ethical or moral activity in a culture. Beauty in art is the idea entered into form; through beauty, and the judgment of beauty, the idea is transformed in the transferal from subjective to objective. Thus Hegel asserts, "for the Idea as such, although it is the essentially and actually true, is yet the truth only in its generality which has not yet taken objective shape; but the Idea as the beautiful in art is at once the Idea when specially determined as in its essence individual reality, and also an individual shape of reality essentially destined to embody and reveal the Idea" (*Introductory Lectures on Aesthetics* CIII). Beauty in art is the confirmation of the presence of mind in the real, the belonging of mind in the world.

Romantic art expresses the alienation of mind from the real which Classical art did not address in its philosophical infancy. Classical art introduced the insertion of mind into the real which the symbolic art of Egypt did not contain; the forms of Egyptian art could only symbolize the real as a concept of mind which did not contain the essence of mind itself in freedom and self-consciousness in relation to the real. Classical art symbolizes the introduction of mind in the real as sensual embodiment, as if mind is body itself, as in the embodied gods of Greek mythology. Classical art does not express the universal in the particular (even the gods are particulars in relation to the universal, as given by the allegorical structure of mythology), while classical philosophy, beginning with Thales and Anaximander and culminating in Plato and Aristotle, does succeed in introducing the universal into the particular. Artistic representation in the Greek world was held behind philosophical development because of political organization, notwithstanding the emergence of representative government; the same can be said of the Roman world, which produced no art which synthesized the universal and the particular, despite the philosophical developments represented by Plotinus in the late empire.

Classical philosophy introduces the universal into the particular by understanding the real, matter and organism, as structured according to reason, as in the geometrical constructs of Anaximander, or the Platonic Solids, or the ascent of the initiate in the *Symposium* in the understanding of beauty as an idea. In understanding matter and organism as a representation in the particular of a universal construct or archetype, the ideal was introduced into the real. In the *Timaeus*, mind is not represented as self-reflective or self-alienated in self-consciousness, but it is represented as ontologically separated from the real, which is not expressed in Greek art. This ontological separation is the foundation for the Neoplatonic metaphysics of Plotinus, and the emergence of the absolute as differentiated from the real and ideal in philosophical contemplation, which becomes the foundation for the self-alienation of mind in the ideal, thought left undeveloped in Christian theology. Beginning with Plotinus, "mind is the infinite subjectivity of the Idea, which, as absolute inwardness, is not capable of finding free expansion in its true nature on condition of remaining transposed into a bodily medium as the existence appropriate to it," as described by Hegel (*Introductory Lectures on Aesthetics* CVII).

Given the complete inwardness of mind in the subjective, the introduction of mind to the real, and the representation of mind in art, becomes problematic, and Classical art is no longer possible, except as an instrument of political propaganda (in Neoclassicism). The irreconcilable split between the subjective and objective is not expressed in art until the Renaissance, because Christian art reveals no such incompatibility, as the absolute itself is seen to be embodied in the real. The attempted synthesis of Classical art and philosophy and Christian theology in the Renaissance involves a dialectical development of subjective and objective that reflects the historical dialectic, in the same way that Hegel frames his project in the *Introductory Lectures on*

Aesthetics. The dialectical development of the Renaissance is a product of the attempted synthesis of the inner spirituality of the subjective in Christianity as a philosophical idea, and the methods of representation of Classical art and philosophy.

The perspectival construction of the Renaissance, for example, the *costruzione leggitima*, applied the classical tenet of the understanding of the real in terms of the mind, in the reason of mathematics and geometry, to the principle in Christian theology of the disembodied absolute in relation to its embodiment in the real. The vanishing point in perspectival construction was the disembodied absolute, the inward spirit of mind, and the lines of projection were the embodiment of the absolute in the real, as given by geometry in reason. Christianity, in recognition of the unity of the absolute and the real, "transforms it from an immediate to a conscious unity," the immediate unity being represented in the sensuous form of Classical art. Renaissance art thus introduces, though does not represent, a self-conscious inward intelligence that can no longer be adequately expressed in sensory form. This philosophical development is not represented, again, because of the political structure of the city-state in the Renaissance, in which freedom and self-consciousness are not completely developed.

Romantic art is similar to symbolic art (of Egypt, for example) in that it treats sensual form as a medium for an attempt to express what cannot be fully expressed in it. In symbolic art, this is a result of the inability to project mind into the real; in Romantic art, it is a result of the self-consciousness of the incompatibility of the mind and the real. The effect, though, is completely different—in Romantic art, the effect of the incompatibility of the real and ideal in form as an expression of the inexpressible, is the sublime. The sublime does not exist in symbolic art, because in symbolic art the possibility of the presence of mind in the real is inconceivable. The subject in Romantic art is fully developed in self-consciousness and subjectivity, as opposed to symbolic art. Thus the essence of Romantic art, the spirit of the idea, is revealed to the mind of the perceiver rather than the eye of the perceiver.

In that the content of Romantic art is the visual representation of the absolute in the indifference of the ideal and the real, as opposed to the visual representation of the ideal as other than the real in symbolic art, the content of Romantic art coincides with the content of the imagination of the perceiving subject, the visual representation of the indifference of the ideal and the real in the mind. The perceiving mind sees itself in the visual representation in Romantic art. In Romantic art, the "artistic object…is revealed in its spirituality to the inner, and not the outer, eye,"[9] as expressed by Hegel in the *Introduction to the Philosophy of Fine Art*. The inner world of Romantic art corresponds to the inner world of the philosophical contemplation of the absolute, unembodied in the real. "The inner life thus triumphs over the outer world," and the sensuous appearances of the outer world are put into perspective in relation to the mind which perceives them.

In Romantic art the sensuous form becomes relatively insignificant in relation to the idea which is communicated, as in symbolic art. The sensuous form is given free reign in relation to organic or material form in the real, corresponding to the freedom of self-consciousness in the imagination. The sensuous form in fact becomes incongruous in relation to the spiritual idea, given the incompatibility of the two in self-consciousness. In Romantic art, as opposed to symbolic art, the idea is allowed to reveal itself in both opposition to and in identity with the real, the sensuous form, and the relation between the idea and the sensuous form is fully revealed. Romantic art displays the incompatibility of idea and form, while the presence of the idea is displayed in the form. Romantic art thus expresses the relation between the perceiving subject and its being, as being one of a constructed sense of belonging, an alienation, and a desire for the fulfillment of the void of being in being itself. Perception itself becomes alienated from mind in consciousness, as it operates within the real in self-consciousness; the finite and the infinite are differentiated in the ideal.

Perception constructs the real as a product of the ideal, as containing the same essence, but in so doing establishes the incompatibility of the real and ideal. "Nature is not thus to be set over against absolute Mind, either as conjoint with a sphere of the Real of equal worth, or as an independent boundary thereto. Rather the aspect which Nature appears to hold in this respect is that which mind or spirit itself sets up, and of which it becomes the product as a Nature in which limit and boundary are themselves determining constituents. In fact, Mind in its absolute or infinite substance can only be apprehended as this free activity, which is manifested in self-development through differentiation" (*Introduction to The Philosophy of Fine Art* [*Introductory Lectures on Aesthetics*], pp. 126–127),[10] differentiation from the absolute, as in *explicato*, manifestation of intelligence in the real. Differentiation, the setting of oppositions, is in fact the activity, the sonority, by which the ideal enters into the real, thus it must be differentiation in the ideal which leads the real in the ideal to the absolute, in the dialectic.

Nature, the real, is the "Idea in *apparent shape*, which mind, in its synthetic power, posits as the object opposed to itself," as described by Hegel (p. 127). Nature is thus "the determination by mind of its own substance, its ideality and power of determination, through a process which no doubt begins with a separation of itself into two factors which apparently negate each other, but which, by the very activity of such negation and separation, passes beyond the contradiction it implies to a unity which heals the fracture." Such is the subject and content of Romantic art, the primordial dehiscence which is mind itself as it perceives itself in consciousness in being. The dialectical synthesis of the differentiation in the absolute in the ideal constitutes the subjectivity of mind, which is the subject of Romantic art. In subjective mind, the real is not "*explicitly* unfolded," as it is in perception, and complete self-consciousness. The real becomes the other to subjective mind in its state of explication, but an other that is defined by finitude rather than the infinity of the absolute. Mind must project itself into its other in order to recover the infinity of the absolute in the subjective, which is the project of Transcendental Idealism. Mind cannot recover its subjectivity in the real through scientific theory or logic in reason, through that which established its finitude in the real. This can only be accomplished in philosophy and art.

In perception, mind always has a sense that what is being given of the real in perception is not being in its completion; the limitations of reason are self-apparent in self-consciousness as well, as in scientific theory. The nature of the human mind is to seek completion in being, whether it be reconciliation of the primordial dehiscence, or recognition of the presence of the absolute in the ideal. Ordinary consciousness is the "entirely finite, temporal, contradictory, and for that reason transitory, unsatisfied, and un-reconciled spirit" (p. 128) which seeks to pacify itself in philosophy and art. In such a consciousness, the satisfactions of reason can only have a "purely relative and isolated validity," a condition which thought must necessarily seek to surpass. Appearance as given by perception is seen as a finite function of reason, and in the perception of the real, the intersection of mind and what is external to it, "mind grasps its finiteness as the negation of its own essential substance, and is aware of its infinity." In this activity mind is subjective because it is self-determinate and the object of its own will, the realization of its own freedom. Romantic art is the expression of the will of the mind in self-determinant activity in relation to its freedom. In this activity mind enacts the principle of differentiation which is the essence of the absolute; reasoning mind doubles itself in relation to the absolute, where the knower and the known are undifferentiated. In this way the infinite is injected into the finite, the ideal into the real, as the real is participant in reason. In absolute mind, the Intellectual Principle of Plotinus, principle and activity are the same, ideal and real. In the ideal, the real is participant in the absolute.

Romantic art is "neither the logical idea, absolute thought, that is, which develops itself in the medium of its freest activity, nor is it the Idea of Nature apprehended under finite categories" (p. 129); it is rather the expression of the independence of the infinite from the finite, the freedom of the subjective mind in relation to logic and perception. As a function of philosophy, Romantic art is the expression of a philosophical freedom, or philosophy *as* freedom, in the enactment of the self-determinant will of thought. Art in its highest manifestation is necessarily the expression of Absolute Spirit, an expression of the Philosophy of Spirit, the highest level of philosophical development, combining the Philosophy of Nature, the Philosophy of Mind, and Identity Philosophy (*Identitätsphilosophie*, Transcendental Idealism), which present philosophy as a science, which is necessary in its development, and equally necessary to synthesize in the dialectic. The Philosophy of Spirit is the philosophy of freedom, freedom of mind from the contingent and determinant factors of the real as given by logic and perception.

Art is the philosophical expression of the absolute in the real, and a complete understanding of the absolute in philosophy is impossible without art, as the ideal can only be understood in relation to the real. Philosophy cannot be disassociated from experience in perception, and art is to experience in perception as philosophy is to mind. As for Schelling, art is not possible without philosophy, and philosophy is not possible without art. In that art is the philosophical expression of the absolute in the real, the synthesis of the universal and the particular in being, art cannot be disassociated from history, which is also the expression of the absolute in the real as given by the ideal, the memory (*Erinnerung*) of the course of events in relation to the present. Art is an instrument of historical memory in the process of philosophical development, an indicator of the philosophical development of a culture.

Through art, the individual subject participates in the Absolute Spirit which is the Absolute Spirit as manifest in mind (*Geist*) and history (*Zeitgeist*), in memory. As art enacts the synthesis of the finite and the infinite, it cannot appear as completely reasonable; in fact, art is better equipped to express the unreason in reason than is philosophy, because as philosophy is given by language, it cannot present unreason as reason. In art, unreason can be expressed in reason because art is not bound to the rational constructs of language, as it occupies the in-between space between the ideal and the real, mind and appearance, the *chôra* as it were in the allegory of becoming, the space of the intersection of language and sensual appearance. Such a space cannot be seen as entirely governed by reason, but also by a mystical connection to unreason, not insanity, but the absence of reason within reason.

In the *Phaedrus* (249), reason gathers the "multiplicity of sense-impressions" and creates from them universals. In order to do this, it must recollect its perception of sense-impressions as archetypes, a kind of perception to which it was initiated in a mystical vision, in the intersection of mind and appearance, ideal and real. Philosophy is the application of the remembrance of archetypal images in perception, the *a priori* synthesis of the real and ideal applied to the real, in the intersection of mind and appearance as given by perception. If the soul of the philosopher dwells in the memory of the archetypal images of the gods, in the presence of the absolute in mind, then it will experience a "continual initiation into the perfect mystic vision." The philosopher in the *Phaedrus* thus appears to ordinary consciousness to be "out of his wits," to be possessed by a god. "This then is the fourth type of madness, which befalls when a man, reminded by the sight of beauty on earth of the true beauty," as in the *Symposium*, "grows his wings and endeavors to fly upward, but in vain, exposing himself to the reproach of insanity because like a bird he fixes his gaze on the heights to the neglect of things below," but beholds his true being.

Art is able to represent this kind of mystical vision in perception which can be described by philosophy. The perception of art, unlike the perception of nature, acts as a catalyst to a mystical vision in philosophy, because in the perception of the art the mind is able to see the absolute in itself, which it cannot see in nature. The unreason of the mystical vision is in contrast to ordinary consciousness in perception, but is necessary for the experience of the absolute in mind, the identity of mind with the appearance in perception, in the philosophical dialectic. The experience of the absolute in mind, which can be enacted in the perception of Romantic art, art in which the ideal can be experienced separately from the ground of the synthesis of the ideal and the real, is described in the *Phaedrus* (250): "But the beauty was once ours to see in all its brightness, when in the company of the blessed we followed Zeus as others followed some other of the Olympians, to enjoy the beatific vision and to be initiated into that mystery which brings, we may say with reverence, supreme felicity. Whole were we who celebrated that festival, unspotted by all the evils which awaited us in time to come, and whole and unspotted and changeless and serene were the objects revealed to us in the light of that mystic vision. Pure was the light and pure were we from the pollution of the walking sepulcher which we call a body, to which we are bound like an oyster to its shell," which could not be transcended in the artistic representation of the classical world, because the absolute was not yet present in mind as distinct from the real, as a product of the self-alienation of mind from reason, and the alienation of mind from being, which could only occur in philosophical development following the conceptualization of the absolute in Christian theology, in Neoplatonism.

The Philosophy of Spirit is the product of a linear development from classical mythology to Platonic philosophy to Christian theology to Neoplatonism. The Philosophy of Spirit is not possible without Neoplatonism, in the reconciliation of classical philosophy and Christian theology, the Platonic Idea with the possibility (though not the realization) of the disembodied absolute. For Hegel, Romantic art is the artistic realization of classical philosophy, which was not achieved in Classical art. It is the artistic realization of the Platonic Idea, the presence of the absolute in the real. The Platonic Idea, and philosophical development toward the Philosophy of Spirit, is not possible without the Olympian gods of Homer and Hesiod, in which the real becomes embodied in the ideal, as opposed to the ideal being embodied in the real. The artistic representation of the Olympian gods in Classical art could not represent the ideal as distinct from the real, as the gods were given in allegory in mythology, because they could still only be given as such, in the identity of the real and ideal. Thus the ideal was represented as distinct from the real in philosophy (in fact, in an un-reconcilable manner, as Hegel points out), but not in art.

Beauty in nature, especially beauty of the body, arouses a desire for absolute beauty, but it does not reveal the absolute, as does beauty in art. The desire for the absolute is the desire for self-knowledge, and the desire for the reconciliation of the self-alienated mind in self-consciousness. Beauty in art is a product of mind, thus it is the absolute made known to mind through mind, through reason and intuition. Beauty in art is the sensuous representation of the idea (*das sinnliche Scheiner der Idee*) in the identity of the real and ideal, the idea being the intuition of the absolute in the Intellectual Principle, the participation of reason, the Reason Principle, in the absolute. The finitude of reason is a function of the infinity of the absolute in the idea. The idea as Spirit is made concrete in reason, following the hypostases of Plotinus represented in Intellectual Principle and Reason Principle, as instruments of the absolute, and in turn the apprehension of the absolute, in the soul, the *anima prima* and *anima secunda* of Marsilio Ficino.

Spirit (*Geist*) as intelligence, is as absolute in the real as in the ideal for Hegel, which allows it to be revealed in the sensuous forms of art. Art is the first manifestation of the absolute, in sensuous form, which leads to the manifestation of the absolute in the ideal, thus art is an instrument of philosophy, and of historicism, being the structure of the manifestation of the absolute in human activity. Beauty in art is the absolute in philosophy in sensuous form; through art, consciousness perceives the absolute within itself as beauty. The absolute is not completely revealed in art, as sensuous form is limited to the real, but it is through the revelation of the absolute in sensuous form that the absolute is revealed in mind. Romantic art is able to reveal an element of the absolute in the idea which does not exist in the real, as the beauty of Romantic art is a product of mind, but not the complete absolute as it is perceived in mind.

Art is propaedeutic to philosophy, and its destiny is to be absorbed into philosophy, which it has been at the end of the twentieth century. In that the purpose of art is to reveal the absolute to the perceiving subject, to manifest the idea in the real, the development of art parallels the development of philosophy, and the development of history. Philosophy progresses toward the understanding of the absolute in the ideal, the relation between thought and being, in both synthesis and alienation; history progresses toward the realization of freedom and self-consciousness in a culture, as the realization of Spirit in activity, as manifest in the level of morality and ethics, expressions of the absolute, which govern that activity. Art is an index of the development of the relation between the idea as manifestation of the absolute in mind and the activity of a culture, the *Zeitgeist*, as it unfolds in history. Art is both the absolute, the same absolute of religious devotion, though unembodied, and the *Zeitgeist* made concrete. The stages of the development of art in history as an index of philosophical and cultural development according to Hegel are the symbolic, the Classical, and the Romantic.

Romantic art represents the absolute as the Christian god unembodied, as pure inner, unrepresentable Spirit. It represents the god as being only realizable as without form, in the absolute unity of form and at the same time the absolute absence of form, as for Schelling. Appearance in perception becomes only contingent to the absolute, as it is contingent to the archetype in the Idea of Plato, which is equally divorced from the real. Romantic art injects both the inner idea of the mind and the inner feeling of the soul into sensuous form. It creates an emotional bond between the sensuous form and the perceiving subject, because the subject sees its inner self in the sensuous form and reaffirms itself, and at the same time recognizes its self-alienation. Romantic art thus stages the pathos of the eternal struggle of mind in relation to mind, the eternal struggle of mind in relation to being. It stages the tragedy of self-consciousness along with the liberation of self-consciousness, in Existentialist terms, the importance of the consequences of freedom. It stages the triumph of self-consciousness and freedom over the real, the triumph of the philosophical development of the perceiving subject, but it raises the stakes of the relation between consciousness and the real, and introduces the modern challenges to self-consciousness, the *horror vacui* of freedom in alienation, the *mise-en-abîme* in the separation of the real and the ideal (as represented in the painting by Friedrich), as the absolute is both absolute form and formlessness, the purest form of reason and unreason.

Because of the contingency of the sensuous form, the least material of the Romantic arts reveal the absolute to the greatest extent—painting, music and poetry. Architecture reveals the absolute in no way, because it does not contain the identity of the real and ideal, and is purely symbolic. It is governed by necessity and cause and effect, by reason and science, and thus contains no element of freedom or self-determination. The only way that architecture could reveal the absolute is if it appeared to be governed by necessity, the laws of structure and architectural form, but in fact is not. But then it would cease to be architecture. In painting the real can appear to be ideal; matter can be transformed into light, or matter and light can be combined in color, as described by Schelling. Painting can create the illusion of space on a plane surface; its perception depends on the construction of perception by mind as it projects the real, as the real is perceived in the construction of the mind, into neutral forms, sensuous forms that exist in the real independent of mind, which are represented in the painting.

Painting mirrors the process of the construction of the real in perception to mind, thus it can be read by mind as existing in the ideal, though it remains in the real. As such, painting achieves the identity of the real and the ideal more than the other visual arts; it enacts the phenomenology of appearance in relation to perceiving mind, as best expressed by Paul Cézanne; painting is able to impart to "phenomenal semblances a higher reality, born of mind." Cézanne expressed to Joachim Gasquet, "Painting is first of all in vision. The material of our art lies there, in what our eyes think."[11] Vision is a form of cognition, mediating with the sensible world. Painting is an enactment of vision in perception, perception as a thought process in the mediation between the ideal and the real. Thus painting is able to express the identity of the ideal and the real. The absolute which painting reveals in the identity of the ideal and the real is a nuance of Spirit, a suggestion of the absolute within the real, a suggestion of its eternal presence in the flux of appearance.

As art is absorbed into philosophy, and is seen as parallel to religion in the contemplation of the absolute, and as art is limited in its revelation of the absolute, being limited to the real, more limited than poetry or music, art loses its central importance as an index and expression of the development of the *Zeitgeist* of a culture. Romantic art appears as the final stage in the development of art as the expression of that *Zeitgeist*, as modern freedom and self-consciousness no longer demand the expression of the absolute in the real, as they are the product of the historical development of consciousness, and their development and realization depend on the obsolescence of their prior stages of becoming. Once the human subject is able to recognize itself as freedom and self-consciousness in the identity of the real and ideal in art, in the representation of absolute beauty, and is able to see itself in self-contradiction in the sublime, it no longer has need of the visualization of that self-consciousness, but rather the need to explore its self-consciousness in being, the relation of thought to being.

In that philosophy and poetry are not limited in the real, they are able to provide a stage for the free exploration of consciousness in being, and thus become more closely reflective of the historical development of consciousness in the *Zeitgeist* of the culture. Visual art seems to have served its purpose in relation to historical development; it no longer serves as a mechanism or expression for universal consciousness in history. It continues to serve as a mechanism of expression of individual self-consciousness in relation to being, but not of the universal self-consciousness of a culture. Visual art no longer has the capacity to symbolize the philosophical progress of a culture, as it has been absorbed into philosophy. The philosophy of visual art, the theory of visual art, in that it is philosophy itself, still plays a role in the progress of the cultural *Zeitgeist*. Visual art is important to a culture in the modern world in terms of how it is conceived by the individual subject of that culture, how its conception plays a role in the philosophical outlook of the individual subject, but visual art in its production is no longer an index of that outlook, because the absolute has become the subject of inner contemplation independent of the real, the subject of philosophical discourse, as given by its historical development in art.

The history of the visual arts remains vital to the philosophical conception of the absolute in the individual subject, because without knowledge of that development the individual would have no knowledge of the basis of self-consciousness, without the role that art has played in history in the formulation of self-consciousness, in the individual subject and the culture. In order to continue to play a vital role in the *Zeitgeist* of the culture, the visual arts must re-discover means to enact the further exploration of self-consciousness. At the end of the twentieth century, architecture borrowed from Deconstruction in philosophy in order to enact the struggle of self-consciousness in relation to being in sculpted forms in the architecture, which staged the dialectic between freedom and necessity, thus contributing to and reflecting the development of the *Zeitgeist* of Western culture.

As an instrument of philosophy, but no longer a catalyst for philosophy in the development of self-consciousness, art can only express self-consciousness and freedom in terms borrowed from philosophy, and mirror the *Zeitgeist*, the manifestation of the absolute, the universal Spirit, in the culture. The visual arts can thus continue to play a secondary role in cultural expression, but a role which is important for the individual subject in the self-identity of the subject in relation to his or her culture, in the understanding of the relation of the philosophical development of the individual in relation to the philosophical development of the culture, of the relation of the experience of thought and perception in the individual subject, the individual thinking mind, and the universal self-consciousness of the culture as a manifestation of the same spirit of the absolute.

Phenomenology of Spirit

The *Phenomenology of Spirit*, first published in 1807, is, in the tradition of Transcendental Idealism, an attempt to establish the manifestation of the absolute in the experience of the real. It is a systematic exposition of the relation between mind and being, though not completely dependent on the categories of science nor the subjective expression of poetry. The Philosophy of Spirit is an attempt to synthesize the classical and modern worlds, and to synthesize science, religion, history and art within the framework of philosophy. It is an attempt to develop the freest form of thought possible, as a product of the development of self-consciousness and freedom, the self-determined will. It is a revision of classical philosophy in relation to the scientific and historical knowledge of the early nineteenth century. The Philosophy of Spirit seeks to define the individual subject in relation to the universal culture; it sees the individual as a microcosm of its culture, in the same way that in classical philosophy the individual was seen as a microcosm of the structure of the universe.

In modern terms the individual can only be seen as a microcosm of the universal principles of history that are manifest in culture, in the *Zeitgeist*, because the human subject only belongs to the world which is constructed by human beings, given by history and culture, as established at the beginning of the Enlightenment by Giambattista Vico. The individual subject can no longer be defined in relation to the organic universal of nature, because the individual subject is an artificial construct, in relation to nature, given by language and history. Nevertheless, the artificial construct of the individual subject is governed by principles which are manifestations of the same universal which underlies nature and all experience in the real, as given by perception. The *Phenomenology of Spirit* lays the groundwork for the epistemological basis of the aesthetics of Hegel, in the dualistic relation between the individual and experience. The Absolute Spirit underlies history as well as nature, and governs the relation between the finite and the infinite, between events and absolute ideas, from which history is constructed.

Events in history are manifestations of the idea of the absolute in the same way that principles of reason are manifestations of those ideas, the archetypal ideas in the Intellectual Principle of Plotinus, as it were. The progress of history is the progress of the realization of the absolute in the particular event and in the individual subject, and in empirical experience, the ideal in the real, in the terms of Schelling. It is through an understanding of the absolute that the events of history, and empirical experience, are understood, as factors which play a role in the definition of being. The individual subject is seen as a universal in a particular form, acting according to the *Zeitgeist* of the culture. All thought, and all artistic expression, is a product of the manifestation of the universal as particular in the individual.

The individual subject is a product of the *Zeitgeist*, as are all forms of artistic expression. The better the individual subject understands the relation between the individual and the universal, between subjective experience and the *Zeitgeist* as manifestations of the absolute, the more resonant and meaningful will be the artistic expression of the individual subject. No individual operates in a void; everyone is a product of the culture and historical time period in which they live; the student of history better understands the relation between the individual and the *Zeitgeist.* The Philosophy of Spirit is a systematic study of history and experience in relation to the absolute; it attempts to lay a groundwork for artistic expression as a form of cultural expression in relation to philosophy, and a groundwork for the understanding of the relation between the particular and the universal and the finite and the infinite in mind.

It is in the self-consciousness of mind, or Spirit, that the absolute is most completely manifested and understood, in the independent activity of mind, the products of which are philosophy and art. The self-consciousness of mind contains the ideas of the universal as archetypes for reason and perception, in the same way as the Intellectual Principle of Plotinus, which is participated in by the absolute, and which dictates forms to Reason Principle, or reason. Self-consciousness allows mind to translate sense experience in perception into idea, as manifestation of the absolute. Perception alone, without the participation of self-consciousness, can only present a limited picture of the real to mind, a picture determined by appearances and inchoate forms. The understanding in self-consciousness makes perceptible a deep structure of signification in relation to perceived forms and appearances, which allows the experience of the real in perception to be integrated with mind to form an experience which synthesizes the real and the ideal, the objective and subjective, and the individual thinking subject and universal principles as manifestations of the absolute.

Consciousness is replaced by self-consciousness, and logic is replaced by a higher form of philosophical reason, combining logic with intuition, conscious and unconscious experience, in the dialectical development of thought in the Philosophy of Spirit. This requires the highest possible development of reason in consciousness, a systematic and scientific understanding in philosophy (*Wissenschaft*) which leads to the understanding of the relation between consciousness and the absolute, and thus self-consciousness. The universal principle of the absolute is made objective and substantial, and is able to be applied to the ethics and morality of the culture, as well as to the principles of artistic expression, in the understanding of the *Zeitgeist* of the culture in the structure of history, and the role of the individual. Self-consciousness in the Philosophy of Spirit raises understanding in reason (*Vernunft*) to the Absolute Spirit (*Geist*), as the historical manifestation of the absolute in the phenomenal experience of the individual, and the ethics and morality and artistic expression of the individual as a function of history and culture.

It is the task of the individual in a culture to pass from phenomenal experience to an understanding of the universal principles at play in the culture which determine and define the phenomenal experience. In the Preface to the *Phenomenology of Spirit*, "The beginning of culture and of the struggle to pass out of the unbroken immediacy of naïve psychical life has always to be made by acquiring knowledge of universal principles and points of view…"[12] The task of philosophy is to aid the individual subject in acquiring a universal point of view in relation to his or her role in a culture, to acquire the knowledge of universal principles in the understanding of the structure of perception in phenomenal experience, the structure of thought in relation to the universal principles, and the structure of history in relation to the absolute. An understanding of the absolute as Spirit or *Geist* is a product of a systematic understanding of these relationships.

Spirit comes to be seen as reality, the inner being of the world which "assumes objective, determinate form, and enters into relations with itself—it is externality (otherness), and exists for self…" (p. 86). It doubles itself in its otherness, but retains its inner essence within itself, "self-contained and self-complete," which is inaccessible to its manifestations in the particular, as the One of Plotinus. The Spirit is implicit in its nature as self-contained (*an sich*); it does not exist in the real, and does not exhibit the qualities of the real, of differentiation in the particular, until the initial doubling of itself as otherness or externality, as in the primordial dehiscence of thought alienating itself from its own being. Spirit becomes object, but as object Spirit is immediately negated. Spirit becomes self-reflected in the object which is the product of its doubling; in the same way, mind is self-reflected in the object which is the product of its doubling, which is reason. Reason is the objective self-reflection of mind, resulting from a primordial dehiscence, a self-alienation of mind in the phenomenal world. Mind as Spirit is negated in reason, but is reflected by reason, so that reason can perceive Spirit in mind.

The inner essence of Spirit as absolute is inaccessible to the laws of reason, which are predicated on the objective self-doubling and negation of the absolute, as the One of Plotinus in inaccessible to both Intellectual Principle and Reason Principle, though it participates in them. Being cannot be realized in a fixed system, although it is only through the fixed system of reason that the unrealizable nature of being in the objective can be perceived. Objective particulars, in the phenomenal and reason, can only have a relation to being in as much as the universal is participant in them; otherwise they only exist as the self-doubling of the absolute, the essence of being, in which the essence of being is negated. The principles and the systems of reason are thus limited in their self-relation to being, and it is the universal which is revealed in them which completes their validation in relation to being. In the universal, particulars are dissolved, but the universal, as source of particulars, can only be predicated on the existence and differentiation of the particulars, in organic nature and in the dialectic.

The organic in existence is a partial revelation of the absolute, in which particulars are dissolved in the universal, in which individual forms participate in universal principles of life, as given by reason in science. The organic in nature is the *Gestalt* in reason, those universal principles which underlie reason and experience, which exceed the sum of the principles of reason, and which cannot be seen to be extracted from them, as in *concinnitas* in the Renaissance. Being, the Spirit of the absolute, is intuited by reason as existing in the unanimated mass of matter in the phenomenal, in what is perceived as the absence of being, the dark ground of existence. Being exists in non-being as the universal exists in the particular; the particulars of matter are animated by Spirit, though undetectable by perception or reason, because they participate in the construction of the universal by reason. Their participation is seen by reason as a principle or a law, a manifestation of the idea of the absolute in reason. The participation of the particulars, as it is perceived by reason, is abstracted into an idea, which differentiates itself from the sensuous existence of the particulars, in the real. The abstraction of the particulars into a universal concept in reason frees mind from the phenomenal, and allows it to develop as self-determinate, though predicated on the systematic abstraction of universals from particulars.

In the abstraction of the universal from the particular, reason gains self-consciousness; it doubles itself as does the absolute in the objective, and the self-doubling, the reason principle in self-consciousness, negates the participation of the particular, objective real from which it is derived. As such mind sets itself against the real which causes its reason principles in self-consciousness, and becomes alienated from it. In modern consciousness, freedom of mind is set against the phenomenological, which is limited to necessity and cause and effect, the principles extracted from it which make it intelligible to mind. The real, matter and organic nature, is determinate, controlled by necessity, while self-reflective mind, in the dialectical process of abstraction, is self-determinate, as the self-alienating double of determinateness. The dialectic, because it moves from the object to the abstraction, from the particular to the universal, is not limited to the necessary laws of cause and effect in matter, nor to the necessary laws of logic in reason, though the dialectic is completely predicated in reason, as the abstracted principle is completely predicated in the real, in the particular.

Organic nature constitutes a preliminary dissolution of the particular into the universal, and a partial revelation of the absolute. Particulars of matter are not connected in the universal in the way that organic bodies are; they are complete in their particularity, and in their absence of being, the absence of the Spirit as absolute. The Spirit as absolute is partially present in organic nature, because organic bodies are particulars of a universal, absorbed into a universal; the particular is partially dissolved in the presence of the universal in the particular. Sensuous forms in art are a more complete revelation of the absolute, because the particulars of artistic representation are more completely dissolved into the universal of the idea, and the universal is more participant in the particular. The presence of the universal in the particular is the presence of law and principle, of the abstractions of the phenomenal in the idea, of the structure of reason. The more the form in nature exhibits the workings of reason in its sensuous form, the more it is defined as animated and organic.

The organic, in scientific reason, is nothing more than the projection of the principles of reason, as a function of the Spirit of the absolute, into nature, into the sensuous form of the real from which reason is in turn extracted. In that the principles of reason are present in the organic structure, the organic being demonstrates an element of self-determination, independent of the isolated particulars of matter. As such, the organic being doubles the principle abstracted from the particular of matter against itself, as in the doubling of the absolute, and both absorbs the abstracted particular and becomes isolated from it. Such is the dialectical process as it develops in the real, as a manifestation of the archetype of the absolute, and its phenomenological ground. "Here, then, law appears as the relation of an element to the formative process of the organic being, which at one moment has the element over against itself, at another exhibits it within its own self-determining organic structure" (p. 294). The organic being doubles against itself as reason doubles against itself, becoming self-determinate and revealing the absolute, in the abstraction from the particular to the universal.

Understanding, as opposed to reason, is the transition from the particular to the universal, given the revelation of the absolute as the universal in the particular. Understanding is the process of the transition which exceeds the sum of the parts of the transition, as in *concinnitas*; it is both the particular and the universal in relation to each other, as opposed to the determinate existence of the particular and universal as combined in reason. The transition from the particular to universal in understanding is the subjective, while the particular and universal identified as such are the objective in reason. The understanding, as subjective, is the self-consciousness of the process of reason, the organic and self-determined aspect of reason. The relation between the particular and universal is the organic unity in reason, the participation of the absolute in Intellectual Principle, and the organic unity in reason, the understanding, itself becomes the object of reason; the object of reason becomes its own process, in self-consciousness. The process of reason becomes its universality, in which particulars become translated into abstract participants in laws and principles. As the particular becomes a universal in the process of reason, the particular comes to be seen as the manifestation of the universal which as object gives the universal to reason in understanding. The universal abstract of the particular exceeds the particular as object in relation to the universal, thus to the absolute; it is the more stable state of the particular in relation to the infinite, as perceived by mind which has isolated itself from the particular in the transitional process in reason. The abstract principle, the universal, becomes the object in relation to understanding, as the understanding is to the absolute as the particular is to reason, in a hierarchy of being reminiscent of the Plotinian hypostases.

The particular as abstracted universal retains the determinate and necessary qualities of the particular in reason. In reason, the relations of cause and effect between particulars have not been subsumed into the self-conscious process of understanding, as in the Intellectual Principle. The understanding is to reason as the organic is to matter, wherein particulars become self-determinate as universals, in the further participation of the absolute. The intersection of mind and the sensible world, between the ideal and the real, occurs in perception. Perception is the enactment of reason in the translation of the particular to the universal. The particulars of the sensible world are immediately present to perception as universals, because perception is the enactment of the constructive process of reason. It is impossible for the perceiving subject to see the particulars of the sensible world as only particulars; that would deny the activity of reason in perception. The process of perception is "immediately self-differentiating" (*Phenomenology* 111),[13] as reason is immediately self-differentiating in relation to itself and in relation to being. Through perception in the self-consciousness of reason, mind perceives sensible particulars as being self-differentiated and self-alienated in the same way that it sees itself in its revelation to itself of the absolute in self-consciousness. This phenomenon of self-differentiation manifests itself as a principle of necessity or cause and effect in reason, as the universal is only given by the particular.

When the object in the sensible world is perceived, it comes into being, because the unfolding of the universal from the particular is enacted in relation to mind. The object is perceived as containing both the particular and universal, and its coming into being is its process of differentiation of the universal from the particular, the process of reason toward understanding, which mind perceives in itself in self-consciousness, which is enacted in perception in relation to the object perceived. The object perceived becomes an element and a catalyst of the dialectical process of mind toward understanding. The act of perceiving is the act of mind in reason toward understanding; the visual arts incorporate the process of perception itself into the objects perceived, and thus act as a further catalyst of mind in reason toward understanding. In the *Phenomenology of Spirit*, "the way we take in perception is no longer something that just happens to us like sense-certainty; on the contrary, it is logically necessitated. With the emergence of the principle, the two moments which in their appearing merely *occur*, also come into being: one being the movement of pointing-out or the *act of perceiving*, the other being the same movement as a simple event or the object perceived. In essence the object is the same as the movement: the movement is the unfolding and differentiation of the two moments, and the object is the apprehended togetherness of the moments" (111). The universal is immediately present in the object which is perceived, because the object cannot be defined as other than being perceived, and thus contains within it the process of perception.

The principle of the universal is the essence of perception. The perceiving subject, and the object which is perceived, are both unessential in relation to the process of perception as particulars, but both contain the principle of the universal within them, and in combination as opposites, constitute the universal principle of perception. The coincidence of opposites is always already present in the universal, as the self-differentiation of the absolute. The act of perception creates the unessential character of both the perceiver and the object perceived in the process of differentiation which must then be reconciled in understanding toward which reason in perception progresses. The variable properties of an object of perception are the exhibition of the universal within the particular as enacted by perception. The properties of an object are constructed by perception, as products of the progression of reason toward understanding, toward the absolute. This is demonstrated in the idea of phenomenal transparency in the twentieth century, in which the mental constructions of space intersect with the space itself, resulting in qualities which are both inherent to the object as perceived and to the object as conceived in its spatial relationships in mind. The variable qualities of an object are the product of the object in perception; it is perception which gives the object a seemingly infinite variety of permutations in the flux of appearance; the flux of appearance is a product of the principle of the universal in perception. Thus, though it is a screen which masks the essential nature of the absolute in the real, as in the *Republic* of Plato, the flux of appearance is the necessary context of the real in perception, in interaction with the ideal, toward the revelation of the absolute.

In perception as the self-consciousness of reason, the object of perception is transformed from the particular which embodies the absence of being into a participant in the principle of the universal which reveals the absolute. Perception negates the existence of the object as a particular, and in the process allows the object to come into being in the universal. Being, as the principle of the universal, contains the negation within it; being is not possible without non-being, as perception is not possible without the object perceived. The negation of being is contained in the differentiation of the object of perception, in the multiple permutations given to the object by perception. Coming to being contains the negation of being as well. The multiple permutations of the object are independent of each other as particulars, and are related to each other through the principle of the universal, which is independent of them. The multiple particulars of the flux of appearance only participate in the universal through reason; in the suspension of reason, the multiple particulars—shadows, reflections, refractions, trajectories, etc. (the qualities of objects in perception)—appear as self-determinate entities, embodying the universal within themselves, independent of the process of reason. The ground of non-being appears as being, in the complete self-alienation of reason from being. The differentiation between reason and being, as given by reason in being, is that which is overcome in the process of perception.

Being mediates the negative within it—this is the principle of the universal in being. The expression of the mediation of negation is the particular in the flux of appearance. All properties of being have a correlate negative in the *coincidentia oppositorum* of becoming, as in the dialectic of reason. The principle of the universal, in contrast, does not have a negative correlate. The particular is not the negative of the universal, because the universal is contained within the particular. The goal of the dialectic is the understanding in the principle of the universal. The universal exists independently of the determinate; as self-determinate, it has no negation; negation can only be what is other to it, not in relation to it. The universal is independent of the particulars which contain it and participate in it, as the absolute is independent of being. In their participation in the principle of the universal, particulars are defined as being both independent from each other and combined in the same organic unity; the particular in being is the either/or or both/and in language, as described in Deconstruction, the scotoma which negates the absolute relation between being and reason, as given in perception or language. The scotoma is the gap in the visual field, and it is present in perception itself, in the gap between the sensible world as intuited by the understanding, as present in the unconscious, for example, and the sensible world as given by perception.

In conscious perception the object of perception is developed in reason, in particular the contradictions contained within the object as it is perceived. The object is perceived as both a particular and a universal; as a universal the object participates in being, in coming into being; as a particular the object is non-being. The object perceived as non-being is also the object perceived as being; being simultaneously co-exists with being in perception, reason with non-reason. As for Schelling, non-being is also the essence of the absolute. The particular as non-being which excludes itself from the community of being in reason contains the same essence which is revealed through reason in understanding, as a product of perception. It is in this way that reason participates in being, and consciousness in perception, which "has a mediated relation to the inner being and, as the Understanding, looks through this mediating play of Forces into the true background of things" (*Phenomenology* 143). That which unites understanding and the essence of being is appearance in perception, which, as understanding and being come together, is "henceforth only a vanishing."

Appearance is in its own self a non-being and a surface show, as in the *Republic*, a non-essential medium of understanding in perception. As a surface show, appearance displays the principle of the universal, a totality in relation to particulars, which is contained in the particulars. In appearance, as given by perception, the particular immediately becomes its own opposite, as the particular is transformed into the universal by reason, thus appearance in perception is unstable and ephemeral. The negative dialectic of appearance becomes a positive in the understanding of the principle of the universal. The being of the object is "mediated by the movement of appearance" (*Phenomenology* 143) in consciousness and becomes the negation of being as a particular. Consciousness sees itself, its own processes, in the negative dialectic of appearance. The negation of being becomes being in reason as self-differentiation; it is activated in the dialectical becoming of being, as the particular is transformed into the universal. The "objective vanishing appearance" given by perception becomes the being-for-self of consciousness in the negative dialectic. The self-differentiation of the absolute, and the self-alienation of reason from being, becomes the being of reason in relation to the absolute.

Reason, in its self-differentiation, is a product of the synthesis of the universal and the particular beyond the particular. The negation of being confirms being beyond appearance and the sensible world, beyond the mechanisms of perception and of reason itself, which is a function of non-reason in the same way. The essence of being is found in the supersensible, as in the Idea of Plato and the intelligible of Plotinus, that which exceeds the dialectic of being and non-being in perception, reason and non-reason in mind, the double negative of the identity of the ideal and the real. Appearance in perception is an element in reason in the dialectic between being and the absolute, and in syllogistic reasoning between the absolute and being, as it is embodied in the particular; "above the vanishing present world there opens up a permanent beyond" (144) in the absolute. The beyond is the inner world in relation to consciousness, where consciousness is unable to find itself. It is the empty nothingness of being in appearance, the self-alienation of reason as manifest in perception, and the simple and unitary universal which is inaccessible to the particulars of perception and logic.

The inner being of things, as a void beyond consciousness, is unknowable to reason in the same way that God is unknowable to consciousness in the negative theology of Christian Neoplatonism. The incomprehensible god was described by Pseudo-Dionysius as "the highest peak of mystic inspiration, eminently unknown yet exceedingly luminous, where the pure, absolute and unchanging mysteries of theology are veiled in the dazzling obscurity of the secret silence, outshining all brilliance with the intensity of their darkness, and surcharging our blinded intellects with the utterly impalpable and invisible splendor surpassing all beauty."[14] Such is the absolute of Hegel in the nothingness of being, as given in perception. The void of Hegel is the "holy of holies," devoid of the relationships and differentiations which constitute reason in the particular, as given in consciousness.

The world of appearance is the essence of the supersensible beyond in the sense that it is through appearance that the absolute comes into being, though appearance at the same time negates the being of the absolute. The world of appearance is the sensible world posited by reason as having been superseded by the universal in perception; appearance itself is the mediation between the real and the ideal in perception, thus appearance is the essence of the absolute in relation to the real, to the sensible world, given that there is a sensible world beyond appearance or perception, which is the first principle of Transcendental Idealism. There must be a sensible world beyond appearance in order that reason be self-determinant, and that consciousness become self-consciousness in the understanding of an absolute. "The supersensible is therefore appearance qua appearance" (*Phenomenology* 147); proof of the supersensible, thus the sensible, is given by appearance, by the double negative of appearance in being, by reason itself, and in particular the limitations of reason.

The double negative of appearance in itself has no significance; it is empty as shadow and reflection. It is only as mediator of being and understanding that appearance in perception, as construct of reason, assumes significance. Appearance is the meeting of being and understanding, through the self-determination of being. The "play of forces" (148) in appearance enacts an interplay or interchange "of the determinateness which constitutes the sole content of what appears: to be either a universal medium, or a negative unity." The content of appearance is the dialectic of being and understanding, of nothingness and the absolute, in the particular and the universal. The interplay constitutes a transformation of the particular to the universal, of the dark ground of being to the ineffable absolute, carried out by the particulars of reason and perception. In the process of being becoming understanding, it is negated in its being by reason and is absorbed into the principle of the universal, by which being is given to understanding. The essence of being is self-differentiated, and what is left in understanding of being is only the self-differentiation of being. The principle of the universal in understanding is an "absolute flux" which "is only difference as a universal difference, or as a difference into which the many antitheses have been resolved."

The understanding is the *différance* of Deconstruction, the "systematic play of differences,"[15] as described by Jacques Derrida in *Positions*, a "generative movement in the play of differences" in appearance, a negation of being in understanding which has only a deferred presence in reason. The play of differences in appearance is a "spacing" in reason, which "designates *nothing*, nothing that is, no presence at a distance; it is the index of an irreducible exterior, and at the same time of a *movement*, a displacement that indicates an irreducible alterity" (p. 81), the movement of the play of differences in perception, the double negation of being in perception, and the self-alienation of reason in being. In the principle of the universal the flux of differences becomes absolute and simple; the universal of the essence of being is both absolute identity and absolute difference, as for Schelling. Negation is an essential aspect of the universal flux of difference, and is itself a universal difference. The negation of being is an essential element in the universal flux of differences as being. In reason, through appearance, the play of differences, the *différance*, is translated into universal principle.

The principle in reason which is the expression of *différance* is the "stable image of unstable appearance" (*Phenomenology* 149), the reconstruction of appearance in perception as given to reason by reason. The only principle of appearance itself is the universal flux of differences, as in the turbulence of the immortal souls thrust into the universal body in the *Timaeus* (43), which "were unable to control it, nor were they controlled by it, and because of the constant violent conflict the motions of the whole creature were irregular, fortuitous and irrational." The supersensible world of the absolute in understanding is the law of stability in identity which corresponds to the law of instability in difference in the sensible world as given by appearance. In the *Timaeus*, the unstable flux of differences is the result of the binding of the soul to the body, of understanding to perception. The regular motion of the Same in the soul is a product of the detachment of the soul from body, when the unstable flux of difference has been transformed into the stable law of identity in understanding. "And because of all this the soul when first bound to its mortal body is as much without reason today as it was in the beginning. But when the stream of growth and nourishment flows less strongly, the soul's orbits take advantage of the calm and as time passes steady down in their proper courses, and the movement of the circles at last regains its correct natural form" (44), that given by the principle of the universal in reason.

In the understanding, in the inner world, as in the Intellectual Principle of Plotinus, the variable and multiple laws of reason in perception, in appearance, are dissolved into the universal idea of law, which, as the absolute, is undifferentiated into the multiple particulars of reason in the intellectual. Differences as well are dissolved into the idea of difference and become indeterminate. The plurality of laws and differences as they are manifest in perception contradict the essence of the understanding, as they are the product of the self-differentiation and self-alienation of the absolute in the understanding. The universal idea of law in the understanding is being itself, undifferentiated in relation to itself and in relation to the sensuous and determinate, in which the particular law corresponds to appearance. The idea of law is related to a particular law as an intelligible archetype, as for the geometers in the *Republic* (511). The determinateness of the particular law is "only a vanishing moment which can no longer occur here as something essential…" (*Phenomenology* 151) as it participates in appearance. The necessity of the law in the particular is its inner unity in the universal idea of law, so necessity and freedom are intertwined in the real, as are absolute being and determinate being. The necessity of difference is also the universal idea of difference, the essence of difference in inner being, the internal self-alienation of being, as manifest in the differentials and particulars of reason.

The flux of differentiation in existence is the product of an antithesis within an antithesis, the possibility of an absolute undifferentiated being, described by Georges Bataille as a "laceration within a lacerated nature,"[16] in which man "can no longer recognize himself in the degrading chains of logic, but he recognizes himself, instead—not only with rage but in an ecstatic torment—in the virulence of his own phantasms," in the manifestation of the absolute of being in the imagination and in the understanding. In differentiated being the thesis is always present in the antithesis; the differentiated is always present in that from which it is differentiated. The absolute must contain the capacity for differentiation within it, though the differentiation is only activated in reason in perception, in appearance. The inner world of being, "the supersensible world, which is the inverted world, has at the same time overarched the other world and has it within it; it is for itself the inverted world" (*Phenomenology* 160); it is the synthesis in the dialectic, the thesis combined with the antithesis, which is the self-differentiation of the thesis. As such, it is absolute difference, and is manifest as the idea of difference in the intelligible.

Infinity is the "absolute unrest of pure self-movement" (163), that which is indeterminate and undifferentiated as particular. Infinity is only present in the absolute, and is only given in intelligence in the understanding, the Intellectual Principle, as that which supersedes the particulars of reason in intelligence. Infinity is present in appearance; it is displayed or revealed, in the same way as the absolute, as the product of mind in perception, but it is not active in appearance, not present as an "explanation," only a phenomenon. Self-consciousness is the presence of infinity in consciousness, the presence of the absolute as given by the understanding, Intellectual Principle. Self-consciousness is the explanation of infinity in consciousness, the presence of unreason in reason, the self-identity of reason differentiated from itself. The explanation of infinity in the understanding "supersedes the differences present in the law," and presents them as a unified force in the absolute. The explanation itself, in unifying differences, creates a new differentiation, a "sundering" or dehiscence, which is both difference and indifference, the thesis and the antithesis. The understanding is subject to the movement of the differentiation of particulars in reason, thus to necessity, in its explanation of indifference in the unification of difference; the understanding is thus still organic in reason, and is not the essence of indifferentiation and infinity in the absolute, though it can explain those qualities as it is recipient of the idea in representation, the *logos* of the intelligible, as it is self-differentiated.

As it is subject to differentiation, the understanding is given through appearance, through reason in perception. As in Deconstruction, there is nothing outside the text. But the understanding, in self-consciousness, sees differentiation as a manifestation of universal differentiation; as self-consciousness, the differentiation which the understanding sees is its own. All differentiation in the real, in matter and the organic, as given by appearance, is perceived by mind as it projects itself, its own self-differentiation, into the real. Differentiation becomes universal in understanding because it is seen as the universal and eternal presence of differentiation in itself; the idea of infinity is the identity of the ideal and the real, the perception of the real as the identity of real and ideal within the ideal. In self-consciousness, in the inner world of mind not given to itself by perception, mind sees itself as identical to the super-sensible, that which precedes the real in perception, as established by Kant, but it is only through the "mediating term of appearance" (165) that mind sees itself as prior to appearance.

The participation of reason in the understanding is predicated on the function of reason in perception; reason cannot see itself as differentiated from perception without the use of perception. Differentiation is only possible in identity, and the absolute in understanding is only possible in the differentiation in reason. In the self-consciousness of reason in perception, "this curtain hanging before the inner world is drawn away, and we have the inner being gazing into the inner world—the vision of the undifferentiated self-same being, which repels itself from itself..." The curtain hanging before the inner world is the luminous embroidered veil in the *Republic*, the curtain along the road next to the cave which separates the cave from the sun, the real from the absolute; in the *Republic* it is "like the screen at puppet shows between the operators and their audience, above which they show their puppets" (514). The curtain is appearance itself as given by perception, through which reason is interfused in the real; when the curtain is drawn away, the mechanisms of reason in relation to the real are drawn away. Reason is stripped of its operative being, and is only left in self-awareness of its inoperative being, its complete alienation from its own being in the world. The "inner being gazing into the inner world" sees the void of the absolute, of absolute non-being, in relation to being as given by appearance.

The void of the inner world is the vision of the immortal souls in the *Phaedrus* (247), which "when they reach the summit of the arch, go outside the vault and stand upon the back of the universe; standing there they are carried around by its revolution while they contemplate what lies outside the heavens....a reality without color or shape, intangible but utterly real, apprehensible only by intellect which is the pilot of the soul." Only intellect can see behind the curtain of appearance constructed by reason, and see reason itself in its process of seeing, in self-consciousness. In the *Enneads* of Plotinus, the vision of the immortal souls is an inner vision which is detached from the sensual world in perception, and is given by intellection, the understanding. "Many times it has happened: lifted out of the body into myself; becoming external to all other things and self-centered; beholding a marvelous beauty; then, more than ever, assured of community with the loftiest order; enacting the noblest life, acquiring identity with the divine; stationing within it by having attained that activity; poised above whatsoever within the Intellectual is less than the Supreme..." (IV.8.1). Reason as it perceives itself in being differentiates itself from itself, as given to itself in consciousness, and sees itself in the illusion of seeing itself see itself, itself as given to itself in perception. The self-differentiated illusion of seeing itself is manifest as the absence of differentiated being, as represented by the intelligible in the absolute.

For Jacques Lacan in *The Four Fundamental Concepts of Psycho-Analysis*, the "*I see myself seeing myself*"[17] of consciousness dissociates reason to itself from perception; consciousness is the "illusion of *seeing itself seeing itself*" (p. 82), which is the gaze, the double negative of reason in appearance. If reason is given by appearance, it is impossible for reason to go behind appearance, behind the curtain into an ulterior reality. But if appearance is given by reason in consciousness, then the revelation of being behind the curtain in the understanding is conceivable to reason. In the *Phenomenology of Spirit*, "For this knowledge of what is the truth of appearance as ordinarily conceived, and of its inner being, is itself only a result of a complex movement whereby the modes of consciousness 'meaning', perceiving, and the Understanding vanish…" (165). As reason in consciousness requires the self-negation of reason, as reason cannot see itself in the manifestation of itself in the illusion of seeing itself seeing itself, appearance cannot be given by reason, and it is impossible for reason to enter behind the curtain of appearance. The essence of being is thus inaccessible to reason, though it can be represented in the intelligible, as in the luminous embroidered veil. "Our existence," as Georges Bataille describes it in *Inner Experience*, "is an exasperated attempt to complete being."[18] Being in fact "is 'ungraspable'—it is only grasped in error."[19]

In the *Phenomenology of Spirit*, self-consciousness is desire in that it wills itself in "superseding this other that presents itself to self-consciousness as an independent life" (174), establishing a certainty in self-consciousness of itself set against the other, which in the negation of reason in perception is nothingness. Desire is the determinate self-perpetuation of self-consciousness around the void of its other, the dark ground of being, described by Bataille as "the dark repulsive core around which all agitation gravitates,"[20] the place of the repulsion of reason in perception from itself. Desire is the objectification of self-differentiation in self-consciousness, the self-determinate process of reason confronting its self-negation in the ideal, which corresponds to the determinate self-perpetuation of self-consciousness. The thinking subject, according to Jacques Lacan in *The Four Fundamental Concepts of Psycho-Analysis*, projects himself into the real and negates himself in relation to the real as given by appearance, thus "sustaining himself in a function of desire" (p. 85). Desire is the continuous reconstitution of reason in non-reason, the continuous enactment of the self-differentiated and self-alienated identity of reason to being in self-consciousness.

The gratification of desire is self-certainty, self-validation, in overcoming the other of non-reason in the continuous self-verification of reason. In the *Phenomenology of Spirit*, "Desire and the self-certainty obtained in its gratification, are conditioned by the object, for self-certainty comes from superseding this other: in order that the supersession take place, there must be this other" (175). It is not possible for reason to exist to itself in consciousness without the perceived presence of non-reason, following Fichte in the *Wissenschaftslehre*, for whom "the self posits itself as determined by the not-self" (§ 4, III: I, 218).[21] The work of art is often the verification of reason to itself in being in the world, but if that verification is not given by the presence of non-reason in the self-confirmation of reason, then reason itself has no being in the world. In that reason in perception is given to self-consciousness as a double negative, the negation of a negation, reason in self-consciousness cannot overcome the other, the self-alienation of reason in being, and thus self-consciousness continually reproduces the other, in that it might be overcome by reason; therein lies desire. The essence of desire lies outside of self-consciousness, because the satisfaction of desire in self-consciousness depends on the inner self-negation of the object of reason, which itself is consciousness in its self-negation and its independence from self-consciousness. Negation is present in desire as it is present in the object of desire; the self-perpetuation of desire in self-consciousness is itself desire.

As it perpetuates desire for the other in itself, self-consciousness can never achieve satisfaction in itself; the only way that self-consciousness can achieve satisfaction is by going outside itself, and by thus negating itself. According to Sigmund Freud, the death instinct is "at work in every living creature and is striving to bring it to ruin and reduce life to its original condition of inanimate matter,"[22] as described by Donald Abel, in the function of desire as self-negation of reason in self-consciousness. The death instinct, the desire to return life to the inorganic, to negate the organic within the organic, is the instinct to abstraction in reason. As described by Wilhelm Worringer in *Abstraction and Empathy*, "every differentiation of organized matter, every development of its most primitive form, is accompanied by a tension, by a longing to revert to this most primitive form."[23]

According to Freud in *The Ego and the Id*, the death instinct in reason is engaged in a continual dialectical struggle with Eros, or sexual instinct, which seeks to evolve and preserve life, as the struggle between the universal and the particular: "We put forward the hypothesis of a death instinct, the task of which is to lead organic life back into the inanimate state; on the other hand, we suppose that Eros, by bringing about a more and more far-reaching combination of the particles into which living substance is dispersed, aims at complicating life and at the same time, of course, preserving it."[24] Differentiation in reason is a function of desire in reason, the necessity of perpetually creating the self-negation of the other in reason, which is a function of the death instinct in desire, the necessity of differentiation and negation. Reason itself is an enactment of the death instinct in desire, as it perpetuates its self-verification in differentiation and negation, the reduction of the organic to the inorganic in the particular, the transference of the form to the principle, embedding the life of the organic, as it is perceived in reason, in the processes of reason, for the purposes of indeterminate self-perpetuation in relation to the real. As Freud explains in *Beyond the Pleasure Principle*,[25]

> If we are to take it as a truth that knows no exception that everything living dies for *internal* reasons—becomes inorganic once again—then we shall be compelled to say that "*the aim of all life is death*" and, looking backwards, that "*inanimate things existed before living ones*"....The tension which then arose in what had hitherto been an inanimate substance endeavored to cancel itself out. In this way the first instinct came into being: the instinct to return to the inanimate state.

In the *Phenomenology of Spirit*, desire is the mediation of the differentiation of the undifferentiated subject in self-consciousness (176). The satisfaction of desire is the reflection of self-consciousness into itself, which is the self-verification of reason in being as existence, which is a double negation in the relation of reason to being, as being manifests itself to reason and reason manifests itself to reason in being. The otherness of reason to itself in consciousness is non-being, or nothingness. The differentiated particulars of existence in reason overcome their independence in relation to being in the function of desire, but in the overcoming of their independence they become doubly negative. "The object of self-consciousness, however, is equally independent in this negativity of itself; and thus it is for itself a genus, a universal fluid element in the peculiarity of its own separate being; it is a living self-consciousness," in the self-determination and self-perpetuation of desire.

In the Organic Rationalism of Gottfried Wilhelm Leibniz, matter in the real is seen as being imbued with a fluid, continuous energy in the ideal, an inner principle which results in the continuous flux of transformation in matter. The inner principle is the *prima materia*, as described in the *Letters to Arnauld*, which is impenetrable and inertial, containing within it a movement of circulatory currents which result in dynamic forces creating compound substances in matter. For the Marquis de Puységur, Armand-Marie-Jacques de Chastenet, roughly contemporary with Hegel, the combination of the continuous flux of matter with the *prima materia* results in a fluid, electrical flow of energy that unites mind and matter, the ideal and the real. "All bodies are saturated, in their own manner, with the fluid we term electrical";[26] the *prima materia* is a watery inwardness, a liquid incandescence which saturates mind and matter in the heterogeneous flux of the universe. Georges Bataille, in "The Pineal Eye," saw existence as a fluid incandescence, glowing with the inner energy of the *prima materia*, linking matter and mind in the heterogeneous, as opposed to a "neatly defined itinerary from one practical sign to another" (*Visions of Excess*, p. 82). The heterogeneous is existence conceived without the differentiation of particulars in the reason process in perception, matter being always already continuously differentiated in the incandescence of being, as opposed to the homogeneous, the undifferentiated *prima materia*, universal substance.

In the *Phenomenology of Spirit*, the object of desire in self-consciousness is "the universal indestructible substance, the fluid self-identical essence" (177), the self-recognition of self-consciousness. Self-consciousness itself becomes the object of self-consciousness; subject is identical to object, in the identity of the ideal and the real, and thus emerges Spirit. Spirit is "this absolute substance which is the unity of the different independent self-consciousnesses which, in their opposition, enjoy perfect freedom and independence." The subject in self-consciousness is absorbed into the collective self-conscious, the universal principle of self-consciousness which binds the subject to the state, and to organic being. "It is in self-consciousness, in the Notion of Spirit, that consciousness first finds its turning point, where it leaves behind it the colorful show of the sensuous here-and-now and the nightlike void of the supersensible beyond, and steps out into the spiritual daylight of the present," in the dialectic of being as existence and nothingness in reason as given by appearance. Spirit belongs to neither appearance nor non-being, but being in the world, in the identity of the ideal and the real.

Reason becomes Spirit when reason is absorbed into self-consciousness, and in the identity of the ideal and the real, reason in self-consciousness is being itself. Reason is absorbed into self-consciousness when the object of consciousness becomes a concept in reason, which is the origin of Spirit, in the identity of the ideal and the real. In reason, the identity of the ideal and the real, of subject and object, is the essence of being, and the origin of the self-consciousness of reason. In reason in perception, reason as intuition or unconscious reason, that is, understanding, the self-consciousness of the identity of the ideal and the real, is superseded in reason, or left behind. Intuition gives the essence of being to consciousness, the self-consciousness of the subject in relation to its otherness, which is revealed behind the curtain of appearance in mind. Being-for-self (existence) is set against being-in-itself (nothingness); differentiation is set against the inner essence, the *prima materia*. The self-reflection of the consciousness of the subject as a universal is an abstraction, the entrance of reason into self-consciousness, the knowledge of the spiritual essence. Reason in self-consciousness is given by law and principle seen by consciousness as absolute. The essence of being-in-itself precedes self-consciousness, as it is undifferentiated. The essence of being-for-self which has become self-consciousness is Spirit.

Spirit is the actuality of the ethical substance of the essence of Spirit, the moral basis of self-consciousness in the thinking subject. It is "the self of actual consciousness to which it stands opposed" (439), which has lost its meaning in reason as alienated or separated, but has been synthesized into being in the dialectical process of reason. Spirit is both the essence and substance of universal being, the "solid ground" of being into which existence in reason is absorbed; Spirit is the "in-itself of every self-consciousness expressed in thought," the essence of differentiation in the undifferentiated, as given by reason. As being-for-self, Spirit is a "fragmented being," as it is manifested in the particulars of existence in appearance, as the One of Plotinus participates in the multiple particulars of the real. In Spirit, essence is resolved into particulars, as the emanation of the One. Spirit is thus the activating force of the universe, the inner essence of all substance; "it is the movement and soul of substance and the resultant universal being." Spirit is the inner principle of the monad of Gottfried Wilhelm Leibniz, as in the *Monadology*, "every created being, and consequently the created monad, is subject to change, and indeed this change is continuous in each. It follows that the natural changes of the monad come from an internal principle, because an external cause can have no influence on its inner being" (10, 11).[27] In *Dialogue sur la pensée*, Nicolas Cusanus expressed, "There can be only one infinite principle, and that one alone is infinitely simple."[28]

Spirit for Hegel, as the inner principle, is self-dependent and absolute being. It is the form of being to which all stages of consciousness act as priors, in the process of abstraction and differentiation. All forms of consciousness are the products of the self-reflection and differentiation of Spirit; all differentiated moments of Spirit in consciousness are contained within Spirit, as all manifestations of Intellectual Principle and Reason Principle are contained within the One of Plotinus. Forms of consciousness abstracted from Spirit are "vanishing quantities" (*Phenomenology* 440), moments in the temporal construction of reason. The essence of Spirit, as in the *prima materia*, is the flux of the movement and resolution of the differentiated and abstracted moments of Spirit, as in what Leibniz calls *appetition*, or desire in perception in reason, the substance of matter which contains the variability of perceptions, manifest as forms of consciousness. In *Letters to de Volder*, *appetition* is described as "the action of the internal principle which brings about the change or the passing from one perception to another,"[29] in the intersection of the ideal and the real.

The self-reflection of Spirit to itself as described by Hegel manifests itself in consciousness, self-consciousness, and reason, as the One of Plotinus manifests itself in Intellectual Principle and Reason Principle. Spirit is consciousness which is manifest in the understanding, Intellectual Principle, and perception in reason. Spirit is consciousness as self-differentiated; if the consciousness of Spirit as self-differentiated is being-for-self in the object, the other of Fichte, as opposed to being-in-itself, then Spirit is self-consciousness. Self-consciousness is a further differentiation of consciousness, which leads to consciousness in reason. Consciousness in reason is given by the consciousness of the identity of consciousness and self-consciousness, of the other as being-for-self and being-in-itself, the participation of the *prima materia* in *appetition*. Spirit is thus a reasoning consciousness; the object of the consciousness of Spirit, the other, is given by reason. Spirit is being-for-self when it intuits that its self-consciousness is given by reason, and it becomes being-in-and-for-itself when it sees reason as a function of itself, when it reconciles itself with its other. As such, Spirit is the existence of the "ethical essence," the self-consciousness of the subject in relation to the universal in the absolute.

The idea of the ethical is the manifestation of Spirit. As Spirit differentiates itself in self-consciousness, the ethical is defined in the principle of the universal in reason. In the self-differentiation of Spirit, culture is set against belief, or faith, as the objective is set against the subjective. As Spirit, as the manifestation of the absolute, is the indifference of the real and the ideal, of the objective and subjective, so Spirit is the indifference of culture and belief, belief being the cultural institution of the intuition of the absolute. The morality of self-consciousness is the indifference that it contains of the real and the absolute, perceived as the essence of being, being-in-itself. Spirit is self-contained and self-dependent, as is the One of Plotinus, self-sufficient being that is the indifference from which all particulars are differentiated. The ethical world is defined as the realization of the self-consciousness of Absolute Spirit.

Spirit is itself consciousness, and differentiates within itself between substance and essence, objective and subjective. The self-consciousness of Spirit is the identity of substance and essence in consciousness. The universal essence united with its "individualized reality" (*Phenomenology* 444) is the basis of ethical action, in the particular abstracted to the universal in reason. The particular abstracted to the universal in reason is a form of self-consciousness, so that the "ethical substance is actual substance, Absolute Spirit realized in the plurality of existent consciousness..." (447). The realization of the Spirit in the plurality of consciousnesses is the ethical community, manifest as the essence of being in the self-consciousness of Spirit in reason. The ethical community is "conscious ethical essence," the identity of the ideal and the real in the self-consciousness of Spirit. Spirit is being-for-self as it preserves itself in the individual members of the community, in the differentiated particulars of the idea of the ethical community, as it is reflected in them. The individual members of the community are in turn preserved within Absolute Spirit; as such, Spirit is being-in-itself, undifferentiated. The substance of Spirit is the nation or the state, while the consciousness of Spirit is the collective of the individual members of the state. The self-consciousness of the state is the self-consciousness of its Spirit, its self-reflection and self-verification as the embodiment of the essence of being.

The essence of the self-consciousness of Spirit is the idea in intellect, in understanding, as the absolute is participant in reason, as in the Intellectual Principle of Plotinus, differentiated from the movement of particulars in abstraction in reason or Reason Principle. The idea, or the Notion, "is, as contrasted with the daylight of this explicit development, the night of its essence" (685), the dark ground of being; "as contrasted with the outer existence of its moments as independent shapes, it is the creative secret of its birth." Spirit as idea is both nothingness and the pregnancy of mind, the *prima materia* which is the inner dynamic force of being in the absolute. The idea of Spirit is the self-consciousness of Spirit; the essence of Spirit is the self-consciousness of Spirit as being-in-itself become being-for-self, the primordial dehiscence, returned to being-in-and-for-itself in the absolute.

The being-in-itself which Spirit sees as itself in self-consciousness is the being of Spirit, as opposed to the "being that is filled with the contingent determinations of sensation" (686) in reason. The form of Spirit in self-consciousness is the absence of form in the absolute, which manifests itself in the real as light, "the pure, all-embracing and all-pervading essential light of sunrise," which for Schelling is the identity of the real and ideal in the absolute, or the self-consciousness of Spirit. The other of Spirit in self-consciousness is darkness, equally absent of form, the non-being that corresponds to the absolute of being. The movements of the externalization of Spirit in its self-differentiation in consciousness are described as "torrents of light," lacerating the lacerated nature of being, as it were. The movements of differentiation as torrents of light are the "genesis of its being-for-self," the self-reflection of Spirit as otherness, and the "return from the existence" of otherness in differentiation back to being-in-itself. The torrents of light are "streams of fire destructive of structured form," the dissolution of differentiated form into the flux of the heterogeneous, in an apocalyptic vision of the self-deception of reason. The differentiation of Spirit in the forms of appearance in reason is infinite; its infinite presence in the finite manifestations of differentiated appearance is the sublime, the absence of reason within reason, into which the differentiated particulars are dissolved.

The differentiated particulars given by perception in reason are an "essence-less by-play" (687) of self-conscious Spirit. "The determinations of this substance are only attributes which do not attain to self-subsistence, but remain merely names of the many-named One," Absolute Spirit as given by language in reason. The variable forms of appearance in sense-perception are adornments of reality, the luminous embroidered veil of the real, indeterminate and insubstantial. The proliferation of differentiated forms, vanishing shapes in the real, is the "reeling, unconstrained Life" (688) of being-for-self. As being-for-self, the real is the negative antithesis of the consciousness of Spirit, through which Spirit gains self-consciousness, as being-in-itself in the other. Pure light sacrifices itself to being-for-self in the multiplicity of forms in the real so that the absolute can participate in the particular form, as for Plotinus, and so that the particular form can see itself as being-in-itself in the other of self-consciousness. Spirit, as such, is an "artificer," like the Platonic Demiurge; it reproduces itself in the objective in consciousness prior to self-consciousness, prior to the double negative of the realization of itself as the essence of Spirit. Its presence in the objective is thus imparticipant in itself; its thrown-ness from itself gives itself to self-consciousness, as the thrown-ness of reason to itself gives itself to itself in self-consciousness.

The objective form of the self-differentiation of Spirit in consciousness is the abstract in the understanding, which is given by the symbolic in art, or the Platonic Solids in the *Timaeus*, the manifestation of the Demiurge, the artificer, in the primordial differentiation of consciousness in reason. According to Anaximander, the universe was created when the opposites of hot and cold separated out from the *stoicheion*, the Unlimited or *archê* which is the source of all things in the material world, in fire, as in streams of fire or torrents of light. The *stoicheion* is the source of everything but accessible to nothing, like the One of Plotinus. As reported by Pseudo-Plutarch in the *Stromata*, Anaximander believed that "at the beginning of the world there separated itself out from the eternal a something capable of producing heat and cold. It took the form of a flame, surrounding the air that surrounds the earth, like the bark of a tree. This sphere became broken into parts, each of which was a different circle; which is how the sun, moon and stars were generated."[30] The primordial self-differentiation of the absolute enters into matter as pure light and results in the further differentiation of particulars in the real. Anaximander held that the stars themselves are hoops of fire breathing out flames, as reported by Aëtius, and that the combination of hot and cold produces dry and wet (earth and sea) (H. Diels, *Die Fragmente der Vorsokratiker*, DK 12 A 27).[31] The generation of the universe is a process of the self-differentiation of the absolute, as is the conception of existence in consciousness.

According to Hegel, in the classical world, the objective form of the self-differentiation of Spirit was represented in the crystalline geometries of pyramids and obelisks, for example, symbols of the differentiation in reason in relation to the absolute in the inorganic, resulting in the self-negation of the other in reason rather than the recognition in the other of the being-in-itself of reason which results in self-consciousness. The significance of the symbolic geometries in the classical world is in their function as symbols in reason, giving the self-differentiation of reason to itself, and the alienation of reason from being, rather than in the being-for-self of the differentiated other. The gods of classical mythology are also symbols, in hindsight, of the self-alienation of reason from being, of the recognition of an other in relation to reason in consciousness. As opposed to the crystalline inorganic, the organic represents the self-consciousness of the self-differentiation of Spirit in its most primitive form, the recognition of Spirit, the artificer, of the being-for-self in its self-differentiation, which allows the particular to be absorbed into the universal, in the identity of the real and the ideal. The organic form "proliferates unchecked in particularity, being itself subjugated by the form of thought" (*Phenomenology* 694); the identity of the real and the ideal is contained in the real, as it is given to the ideal, to reason in mind.

The Sprit as artificer realizes being-for-self in consciousness in the organic, in the "animal shape" (695). Spirit becomes self-consciousness when the differentiated other of itself is seen as being-in-itself and as a product of itself, that is, when Spirit sees itself as artificer, and the organic is seen as a symbol of the differentiation of the artificer, as a hieroglyph in thought, as it were, the revelation of being-in-itself in the differentiated other in intuition, or the understanding, Intellectual Principle. In the organic the form of the organic is dissolved into the thought of the organic as *logos*, the absolute in the identity of mind and form. The organic form does not express itself, as in Classical sculpture, because its being-in-itself is contained within form in the real, as the form of being-for-self; the being-in-itself of the organic enters into the ideal through light, the element of the ideal in the real, which enables the expression of the inner self in picture-thinking, thus in language. The organic form without language is "still the soundless shape which needs the rays of the rising sun in order to have sound…" The inner being in relation to language and the "self-particularizing, self-entangling manifold existence" (696) of the real is the "still simple darkness, the unmoved, the black, formless stone," the identity of absolute being and absolute non-being.

The self-entangling manifold existence is the result of the binding of the being-in-itself of Absolute Spirit to the organic form, to the body, which causes, as described in the *Timaeus*, "every possible kind of shock and damage" (43) to the soul, being "twisted in all directions." The realm of organic form, of nature in the real, is a corruptible and sublunary world, as in Neoplatonism. As described by Erwin Panofsky in *Studies in Iconology*, the Neoplatonists saw that "the Realm of Nature, so full of vigor and beauty as a manifestation of the 'divine influence', when contrasted with the shapelessness and lifelessness of sheer matter," as in the formless stone of Hegel, "is, at the same time, a place of unending struggle, ugliness and distress, when contrasted with the celestial, let alone the supercelestial world" (p. 34).[32] The undifferentiated absolute becomes the differentiated entanglement of particulars in Neoplatonism in the *circuitus spiritualis*, in the infusion of the *prima materia*, the dynamic life force, in the organic by way of the *logos*, the intelligible in reason, as described by Hegel. The infinite differentiation of particulars in the organic is the result of the binding of the body to soul, of the entrance of the absolute into the real. Panofsky explains: "The Cosmic Soul in turn converts the static ideas and intelligences comprised in the Cosmic Mind into dynamic causes moving and fertilizing the sublunary world, and thus stimulates nature to produce visible things" (p. 132), organic form as given in picture-thinking, reason in perception. "With all its corruptibility the sublunary world participates in the eternal life and beauty of God imparted to it by the 'divine influence'. But on its way through the celestial realm the 'splendor of divine goodness', as beauty is defined by the Neoplatonists, has been broken up into as many rays as there are spheres or heavens," in infinite differentiation. "There is therefore no perfect beauty on earth," as represented in the aesthetics of the Baroque.

In the *Phenomenology of Spirit*, the soul and the body are simultaneous and antithetical expressions of Spirit; the self is both inner and outer. In Transcendental Idealism, the identity or unification of soul and body is necessary. In the Classical statue, in the perfection of the human form in representation, the soul is contained in the inner and is not manifest, because it is not allowed to speak, because Spirit has not yet recognized itself in its self-differentiation as being-in-itself; the identity of soul and body has not been achieved. In the Classical statue "the inner being of multiform existence is still soundless, is not immanently differentiated and is still separated from its outer existence to which all differences belong" (697). The same can be said of the citizen of the polis in relation to the state in the lack of identity between universal and particular in Spirit. Spirit, as artificer, therefore must unite body and soul by "blending the natural and the self-conscious shape," allowing the unified inner and unconscious soul to speak, so that "the conscious wrestling with the non-conscious, the simple inner with the multiform outer, the darkness of thought mating with the clarity of utterance, these break out into the language of a profound, but scarcely intelligible wisdom." The expression of the unconscious through the conscious is given by the self-consciousness of Spirit, the double negative in reason of being-in-itself in the other, the self-identity of reason in Spirit as self-alienated, seeking reconciliation. The Christian god established Spirit as inaccessible to reason, thus established reason as self-alienated, though Spirit was still embodied in the real.

The indifference of body and soul is the indifference of self-conscious Spirit with itself. The identity of the unconscious with the conscious is not revealed in organic form. The organic shapes of nature, forms of the real, are "monsters in shape, word, and deed" (698) which are "dissolved into spiritual shape," as particulars into the universal, in the identity of the conscious and unconscious, being-for-self and being-in-itself. In the spiritual shape, "the outer has retreated into itself," and the inner "utters or expresses itself out of itself and in its own self," as being-in-itself absorbed into language, the mechanism of being-for-self. The organic forms of nature are dissolved "into thought which begets itself, which preserves its shape in harmony with itself and is a lucid, intelligible existence. Spirit is Artist," art is idea.

In the *Republic*, Plato conceived of forms in art as invested with idea, with concept, as *poietic* (forming, making) or *heuretic* (uncovering). Socrates describes the process of the artist as such: "Our artist will, I suppose, as he works, look frequently in both directions, that is, at justice and beauty and self-discipline and the like in their true nature, and again at the copy of them he is trying to make in human beings, mixing and blending traits to give the color of manhood, and judging by that quality in men that Homer too called godly and godlike" (501). The work of art is seen as the identity of soul and body, of the divine Idea in the intelligible and human form, though in Hegel's terms the lack of the development of the self-consciousness of Spirit, or the divine, in the idea prevents the complete expression of the idea in the form. Aristotle, in the *Metaphysics*, also saw art as the identity of soul and body: "By art are produced the things of which the form is in the soul of the maker. By form I mean the essence of the thing and its primary substance."[33] Art is seen as a form of thought, as the identity on the interior and exterior, soul and body. Form in the idea is the *prima materia*, to which all matter in the real can be reduced. According to Aristotle, the work of art is invested with universal intelligence, the divine Idea; the universal intelligence is present in the art as the substance of form, the *prima materia*, simultaneously with the differentiated forms which are the manifestations of the idea in the real.

For Hegel, the form of the self-consciousness of Spirit is produced by consciousness. The self-consciousness of Spirit cannot be expressed in form which contains the indifference of "the heterogeneous forms of thought and natural objects" (*Phenomenology* 699), soul and body, because as such soul has not been given adequate means to express itself through body. The self-consciousness of Spirit can only be expressed by the form of consciousness, "the form of the self-conscious activity" of the artificer, which manifests itself as "the consciousness of its absolute essence in the religion of art" (700). The Spirit which manifests itself as the consciousness of its absolute essence in art is the ethical Spirit, and it is the ethical community, the realization of the ethical Spirit as the universal in the particular, which enables the expression of the essence of the Absolute Spirit in art. The ethical community in which art can express Absolute Spirit in self-consciousness is "the free nation in which hallowed custom constitutes the substance of all, whose actuality and existence each and everyone knows to be his own will and deed." Art as an expression of the spiritual is only possible in a community in which the indifference of freedom and necessity is achieved; the indifference of freedom and necessity is necessary within the spiritual form of the work of art.

The religion of the ethical Spirit, beginning with Christianity, is the withdrawal of Spirit from the real into itself in self-consciousness. The relation of particulars to universals in the work of art parallels the relation of particulars to universals in the community, and the dialectic of the particular and universal, of knowledge and thought, as in the *Republic*, in reason. Thus "the multiplicity of rights and duties, like the restricted activity, is the same dialectical movement of the ethical sphere as the multiplicity of things and their specific natures..." (*Phenomenology* 701). The individual subject in the ethical community withdraws into itself in self-consciousness in reason as Absolute Spirit reflects itself; the individual subject, like Spirit, is being-in-itself or essence in its self-reflection in reason. The organization of the ethical community is not the organization of the organic world of nature; it must supersede nature in its expression of Spirit in self-consciousness, and invent its own laws of organization in relation to self-consciousness, as established by Giambattista Vico.

The differentiated laws of organization are dissolved into the absolute essence of Spirit as given by the universal principles in the Idea, the *logos* of the absolute. "The consummation of the ethical sphere in free self-consciousness, and the fate of the ethical world, are therefore the individuality that has withdrawn into itself, the absolute levity of the ethical Spirit which has dissolved within itself all the firmly established distinctions of its stable existence and the spheres of its organically ordered world and, being perfectly sure of itself, has attained to unrestrained joyfulness and the freest enjoyment of itself." Freedom is contrasted with necessity in the dialectic of Spirit as universal self-consciousness is contrasted with the organic, and it is freedom from the laws of the organic in reason which allows for the expression of the self-consciousness of Spirit in language and in art. "In such an epoch, absolute art makes its appearance" (702), freed from the "world of determinate being," Spirit unrevealed in form. Ultimately, Spirit cannot achieve complete expression in art, as for Schelling, and must free itself from the limitations of the real altogether in philosophy and religion.

The content of art must thus move from abstraction toward self-consciousness in the same way that the individual subject must move from reason toward self-consciousness through the understanding. A work of art is self-animated in which the identity of the particular and universal is achieved as the identity of individual subject and Absolute Spirit, and an identity, as it were, or a dialectical synthesis, is achieved between the crystalline forms of reason in understanding and the organic forms of nature, where "the ensoulment of the organic is taken up into the abstract form of the understanding" (706), resulting in "incommensurable ratios" of an essential nature. As such the "indwelling god" is "drawn forth from its animal covering and pervaded with the light of consciousness" (707). The human body becomes only a symbol in the ideal, in the understanding, rather than an embodiment of Spirit, or divine Idea. Nature is "transfigured by thought and united with self-conscious life," self-conscious Spirit and the universal spirit of a community. The anthropomorphism of the god is a "transcended moment" and a "dim memory," necessary in the development toward the self-consciousness of Spirit, but also necessary to abandon in the understanding in order to achieve the identity of Spirit and nature, and the expression of Spirit in form beyond the organic.

As form in art rids itself of organic form, as the embodiment of Spirit, it frees itself from necessity in the ideal; it is able to "rid itself of the unrest of endless individuation" (708) and its existence as contingency, as subject to the laws of cause and effect. The freeing of the form from the contingent real is a "moment of unrest" as an expression of self-consciousness, the realization of the self-alienation of reason from being. Self-consciousness is the "birthplace of that unrest," the cause of the self-alienation of reason. The self-alienation of reason in self-consciousness is the loss of the individual subject as embodied in the particular and contingent; it is the re-invention of the individual subject as participant of Absolute Spirit and universal self-consciousness, "by emptying himself of his particularity, depersonalizing himself and rising to the abstraction of pure creation" in reason. The form in the work of art becomes identical to the idea in the mind of the artist, which is participant of the divine Idea, as in the *scintilla della divinità* of the sixteenth century, the spark of the divine in the mind, but the Idea is not the Idea of Plato and Aristotle, in the identity of soul and body, but rather the Idea freed from body in the inner withdrawal toward the self-consciousness of Spirit.

The Idea, the *logos* in the understanding, the symbolic in language, becomes the mediator between Spirit and matter rather than the identity of the two. The human subject, no longer the connector between the celestial and terrestrial worlds, as represented in the Renaissance, by Giovanni Pico della

Mirandola, for example, in the *Oration on the Dignity of Man*, or Leonardo da Vinci in the drawing of the *Vitruvian Man*, is eternally alienated from both, and can only find identity as mediating instrument between the spiritual and the physical, in either of which reason no longer partakes. Reason is no longer defined as distinct from the divine or the material in its capacity to partake of both, but rather in its capacity to partake in neither. The dignity of the human soul, the invention of the Renaissance, in man as the measure of all things, condemns man to absolute estrangement from the factors which determine his existence. Body and soul are no longer compatible in the self-alienation of Spirit in reason in self-consciousness.

Through language in reason, as mediating instrument, which is self-conscious existence, Spirit descends into externality. Individual self-consciousness is immediately present in language as a universal. Language is the shape of Spirit in the work of art, the artificial construct of reason as mediator between Spirit and matter. Self-consciousness retains itself in the objectification of its essence as being-for-self in language. The form of self-consciousness in language is pure thought, like the *epistēmē* of Plato in relation to reason, though given by self-consciousness in intuition or the unconscious rather than as the dialectical synthesis of reason and knowledge, *noēsis*. In the objectification of the essence of Spirit in self-consciousness in language, Spirit as self-consciousness is itself, being-for-self, in the identity of the universal and particular as given in the understanding, the identity of pure inwardness and determinate activity, which can be represented in the form of art which corresponds to the *logos* in language in reason.

The *logos* in the understanding is the language of Spirit as self-alienated in self-consciousness, not yet re-unified in the recognition of itself as being-in-itself, as opposed to the Oracle, immediate revelation, which is possible in the embodiment of Spirit. Immediate revelation becomes the mystical experience, the self-consciousness of the individual subject as participated in by the absolute, in the embodiment of Spirit. The identity of Spirit and self-consciousness in the understanding is the identity of the universal and the particular in the artform. The identity of Spirit and self-consciousness is represented in the understanding as picture-thinking (*Vorstellung*), or reason in perception. Picture-thinking is the Ur-language of existence, of being in the world. From the beginning, picture-thinking and language are not manifestations of nature, of organic form, but rather of Mnemosyne, the manifestation of Spirit in reason.

Philosophy of Mind

The relations between perception and language and thought and nature are further explored by Hegel in the *Philosophy of Mind*, the third part of the *Encyclopedia of the Philosophical Sciences*, published in 1830. Mind (*Geist*) is a product of nature, but nature vanishes in the self-consciousness of mind, in the being-for-self of the idea in mind. In self-consciousness the subject and object of the idea are the same, and the necessity of nature in the Principle of Sufficient Reason is no longer adequate or appropriate for the phenomenon of mind, as it sees itself in self-consciousness. The identity of subject and object in the idea, which does not occur in nature, is "absolute negativity" (*Philosophy of Mind*, § 381)[34] because it does not consist of the externalization of essence which is necessary in nature as a function of material reproduction and the laws of necessity in reason. The identity of subject and object is only possible outside of nature, and only possible in mind. In nature, idea is in a state of "asunderness" where subject and object are not unified in it; it is external to both itself and mind, and the essential nature of mind, in its self-conscious otherness which is not possible in nature, because of the lack of the revelation of the absolute in nature, because of the material necessity of the particular.

In the material necessity of nature "all things are mutually external, *ad infinitum*" (§ 381, *Zusatz*). There is no identity of subject and object because there is no identification of object by subject in consciousness. Mind sees itself as separate from nature; the subjectivity of mind sees the objectivity of nature as resistant to it. The operations of nature are seen as the mechanical operations, following Leibniz, of mutually external particulars against each other, as nature "divides itself into concrete points, into material atoms, of which it is composed." Differentiations in nature are "mutually independent existences"; the connections between the points or atoms of nature, the differentiated particulars, are only existent external to them; in the operations of the particulars there is no consciousness of universality, of community, beyond the laws of necessity in externalized relations. Nature is the realm of necessity, and the idea of freedom as being that which precludes necessity is not present in natural relations. Necessity is defined as the "merely external connection of mutually independent existences," as in the atomic structure of nature and its material elements. Mind differentiates itself from nature in self-consciousness; as mind sees itself, it sees itself in itself, in *Ansichsein*. Its doubling is an internal connection, and a negation of the external material condition of nature, of which mind is a product. In universal self-consciousness, Objective Spirit, the individual mind is no longer in a mutually independent existence, and is absorbed into the ethical community, which is a product of mind and which is not possible in nature, beyond the necessities of material reproduction. The product of the ethical community of mind in self-consciousness is culture, artistic expression, which is a uniquely human phenomenon, and which in fact is the definition of being human as mind in relation to nature.

The self-differentiation of mind in self-consciousness constitutes a "higher necessity" than that which exists in nature. Reproduction in nature is a systematic process of self-differentiation governed by *Trieb*, drive or urge, but the differentiation is limited to repetition of particulars with no subjective unity or universal participation in the self-manifestation of "coming-forth-from-self." The externality of the differentiation in nature is rendered as a unity, which creates the illusion of universality. Each individual act of differentiation in nature occurs as an independent manifestation of a universality which is external to the individual act. In the universal the individual agent in organic nature is self-determined, "being-with-itself" and reflected into self, governed by urge or instinct, towards externalization, and the denial of the universal in the particular. The externalization of the self-determination of the organic being in nature is the instinct of self-preservation, like the Eros of Freud, which is a limited form of subjectivity. The organic being in subjectivity contains the possibility of self-differentiation in its subjectivity as well as its material externality, but the self-differentiation in subjectivity remains resolved and unified in the externalized universality. The difference of the subjective self-differentiation in the organic being remains a difference in which the self-differentiation resolves itself; the subjectivity of the organic being, without mind, cannot pass from being-for-self to being-in-itself in self-consciousness because of its universal particularity. In its particular self-differentiation the organic being is set against nature as well; the organic being will consume whatever it has to in nature for the instinctual purpose of self-preservation.

The particular self-differentiation of the organic being is preserved in the direct "annihilation of the Other" in the survival of the species, which precludes the manifestation of the absolute universal in nature, and the possibility of freedom in the organic being. The only point at which the alienation of the other is overcome in the self-differentiation of the organic being is in the sexual relation, which is the highest manifestation of freedom in nature, the only point at which the relation between particulars is not one of complete externality and mutual exclusion. The sexual relation is always only one of determinateness, though, governed by necessity, and subject to the self-differentiation of the particular, governed by but imparticipant in the universal. In organic nature, the sexual relation and death are functions of the perpetual cycle of cause and effect in self-preservation, perpetuating the particular in opposition to the universal, precluding the possibility of individual subjectivity, and preserving externality as a function of the finitude of biological life. Only in mind does the organism distinguish itself from nature to which it is opposed, and become self-conscious of this distinction. The self-consciousness of the opposition of mind to nature, a biological necessity, is the first premise of freedom and artistic expression in human culture.

The "triumph over externality" of mind is the "ideality of mind," the self-consciousness of mind in its opposition to causal necessity and to itself, as in the ideal of Schelling. The ideality of mind is itself a necessary product of the relation between mind and what is external to it, and the self-consciousness of mind in its relation to its externality, in its translation of its externality to its inner function, as philosophy entails primarily the translation of the particular to the universal. Mind defines itself in its translation of that which is external to it, and is thus, like any organic being, set against nature. Language is a function in mind of the translation from the external to the subjective, and from the particular to the universal. The very nature of the sign in language is that the particular becomes subject to the universal in the transition of the perceived object into the word, and the simultaneous transition of the word into the idea. The formulation of language is a process of the externalization of perception, of *Vorstellung*, into the particulars which mask the unified universality of existence and render existence fragmented and self-alienated, in the same way that the instinct for self-preservation in the organic being renders the universal impossible in a nature composed of fragmented and self-alienated particulars.

The word in language abstracts the universal from the particular; meaning is a product of the self-differentiation of the particular in language, the primordial dehiscence of the universal in nature. Any word in language given to designate a particular is automatically taken as a universal in abstract thought. The universal is only given by the external manifestation of the particular in the word, and is thus necessarily a negation, a double negation, of consciousness in language in relation to externality. Self-conscious mind for Hegel "sets itself over against itself, makes itself its own object and returns from this difference, which is, of course, only abstract, not yet concrete, into unity with itself." Mind is thus necessarily given to itself in ideality, as a function of language. In its ideality, mind abstracts particulars into universals; it transforms the reality with which it is confronted, leaving it "poisoned and transfigured," transformed into a spiritual existence of the abstracted universal. The universality in abstract mind in fact prevents the material reality with which it is confronted to exist as independent of that universality and abstraction; mind is condemned to its own mechanisms in self-consciousness and self-differentiation. There is no possibility of mind overcoming itself, of knowing anything beyond itself, beyond its own premise of operations. In that mind sees itself as differentiated from nature, there is no possibility that mind can know nature beyond the premise of its self-differentiated relation to it, just as in the pre-scientific era mind could only know nature in so far as it could project itself into it.

In the biological necessity of self-differentiation, the *Trieb*, mind can never be satisfied with its own limited activity in the abstraction of the particular to the universal, material reality in perception to the idea, in language and thought. The product of this restlessness and dissatisfaction in philosophy is the desire for an absolute, the universal which is hidden by the externality of language in thought. Mind seeks the essence of the material in perception which is lost in language; philosophy is thus, like poetry and the visual arts, a seeking beyond language, an attempt to rescue the essence and universal which has been lost by the activity of thought in its self-consciousness. The idea is the perceived resurrection of the essence of being in reason, or finite thought, the re-entrance of the absolute into the self-differentiated and sundered structure of rational thought, as the Intellectual Principle is to the Reason Principle of Plotinus. In reason, ideality in self-consciousness develops toward the absolute in the dialectic, and is thus dependent on the self-differentiation and negation given by reason in perception.

As reason returns to itself from the other in the dialectic, it discovers itself as simultaneously "absolute negativity" and "infinite self-affirmation," as described by Hegel. Reason is thus the infinite self-affirmation of absolute negativity, the perpetuation of the externality of language in the void of being which language creates. The consummation of the dialectic in reason, in the ideal, is the absolute, which is itself an infinite self-affirmation of absolute negativity, as in the *via negativa* of Pseudo-Dionysius. Reason appears as universal to itself, as it is the product of abstraction in language; language, like the organic being, hides the absence of universality in the unified externality of its existence. The absolute in mind is that which is not present in mind to reason, the absence of the universality, and the impossibility of a reconciliation between mind and nature in abstraction. The absolute in mind is the synthesis of the subjective and the objective, the synthesis of thought and the object of thought, in which the seer becomes the seen, the knower becomes the known.

Absolute knowledge as reason in mind is only given by philosophy, and suggested in art. It cannot be confirmed in ordinary consciousness, in the processes of reason, in scientific or empirical reasoning, but in the dialectical reason of philosophy, the reasoning of the self-consciousness of mind in its return from its other. Finite reason preserves the externality and negation of nature in relation to itself, and the indifference of nature to mind. Spirit in mind, on the other hand, seeks to transcend the externalization and alienation of its other in self-consciousness, in the synthesis of subject and object, and the universal and the particular in history. The absolute which is present in mind is also present, though unrevealed, in nature. In Spirit, nature is seen as other than its external manifestation as differentiated and particular; Spirit sees itself in the possibility of the revelation of the absolute in nature—it sees a reflection of itself in its negation and self-alienation in nature. The double negation of mind in the absolute binds it to nature in a way different than empirical observation, but premised on perception and language, the return to the particular forms of nature through the process of the abstraction of them in mind.

Mind sees itself in nature in the process of destroying it. Nature overcomes it own externality in mind in the same way that mind overcomes its externality in its subjectivity toward the absolute, in the transition from necessity to freedom. The transition from reason to Spirit in mind, from necessity to freedom, is a philosophical transition necessitating the dialectical process in self-consciousness. Mind attains freedom from the cause and effect of nature in the attainment of being-for-self in consciousness, but mind in being-for-self is still governed by the particular in its consciousness as abstraction. It is only in the self-consciousness of being-for-self and the attainment of being-in-itself, towards being-in-and-for-itself, Absolute Spirit, as in the Intellectual Principle of Plotinus, that mind attains to the universal in abstraction, as given by language, and it is the return of mind from being-for-self to being-in-itself, in the dialectical abstraction, that the universal is achieved in mind for itself in the synthesis of subject and object in self-consciousness, and thus freedom.

In this process it becomes evident that rather than mind being posited by nature, nature is seen as being posited by mind. Mind as being-for-self can be seen as being predicated by nature, but mind as being-in-itself has no basis in nature. In its doubling of itself in self-consciousness, mind discovers itself as other than nature, and the product of its own abstraction in language. Mind "brings forth itself from the presuppositions which it makes for itself, from the logical Idea and external Nature..."; mind re-invents itself as the product of its own processes. The other (nature, material reality as given by perception) which mediates mind in self-consciousness disappears, in the same way that it disappears in the external manifestations of nature, and mind sees itself as given by abstraction in language, in which the synthesis of subject and object, perceiving mind and word, takes place, revealing the absolute in Spirit. Mind becomes self-subsistent to itself in self-consciousness, eliminating that which mediated it in self-differentiation (necessity in nature), and thus sees itself as a totality reconstructed from the fragmentation of the self-differentiation. Mind dies as nature (real) and is reborn as ideal; it sees itself as ideal, and seeks the reconciliation of the real and the ideal within the ideal, in philosophy and art.

The transition from nature to mind is thus a "coming-to-itself of mind out of its self-externality in Nature." The transition from nature to Spirit occurs in mind; it is not a natural transition, not governed by the Principle of Sufficient Reason in the real. It has been seen that perception is constructed by reason, and it can now be seen that Spirit in mind is constructed by mind in self-consciousness. Though reason can be seen to be governed by necessity, in cause and effect, the scaffolding of reason, that is, language, which is an abstraction of perception in mind (a transition from "the singleness of sensation to the universality of thought"), comes to be seen more and more as a construct of mind in its development toward self-consciousness, and in the revelation of the absolute in mind. The revelation of the absolute in mind in fact dissolves the scaffolding of language in reason in mind, in the same way that light dissolves the material solidity of particular objects in the real. Language comes to be seen as an element in the mediating process of nature in mind, which begins to disappear in the development of self-consciousness. Mind reveals itself as the negative, the void, underneath the scaffolding of language in reason, and it is in that void that the absolute is revealed.

Freedom is thus the absolute negativity of mind, in which the only object of thought is thought itself. The other of mind is still present in it, but the other is overcome in the presence of the absolute, in the dark night of being within mind. Mind still has the capacity to "step out of its abstract, self-existent universality, out of its simple self-relation" (§ 382, *Zusatz*), and to "posit within itself a determinate, actual difference..." In so doing mind authenticates itself, defines itself in relation to the other, as the ideal in relation to the real, and the "Idea which returns to itself out of its otherness." Mind legitimizes itself in its construction of itself in language. In self-consciousness mind *must* legitimize itself as against nature, and celebrate its artificiality, its thrown-ness from anything external to it on which it might be predicated.

The dialectical synthesis of the self-conscious mind as artificially constructed and the other as any premise which was lost in the process of abstraction, becomes the basis for the presence of the absolute, as both an all-encompassing totality and as an absolute void in subjectivity. The absolute, especially in religion, but also in ethics and even art, prevents mind in its solipsistic state of self-existent universality and simple self-relation from detaching itself from the totality of mind and doing harm to it. Though the absolute provides an ethical basis for the activity of mind in self-consciousness, in self-constructed negation, it precludes any possibility for a moral basis of activity, that is, the activity of mind in self-consciousness can have no meaning in relation to itself or to its other. Freedom in mind entails mind's "freeing of itself from all its existential forms which do not accord with its Notion," including all elements of mind which are contradictory or self-contradictory. In its freedom mind has no existential responsibility, and thus no moral responsibility, in relation to nature, reason, or the real. The religious absolute entails moral responsibility because of the possibility of the embodiment of the absolute in the real.

Spirit in mind is an infinite and absolute actuality, as opposed to a realization, because it is not governed by self-differentiation or universalization in abstraction. Spirit in mind is the element of thought which is not self-differentiated or universalized in reason, which precedes self-consciousness as an always already, as in the *chôra* of Plato and the *différance* of Deconstruction. Spirit in mind is manifest to itself in itself as other than reason, as other than the scaffolding of its perception, as other than that which "is poured out into the asunderness of Nature and only ideally present therein..." (§ 383, *Zusatz*). In being-for-self mind converts the other of itself to itself; it reinvents the real as within the ideal. In its manifestation of itself in its other, it destroys the other (the real) as an independent entity, and re-affirms itself in the negation of the other as other. What is left of the other is the sublime, the trace of the absence of reason within reason and within the real. Mind converts the other to a form which corresponds to its own content, through abstraction in language, and perception.

In perception, mind orders the world according to its own mechanisms, its reason, and forms in perception, like forms in language, correspond to the self-affirmation of mind in the negation of the other. Beauty in nature and art, as the self-affirmation of mind, is also the negation or destruction of the other, what is other to reason. Through language and perception, form and content become identical in mind. Content only becomes differentiated from form in mind in Spirit, in the dialectical transcendence of reason in the return of mind to itself from being-for-self in self-consciousness. Content (being-within-itself)) is only given to mind as separate from form in the manifestation of mind only to itself, in self-consciousness in the return from the other. The separation of content and form in mind cannot be represented in art, except in the representation of light, which itself retains a trace of the form in relation to the content, being confined by the real. Metaphysical philosophy seeks to discover content as separate from form; whether such an independent existence is possible is irrelevant to the necessity of mind to discover itself in its own negation.

The unity of content and form in mind, as given by mind in being-in-and-for-itself, is the unity of actuality and possibility, inwardness and externality. If mind is reconstituted to itself as not predicated by nature, but rather preceding nature, then mind gives to itself the possibility of origin, the basis of the theory of creativity in Romantic art. Mind only exists in the ideal as it manifests itself to itself, which is its actuality, the possibility of origin within itself: actuality contains the possibility of possibility. The unity of actuality and possibility in mind, the product of mind's reconstruction of itself in its return from its differentiation in its other, is the absolute. In self-consciousness mind sees nature as an independent reality, a reality governed by necessity in relation to the freedom of the self-differentiated mind. Mind can thus never reveal nature or the real as it is, but only as it is constructed by mind, as a product of its self-construction. "In the intellectual sphere to reveal is thus to create a world as its being—a being in which the mind procures the affirmation and truth of its freedom" (§ 384). Mind can only see nature as necessity as a re-affirmation of its own freedom in relation to it, and it must see the real as necessity in order to see itself as freedom. In that Spirit entails the synthesis of actuality and possibility in mind, the synthesis of freedom and necessity, Spirit, the absolute in mind, entails the synthesis of mind (reason) and its self-perceived and self-manufactured other, in the attempt to form a totality based in differentiation and negation. That is not to say that such a totality exists, but only that it is the nature of mind to seek such a totality, in the universalizing processes of abstraction in reason. The premise of Deconstruction that such a totality might actually exist in the thought of Hegel is only a partial interpretation; much of post-Hegelian thought is always already present in Hegel's writings.

Mind manifests itself to itself in three stages or forms, according to Hegel. The first stage is the release of reason (*Umschlagen*), mind-in-itself, to the real, to the particularized forms of nature, which is seen as the coming-to-be, the possibility, of nature. Nature becomes a posited existence within the realm of the idea, and the idea as posited in nature vanishes. In order to do this, the idea in mind must overcome its externality and separateness, and recreate itself as being-in-itself, as self-determinate and self-justified, predicated on inwardness and actuality, rather than determinateness and possibility. It is the natural inclination of mind to do so, the *Trieb* within abstraction in language. Mind is thus self-reflected into itself in self-consciousness. In its self-consciousness, mind opposes itself to the nature which was the repository of its possibility.

In the second stage of self-consciousness, mind sees itself as opposed to nature, and incorporates the otherness of nature, of the real, in itself, in its self-consciousness as ideality. In so doing mind denies the presence of mind in nature. The incorporation of nature as other, as real in the ideal, is an abstraction, a movement from particular to universal in language. Seeing itself as differentiated in relation to nature or the real, consciousness and self-consciousness of mind remain distinct, and mind still sees itself in relation to the other. The other is not yet for mind, and the possibility of mind in the other is not yet recognized. Nature remains seen as a "reflectedness-into-self" (§ 384, *Zusatz*) in the same way that mind sees itself. Nature, though independent of mind, is seen as something presupposed by mind, and something which is other in relation to mind, rather than as participating in a dialectical relationship with mind. Nature is not seen as absolute, or as participating in the absolute, as it is "effected only in the reflective consciousness" of mind. Nature is therefore not yet seen as the creation of absolute mind, and is seen as the function of reason in mind, in mechanistic terms.

The absolute in mind, Spirit, allows nature to be seen by mind as other than the function of reason, though still other to mind. Absolute knowledge is the third stage or form of self-consciousness. In absolute knowledge, the previous dualism of nature and mind is transcended. Absolute mind sees itself as the creator of nature as it is given to mind, and the creator of reason, as manifest in perception and language. As such absolute mind is no longer limited in its relation to nature or reason; it is no longer limited to the asunderness of nature, or the self-awareness of reason in perception. Rather than being independent of mind, nature and reason, as the other of absolute mind, are seen as facilitating the being-for-self of absolute mind, the freedom of Spirit, the synthesis of actuality and possibility, subject and object, being-in-itself and being-for-self of mind. Such is the highest stage or form of self-consciousness in mind, which manifests mind as "infinitely creative" in its self-consciousness, and thus capable of the highest form of cultural expression, reflecting both philosophical and historical development, as manifestations of the development of the self-consciousness of Spirit. It is the role of philosophy in history to raise the content of reason and perception to the form of absolute knowledge, which is seen as the highest manifestation of the content of reason.

Spirit in mind thus develops in three stages: as self-reflected in the ideal, as Subjective Spirit; as become necessity in the real, as Objective Spirit; and in the synthesis of objectivity and ideality, necessity and freedom, as Absolute Mind. Mind is universal as Subjective Spirit, undifferentiated in the other, in the relationship of particulars, but the universality of undifferentiated mind can only be given by Philosophy of Mind, in the dialectic of differentiation, return and synthesis. In the particularity of differentiation, in the abstract, mind is objective and undeveloped, not yet realizing the synthesis that is Spirit, which is given by the three stages, of the dialectic, as it were. The reality of mind is only given in its return from its other, in the abstract differentiation which is governed by necessity, as in nature. Undifferentiated mind is un-self-conscious mind, as in nature, unaware of itself; mind only knows itself when it sees itself in its differentiation, in its other. "That mind comes to a knowledge of what it is, this constitutes its realization" (§ 385, *Zusatz*).

Mind actualizes itself in its being-for-self, in the particular and determinate, "making itself into its own presupposition, into the Other of itself."

Mind can only define itself in relation to itself, as it has differentiated itself from causal necessity; therein lies its freedom. Mind finds its freedom in its releasing itself from its other, releasing itself from its self-knowledge in abstract thought, in reason. In its relationship to itself, mind is Subjective Spirit, governed by necessity. Mind becomes Objective Spirit when it has released itself from its other. The activity of Subjective Spirit is mind coming to know itself as itself, as its other. Subjective Spirit becomes Objective Spirit when mind has come to know itself as its other, and attains freedom from necessity, the causal relations of natural mind. As mind becomes free in the self-knowledge of Subjective Spirit in the other, thus Objective Spirit, mind sees itself as universal, in its natural state of universality, and understands itself as participating in universal mind, and thus in the state or community, in particular in the ethical community. The self-knowledge of universality of Subjective Spirit in Objective Spirit, the participation of mind in community, allows mind to return to itself from its other, and become Absolute Mind, which is manifest in the art, religion and philosophy of the community, of the culture of mind in philosophical development.

Mind seeing itself in its other as Objective Spirit is a "shadow cast by the mind's own light—a show or illusion which the mind implicitly imposes as a barrier to itself" (§ 386) in order to realize its freedom. Infinite mind, or Absolute Mind, discovers itself through the finitude of its operations in reason, the light which casts the shadow, which discovers that which is other to itself. When mind discovers the presence of that which is other to itself, the light of its reason becomes its barrier to itself, through which mind withdraws from its limitations into itself. The passage from Subjective Spirit to Absolute Mind entails "finding a world presupposed before us, generating a world as our own creation, and gaining freedom from it and in it." Hegel's Transcendental Idealism thus combines Idealism and Identity Philosophy in a dialectical movement. "To the infinite form of its truth the show purifies itself till it becomes a consciousness of it." Mind is only free in the reality which it constructs, in the attempt to negotiate the reality to which it is subject, but on which it cannot predicate itself. It is immoral, in Hegel's mind, to limit the functions of mind to (dogmatic) reason and logic, following Giordano Bruno: "a modesty of thought, as treats the finite as something altogether fixed and absolute, is the worst of virtues..." The finite is "not the truth, but merely a transition and an emergence to something higher." The infinitude of mind opposes itself to the finitude of nature. The finitude of mind is a form of vanity of mind in reason, the inability of mind to move beyond Objective Spirit. The vanity of mind in objective thought manifests itself as "wickedness" at the arrival of Objective Spirit, when the mind is most immersed in itself in its self-reflection, and most contradictory to itself in its self-knowledge as other.

The finitude of mind in Subjective and Objective Spirit, and reason and logic, is given by the fact that mind does not exist outside of its definition in reason. The existence of mind as finitude can only be seen as a temporary moment in the flux of matter, while the ideal, Absolute Spirit in mind, constitutes the negation of finitude, in the return of mind to itself from its other, which is in the realm of the finite. The ideal is thus the double negative of the finite, the finite itself doubled over onto itself, revealing the void within the finite of the infinite. The existence of the finite in the flux of being is not an affirmation of being, but only an affirmation of reason in being. The finite is seen as a moment within the infinite, encompassing nature and the real. Mind contains the finite, and manifests itself to itself as finite, but it is not finitude itself. A work of art, as a finite manifestation in the real of the infinitude of the ideal, cannot reveal completely Absolute Spirit, while philosophy, in its appearance to itself as the temporal succession of the idea, sees itself from within the temporal succession of thought as infinite, as preceding the idea, and the temporal succession of thought, and revealing its pre-existence to thought in thought, in the illusion of the doubling of Subjective Spirit in reason, in the light cast by reason.

The finitude of nature as it is perceived by mind does not correspond with the idea of nature in the ideal, because the idea of nature does not correspond to nature, because idea does not correspond to reason in perception, because reason has doubled itself in the process of reason in perception, and has alienated itself from the finitude by which it defines its perception to itself. The only reality of mind to mind is its ideality, its self-identity as other, as constructed reality, which cannot be finite, and is therefore infinite. The infinity, as Absolute Spirit, is the synthesis of the real and the ideal, finitude and mind. The finite is impossible in the self-consciousness of finitude; if the finite sees itself as finite, it is non-finite, or infinite. If necessity sees itself as necessity, it is non-necessity, or freedom. Mind identifies itself as finite in its other, in Subjective Spirit, and in seeing itself as other, in Objective Spirit, mind ceases to be finite, in Absolute Mind. The self-knowledge of mind of its limitation in reason is its unlimit; as in the *docta ignorantia* of Cusanus, "to know one's limitation means to know of one's unlimitedness" (§ 386, *Zusatz*), and one's freedom. It is not that mind is free *from* limitation, but that mind is free *in relation to* limitation, so that it can make itself finite, rather than be determined by finitude.

The relation between the finite and the infinite in mind is not static or fixed, but participates in the dialectic of Subjective and Objective Spirit, as has been seen. The finite is contained in the infinite, and the infinite is contained in the finite, as the real is contained in the ideal, and the ideal is contained in the real, in Transcendental Idealism. In seeing itself as its other, mind is contained in its other, and its other is contained in mind. The self-alienation of mind from its other is the self-alienation from itself. The self-alienation from itself within mind, which it sees in its other, is that which reveals the void within mind which is the infinite, the ground of being which is identical to the absolute. The absolute finite is identical to the absolute infinite. Mind cannot cease to be infinite in the finitude of reason; in reason the infinite becomes the moment of the finite, in temporal succession and determinateness. In the finite, in reason, "everything is only an ideal moment, only an appearance," given by reason in perception, the relationship of reason to the real, in which it is tied to the finite. On the other hand, mind cannot cease to be finite in Absolute Mind or Spirit in mind, though the infinitude of the absolute can be revealed to mind in the finitude of its reason. Finitude is in fact as much a constructed reality of mind as is infinitude, the reality constructed by mind in Subjective Spirit as it becomes Objective Spirit, through reason in perception, or *Vorstellung*.

Both the finite and the infinite are elements of the ideal which are projected into the real, functions of the dialectical struggle of mind with itself in the construction of a reality in relation to the reality which it presupposes. As both the finite and infinite are products of the constructed reality of the ideal, mind can know itself to be both finite and infinite. The absolute is neither the finite nor the infinite, but the synthesis and transcendence of both. In the transition from the finite to the infinite in the transition from Subjective and Objective Spirit to Absolute Mind, "mind wrests itself out of this progress to infinity, frees itself absolutely from the limitation, from its Other, and so attains to absolute being-for-self, makes itself truly infinite." Mind must be finite in order to be infinite. Mind becomes truly infinite when it frees itself from the relation between finite and infinite; it is both finite and infinite, not beyond limitation but outside of limitation, outside of the relation between the finite and the infinite.

In *Reason in History, A General Introduction to the Philosophy of History* (1837), Hegel asserts that world history, human history, develops within the realm of Spirit, and that "world" is constituted by a combination of the physical and the psychical. Spirit is the substance of history as it develops, as the human being constitutes the "antithesis to the natural world" (III).[35] The realm of Spirit in universal consciousness is that which is produced by the human being, including the reality created by mind. The most concrete realization of Spirit is human history, the course of events determined by Spirit, as it is unified by nature in "human nature." Spirit is seen as opposed to matter, as freedom, the quality of Spirit, is seen as opposed to gravity, the laws of necessity. Spirit is self-encentered, non-determinate, as opposed to matter, and is given to reason through self-consciousness; thus the only knowledge for which Spirit strives in reason is knowledge of itself, and history can be described as the progress of the realization of self-knowledge in the self-consciousness of Spirit. The self-consciousness of Spirit is freedom, the non-necessary and determinate, thus the purpose of history is the actualization of the freedom in the self-consciousness of Spirit. Freedom "comprises within itself the infinite necessity of bringing itself to consciousness..."; necessity is contained within freedom and the finite is contained within the infinite, as the physical world is contained within the psychical world. Freedom is the purpose of Spirit and the purpose of human history. Freedom is the only purpose in history and reality which is able to realize and fulfill itself, because it is a function of Spirit, Absolute Mind, which alone is being-in-and-for-itself.

History begins its purpose as the realization of the idea of Spirit, like consciousness itself, as unconscious instinct in nature, which is implicit form (*an sich*), being-in-itself in its prior state. History is the process of making conscious the unconscious instinct in reason, and reconciling conscious reason with unconscious instinct, Subjective Spirit with Objective Spirit. Subjective Spirit is natural will, "immediate, actual existence (*für sich*): need, instinct, passion..." (III.2). The mechanisms of history, "these vast congeries of volitions, interests and activities," including war, slavery, genocide, colonization, etc., are "the tools and means of World Spirit for attaining its purpose, bringing it to consciousness and realizing it." The mechanisms of history are the means by which Subjective Spirit becomes Objective Spirit, unconscious instinct becomes conscious reason, and the two are reconciled in Absolute Mind. History allows Sprit to discover itself and contemplate itself in "concrete reality." History is the stage on which are acted out the events of the constructed reality of mind in its self-alienation from nature and from its other, in Objective Spirit, for the purpose of Spirit finding itself in self-consciousness.

The events of world history are exterior manifestations of the interior purposes of Spirit in human consciousness; they are the material correlate to the psychical struggles in the mind, the struggle between reason and instinct, the conscious and unconscious forces that make up the synthesis of reason and instinct. Spirit, Absolute Mind, is not a fixed or permanent state of being, not a stable moment within the infinite, but rather the continuing process of the struggle between reason and instinct and the attempt to achieve a synthesis, of Subjective Spirit and Objective Spirit. Absolute Mind is itself the dialectical process, of both individual self-consciousness and universal self-consciousness, of the ethical individual and human history. Historical subjects are puppets of the dialectical self-realization of Spirit; historical events have an underlying significance in relation to the development of human nature. All physical matter and physical activity, in the realm of the real, has a psychical correlate in Spirit, in the realm of the ideal.

It is as for Plato, where all manifestations in the physical world have an underlying reality in the ideal world, in the idea, but for Hegel the ideal is not just the idea, but the idea and instinct, thought in synthesis with the absence of thought in nature, the conscious in synthesis with the unconscious, the crystalline purity of light in synthesis with the dark night of being. The ideal of Hegel is closer to the Intellectual Principle of Plotinus, as an intermediary between Reason Principle and the One, as Objective Spirit is an intermediary between Subjective Spirit and Absolute Mind. The Intellectual Principle of Plotinus suggests the presence of an unconscious, or the presence of the unconscious in the conscious, of unreason in reason; Plotinus is therefore called the first psychological philosopher. The philosophies of both Plotinus and Hegel, along with Schelling, are important precursors to the psychological philosophies and psychoanalysis (a form of Hegelian *Kunstreligion*) in the twentieth century.

In the dialectical development of the self-consciousness of Spirit as it is manifest in the course of events in human history, the dominant factor in the ideal is always reason, and reason realizes itself in the course of events of history, as the instrument in the synthesis of the universal and the particular, of Subjective Spirit and Objective Spirit. Reason, as "abstract action," is the mediator between Spirit (universal Idea) and the real, the course of external events. It is through reason that the idea becomes material in events, that the universal becomes particular, and through which, conversely, the particular becomes universal. The immanent becomes existent through action. It is the activity of reason which "elevates the empty objectivity of nature to be the appearance of the essence which is in and for itself," which reveals the essence of being in the matter of being, in the relation between the ideal and the real.

The struggle between reason and unreason in human consciousness is manifest in history as the struggle between necessity and freedom and between the individual and fate in the course of events. Freedom is attained through reason, through abstraction, which translates into the will of the individual in the historical event. The individual will is a product of a culture, as the particular is a product of the universal. It is only through individual will that the actions of an individual reflect the *Zeitgeist* of the culture in a positive way, as an instrument in historical development, because it is through the individual will that the universal consciousness enters into the individual consciousness. The individual historical subject can only act in relation to his or her position in history and universal consciousness, and in relation to the universal consciousness: "The individual does not invent his own content; he is what he is by acting out the universal as his own content" (III.2.b). Any action which contributes to the course of historical development of a culture on the part of an individual is a consequence of that individual interpreting and carrying out the universal will of the culture in particular events.

As such, each individual member of a culture must activate the universal content of the culture within himself or herself, and this activation constitutes the ethical dimension of the individual. But the universal content of the culture does not originate in the ethical activity of the culture, its particular events, but rather in universal Spirit, universal self-consciousness. Thus there is a necessary dehiscence between the universal Spirit of a culture and its manifestation in ethical events through individual will; the struggle between the ethics and Spirit of a culture reflects the inner struggle between reason and being-in-itself in individual consciousness. The culture is a macrocosm of the individual, and conversely the individual is a microcosm of the culture, both being stages in which the dialectical struggle between freedom and necessity and Objective and Subjective Spirit are carried out. The relation between universal Spirit and ethical activity is thus a volatile and unstable one, filled with temporary manifestations and contradictions, in the transition from the potential to the actual. "This makes all existing reality unstable and disunited," in the same way that individual consciousness is unstable and disunited in its self-alienation from its other in being-for-self, the actuality of the potential.

In the transition from the potential to the actual, from the universal to the particular, the element of unreason is always present in reason, the mediating element. Unreason is manifest in historical events as passion and instinct. In the transition from the particular to the universal in reason towards Spirit, the particular must be negated; mind must destroy nature, and the nature within it. The particular exhausts itself in the dialectical struggle between necessity and freedom in history, as well as between Subjective Spirit and Objective Spirit in consciousness. It is from the negation of the particular that the universal arises, only to be re-united with the resurrected particular in Spirit. In self-consciousness, mind must negate itself as other before it can return to itself as essential being. The universal itself never enters into the struggle between necessity and freedom in history, as it never enters into the struggle between Subjective Spirit and Objective Spirit in consciousness. Particular events are acted out in history, and logic operates in reason, as pawns of universal Spirit, which never enters into the dialectic, as the One of Plotinus never enters into the dialectic of Intellectual Principle and Reason Principle, though it participates in each to various degrees. This for Hegel is the "*cunning of Reason*" (III.2.c), that which "sets the passions to work for itself, while that through which it develops itself pays the penalty and suffers the loss." Reason itself is seen as abstraction in the ideal, removed from the physical struggle of material reality, though reason itself is engaged as an instrument in the dialectical struggle within consciousness.

The phenomenal is both positive and negative in relation to reason; as the particular, it must be negated in the dialectical movement toward Spirit, but it is also the material enactment of that dialectical movement. The particular is sacrificed to the universal in the same way that the historical subject is sacrificed to history. It is the individual subject which determines the course of history through individual will as the enactment of universal consciousness, but the action of the individual subject is negated in the development of history towards the universal, as the particular is negated in consciousness, in the mediation of abstract thought. "The Idea pays the tribute of existence and transience, not out of its own funds but with the passions of the individuals." The passion of the individual is sacrificed to the idea as unreason is sacrificed to reason and the unconscious is sacrificed to the conscious, in the dialectical development toward Spirit in history and consciousness, to be reconciled in Spirit itself.

It is necessary that the passions of individuals, their "purposes and gratifications," and their happiness be sacrificed to the universal in historical development. The only element which is seen as existing in the individual which is not sacrificed to the universal, in that it is the only element which exists in the individual as the essence of the universal, rather than its particular manifestation, is morality, intrinsic morality (*Moralität*) as opposed to extrinsic morality (*Sittlichkeit*), which is morality as it is applied to human relations. *Moralität* is the consciousness of the essence of the universal, of Spirit as Absolute Mind, in reason, consciousness of the purpose of the dialectical development of reason in mind and history. *Sittlichkeit* is the applied morality of ethics and religion, which are manifestations of the universal as particular in the real, in historical events and relations. *Moralität* is the consciousness of reason itself as instrument of Absolute Mind, and the consciousness of reason as self-determination and freedom in relation to necessity. *Moralität* is the universal within the particular, as opposed to the particular within the universal, which is as being-in-itself in mind, the essence of being from which the particular is differentiated in the process of negation and reconciliation, as in the allegory of *Moralität* in Christianity.

The application of *Moralität* in *Sittlichkeit*, and the virtues and fortunes of individuals within a culture, are ultimately irrelevant to historical development, and to the "rational order of the universe." The purpose of historical development is unfolded in the manifestation of *Moralität* in the particular, in particular actions and forces of will, as the individual participates in universal Spirit. The goal of the creative artist, as in any other cultural role, is to participate in the universal Spirit through the creative act as a force of will and a manifestation of freedom, and to manifest the *Moralität* in the particular act, as the universal being-in-itself in the individual being-for-self, in the self-consciousness of mind as enacted in reason. The artistic struggle is the dialectical struggle of the individual in culture and history, and the dialectical struggle of Subjective Spirit and Objective Spirit in mind, involving the perpetual cycle of negation and reconciliation, in the thrown-ness of being in consciousness from itself.

The instrument of the understanding of the role of reason and *Moralität* in the dialectical struggle, on both a microcosmic and macrocosmic level, is philosophy. Philosophy precedes art, and all ethical action in a culture. Philosophy is the attempt to understand the "rational order of the universe," the mind of the Demiurge, as from Plato, as a symbol for the workings of the synthesis of the real and the ideal, which is Spirit. "Philosophy wished to recognize the content, the reality of the divine Idea, and to justify the spurned actuality; for Reason is the comprehension of the divine work." As the subject of philosophy is now the synthesis of the real and the ideal, and the inherent negation and self-alienation of reason within the ideal, the subject of philosophy becomes psychological, in light of the psychoanalysis developed in the twentieth century, beginning with Sigmund Freud. Hegelian philosophy can be called metaphysical psychology, an attempt to come to terms with human reason in relation to perceived reality, based in the relation between perception and reason (principally the instrument of *Vorstellung*), within the framework of the Idealist and metaphysical (Platonic) presupposition of the precedence of the ideal in relation to the real. In such a framework, human reality is taken as a construction within the ideal, and following that, human psychology is taken as a construction within the ideal as well.

Moralität is seen as the one essential element within the real, in human events in history, which is not "subject to the sway of chance," and not "transitory and exposed to atrophy and corruption." *Moralität* is thus seen as an *archê* in the ideal realm of human psychology, the originary element as the presence of the essence of being in human activities. *Moralität* as *archê* is the essential determinate factor in the synthesis and re-unification of Subjective Spirit and Objective Spirit in Absolute Mind, in the transition from being-in-itself to being-for-self (thus the essential determinateness), and of the synthesis of freedom and necessity in culture, universal and particular. In culture, Objective Spirit is the state, the universal organization of particulars, being-in-itself made being-for-self, the negation of the individual in the dialectic between freedom and necessity as subjective and objective. The state contains within it all concrete activity in the realization of Spirit, through art, religion, science and law. All activity in the state becomes conscious of the synthesis of necessity and freedom within it.

In the realization of the consciousness of Absolute Spirit in the state, of being-in-and-for-itself as the synthesis of the real and ideal, the particular interests of the individual are negated. In self-consciousness the individual sacrifices property, sentiment, and even value. The synthesis of the subjective and objective is manifest in philosophy, in its purest form through the instrument of reason; in religion, in the suspension of reason in the embodiment of the ideal in the real; and in art, in the synthesis of the ideal and the real in the real (the beautiful), and the presentation of the absence of the ideal in the real (the sublime). The culture of the state is the manifestation of the universal in the particular, as expressed in philosophy, religion and art. The expression of the universal in culture is the spirit of the people, the *Zeitgeist* and *Volksgeist*. In the ideal state, all the affairs of the state are manifestations of the universal Spirit, and all particular activities of the individuals within the state are enactments of the universal Spirit, as for Plato the well-ordered and lawful state is a macrocosm of the well-ordered and lawful mind of the individual within it, which is a product of the discipline of mind in reason as given by philosophy.

The essential element in the identification of the universal Spirit of the state and the individual will is the *Moralität*, the element of being-in-itself in the psychology of mind. Freedom in the state depends on both the identification of the universal Spirit and individual will, and the differentiation of the two, in the same way that Objective Spirit in mind is both the self-identification of consciousness in the other and its alienation from it. The actions of the individual will can only be justified in relation to universal Spirit, and as distinct from it at the same time, as particulars in relation to the universal, as there can be no universal without particulars. The universal Spirit of the state as manifest in the individual is the *Sittlichkeit*; the *Moralität* co-exists in state and individual, and is not a function of the particular manifestation of the universal, but rather the necessary grounds for their being.

The universal Spirit of the state becomes a particular in relation to the overall course of world history as the universal, the complete manifestation of Absolute Spirit. The dialectical struggle between states in the course of history mirrors the struggle between freedom and necessity within the states, which mirrors the struggle between the subjective and objective within the individual. The underlying basis of all human activity is reason, and the underlying basis of all human reason is being-in-itself, consciousness and self-consciousness, those elements which define human reason to itself. Human reason is unstable and in flux as it is manifest in varying states and periods of history, and the role of subjective and objective, consciousness and self-consciousness, necessity and freedom, in reason varies with the variances of the actuality of different cultural states, in the dialectical relation between real and ideal. As in Structural Anthropology and Structural Linguistics, there are underlying bases in reason for all human activity. All of world history is seen by Hegel as "the development of the principle whose *content* is the consciousness of freedom" (IV.1), the manifestation of Absolute Spirit. The analysis of such a development is (non-dogmatic) logic in reason (as differentiated in the *Wissenschaft der Logik*), the subject of philosophy; the analysis of the actuality of such a development is the subject of the *Phenomenology of Spirit* (*Phänomenologie des Geistes*). In the process of the analysis Spirit enters nature (the ideal enters the real), then steps out of the real into consciousness, then detaches itself from its relationship with the real, the particular, in consciousness, and enters into the "pure universality of freedom," Absolute Mind, where Spirit attains self-consciousness, the goal of historical development. Absolute Mind is the continual dialectical process of Spirit realizing itself in self-consciousness in world history.

6
Architecture and the Philosophy of Spirit

In the Introduction to the *Philosophy of Fine Art* (or the *Introductory Lectures on Aesthetics*), delivered in 1818, Georg Wilhelm Friedrich Hegel described the task of architecture as "shaping external inorganic nature that it becomes homogeneous with mind."[1] Architecture is the first step toward the realization of the absolute, the identity between the organic and inorganic, that is, Spirit (*Geist*). Architecture overcomes the duality between mind and nature, and purifies and coordinates the external world through mathematics and geometry. But because the forms of architecture are inorganic, and can only imitate the organic, they are symbolic, and cannot achieve an identity between the organic and inorganic, between the universal and particular, in the way that other artforms, and philosophy, can. Spirit cannot be contained in the material forms of architecture, and idea and form remain distinct, and can only be related abstractly.

Earlier, in lectures delivered in Jena in 1802, collected in *The Philosophy of Art*, Friedrich Wilhelm Joseph von Schelling also described the forms of architecture as inorganic, and constructed according to geometry and mathematics, which make the forms schematic, and allow them to symbolize the particular through the universal. As with Hegel, only organic form can express Spirit, or the absolute, as the expression of the Idea. Reason is only indirectly related to the inorganic, and thus to architecture; it is only mediated through the schema or concept. In order to be an absolute art of the Spirit, architecture must be in identity with reason, without mediation. In the organic, form and concept are identical, the subjective and the objective. Architecture can be beautiful (reflecting Hegel's definition of beauty in art as that which is born of Spirit, in the identity of the real and ideal), but only when it becomes independent of purpose or need, as a mechanical art. It must thus become independent of itself, and an imitation of itself. Architecture is fine art only when it appears to be purposeful and symbolic, but in reality is not.

According to Schelling, architecture can only be an idea or an allegory of the organic. It can never achieve an absolute identity ("indifference" in Spirit) between idea and matter. The only way that architecture can achieve an identity of particular (form) and universal or absolute (Idea), an identity between subjective and objective, is when it imitates its own requirements of necessity, satisfying necessity and being independent of it at the same time. Only in this way can architecture express Spirit, the identity of the universal and particular in the organic, and go a step beyond that allowed by Hegel toward the realization of the absolute, that which unifies and transcends both mind and matter, which is the object of philosophy. In *The Philosophy of Art*, § 107, Schelling describes architecture as the "anorganic art form"[2] within the plastic arts, and as necessarily based in geometry and mathematics, functions of the relations of logic within the real, unable to represent the presence of unreason in reason, or the sublime. The presence of the absolute in the real is only possible in light and color in painting, the dematerialization of substance. Qualities of the real which contain the representation of the sublime, light and vastness, are possible in the perception and experience of architecture, as in the perception and experience of nature, but they are not possible in the architecture itself.

According to Schelling, communication in the arts depends on the sequential development from schematic representation, as in signification in language, to the allegorical, the placing of the schematic representation in a narrative, and then to the symbolic, the reading of the artform as in the ideal, divorced from the real, in the same way that, for Hegel, mind becomes alienated from itself in being-for-self in self-consciousness, and the real and ideal become separated in mind, only to be reconciled in Absolute Mind or Spirit. The symbolic is the self-realization of the artificial construction of meaning, preceding the trope of irony in cultural development as the signification of the impossibility of meaning in language. Such an impossibility is already embedded in the symbolic. Arithmetic constitutes the "most primal schematism," as for Plato arithmetic results from the necessity of the mind in engaging in the alteration of day and night. In the schematic, the particular is automatically symbolized in the universal. As soon as the alteration of day and night becomes schematized as odd and even in the tetractys, for example, the particular is subsumed in the universal. Such is the function of thought, and philosophy in general. The relation between the particular and the universal in the schematic is symbolic, as in language, in Structural Linguistics, a word which corresponds to an idea, in an arbitrary correspondence, becomes a symbol of the idea. It is in the symbol that the relation between the real and the ideal is expressed.

Because architecture is composed of spatial relationships, arithmetic is necessarily manifest as geometry. Architecture is "solidified music," or "music in space," the spatial realization of proportional relations in music through geometry. None of the other visual arts are possible without the underlying role of arithmetical or geometrical relationships, as in the most substantial element of painting, drawing, and in especially the use of linear perspective. In order to become symbolic, though, that is in order to express a relation between the real and ideal, between matter and thought, forms in both nature and art must cast off "the limitations of a merely finite regularity," which can only express the presence of the real in the ideal, in the realm of logic in reason. Forms in nature and art which go beyond the limitations of finite regularity display the "chaos within the absolute," the unreason within reason in the identity or indifference of the real and ideal which is Absolute Spirit in mind. The chaos within the absolute is the void within being, the aporetic gap between mind and its other in self-consciousness, as it symbolizes the real to itself. Chaos within the absolute is lack of form within form, the *informe*, and that which exceeds reason in mind, the crisis of the symbol.

The crisis of the symbolic is the manifestation of self-consciousness in the absolute, and represents that which is exceeded by reason as logic. Philosophy is the "symbolic science," and philosophy as a science is necessary for the understanding of the symbolic as science is necessary for the understanding of the higher principles of nature. The symbolic is the subject of philosophy as reason in understanding; the beauty of form and figure in nature is the subject of philosophy as reason in imagination, the product of *Vorstellung*. Nature can no longer be understood in reason in logic as "the expression of a merely finite regularity of form," as given by geometric regularity. Nature becomes rather "the image of absolute identity, the chaos within the absolute." The plastic arts are generally "independent of geometric relationships," and are thus able to "consider and portray with complete freedom only the relationships of beauty in and for themselves," that is, the plastic arts are able to represent the chaos within the absolute and the image of absolute identity, the identity of the ideal and the real, of thought and matter, in Transcendental Idealism. Architecture, on the other hand, is necessarily governed by geometric regularity, and thus constitutes a "reversion of the plastic arts to the anorganic"; architecture is limited in relation to the plastic arts in its ability to represent absolute identity, in particular the sublime, and the chaos within the absolute, within self-consciousness in human thought, in the self-alienation of thought in its being-for-self as it returns to being-in-itself, in Hegelian terms.

The highest form which architecture can take as an art is in the expression of an abstract idea in reason as an image or representation of absolute identity. "Architecture can appear as free and beautiful art only insofar as it becomes the expression of *ideas*, an image of the universe and of the absolute." A true image of the absolute and an immediate expression of the Idea is only possible in organic form, which can only be achieved in the plastic arts. Unlike music, the conceptual counterpart of architecture, architecture cannot free itself from the representation of form in the real; it cannot free itself from matter, and the insertion of thought as reason into matter, the ideal into the real, as geometric regularity. Architecture cannot represent the absolute in form alone; it can only represent the absolute in both form and essence simultaneously, that is, it must express an idea. The organic form in the plastic arts is an immediate representation of reason, because the organic form itself is "reason perceived in the real," reason's perception of itself in the real, the definition of beauty. The anorganic form is not an immediate representation of reason, because reason cannot perceive itself in the real in the anorganic form; the anorganic form is a product of reason, a product of the ideal. The relation between reason and architecture is thus an indirect one, and must be mediated by the organic, seen in relation to the organic, and as such mediated by the concept or the idea. Reason perceives itself directly in the real, in nature, in absolute identity, in the organic form of the plastic arts; reason can only perceive itself indirectly in nature in the anorganic forms of architecture. Architecture thus stages the problematic relation between reason and nature, the inability of mind to perceive itself in the real, and the forms of architecture are the product of the struggle between mind and its self-perception in the real. The forms of architecture are the product of the problematic relation between the real and the ideal in Transcendental Idealism.

Architecture can only represent through the mediation of the concept, the idea, in reason. In order to exist within the realm of absolute identity, in the realm of Spirit, architecture must achieve an absolute identity with reason itself, it must "in itself and without mediation be in identity with reason." An identity with reason cannot be achieved in materiality alone, in the realm of matter or the real, and in the concept of purpose associated with matter, the laws of cause and effect and necessity, as in the Principle of Sufficient Reason, as given by logic in the real. The concept cannot be found within the matter or emerge from it; it must be external to it. In order to represent absolute identity, architecture must communicate an idea which is external to its material presence. It must enact the presence of an idea, or the possibility of an idea, in the Platonic sense of an *archê*, an idea which precedes its material manifestation, an idea of which its materiality is a manifestation, but which is external to its manifestation in the materiality, external to both nature and the identity of mind as perceived in nature or the real. In organic form in the plastic arts, the idea is not external to the material; the concept is infused into the material, creating a synthesis of the subjective and objective in mind, Hegelian being-in-itself and being-for-self in consciousness, and thus a synthesis of the infinite and finite. The organic form is thus an image of reason; the most ideal form of the organic is the human body, and the representation of the human body was seen in Classical art to be the most complete synthesis of the real and ideal in the plastic arts, and the synthesis of the real and the ideal in the anthropomorphized mythological figure. Architecture cannot achieve the synthesis of the subjective and objective and the infinite and finite in form; architectural form always displays the incompatibility of the ideal and the real within reason, to which it is bound. Architecture as art depends on its identity with reason in the realm of the ideal, and thus of the existence of the real within the ideal, and the presupposition of the ideal in the perception of the real, which is the basis of Idealist philosophy.

Architecture can only be beautiful, that is, it can only achieve a synthesis of the ideal and real, mind and matter, within the ideal, when it becomes independent of its purpose or function in its representational forms. In order to be beautiful, architecture must appear to be functional, but in fact must not be functional. Architectural forms must appear to obey the laws of cause and effect in the real, but at the same time be independent of those laws within the ideal. This in fact is the Hegelian definition of freedom, the independence in mind from the laws of necessity in the real, as given by self-consciousness. The Parthenon is beautiful because the colonnade, entablature and pediment appear to support the structure, but in fact do not. Those elements of the building assume only the form of structure, and not purpose. The building communicates the discrepancy of the real and ideal, function and idea, within the ideal, within the concept which is communicated in connection to the material. In that way the building assumes an identity with reason in relationship to nature; reason perceives itself in the forms of the building and judges it to be beautiful. The façades of the Palazzo Rucellai, Santa Maria Novella, and Sant'Andrea in Mantua by Leon Battista Alberti are the epitome of architectural beauty in the Renaissance because the forms which are based in structural necessity do not function in any structural way. The same can be said of the Villa Rotunda of Andrea Palladio and the Palazzo del Tè of Giulio Romano in the Renaissance, or the Villa Savoye of Le Corbusier, the Seagrams Building of Ludvig Mies van der Rohe, and the Wexner Center of Peter Eisenman in the twentieth century. Peter Eisenman has in fact put forward this argument as a defense of compositional strategies in architecture.

For Schelling, "architecture is beautiful," that is, represents the self-identity of the ideal within the real, only when it becomes independent of need," as opposed to the other plastic arts, in which the organic form displays the identity of the real and ideal within the realm of necessity, the realm of the real. Organic form is taken as a symbol of the real, which contains within itself, the symbol, the possibility of the identity of the real and ideal. Architecture can never be completely independent of the real, of necessity and cause and effect, thus in order to be beautiful it must be "simultaneously becoming independent *of itself*." Architecture achieves its communicative potential when it becomes a "free imitation of itself." Architecture achieves freedom in mind, Absolute Spirit, in the same way that mind attains freedom as Absolute Spirit, in Hegelian terms: architecture becomes conscious of itself in its being-in-itself, its essential being in the real, and it becomes alienated from itself in its doubling of itself, its self-recognition as other to itself, and through its being-for-self becomes self-conscious in its return to itself, achieving a being-in-and-for-itself, which is freedom in mind as the absolute. In such a way architecture mirrors the activity of mind in self-consciousness; it enacts the process of reason in imagination and understanding, and in that way is identical to reason itself, and can thus represent the absolute within the ideal.

According to Schelling, as soon as architecture "attains through appearance both actuality and utility without intending these *as* utility and as actuality," that is, as soon as it imitates itself in its forms, it "becomes free and independent art." Architecture imitating itself is as the real imitating itself in the ideal, or the laws of necessity and cause and effect imitating themselves in reason. In that way reason in imagination is able to perceive the presence of the real, that which is external to it, within itself, and then to transcend the self-presence of the real in self-consciousness, to attain freedom from it, which is the purpose of philosophy, and the purpose of the development of mind in Transcendental Idealism. The object associated with the concept of purpose is transformed into an object of art devoid of purpose, or independent of the concept of purpose with which it was previously associated, as in the conceptual art of Marcel Duchamp. The concept of purpose itself becomes disassociated with purpose, and the presence of the ideal within the real is revealed, the perception of the real based in the presupposition of the ideal. The concept of purpose itself becomes an artistic object, an idea which displays the synthesis of ideal and real within the ideal within the framework of the discrepancy of the ideal and the real, between thought and that which is external to it as given by thought in perception, in the doubling of mind in consciousness in being-for-self and the consequent self-alienation of mind.

The work of art as concept, as in architecture, achieves an objective identity between subjective and objective, between ideal and real, as concept in being-for-self, and thus is able to return to itself in being-in-itself, unconscious existence and essential reality. The objective identity achieved in architecture is in the objective purposiveness of the architecture. All art is the objective representation of the identity between the subjective and the objective, between the universal and the particular, in the real, in the object. Architecture achieves the representation of the universal by representing that which is other to itself within its form, in the discontinuity between the subjective and the objective, while the other forms of the plastic arts are able to represent the continuity of the subjective and objective as far as it is possible in the real, in the organism, as given by reason in perception. As art, architecture must present the possibility of the precedence of the anorganic to the organic, the crystalline to the organism, and thus it must present the organic as the essence of the anorganic. The precedence of the anorganic to the organic in representation contains the essence of thought, its being-in-itself, in the ideal, because as thought is a process of abstraction, the universal derived from the particular in the schematic, as given in language, then thought itself entails a return to the anorganic which precedes the organic, the crystalline forms of mineral matter which precede life forms, which are the model in the real for abstraction as a reduction of the particularity of life forms in the organic to the universality of schematic forms in thought.

In architecture, organic forms are displayed as preformed in the anorganic in the same way that the organic forms of life are understood to be preformed in the crystalline forms of the mineral, and the particular is seen to be preformed in the universal, as in the Platonic *archê*. It is necessary for architecture to present the organic as the result of the anorganic in order for architecture to appear to reason as reason, as the synthesis of the subjective and objective, in the real. Architecture cannot represent reason alone in the organic because the forms of architecture cannot escape their necessity in matter, except as imitations of that necessity. The representation of reason in architecture requires both the organic and anorganic, that which precedes necessity in logic in reason in the real, that is, the essential being-in-itself, unconscious being which precedes conscious being, the dark ground of being which contains the chaos and formlessness of the absolute. As absolute formlessness is the equivalent of pure form in the ideal, as absolute chaos is the equivalent of absolute identity, so absolute formlessness is the equivalent of the abject crystalline forms of the anorganic, and as they are represented in the geometry and mathematics of logic in the real. The crystalline form of the anorganic in reason is the reduction to ground zero of form in being, the primordial state of form which has no prior, because it has no necessity. It is the crystalline anorganic form of geometry and mathematics which architecture imitates as itself in its representation of the identity of the infinite and finite within reason. The architectural form is a form which has no necessity of itself as geometry, but assumes necessity in the enactment of the geometry in function, then doubles and imitates the necessity as a form of expression, and separates itself from the necessity as art. This is the same process which mind follows from unconscious being, to consciousness and self-consciousness in absolute being, being-in-and-for-itself, the forms of which are equivalent to the forms of unconscious being.

Thus architecture as art must contain a representation of the relation between the organic and the anorganic, between reason in the real and the absence of reason in the real, between belonging in the world and alienation from it. In architecture the organic can only be represented as preformed within the anorganic, belonging in the world as preformed within the alienation of reason from the world. As the human being builds a place for himself in the world, he constructs the incompatibility between himself and the world. In order for the organic to be present in architecture, in order for belonging in the world to be present, for reason to recognize itself in the real in the identity of the subjective and objective in architecture, the organic must be represented by the anorganic allegorically. The anorganic forms of architecture must signify the organic, must suggest their opposite or their other, the presence of reason in the real, as linguistic tropisms, and organize them in a temporal progression to represent the process of thought, so that thought can see itself in the real, in the anorganic forms of the architecture, from which it is *a priori* absent. Architecture as art is necessarily allegorical; it necessarily represents that which it is not, in order to participate in the absolute, in the indifference of the real and ideal.

In *The Philosophy of Art*, § 111, "architecture, to be fine art, must be the potence or imitation of itself as the art of need." Architecture imitates itself allegorically. The anorganic form in itself cannot be symbolic, because it does not have a direct relation to reason; reason cannot see itself in the anorganic form, though the anorganic form is a product of logic in reason. Thus it is impossible for reason to see itself in a synthesis with matter in the anorganic form, and the anorganic form cannot be other than what it is to reason. It is only the organic form, that which is achieved in the plastic arts in the synthesis of the material and immaterial, the particular and universal, which can be symbolic to reason, which can suggest to reason the participation of reason in the real, and thus become to reason other than what it is. As will be seen, for Hegel it is precisely the anorganic form of architecture which contains the first possibility of the symbolic. For Schelling, "the anorganic as such can have only an indirect relationship to reason and thus can never possess symbolic significance." The anorganic can only be symbolic in imitation of itself.

The pyramids, the primal form of architectural expression, are symbolic not in their materiality as necessity in the real, but as imitation of their materiality as necessity in the real, as enacted in the symbolic representation in language of the trope, in reason in understanding. The symbolic function of the pyramid, as the primordial mound, or the rays of light from the sun emanating to the four corners of the world, is extraneous to the material function of the pyramid as an anorganic form. The anorganic form of the pyramid must double itself, through the symbolic in language, in metaphor and allegory, in order to symbolize something. In other words, the anorganic form is not symbolic in itself, but only in how it is perceived by reason, as it is extraneous to the perception of reason of itself in the real, because the anorganic form is always already reason in the real. The symbolic in language functions as a product of the inability of reason to see itself as itself in the real outside of its relation to the real, that which it perceives. It is a product of the thrown-ness of reason from itself and from the real in self-consciousness, thus the symbolic for Hegel becomes an instrument for the return of reason to itself. The same can be said for the allegorical, which is the narrativization of the symbolic.

In architecture the organic form is only presented as an idea, as representation or imitation of itself, the representation of the real within the ideal. The organic is not present in architecture outside the framework of the anorganic, outside the framework of the anorganic as allegory of the organic, thus outside the framework of language. Thus the symbolic is only given in architecture as a product of language. The identity between the idea or concept and the materiality of the architecture is an objective identity rather than a subjective identity, an identity which is facilitated by the relationship between thought and matter, rather than the indifference of thought and matter in both the real and the ideal, which is the absolute. The symbolic in architecture is the being-for-self of consciousness in Hegelian terms, a product of mind seeing itself as other, and attempting to return to itself. The symbolic in architecture thus signifies the self-alienation of mind in consciousness, and the inability of reason to see itself in the real, in that which it perceives. This is similar to Hegel's explanation for the symbolic character of architecture in Egypt as a reflection of the culture, in which it was impossible for human reason to identify itself in nature, in the real, and thus the synthesis of reason and nature, the ideal and the real, required a symbolic mediation, which made possible Absolute Spirit.

In that the symbolic in architectural form is a function of language, language itself is a symbolic mediation between the real and the ideal in the impossibility of reason to identify itself in the real. Language is an allegorical construct of thought in imitation of the perception of the real in the ideal, or nature in relation to thought; language imitates nature as the symbolic imitates the organic in architectural form. In the hieroglyph, allegorical language, or alphabetical language, can be seen to be a product of symbolic language, or picture thinking, reason as perception. In the symbolic element of the hieroglyph, the organic form is presented as an imitation of itself in the anorganic as the organic is present in the architecture. Symbolic architectural forms can be seen as hieroglyphics, in that their communicative function is based in the tropics of language.

The subjective indifference of the ideal and the real is not possible in the imitation of symbolic mediation in architectural forms, but it is possible in the organic forms of the plastic arts, which can directly symbolize the presence of reason in the real. Architecture can only generate such an identity in its mechanisms, as is the case with language. The plastic arts are therefore seen as being able to communicate an identity between the ideal and the real which language cannot, though ultimately poetry is the most absolute form of artistic expression, because it is completely within the ideal, while the plastic arts are limited in their existence in the real. Nevertheless, their ability to communicate the indifference of the ideal and the real within the real exceeds the possibility of such an indifference in language. The contemplation of the sublime as represented in a painting, for example, in the use of color and light, exceeds the symbolic mediation of language in the real, and represents the return of thought to itself in self-consciousness, to essential, unconscious being, the ground of being prior to language. Light and color are seen by Schelling as those elements in painting which contain the indifference of the ideal and the real most directly, because they signify the presence of the absolute in the real, outside the structure of the symbolic in language.

The signification of color and light allows mind to see itself in the real in intuition rather than the symbolic structures of logic, based on Kant's definition of the schematic in the *Critique of Judgment.* According to Kant, "In schematic hypostasis [exhibition] there is a concept that the understanding has formed, and the intuition corresponding to it is given a priori. In symbolic hypostasis there is a concept which only reason can think and to which no sensible intuition can be adequate....Schemata contain direct, symbols indirect, exhibitions of the concept. Schematic exhibition is demonstrative. Symbolic exhibition uses an analogy (for which we use empirical intuitions as well), in which judgment performs a double function: it applies the concept to the object of a sensible intuition; and then it applies the mere rule by which it reflects on that intuition to an entirely different object, of which the former object is only the symbol..."[3] The double function of judgment in the symbolic is as the imitation of the organic of itself in the anorganic in architecture. Symbolic mediation is the product of the doubling of thought in the consciousness of its other. In the schematic, in signification, the perception of thought in intuition is a function of its return to itself, in its rediscovery of itself as prior to consciousness, in Hegelian terms, prior to symbolic mediation. In Structural Linguistics, language is seen as systematized signification, where in fact language is not possible without the mediation of the symbolic as the doubling of thought of itself, as the organic imitates itself in the anorganic in architectural forms.

According to Schelling, when architecture as art is both the enactment of necessity and the freedom from necessity, it achieves a synthesis between the particular and the universal, which is the identity of the subjective and objective. If the "allegory of the organic is expressed through the anorganic" (*The Philosophy of Art*, § 111), then the architecture achieves an identity between the subjective and objective, between the ideal and the real, and the forms of the architecture are beautiful, reinforcing that identity. As such, in the imitation of the organic in the anorganic, in the imitation of necessity in free form, architecture is a "parody of the mechanical building arts," an imitation of the act of building in allegorical representation. It is impossible for architecture as art to take building seriously in its imitation of it, because that would make necessary the realization on the part of reason that it does not exist in the real, which would negate being-in-the-world altogether. Architecture is a parody of necessity because thought as given by language is a parody of the real, that which is perceived by reason. Thought in language cannot overcome its alienation from the real in its being-for-self, in the necessity of symbolic mediation; it is only in intuition and signification that the possibility exists for an identity between reason and the real, and such an identity is only found in the organic, according to Schelling, which is impossible in architecture. Architecture is thus the expression of the most self-alienated form of reason in mind, which is why, in a certain respect, it is the most representative of the human condition as an art.

The organic form which best serves architecture, which architecture is best suited to imitate in the anorganic, is the plant form, according to Schelling, because the plant form is already seen only as an allegory of the organism of the animal or human body. The plant form is easily reducible to arithmetic and geometric structures, as in the Fibonacci Series, symbolic structures which are easily translated into the anorganic forms of architecture. The plant form is the closest form in nature to the crystalline, mineral form, the anorganic in nature; it is the most anorganic of organic forms. The plant form displays the most objective identity of the particular and the universal in nature, that is, it displays the identity in which the universal is most subjugated to the particular, and seen as being "prefigured or preformed through particularity" (§ 112). The plant form is thus the closest of the organic forms to necessity, as it is identified in the real by reason. The proportions and relationships in the mathematics and geometries of architectural forms are closest to those of the plant organism, but the basis of the judgment of beauty in architectural proportions and relationships traditionally is the analogy to the human body rather than the plant organism, because, as seen in Classical art, it is the human body which represents the most complete indifference of the ideal and the real in form.

The proportions and relationships of architecture constitute its "harmonic part" (§ 117), in analogy to the rhythm and harmony of music, which, like architecture, consists of a "periodic subdivision of equal elements..." (§ 115). Proportions in architecture are primarily analogous to the proportions of the human body, and it is primarily through the analogy of proportions to the human body that the anorganic forms of architecture can imitate the organic. The proportional analogy between architecture and the human body must be seen as a parody as well, as the analogy again depends on the symbolic mediation of language, and the alienation of reason from the real. The harmony of proportions in architecture exists only in the ideal, in mind, and cannot be seen as the indifference of the ideal and the real, as the expression of Absolute Spirit in mind, self-consciousness in being-in-and-for-itself, in Hegel's terms. Harmonic Proportions in architecture are only allegorical, a poetic function of language, and must be seen as reinforcing the incompatibility of reason and nature, the exact opposite of the function of the analogy in the Renaissance, a distinction which defines the principal difference between Classical (Renaissance) and Romantic art and architecture. Romantic forms of architecture deny the allegorical role of the forms in establishing an identity of the ideal and the real through the imitation of the organic; in fact, in Romantic forms of architecture, the purpose of the imitation of the organic is to emphasize the incompatibility of reason and nature, as in the sublime and the grotesque, the *Carceri* of Giambattista Piranesi, the neo-Gothic forms of Horace Walpole in both building and literary description (*The Castle of Otranto*).

According to Schelling, the symbolic facilitates the representation of the identity or indifference of the universal and particular within the particular (*The Philosophy of Art*, § 39), or the identity of the ideal and the real within the real. As in all of the plastic arts, the forms of architecture are limited to the real, to matter, and only contain the universal in perception, in the interaction of reason, and the structure of the interaction is the symbolic. Representation of the identity of the universal and particular within the ideal is the idea, the subject of philosophy. Architecture can be seen as the equivalent of philosophy in the real. The symbolic, the mediation between the real and the ideal, which allows architecture to function as philosophy within the real, can be seen as a "synthesis of two opposing modes, the schematic and the allegorical..." The schematic is that form of representation in which the particular is intuited through the universal. The allegorical is that form of representation in which the universal is intuited through the particular. The symbolic is the form of representation in which the synthesis of the universal and particular is achieved. In the symbolic, the universal is not intuited through the particular, nor is the particular intuited through the universal, but the two are seen as the same.

The schema is the means by which the concept or the idea becomes a particular form or image in the plastic arts, the means by which particular forms are chosen and arranged in relation to the universal, so that they contain an identity of the particular and universal. Mathematical and geometrical structures are schemas which are translated into architectural forms; if the arrangement of architectural forms corresponds to a mathematical or geometrical structure, then the particular forms are understood through the universal concept. According to Schelling, Kant defined the schema in the *Critique of Pure Reason* as the "sensually intuited rule for the production of an object." The schematic transition between idea and form in the art has a linguistic basis. Language is "nothing more than perpetual schematization." In language, "we make use of merely universal designations even for the designation of the particular." In other words, most often when a word is used to describe an object, the word used can describe any object of that type. The object described is understood as a particular only through the universal, the idea or concept of the object preformed in the mind, as described by Plato. Schematization is the correlate of signification in language, in which a word with no particular relation to that which it designates substitutes for that which is designated; the idea substitutes for the object, and, in architectural terms, the anorganic imitates the organic. In the schematic the ideal becomes a parody of the real; the ideal assumes a life of its own, in imitation of the real, in order to describe the real, with which it has lost an identity through the intervention of the schematic or the signifying in language. The schematic in language and thought is at the core of architectural production, because the organization of architectural forms always corresponds to an idea or a concept, and thus always represents the presence of the universal within the particular.

The allegory is seen as the reverse of the schema. Like the schema, allegory contains the identity of the universal and particular, but in allegory the universal is understood through the particular, while in the schematic the particular is understood through the universal. In allegory the particular signifies the universal without being the universal. All language is allegorical in signification, because a particular word in language has no universal quality in and of itself; its universal quality is only given to it by the idea or concept which is applied to it, as in the "deep structure" of transformational grammar in Structural Linguistics. Forms in the plastic arts are allegorical in signification because they are always particular forms within the real which only participate in the universal as they are perceived by reason. The same can be said of nature; the particular forms of nature only participate in the universal in perception and reason, thus nature is communicated allegorically to reason in language. The schematic and the allegorical represent to Schelling the two directions of transference between the ideal and the real, mind and matter. The schematic is the transition in signification from the ideal to the real, and the allegorical is the transition in signification from the real to the ideal. Thus all concepts in mind, and all particular forms of the real, and particular forms in the plastic arts, are seen within the framework of the schematic and the allegorical. Such a framework can be taken as a compositional tool for the architect, for example, particularly in the arrangement of forms schematically, in the ideal, to the end of representing the universal in the particular, and the arrangement of forms allegorically, in the real, to the end of representing the particular in the universal. The allegorical content of an architectural composition allows the particular forms of the architecture to participate in the universal, as individual expression, in the same way that language in individual expression participates in the universal through allegory.

Allegory in language is defined as the narrativization of the symbolic, thus allegory in architecture would involve the introduction of the temporal element of language into the spatial relationships of architecture. Schelling defines architecture as the spatial correlate in the real of the temporal relations in music in proportion and harmony, intervals of rhythm and arrangements of scale. The structural elements of music can thus play a direct allegorical role when translated into the spatial relationships of architecture. The same can be said for mathematical and geometrical structures. For example, in the Renaissance, in the treatise *De circuli quadratura*, Nicolas Cusanus described the relationship between reason and the absolute (the ineffable god) as the relationship between a succession of polygonal figures and the circle in which they are inscribed.[4] As the sides of the polygonal figure are multiplied, the polygonal figure approaches the circle, but no matter how many times the sides of the polygonal figure are multiplied, within the limited domain of exponential mathematics in logic, the polygonal figure can never arrive at the circle; the circle always exceeds the polygonal figure, as the absolute always exceeds reason, as in the dialectic of the universal and particular in the Transcendental Idealism of Schelling and Hegel. The polygon and the circle are a schematic representation of the concept of reason in relation to the absolute; the circle signifies the absolute which is inaccessible to reason, and the polygon signifies the systematic processes of reason. The circle and the polygon are symbolic as well, because there is a quality in both which is implicit in relationships to what they represent, which is not always the case with words in language, although oftentimes an implicit relationship between a word and the idea which it signifies can be found in the origin of the word.

In the treatise on architecture in the Renaissance, *De re aedificatoria*, Leon Battista Alberti prescribed the inscription of the polygonal figure within the circle as a template for the composition of the temple plan, perhaps for the purpose of inscribing the symbolic relationship in the architecture, following Cusanus or in relation to the same concept, as Alberti and Cusanus were familiar with each other's writings. Following such an inscription, the plan of the temple becomes an allegorical representation of the universal idea which is translated schematically in the mind of the architect in the form of a diagram. An example of the application of such an inscription is the plan for the Church of San Carlo alle Quattro Fontane in Rome by Francesco Borromini (as represented in Drawing 173 in the Albertina collection in Vienna), who was certainly familiar with the *De re aedificatoria*, and whose architecture contains many references to the concepts of Alberti.[5] The plan of San Carlo contains an oval inscribed into a rectangle which has been chamfered at the corners to form an octagon to circumscribe the oval. The circle of the Renaissance, the schema of the perfection and ineffability of the absolute, has been elongated into an oval. The circle is seen, in Platonic terms, as the *archê* of the material world, but as such it is imperceptible in the material world. If the circle in the celestial world is illuminated by a celestial light, the shadow that it would cast in the material world would be in the shape of the oval; the oval is thus the form of the circle which is perceptible to reason in the material world. The polygons have been elongated accordingly in relation to the oval.

The relation between the oval and the octagon and rectangle which are circumscribed around it seems to be functioning in the same allegorical context as intended by Leon Battisa Alberti in his prescription for the plans of temples, enacting the relation between the absolute and human reason. Other geometries inscribed within Borromini's oval, in particular intersecting triangles, indicate that the composition is also a schematic allegory for the process of creation. Intersecting triangles were used schematically by Nicolas Cusanus in the treatise *De coniecturis* to signify the coincidence of opposites, particularly light and dark, in the process of creation. In inscribing the intersecting triangles in the oval which is circumscribed by the polygonal figures in the plan of San Carlo, Borromini seems to be constructing an allegory of the relation between the absolute and human reason in the context of creation, wherein the absolute is the formless void of being at the core of creation, as for Schelling, and human reason circumscribes itself around the void of the absolute in the allegorical construction, through language, of the identity of reason and that which is external to it, in the terms of Transcendental Idealism. Borromini's plan can be seen as a model for the allegorical function of architectural forms, in representing the universal in the particular, which Schelling prescribes.

To take another example from the twentieth century, in the treatise *Syntactic Structures*, published in 1965, Noam Chomsky formulated a schematic relation between the syntax of linguistic structure, the way words are arranged in a sentence, and the semantic content of the syntax, the meaning that is generated by the arrangement of words in a sentence, to which he referred as the surface aspect of a language and the deep level aspect of a language, derived from his reading of the linguistic theory of the Port-Royal *Grammar*. In *Aspects of the Theory of Syntax* and *Language and Mind*, Chomsky formulated what he called "grammatical transformations," which were schematic representations for the transferal of meaning between the deep structure and surface structure of a language. In *Language and Mind*, grammatical transformations consist of "a system of rules that characterizes deep and surface structures and the transformational relations between them" (p. 17).[6] With this set of rules, it is possible to have "control of a grammar that generates (that is, characterizes) the infinite set of potential deep structures, maps them into associated surface structures, and determines the semantic and phonetic interpretations of these abstracted objects" (p. 30), to understand the universal through the particular, as in allegory. Chomsky's grammatical transformations are an allegorical structure within the allegorical structure of language for the purpose of understanding the relation between the universal, or idea, and particular, or word and syntax, in language.

Peter Eisenman applied the schema of the grammatical transformations of Chomsky to the analysis of a work of architecture, the Casa Giuliani Frigerio in Como by Giuseppe Terragni, as described in the article "From Object to Relationship II: Giuseppe Terragni, Casa Giuliani Frigerio," in *Perspecta*, The Yale Architectural Journal, in 1971.[7] Eisenman perceived the architecture as containing a surface aspect, the material elements of the architecture which function as words in a sentence, and a deep aspect, which is a set of "conceptual relationships which are not sensually perceived; such as frontality, obliqueness, recession, elongation, compression, and shear, which are understood in the mind. These are attributes which accrue to relationships between objects, rather than to the physical presence of the objects themselves,"[8] in the same way that a deep structure of a language is not immediately present in the words or the syntax of the language, but can be construed from the syntax and constructed in the mind, as the universal is construed from the particular and constructed in the mind in allegory. The composition of Terragni at the Casa Giuliani Frigerio, according to Eisenman, is an allegorical composition, where the particulars of the architectural forms are arranged in such a way that they lead the perceiver to universal concepts in the mind which are not present in the architecture as it is perceived. This is accomplished by Terragni, according to Eisenman, in the simultaneous centripetal and centrifugal organization of solids and voids in the centralized plan, and the simultaneous additive and subtractive relation between the solids and voids. Such a layering of compositional relationships suggests the possibility of layering of significance in language, in particular in the creation of what is called "pictorial ambiguity" by Eisenman in the composition, the possibility of multiple significations by a single signifier, which reveals the relation between a surface and deep structure, and can be seen as a transformational device, corresponding to syntactical ambiguity in language, as in the phrase "the shooting of the hunters," which creates two conflicting conceptual structures corresponding to the syntax.

The pictorial ambiguity of Terragni as perceived by Eisenman in the Casa Giuliani Frigerio, in the simultaneous centripetal and centrifugal, and additive and subtractive organizations, is not dissimilar to the diagrammatic basis of the plan of San Carlo alle Quattro Fontane of Francesco Borromini. In both cases a schematic representation of a conceptual structure is enacted by the architect, or at least read by its interpreters, and as enacted the schematic structure functions allegorically to lead the perceiver from the particulars of the architecture to the universal concepts which they enact in the real. The architects compose in the schematic, that is they translate universals into particulars, in the same way that a writer composes a sentence, and then the architecture is read allegorically, leading the perceiver from the particular to the universal, from the real to the ideal, in the same way that a text or a poem is read. The transition from the schematic to the allegorical and vice versa are functions of the identity of the universal and particular in the absolute, in Absolute Spirit in mind, in the terms of Transcendental Idealism.

The linguistic transformations as enacted in architecture are devices for the self-perception of reason in the real in consciousness; the product of the devices is the doubling of reason in consciousness, its becoming being-for-self, the self-perception of reason as other to itself and its self-alienation from itself, and its return to itself in being-in-and-for-itself, as Absolute Spirit, as described by Hegel in *Phenomenology of Spirit.* In that architectural representation is limited to the allegorical and schematic, or the symbolic as the combination of the two, in Schelling's terms, architecture cannot transcend the symbolic mediation of Spirit which is possible in the other plastic arts; architectural representation thus displays, in particular, the self-alienation of reason from itself at the point of self-recognition in its other, which is that in mind which is given by the symbolic. Architecture is the art of the self-alienation of reason, the representation of the thrown-ness of reason from being, in the process of reason attempting to return to itself, but not being able to overcome the symbolic mediation, as given by the anorganic forms of architecture, which can only imitate the organic.

Allegory was described by Fredric Jameson in the article "From Metaphor to Allegory" in *Anything* as "a structure that designates difficulties, if not outright impossibilities, in meaning and representation, and also designates its own peculiar structure as a failure to mean and to represent in the conventional way" (p. 27).[9] Allegory is a product of a "crisis in representation," as the expression of the crisis of reason in its self-alienation. As a narrative process, allegory stages the crisis of representation as a dialectical struggle between the ideal and the real, in Idealist terms. Jameson explains:

> Allegory is a narrative process precisely because it needs to tell the narrative of the solution to its representational dilemma. Or, if you prefer, in allegory the crisis of representation and of meaning is conceived precisely as a dramatic situation that the allegorist is called upon to resolve in some way. The narrative here is thus very often a dialectical one: the crisis embodies a contradiction, which is articulated as a binary opposition, and the allegorical narrative will consist in the attempt to overcome this opposition in one way or another, which obviously does not always have to involve a synthesis between the two allegedly irreconcilable terms.

Allegorical representation itself is the product of the struggle of reason in relation to the real in self-consciousness, in Hegelian terms. It is the drama unfolding in the real, in language and architectural forms, of the struggle between reason and non-reason in the ideal. In Transcendental Idealism, the dialectical struggle ideally resolves itself in the perception of the identity and synthesis of the ideal and the real, which cannot be accomplished through allegory. Architecture, as an allegorical art, stages this crisis of representation, in its limitation to the symbolic. The drama of architecture is the drama of the crisis of representation in the symbolic, reason struggling with itself in its relation to the real, and in its self-alienation in self-consciousness, which precludes the possibility of a resolution in the framework of symbolic representation.

As Jameson describes, "If the allegorical is attractive for the present day and age it is because it models a relationship of breaks, gaps, discontinuities, and inner distances and incommensurabilities of all kinds. It can therefore better serve as a figure for the incommensurability of the world today than the ideal of the symbol, which serves to designate some impossible unity" (p. 25). Much of the composition of Deconstructivist architecture is a simple allegory of the incommensurabilities of human reason in relation to the real, but the incommensurabilities allegorized in Deconstructivism are outside of the linguistic structure of the symbolic manifestation of reason to itself, and appear as anorganic parodies or imitations of organic forms, which architecture is prone to do in its most basic textual form, as described by Schelling, in its limitation in the symbolic. A more complete allegorical representation in architecture must involve the mechanisms of the allegory itself in relation to reason, in order to stage the crisis of reason in the crisis of representation. The anorganic imitation of organic forms in architecture represents no crisis in representation, but rather celebrates representation in imitation, and preserves the perception of the identity of the ideal and the real in the real, the belonging of reason in the world.

Architecture at the beginning of the twenty-first century requires a more thorough development of its capacity for allegorical representation if it is to continue to expand as a form of human expression. Allegorical representation in architecture requires the symbolic enactment of the relation between the ideal and the real, between mind and nature, between reason and that which it perceives. Along with music, mathematics and geometry, architectural compositions are capable of enacting allegories of perception, linguistic structures, conceptual structures in logic, philosophical and theological structures, social relations, ethical and moral values, and dramatic and performative structures. All of these conceptual structures can be translated into particular forms through schematic devices, enacted in architectural materials and compositions, and then read as allegories in the transference of the particular back to the universal, in the two-way transference between the schematic and allegorical and the universal and particular which defines artistic expression in the enactment of the dialectical struggle between reason and that which reason perceives in the real, between reason and its self-alienation from itself in being-for-self in self-consciousness, and between reason and the absence of reason which it perceives in the real, in the terms of Transcendental Idealism. Transcendental Idealism, the thought of Schelling and Hegel, and its precedent, Neoplatonism, in particular in the thought of Plotinus, deserve to be rediscovered in art and architectural theory, for the purposes of designing strategies for composition and expression in art and architecture, for the purpose of continuing to express the human condition through art and architecture in the twenty-first century, regardless of the mechanisms of production, and the external subject matter of the work.

Notes

1
Introduction

1. Michael G. Vater, "Schelling's Neoplatonic System-Notion: '*Ineinsbildung*' and Temporal Unfolding," in R. Baine Harris, ed., *The Significance of Neoplatonism*, Norfolk: International Society for Neoplatonic Studies, 1976.
2. Friedrich Wilhelm Joseph von Schelling, *System of Transcendental Idealism* (1800), trans. Peter Heath (Charlottesville: University Press of Virginia, 1978), p. 231.
3. Johann Gottlieb Fichte, *The Science of Knowledge*, ed. and trans. Peter Heath and John Lachs (Cambridge: Cambridge University Press, 1982).
4. Johann Gottlieb Fichte, "Letter to Jens Baggeson," 1795, in *Early Philosophical Writings*, ed. and trans. Daniel Breazeale (Ithaca and London: Cornell University Press, 1988), p. 385.
5. Georg Wilhelm Friedrich Hegel, *Phenomenology of Spirit*, trans. A. V. Miller (Oxford: Oxford University Press, 1977).
6. Georg Wilhelm Friedrich Hegel, *The Encyclopedia Logic* (*Wissenschaft der Logic*, 1830), trans. T. F. Geraets, W. A. Suchting, and H. S. Harris (Indianapolis/Cambridge: Hackett Publishing Company, Inc., 1991).
7. Georg Wilhelm Friedrich Hegel, *Introductory Lectures on Aesthetics* (*The Introduction to Hegel's Philosophy of Fine Art*, 1886), trans. Bernard Bosanquet, ed. Michael Inwood (London: Penguin Books, 1993).
8. Eric von der Luft, "Comment," in Robert L. Perkins, ed., *History and System: Hegel's Philosophy of History* (Albany: State University of New York Press, 1984), p. 40.
9. Jon Mills, *The Unconscious Abyss: Hegel's Anticipation of Psychoanalysis* (Albany: State University of New York Press, 2002), p. 31.
10. Terry Pinkard, *Hegel, A Biography* (Cambridge: Cambridge University Press, 2000), p. 27.
11. George di Giovanni and H. S. Harris, trans. and annotated, *Between Kant and Hegel: Texts in the Development of Post-Kantian Idealism* (Albany: State University of New York Press, 1985), p. 253.

2
The *Symposium* and the Aesthetics of Plotinus

1. Plato, *Symposium*, trans. Christopher Gill (London: Penguin Books, 1999).
2. Plotinus, *Enneads*, trans. Stephen MacKenna (London: Penguin Books, 1991).
3. Giovanni Pico della Mirandola, *Oration on the Dignity of Man*, trans. A Robert Caponigri (Washington, D.C.: Regnery Publishing, 1956 [1496]), pp. 25–26.
4. Plato, *Phaedrus*, trans. Walter Hamilton (London: Penguin Books, 1973).
5. Thomas Mann, *Death in Venice*, ed. Naomi Ritter (Boston: Bedford Books, 1998).
6. Plato, *The Republic*, trans. Desmond Lee (New York: Penguin Books, 1955).
7. Leon Battista Alberti, *On the Art of Building in Ten Books*, trans. Joseph Rykwert, Neil Leach and Robert Tavernor (Cambridge, MA: MIT Press, 1988).
8. Hesiod, *Theogony*, trans. M. L. West (Oxford: Oxford University Press, 1988).
9. This quotation was given to me by the procurator of the church, Giovanni Pujana.
10. Quoted from the translation in Ernst Cassirer, ed., *The Renaissance Philosophy of Man* (Chicago: University of Chicago Press, 1948), p. 233.
11. Plato, *Timaeus*, trans. Desmond Lee (London: Penguin Books, 1965).
12. Jacques Lacan, *The Four Fundamental Concepts of Psycho-Analysis*, trans. Alan Sheridan (New York: W. W. Norton, 1981).

3
The Aesthetics of Schelling

1. Plato, *Symposium*, trans. Christopher Gill (London: Penguin Books, 1999).
2. Plato, *Timaeus*, trans. Desmond Lee (London: Penguin Books, 1965).
3. Plato, *Phaedrus*, trans. Walter Hamilton (London: Penguin Books, 1973).
4. Friedrich Wilhelm Joseph von Schelling, *Bruno, or On the Natural and the Divine Principle of Things, 1802*, trans. Michael G. Vater (Albany: State University of New York Press, 1984).
5. Friedrich Wilhelm Joseph von Schelling, *System of Transcendental Idealism* (1800), trans. Peter Heath (Charlottesville: University Press of Virginia, 1978).
6. Georg Wilhelm Friedrich Hegel, *Phenomenology of Spirit*, trans. Arnold Vincent Miller (Oxford: Oxford University Press, 1977).
7. Friedrich Wilhelm Joseph von Schelling, *The Philosophy of Art* (*Die Philosophie der Kunst*), trans. Douglas W. Stott (Minneapolis: University of Minnesota Press, 1989 [1859]).
8. Jacques Lacan, The *Four Fundamental Concepts of Psycho-Analysis*, trans. Alan Sheridan (New York: W. W. Norton, 1981).
9. Leon Battista Alberti, *On the Art of Building in Ten Books*, trans. Joseph Rykwert, Neil Leach and Robert Tavernor (Cambridge, MA: MIT Press, 1988).
10. Plotinus, *The Six Enneads*, trans. Stephen MacKenna (Chicago: Encyclopedia Britannica, 1952).

11. Giovanni Pico della Mirandola, *Oration on the Dignity of Man*, trans. A. Robert Laponigri (Washington, D.C.: Regnery Publishing, 1956 [1496]).
12. Plato, *Republic*, trans. Desmond Lee (London: Penguin Books, 1955).
13. Immanuel Kant, *Critique of Judgment*, trans. Werner S. Pluhar (Indianapolis/Cambridge: Hackett Publishing Company, 1987).
14. Marsilio Ficino, *Commentary on Plato's Symposium on Love*, trans. Sears Jayne (Dallas: Spring Publications, 1985).
15. Quoted in Gloria K. Fiero, *The Humanistic Tradition*, Volume III (New York: McGraw Hill, 2002), p. 147.
16. Georges Bataille, *Visions of Excess, Selected Writings, 1927–1939*, trans. Allan Stoekl (Minneapolis: University of Minnesota Press, 1985), p. 128.
17. Thomas Mann, *Death in Venice*, ed. Naomi Ritter (Boston: Bedford Books, 1998).
18. Hesiod, *Theogony*, trans. M. L. West (Oxford: Oxford University Press, 1988).
19. Edward F. Fry, *Cubism* (New York: Oxford University Press, 1966), p. 147.
20. Roger Caillois, *The Necessity of the Mind* (Venice, CA: The Lapis Press, 1990).
21. Roger Caillois, "Mimicry and Legendary Psychasthenia," in *October* 31 (Cambridge, MA: MIT Press, 1993), p. 17.
22. Georg Wilhelm Friedrich Hegel, *The Difference Between Fichte's and Schelling's System of Philosophy*, trans. H. S. Harris and Walter Cerf (Albany: State University of New York Press, 1977).
23. Athanasius Kircher, *Primitiae Gnomonicae Catopticae* (Avenione: Ioannis Piot Ex Typographia, 1633), p. 33: "Et cum descendit lux a corpore luminoso per foramen aliquod ad corpus politum; si in superficie foraminis ex parte luminosi intelligatur punctum, a quo puncto intelligantur duae pyramides basis unius in luminoso, alterius in polito…"
24. Ibid., p. 2: "In iis denique quae sensu carent, nil nisi caelitus quaedam diffusa gratia, ubique divinae bonitatis, veritatisque typus et imago."
25. René Descartes, *Treatise of Man*, trans. Thomas Steele Hall (Cambridge, MA: Harvard University Press, 1972), p. 60.
26. Athanasius Kircher, *Primitiae Gnomonicae Catopticae*, p. 31: "…omnes istae lineae productae in diversis oculi punctis superficiem sphaericam oculi fecent, et omnes in centrum concurrant, atque adeo omnes istae lineae contineantur in uno quasi continuo corpore, et a punctis quasi continuis unius superficiei res visae ad unum punctum, qui est centrum oculi terminentur…"
27. Nicolai de Cusa, *De coniecturis* (Hamburgi: In Aedibus Felicis Meiner, 1972), p. 37: "Solida atque compositissima est haec sensibilis unitas, uti ipse millenarius. Et ut harum unitatum conceptum subintres, eas concipe differentes, quasi prima sit unitas simplicissimi puncti, secunda simplicis lineae, tertia simplicis superficiei, quarta simplicis corporis. Scies post haec clarius unitatem puncti simplicissimi omne id esse, quod in lineali, superficiali atque corporali exstat unitate; sed unitas lineae est id omne, quod in superficiali et corporali est, atque superficialis pariformiter est id omne, quod in corporali."
28. Leon Battista Alberti, *On Painting* and *On Sculpture*, trans. Cecil Grayson (London: Phaidon, 1972).

29. Piero della Francesca, *De Prospectiva Pingendi* (Firenze: Sansoni Editore, 1942), p. 64: "che con line angoli et proportioni se po dimostrare, dicendo de puncti, linee, superficie et de corpi."
30. Ibid.: "La qual parte contiene in sè cinque parti: La prima è il vedere, cioè l'ochio; seconda è la forma de la cosa veduta; la terza è la distantia da l'ochio a la cosa veduta; la quarta è le linee che se partano da l'estremità de la cosa e vanno a l'ochio; la quinta è il termine che è intra l'ochio e la cosa veduta dove si intende ponere le cose."
31. Ibid.: "...le linee, le quali s'apresentano da l'estremità de la cosa e terminano nell'ochio, infra le quali l'ochio le receve e discerne..."
32. Ibid.: "...è necessario sapere lineare in propria forma sopra il piano tucte le cose che l'omo intende fare..."
33. Proclus, *A Commentary on the First Book of Euclid's Elements*, trans. Glenn R. Morrow (Princeton: Princeton University Press, 1970).
34. Quoted in Gloria K. Fiero, *The Humanistic Tradition*, Volume IV (New York: McGraw Hill, 1998), p. 35.
35. Marsilio Ficino, *Sopra lo Amore, ovvero Convito di Platone* (Lanciano: Carabba), p. 20: "Il perchè l'occhio, primamente oscuro e informe a similitudine di caos, ama il lume mentre che ei guarda, e guardando piglia i raggi del sole: e quelli ricevendo, de' colori e delle figure delle cose s'informa..."
36. Athanasius Kircher, *Oedipi Aegyptiaci* (Roma, 1653), p. 116: "Nam ut a Deo incipit, et allicit, perfectae pulchritudinis rationem praefefert; ut autem in Mundum transit, amor potissimum dicitur; voluptas denique, prout in authorem remeans pulchro exemplari, pulchram imaginem, pulchra revolutione convertit. In hoc circuitu per omnia penetrans, sursum eadem fecum, deorsumque volui continuo facit; non fecus ac Solis simplex radius per se uniformis in coelo lucem, splendorem in aethere, in elementis lumen, in mistis corporibus colorem lucidum creat. Patet itaque quod amatorius ordo sit causa conversionis in rebus omnibus ad divinam pulchritudinem et formam principem, atque (ut verbis Procli utar) reducat sequentia ad illam omnia, eique coniungens, et coniuncta, confirmans, et mox inde sequentia replens, divini luminis dotes inde scaturientes per universa distribuat."
37. Marsilio Ficino, *Sopra lo Amore, ovvero Convito di Platone*, p. 18: "Voltandosi a Dio, dal suo raggio è illustrata, e per lo splendor di quel raggio si accende l'appetito suo: acceso, tutto a Dio s'accosta: accostandosi, piglia le forme: imperocchè, Iddio che tutto può, nella Mente, che a lui si accosta, scolpisce le nature di tutte le cose che si creano. In quella adunque spiritualmente si dipingono tutte le cose, che in questo Mondo sono."
38. H. Diels, *Die Fragmente der Vorsokratiker*, DK 12 A 14, quoted in Elizabeth Asmis, "What is Anaximander's *Apeiron*?," in *Journal of the History of Philosophy*, Vol. 19 (Berkeley: University of California Press, 1981), p. 281.
39. Pseudo-Dionysius, *The Complete Works*, trans. Colin Luibheid (New York: Paulist Press, 1987).
40. Jacques Lacan, *Écrits*, trans. Alan Sheridan (New York: W. W. Norton, 1977).
41. Colin Rowe and Robert Slutzky, "Transparency: Literal and Phenomenal," in Colin Rowe, *The Mathematics of the Ideal Villa and Other Essays* (Cambridge, MA: MIT Press, 1976), p. 163.

42. Gyorgy Kepes, *Language of Vision*, Chicago, 1944, p. 77, quoted in Rowe and Slutzky, Transparency: Literal and Phenomenal," in Colin Rowe, *The Mathematics of the Ideal Villa and Other Essays*, pp. 160–1.
43. Federico Zuccari, *L'Idea de' Pittori, Scultori e Architetti* (Torino, 1607), in Detlef Heikamp, ed., *Scritti d'Arte di Federico Zuccaro* (Firenze: Leo S. Olschki Editore, 1941), p. 25: "...Cosi la virtu intelletiva batte la pietra de i concetti nella mente humana; e il primo concetto, che svavilla accende l'esca dell'imaginatione, e move i fantasmi, e imaginationi ideali..."
44. Edmund Burke, *A Philosophical Enquiry into the Origin of Our Ideas of the Sublime and Beautiful* (London: Routledge and Kegan Paul, 1958), p. 63.
45. Quoted in Edmund Burke, *A Philosophical Enquiry into the Origin of Our Ideas of the Sublime and Beautiful*, p. 58.
46. Quoted in Edmund Burke, *A Philosophical Enquiry into the Origin of Our Ideas of the Sublime and Beautiful*, p. 71.
47. John Gage, *Colour and Culture* (London: Thames and Hudson, 1993), p. 210.
48. Michael Doran, ed., *Conversations with Cézanne* (Berkeley: University of California Press, 2001), p. 111.
49. Ibid., p. 110.
50. Sigmund Freud, *The Interpretation of Dreams*, trans. James Strachey (New York: Avon Books, 1965), p. 545, Note 2.
51. Sigmund Freud, *On Dreams*, trans. James Strachey (New York: W. W. Norton, 1952), p. 40.
52. Jacques Derrida, "Semiology and Grammatology, Interview with Julia Kristeva," in *Positions*, trans. Alan Bass (Chicago: University of Chicago Press, 1981), p. 27.
53. Jacques Derrida, *Speech and Phenomena, and Other Essays on Husserl's Theory of Signs*, trans. David B. Allison (Evanston: Northwestern University Press, 1973), p. 130.
54. Georges Bataille, "The College of Sociology," in *Visions of Excess*, p. 253.

4
Plotinian Hypostases in Hegel's *Phenomenology of Spirit*

1. George Wilhelm Friedrich Hegel, *Reason in History, A General Introduction to the Philosophy of History*, trans. Robert Hartman (New York: The Liberal Arts Press, 1953 [1837]), p. 21.
2. George Wilhelm Friedrich Hegel, *The Phenomenology of Mind*, trans. J. B. Baillie (London: George Allen and Unwin Ltd., 1966 [1910]), p. 70.
3. Hegel, *Reason in History*, p. 11.
4. Plotinus, *The Six Enneads*, trans. Stephen Mackenna and B. S. Page (Chicago: Encyclopedia Britannica, 1952).
5. George Wilhelm Friedrich Hegel, *Phenomenology of Spirit*, trans. Arnold Vincent Miller (Oxford: Oxford University Press, 1977).

6. Nicolai de Cusa, *De coniecturis* (Hamburgi: In Aedibus Felicis Meiner, 1972), p. 61: "Universum igitur sic erit ex centraliori spiritualissimo mundo atque ex circumferentialiori grossissimo et ex medio. Centrum primi deus, centrum secundi intelligentia, centrum tertii ratio."
7. Proclus, *A Commentary on the First Book of Euclid's Elements*, trans. Glenn R. Morrow (Princeton: Princeton University Press, 1970).
8. Plato, *The Dialogues of Plato*, trans. Benjamin Jowett (Chicago: Encyclopedia Britannica, 1952).
9. Hegel, *Reason in History*, p. 23.
10. Nicholas of Cusa, *On Learned Ignorance*, trans. Jasper Hopkins (Minneapolis: Arthur Banning Press, 1981).
11. Hegel, *Reason in History*, p. 32.
12. Nicolai de Cusa, *De coniecturis* (Hamburgi: In Aedibus Felicis Meiner, 1972), p. 61: "Universum igitur sic erit ex centraliori spiritualissimo mundo atque ex circumferentialiori grossissimo et ex medio. Centrum primi deus, centrum secundi intelligentia, centrum tertii ratio."
13. Philip Wheelwright, ed., *The Presocratics* (Indianapolis: Bobbs-Merrill Educational Publishing, 1960), p. 57.
14. Charles H. Kahn, *Anaximander and the Origins of Greek Cosmology* (Philadelphia: Centrum, 1985), p. 85.
15. Plato, *Republic*, trans. Desmond Lee (New York: Penguin Books, 1955).
16. Erwin Panofsky, *Studies in Iconology, Humanistic Themes in the Art of the Renaissance* (New York: Harper and Row, 1962), p. 132.
17. Plato, *Phaedrus*, trans. Walter Hamilton (New York: Penguin Books, 1973).
18. Gottfried Wilhelm Leibniz, *Discourse on Metaphysics, Correspondence with Arnauld and Monadology* (Chicago: Open Court Publishing, 1918).
19. Pseudo-Dionysius, *The Works of Dionysius the Areopagite*, trans. John Parker (London: James Parker, 1897).
20. Translated in Fran O'Rourke, *Pseudo-Dionysius and the Metaphysics of Aquinas* (New York: E. J. Brill, 1992), p. 19.
21. Jacques Derrida, *Writing and Difference* (Chicago: University of Chicago Press, 1978), p. 114.
22. Jacques Lacan, *Écrits* (New York: W.W. Norton, 1977), p. 22.
23. Charles H. Kahn, *Anaximander and the Origins of Greek Cosmology* (Philadelphia: Centrum, 1985), p. 85.
24. H. Diels, *Die Fragmente der Vorsokratiker*, B27–B29, quoted in D. R. Dicks, *Early Greek Astronomy to Aristotle* (Ithaca: Cornell University Press, 1970), p. 52.
25. Philip Wheelwright, ed., *The Presocratics* (Indianapolis: Bobbs-Merrill Educational Publishing, 1960), p. 54.
26. Ibid., p. 57.
27. Ibid., p. 55.
28. Elizabeth Asmis, "What is Anaximander's *Apeiron*?," in *Journal of the History of Philosophy*, Volume 19 (Berkeley: University of California Press, 1981), p. 281.
29. Ibid.

30. Jacques Lacan, *The Four Fundamental Concepts of Psycho-Analysis* (New York: W.W. Norton, 1973), p. 15.
31. Jean-Louis Baudry, "Bataille and Science: Introduction to Inner Experience," in Leslie Anne Boldt-Irons, ed., *On Bataille, Critical Essays* (Albany: State University of New York Press, 1995), p. 277.
32. Georges Bataille, "The Pineal Eye," in *Visions of Excess, Selected Writings* (Minneapolis: University of Minnesota Press, 1985), p. 80.
33. Georges Bataille, "The Sorcerer's Apprentice," in *Visions of Excess*, p. 231.
34. Georges Bataille, "The Notion of Expenditure," in *Visions of Excess*, p. 128.

5
The Aesthetics of Hegel

1. Plato, *Symposium*, trans. Christopher Gill (London: Penguin Books, 1999).
2. Georg Wilhelm Friedrich Hegel, *Introductory Lectures on Aesthetics* (*The Introduction to Hegel's Philosophy of Fine Art*, 1886), trans. Bernard Bosanquet, ed. Michael Inwood (London: Penguin Books, 1993).
3. Plato, *Timaeus and Critias*, trans. Desmond Lee (London: Penguin Books, 1965).
4. Plato, *Republic*, trans. Desmond Lee (London: Penguin Books, 1955).
5. Plotinus, *The Enneads*, trans. Stephen MacKenna (London: Penguin Books, 1991).
6. Plato, *Phaedrus*, trans. Walter Hamilton (London: Penguin Books, 1973).
7. Michael Doran, ed., *Conversations with Cézanne* (Berkeley: University of California Press, 2001), p. 110.
8. For the difference between the sign and symbol in Hegel's philosophy, see Kathleen Dow Magnus, *Hegel and the Symbolic Mediation of Spirit* (Albany: State University of New York Press, 2001).
9. Georg Wilhelm Friedrich Hegel, *Introduction to the Philosophy of Art*, trans. Jacob Loewenberg, in *Hegel: Selections*, ed. Jacob Loewenberg (New York: Charles Scribner's Sons, 1929), p. 327.
10. Georg Wilhelm Friedrich Hegel, "Introduction" (*Introductory Lectures on Aesthetics*) in *The Philosophy of Fine Art*, trans. F. P. B. Osmaston (New York: Hacker Art Books, 1975 [1920]).
11. Michael Doran, ed., *Conversations with Cézanne*, p. 120.
12. Georg Wilhelm Friedrich Hegel, *The Phenomenology of Mind*, trans. J. B. Baillie (London: George Allen & Unwin Ltd., 1966), p. 70.
13. Georg Wilhelm Freidrich Hegel, *Phenomenology of Spirit*, trans. A. V. Miller (Oxford: Oxford University Press, 1977).
14. Translated in Fran O'Rourke, *Pseudo-Dionysius and the Metaphysics of Aquinas* (New York: E. J. Brill, 1992), p. 9.
15. Jacques Derrida, "Semiology and Grammatology, Interview with Julia Kristeva," in *Positions*, trans. Alan Bass (Chicago: University of Chicago Press, 1981), p. 27.

16. Georges Bataille, "The Pineal Eye," in *Visions of Excess: Selected Writings, 1927–1939*, trans. Allan Stoekl (Minneapolis: University of Minnesota Press, 1985), p. 80.
17. Jacques Lacan, *The Four Fundamental Concepts of Psycho-Analysis*, trans. Alan Sheridan (New York: W. W. Norton, 1978), p. 80.
18. Georges Bataille, *Inner Experience*, trans. Leslie Anne Boldt (Albany: State University of New York Press, 1988), p. 89.
19. Quoted in Jean-Louis Baudry, "Bataille and Science: An Introduction to Inner Experience," in Leslie Anne Boldt-Irons, ed., *On Bataille, Critical Essays* (Albany: State University of New York Press, 1995), p. 276.
20. Rodolphe Gasché, "The Heterological Almanac," in Leslie Anne Boldt-Irons, ed., *On Bataille, Critical Essays*, p. 112.
21. Johann Gottlieb Fichte, *The Science of Knowledge*, ed. and trans. Peter Heath and John Lachs (Cambridge: Cambridge University Press, 1982).
22. Donald C. Abel, *Freud on Instinct and Morality* (Albany: State University of New York Press, 1989), p. 45.
23. Wilhelm Worringer, *Abstraction and Empathy, A Contribution to the Psychology of Style* (New York: Meridian, 1948), p. 34.
24. Sigmund Freud, *The Ego and the Id*, trans. Joan Riviere, ed. James Strachey (New York: W. W. Norton & Company, Inc., 1962), p. 30.
25. Sigmund Freud, *Beyond the Pleasure Principle*, trans. and ed. James Strachey (New York: Liveright Publishing Corporation, 1961 [1920]), p. 32.
26. Quoted in Barbara Maria Stafford, *Body Criticism, Imagining the Unseen in Enlightenment Art and Medicine* (Cambridge, MA: MIT Press, 1991), p. 461.
27. Gottfried Wilhelm Leibniz, *Discourse on Metaphysics, Correspondence with Arnauld and Monadology* (Chicago: Open Court Publishing, 1918), p. 250.
28. Quoted in Gilles Deleuze, *The Fold, Leibniz and the Baroque*, trans. Tom Conley (Minneapolis: University of Minnesota Press, 1993), p. 162, n. 15.
29. C. D. Broad, *Leibniz, An Introduction* (Oxford: Cambridge University Press, 1975), p. 94.
30. Philip Wheelwright, ed., *The Presocratics* (Indianapolis: Bobbs-Merrill Educational Publishing, 1960), p. 57.
31. Paul Seligman, *The* Apeiron *of Anaximander, A Study in the Origin and Function of Metaphysical Ideas* (Westport, CT: Greenwood Press, 1962), p. 17.
32. Erwin Panofsky, *Studies in Iconology, Humanistic Themes in the Art of the Renaissance* (New York: Harper and Row, 1962), p. 131.
33. Aristotle, *Metaphysics*, in Louise Ropes Loomis, ed., *On Man in the Universe: Metaphysics, Parts of Animals, Ethics, Politics, Poetics* (New York: Walter Black, 1943), p. 27.
34. Georg Wilhelm Friedrich Hegel, *Hegel's Philosophy of Mind, Being Part Three of the Encyclopedia of the Philosophical Sciences* (1830), trans. William Wallace (Oxford: Clarendon Press, 1971).
35. Georg Wilhelm Friedrich Hegel, *Reason in History, A General Introduction to the Philosophy of History* (1837), trans. Robert Hartman (New York: The Liberal Arts Press, 1953).

6
Architecture and the Philosophy of Spirit

1. Georg Wilhelm Friedrich Hegel, *Introductory Lectures on Aesthetics* (*The Introduction to Hegel's Philosophy of Fine Art*, 1886), trans. Bernard Bosanquet, ed. Michael Inwood (London: Penguin Books, 1993).
2. Friedrich Wilhelm Joseph Schelling, *The Philosophy of Art* (*Die Philosophie der Kunst*, 1859), trans. Douglas W. Stott (Minneapolis: University of Minnesota Press, 1989).
3. Immanuel Kant, *Critique of Judgment* (1790), trans. Werner S. Pluhar (Indianapolis/Cambridge: Hackett Publishing Company, 1987), § 51.
4. For a more complete analysis of the relation between the circle and the polygonal figures in the *De circuli quadratura* of Nicolas Cusanus, see the discussions in my previous books: "Cusanus and Proclus" in *Platonic Architectonics: Platonic Philosophies and the Visual Arts* (New York: Peter Lang Publishing, 2004); "Francesco Borromini and the Construction of Meaning" in *Architectural Forms and Philosophical Structures* (New York: Peter Lang Publishing, 2003); and "The Transmutation of Geometries" in *The Relation Between Architectural Forms and Philosophical Structures in the Work of Francesco Borromini in Seventeenth-Century Rome* (Lewiston, NY: Edwin Mellen Press, 2002).
5. For a more complete analysis of Francesco Borromini's plan for San Carlo alle Quattro Fontane, see the discussions in "Francesco Borromini and the Construction of Meaning" in *Architectural Forms and Philosophical Structures*; and "The Transmutation of Geometries" in *The Relation Between Architectural Forms and Philosophical Structures in the Work of Francesco Borromini in Seventeenth-Century Rome.*
6. Noam Chomsky, *Language and Mind* (New York: Harcourt Brace Jovanovich, Inc., 1968).
7. For a more complete analysis of the relation between Chomsky's theories and Eisenman's analysis of Terragni's architecture, see "Cubism and Deep Structure" in *Platonic Architectonics: Platonic Philosophies and the Visual Arts.*
8. Peter D. Eisenman, "From Object to Relationship II: Giuseppe Terragni, Casa Giuliani Frigerio," in *Perspecta* 13 (The Yale Architectural Journal, 1971), p. 38.
9. Fredric Jameson, "From Metaphor to Allegory," in *Anything*, ed. Cynthia Davidson (Cambridge, MA: MIT Press, 2001).

Bibliography

Donald C. Abel, *Freud on Instinct and Morality*, Albany: State University of New York Press, 1989.

Leon Battista Alberti, *On the Art of Building in Ten Books* (*De re aedificatoria*), trans. Joseph Rykwert, Neil Leach and Robert Tavernor, Cambridge, MA: MIT Press, 1988.

———, *On Painting* and *On Sculpture*, trans. Cecil Grayson, London: Phaidon, 1972.

Aphrodite Alexandrakis, ed., *Neoplatonism and Western Aesthetics*, Albany: State University of New York Press, 2002.

Aristotle, *De anima*, trans. J. A. Smith, in *The Works of Aristotle*, Chicago: Encyclopedia Britannica, 1952.

———, *Metaphysics*, in Louise Ropes Loomis, ed., *On Man in the Universe: Metaphysics, Parts of Animals, Ethics, Politics, Poetics*, New York: Walter Black, 1943.

———, *Metaphysics*, trans. W. D. Ross, in *The Works of Aristotle*, Chicago: Encyclopedia Britannica, 1952.

Elizabeth Asmis, "What is Anaximander's *Apeiron*?," in *Journal of the History of Philosophy*, Volume 19, Berkeley: University of California Press, 1981.

Stuart Barnett, ed., *Hegel after Derrida*, London and New York: Routledge, 1998.

Georges Bataille, *Inner Experience*, trans. Leslie Anne Boldt, Albany: State University of New York Press, 1988.

———, *Visions of Excess, Selected Writings*, trans. Allan Stoekl, Minneapolis: University of Minnesota Press, 1985.

Jean-Louis Baudry, "Bataille and Science: Introduction to Inner Experience," in Leslie Anne Boldt-Irons, ed., *On Bataille, Critical Essays*, Albany: State University of New York Press, 1995.

Daniel Berthold-Bond, *Hegel's Grand Synthesis: A Study of Being, Thought, and History*, Albany: State University of New York Press, 1989.

———, *Hegel's Theory of Madness*, Albany: State University of New York Press, 1995.

Leslie Anne Boldt-Irons, *On Bataille, Critical Essays*, Albany: State University of New York Press, 1995.

Andrew Bowie, *Schelling and Modern European Philosophy*, London and New York: Routledge, 1993.

Charlie Dunbar Broad, *Leibniz, An Introduction*, London: Cambridge University Press, 1975.

Stephen Bungay, *Beauty and Truth: A Study of Hegel's Aesthetics*, Oxford: Oxford University Press, 1984.

Edmund Burke, *A Philosophical Enquiry into the Nature of Our Ideas of the Sublime and Beautiful*, London: Routledge and Kegan Paul, 1958.

Roger Caillois, "Mimicry and Legendary Psychasthenia," in *October* 31, Cambridge, MA: MIT Press, 1993.

———, *The Necessity of the Mind*, Venice, CA: The Lapis Press, 1990.

Liana De Girolami Cheney and John Hendrix, ed, *Neoplatonic Aesthetics: Music, Literature, and the Visual Arts*, New York: Peter Lang Publishing, 2004.

———, *Neoplatonism and the Arts*, Lewiston, NY: Edwin Mellen Press, 2002.

Noam Chomsky, *Aspects of the Theory of Syntax*, Cambridge, MA: MIT Press, 1965.

———, *Language and Mind*, New York: Harcourt Brace Jovanovich, Inc., 1968.

Malcolm Clark, *Logic and System: A Study of the Transition from "Vorstellung" to Thought in the Philosophy of Hegel*, The Hague: Martinus Nijhoff, 1971.

Daniel J. Cook, *Language in the Philosophy of Hegel*, The Hague: Morton and Co., 1973.

Jonathan Culler, *Structuralist Poetics: Structuralism, Linguistics, and the Study of Literature*, Ithaca, NY: Cornell University Press, 1975.

Nicolai de Cusa, *De circuli quadratura* in *Opera Omnia*, Hamburgi: In Aedibus Felicis Meiner, 1994.

———, *De coniecturis*, Hamburgi: In Aedibus Felicis Meiner, 1972.

Nicholas of Cusa, *On Learned Ignorance*, trans. Jasper Hopkins, Minneapolis: Arthur Banning Press, 1981.

Gilles Deleuze, *The Fold, Leibniz and the Baroque*, Minneapolis: University of Minnesota Press, 1993.

Jacques Derrida, *Glas*, trans. John P. Leavey, Jr., and Richard Rand, Lincoln: University of Nebraska Press, 1986.

———, *Margins of Philosophy*, trans. Alan Bass, Chicago: University of Chicago Press, 1982.

———, "Semiology and Grammatology, Interview with Julia Kristeva," in *Positions*, trans. Alan Bass, Chicago: University of Chicago Press, 1981.

———, *Speech and Phenomena, and Other Essays on Husserl's Theory of Signs*, trans. David B. Allison, Evanston: Northwestern University Press, 1973.

———, *Writing and Difference*, Chicago: University of Chicago Press, 1978.

René Descartes, *Treatise of Man*, trans. Thomas Steele Hall, Cambridge, MA: Harvard University Press, 1972.

William Desmond, *Art and the Absolute: A Study of Hegel's Aesthetics*, Albany: State University of New York Press, 1986.

Willem A. DeVries, *Hegel's Theory of Mental Activity: An Introduction to Theoretical Spirit*, Ithaca and London: Cornell University Press, 1988.

D. R. Dicks, *Early Greek Astronomy to Aristotle*, Ithaca: Cornell University Press, 1970.

Michael Doran, ed. *Conversations with Cézanne*, Berkeley: University of California Press, 2001.

Peter D. Eisenman, "From Object to Relationship II: Giuseppe Terragni, Casa Giuliani Frigerio," in *Perspecta* 13 (The Yale Architectural Journal), 1971.

Johann Gottlieb Fichte, *Early Philosophical Writings*, ed. and trans. Daniel Breazeale, Ithaca and London: Cornell University Press, 1988.

———, *Foundations of Transcendental Philosophy: (Wissenschaftslehre) Nova Methodo (1796/99)*, trans. and ed. Daniel Breazeale, Ithaca and London: Cornell University Press, 1992.

———, *The Science of Knowledge*, ed. and trans. Peter Heath and John Lachs, Cambridge: Cambridge University Press, 1982.

Marsilio Ficino, *Commentary on Plato's Symposium on Love*, trans. Sears Jayne, Dallas: Spring Publications, 1985.

———, *Platonic Theology, On the Immortality of Souls*, Paris: Humanities, 1964.

———, *Sopra lo Amore, ovvero Convito di Platone*, Lanciano: Carabba.

Gloria K. Fiero, *The Humanistic Tradition*, New York: McGraw Hill, 2002.

Piero della Francesca, *De Prospectiva Pingendi*, Firenze: Sansoni Editore, 1942.

Sigmund Freud, *Beyond the Pleasure Principle*, trans. and ed. James Strachey, New York: Liveright Publishing Corporation, 1961 (1920).

———, *The Ego and the Id*, trans. Joan Riviere, ed. James Strachey, New York: W. W. Norton & Company, Inc., 1962.

———, *The Interpretation of Dreams*, trans. James Strachey, New York: Avon Books, 1965.

———, *On Dreams*, trans. James Strachey, New York: W. W. Norton, 1952.

Edward F. Fry, *Cubism*, New York: Oxford University Press, 1966.

Hans-Georg Gadamer, *Hegel's Dialectic, Five Hermeneutical Studies*, trans. P. Christopher Smith, New Haven: Yale University Press, 1976.

George di Giovanni and H. S. Harris, trans. and annotated, *Between Kant and Hegel: Texts in the Development of Post-Kantian Idealism*, Albany: State University of New York Press, 1985.

Kai Hammermeister, *The German Aesthetic Tradition*, Cambridge: Cambridge University Press, 2002.

R. Baine Harris, ed., *The Significance of Neoplatonism*, Norfolk: International Society for Neoplatonic Studies, 1976.

Georg Wilhelm Friedrich Hegel, *The Difference Between Fichte's and Schelling's Systems of Philosophy*, ed. H. S. Harris and Walter Cerf, Albany: State University of New York Press, 1977.

———, "The Doctrine of Essence," trans. William Wallace, from the *Encyclopedia of the Philosophical Sciences*, in Jacob Loewenberg, ed., *Hegel: Selections*, New York: Charles Scribner's Sons, 1929.

———, *The Encyclopedia Logic* (*Wissenschaft der Logik*, 1830), trans. T. F. Geraets, W. A. Suchting, and H. S. Harris, Indianapolis/Cambridge: Hackett Publishing Company, Inc., 1991.

———, *Faith and Knowledge*, trans. Walter Cerf and H. S. Harris, Albany: State University of New York Press, 1977.

———, *Hegel's Philosophy of Mind, Being Part Three of the Encyclopedia of the Philosophical Sciences* (1830), trans. William Wallace, Oxford: Clarendon Press, 1971.

———, *Introductory Lectures on Aesthetics*, trans. Bernard Bosanquet, ed. Michael Inwood, London: Penguin Books, 1993.

———, *The Phenomenology of Mind*, trans. J. B. Baillie, London: George Allen and Unwin Ltd., 1966 (1910).

———, *Phenomenology of Spirit*, trans. Arnold Vincent Miller, Oxford: Oxford University Press, 1977.

———, *The Philosophy of Fine Art*, trans. F. P. B. Osmaston, London, 1975 (1920).

———, "The Philosophy of Mind," trans. William Wallace, from *The Encyclopedia of the Philosophical Sciences*, in Jacob Loewenberg, ed., *Hegel: Selections*, New York: Charles Scribner's Sons, 1929.

———, *Reason in History, A General Introduction to the Philosophy of History*, trans. Robert Hartman, New York: The Liberal Arts Press, 1953 (1837).

———, *Science of Logic*, trans. A. V. Miller, New York: Humanities Press, 1969.

Martin Heidegger, *Hegel's Phenomenology of Spirit*, trans. Parvis Emad and Kenneth Maly, Bloomington: Indiana University Press, 1988.

Detlef Heikamp, ed., *Scritti d'Arte di Federico Zuccaro*, Firenze: Leo S. Olschki Editore, 1941.

John Hendrix, *Architectural Forms and Philosophical Structures*, New York: Peter Lang Publishing, 2003.

———, *Platonic Architectonics: Platonic Philosophies and the Visual Arts*, New York: Peter Lang Publishing, 2004.

———, *The Relation Between Architectural Forms and Philosophical Structures in the Work of Francesco Borromini in Seventeenth-Century Rome*, Lewiston, NY: Edwin Mellen Press, 2002.

Hesiod, *Theogony*, trans. M. L. West, Oxford: Oxford University Press, 1988.

Homer, *The Iliad* and *The Odyssey*, trans. Richmond Lattimore, Chicago: Encyclopedia Britannica, 1990.

Fredric Jameson, "From Metaphor to Allegory," *Anything*, Cynthia Davidson ed., Cambridge, MA: MIT Press, 2001.

Charles H. Kahn, *Anaximander and the Origins of Greek Cosmology*, Philadelphia: Centrum, 1985.

Howard P. Kainz, *Hegel's* Phenomenology, Part I: *Analysis and Commentary*, University, AL: The University of Alabama Press, 1976.

Jack Kaminsky, *Hegel on Art: An Interpretation of Hegel's Aesthetics*, Albany: State University of New York Press, 1962.

Immanuel Kant, *Critique of Judgment* (1790), trans. Werner S. Pluhar, Indianapolis and Cambridge: Hackett Publishing Company, 1987.

———, *Critique of Pure Judgment*, trans. J. H. Bernard, New York: MacMillan, 1914.

———, *Prolegomena to Any Future Metaphysics*, trans. Paul Carns, Chicago: University of Chicago Press, 1929.

S. S. Kerry, *Schiller's Writings on Aesthetics*, Manchester: Manchester University Press, 1961.

Athanasius Kircher, *Ars Magna Lucis et Umbrae*, Roma: Sumptibus Hermanni Schens, 1645.

———, *Oedipi Aegyptiaci*, Roma, 1653.

———, *Primitiae Gnomonicae Catopticae*, Avenione: Ioannis Piot Ex Typographia, 1633.

Israel Knox, *The Aesthetic Theories of Kant, Hegel, and Schopenhauer*, New York: Humanities Press, 1958.

T. M. Knox, *Hegel's Aesthetics*, Oxford: Clarendon Press, 1975.

Alexandre Kojève, *Introduction to the Reading of Hegel*, trans. James H. Nichols, Jr., New York: Basic Books, 1969.

Julia Kristeva, *Desire in Language: A Semiotic Approach to Literature and Art*, ed. Leon S. Roudiez, New York: Columbia University Press, 1980.

Jacques Lacan, *Écrits*, New York: W. W. Norton, 1977.

———, *The Four Fundamental Concepts of Psycho-Analysis*, trans. Alan Sheridan, New York: W. W. Norton, 1981.

Erika Langmuir, *Allegory*, London: National Gallery Company, 1997.

Gottfried Wilhelm Leibniz, *Discourse on Metaphysics, Correspondence with Arnauld and Monadology*, Chicago: Open Court Publishing, 1918.

Jacob Loewenberg, ed., *Hegel: Selections*, New York: Charles Scribner's Sons, 1929.

Kathleen Dow Magnus, *Hegel and the Symbolic Mediation of Spirit*, Albany: State University of New York Press, 2001.

William Maker, ed., *Hegel and Aesthetics*, Albany: State University of New York Press, 2000.

Thomas Mann, *Death in Venice*, ed. Naomi Ritter, Boston: Bedford Books, 1998.

John McCumber, *The Company of Words: Hegel, Language, and Systematic Philosophy*, Evanston: Northwestern University Press, 1993.

Jon Mills, *The Unconscious Abyss: Hegel's Anticipation of Psychoanalysis*, Albany: State University of New York Press, 2002.

Giovanni Pico della Mirandola, *Oration on the Dignity of Man* (1496), trans. A. Robert Camponigri, Washington, D.C.: Regnery Publishing, 1956.

Judith Norman and Alistair Welchman, ed., *The New Schelling*, London: Continuum, 2004.

Richard Norman, *Hegel's Phenomenology: A Philosophical Introduction*, New York: St. Martin's Press, 1976.

Fran O'Rourke, *Pseudo-Dionysius and the Metaphysics of Aquinas*, New York: E. J. Brill, 1992.

Erwin Panofsky, *Studies in Iconology, Humanistic Themes in the Art of the Renaissance*, New York: Harper and Row, 1962.

Robert L. Perkins, ed., *History and System: Hegel's Philosophy of History*, Albany: State University of New York Press, 1984.

Terry Pinkard, *Hegel, A Biography*, Cambridge: Cambridge University Press, 2000.

Robert B. Pippin, *Hegel's Idealism: The Satisfactions of Self-Consciousness*, Cambridge: Cambridge University Press, 1989.

Plato, *The Dialogues of Plato*, trans. Benjamin Jowett, Chicago: Encyclopedia Britannica, 1952.

———, *Phaedrus*, trans. Walter Hamilton, London: Penguin Books, 1973.

———, *The Republic*, trans. Desmond Lee, London: Penguin Books, 1955.

———, *The Symposium*, trans. Christopher Gill, London: Penguin Books, 1999.

———, *Timaeus and Critias*, trans. Desmond Lee, London: Penguin Books, 1977.

Plotinus, *The Enneads*, trans. Stephen MacKenna, London: Penguin Books, 1991.

———, *The Six Enneads*, trans. Stephen MacKenna and B. S. Page, Chicago: Encyclopedia Britannica, 1952.

Proclus, *A Commentary on the First Book of Euclid's Elements*, trans. Glenn R. Morrow, Princeton: Princeton University Press, 1970.

Pseudo-Dionysius, *The Complete Works*, trans. Colin Luibheid, New York: Paulist Press, 1987.

———, *The Works of Dionysius the Areopagite*, trans. John Parker, London: James Parker, 1897.

David Pugh, *Dialectic of Love: Platonism in Schiller's Aesthetics*, Montreal and Kingston: McGill-Queen's University Press, 1996.

Herbert Read, ed., *The True Voice of Feeling, Studies in English Romantic Poetry*, New York: Pantheon Books, 1953.

Colin Rowe, *The Mathematics of the Ideal Villa and Other Essays*, Cambridge, MA: MIT Press, 1976.

Friedrich Wilhelm Joseph von Schelling, *Bruno, or On the Natural and the Divine Principle of Things, 1802*, trans. Michael G. Vater, Albany: State University of New York Press, 1984.

———, "Concerning the Relation of the Plastic Arts to Nature," trans. Michael Bullock, in *The True Voice of Feeling*, ed. Herbert Read, New York: Pantheon Books, 1953.

———, *The Philosophy of Art* (*Die Philosophie der Kunst*, 1859), trans. Douglas W. Stott, Minneapolis: University of Minnesota Press, 1989.

———, *System of Transcendental Idealism* (1800), trans. Peter Heath, Charlottesville: University Press of Virginia, 1978.

———, *The Unconditional in Human Knowledge: Four Early Essays*, trans. Fritz Marti, Lewisburg: Bucknell University Press, 1980.

Friedrich Schiller, *Naïve and Sentimental Poetry, and On the Sublime*, trans. Julius A. Elias, New York: F. Ungar, 1967.

———, *On the Aesthetic Education of Man*, ed. and trans. Elizabeth M. Wilkinson and L. A. Willoughby, Oxford: Oxford University Press, 1967.

George J. Seidel, *Fichte's Wissenschaftslehre of 1794: A Commentary on Part I*, West Lafayette: Purdue University Press, 1993.

Paul Seligman, *The* Apeiron *of Anaximander, A Study in the Origin and Function of Metaphysical Ideas*, Westport, CT: Greenwood Press, 1962.

Barbara Maria Stafford, *Body Criticism, Imagining the Unseen in Enlightenment Art and Medicine*, Cambridge, MA: MIT Press, 1991.

Peter G. Stillman, ed., *Hegel's Philosophy of Spirit*, Albany: State University of New York Press, 1987.

Charles Taylor, *Hegel*, Cambridge: Cambridge University Press, 1975.

Michael G. Vater, "Schelling's Neoplatonic System-Notion: '*Ineinsbildung*' and Temporal Unfolding," in *The Significance of Neoplatonism*, ed. R. Baine Harris, Norfolk: International Society for Neoplatonic Studies, 1976.

Donald Phillip Verene, *Hegel's Recollection: A Study of Images in the* Phenomenology of Spirit, Albany: State University of New York Press, 1985.

Ton Verstegen, *Tropisms, Metaphoric Animation and Architecture*, Rotterdam: NAi Publishers, 2001.

Giambattista Vico, *New Science*, trans. David Marsh, London: Penguin Books, 1999.

Merold Westphal, *History and Truth in Hegel's Phenomenology*, Atlantic Highlands, NJ: Humanities Press, 1978.

Philip Wheelwright, ed., *The Presocratics*, Indianapolis: Bobbs-Merrill Educational Publishing, 1960.

Robert Wicks, *Hegel's Theory of Aesthetic Judgment*, New York: Peter Lang Publishing, 1994.

Robert R. Williams, *Recognition: Fichte and Hegel on the Other*, Albany: State University of New York Press, 1992.

Heinrich Wölfflin, *Principles of Art History*, trans. M. D. Hottinger, New York: Dover Publications, 1950.

Federico Zuccari, *L'Idea de' Pittori, Scultori e Architetti*, Torino, 1607, in Detlef Heikamp, ed., *Scritti d'Arte di Federico Zuccaro*, Firenze: Leo S. Olschki Editore, 1941.

Index